FULFILLMENT IN CHRIST

FULFILLMENT IN CHRIST

A Summary of Christian Moral Principles

Germain Grisez
and
Russell Shaw

UNIVERSITY OF NOTRE DAME PRESS
NOTRE DAME

Paperback reprinted in 1997 and 2001, 2005, 2009

Nihil Obstat
Rev. Kevin T. McMahon, S.T.D.
Censor Deputatus

Imprimatur
His Eminence,
†James Cardinal Hickey
Archbishop of Washington
20 August 1990

The *nihil obstat* and *imprimatur* are official declarations that a book or pamphlet is free of doctrinal or moral error. No implication is contained therein that those who have granted the *nihil obstat* and *imprimatur* agree with the content, opinions, or statements expressed.

Quotations from the Constitutions, Decrees, and Declarations of the Second Vatican Council in this book are taken, unless otherwise noted, from *The Documents of Vatican II,* ed. Walter M. Abbott, S.J., and Joseph Gallagher, and are reprinted with permission of America Press, Inc., 106 West 56th Street, New York, New York 10019. Copyright © 1996. All rights reserved.

Quotations from Scripture in this book are from the New Revised Standard Version of the Bible, copyright © 1989 by the Division of Christian Education of the National Council of the Churches of Christ in the U.S.A., and are used by permission.

Library of Congress Cataloging-in-Publication Data
Grisez, Germain Gabriel, 1929–
    Fulfillment in Christ : a summary of Christian moral principals / Germain
Grisez and Russell Shaw.
      p. cm.
    Includes bibliographical references and index.
    ISBN 0-268-00980-5
    ISBN 13: 978-0-268-00981-6 (pbk. : alk. paper)
    ISBN 10: 0-268-00981-3 (pbk. : alk. paper)
    1. Christian ethics—Catholic authors. 2. Christian life—Catholic authors.
3. Catholic Church—Doctrines. I. Shaw, Russell B. II. Title
BJ1249.G75   1991
241'.042—dc20   90-50970
                                            CIP

∞ *This book was printed on acid-free paper.*

Contents

Preface

In 1983 Germain Grisez published the first volume of a projected comprehensive treatment of Catholic moral theology in four volumes: *The Way of the Lord Jesus*, volume one: *Christian Moral Principles* (Chicago: Franciscan Herald Press). Intended primarily, though not exclusively, as a textbook for students in Catholic seminaries, it is now in use in several such institutions in the United States and has reached a growing number of other readers.

That text is a work of nearly a thousand closely printed pages including detailed arguments supporting all its major positions, appendices on special questions, extensive footnotes, and other scholarly apparatus. While its purpose makes all this material necessary, the resulting length and density of the book limit its audience to the comparatively small number of persons willing and able to make the effort which its assimilation undoubtedly requires. Yet the work contains something interesting to a far wider audience: an original, contemporary treatment of moral theology which is faithful to received Catholic teaching and the magisterium of the Church. Thus, it seemed desirable to rework the main elements of its treatment into a more accessible form.

Hence the present volume: a summary of *Christian Moral Principles* from volume one of *The Way of the Lord Jesus*. Although not a substitute for the larger work, which covers more ground in greater detail and which remains the appropriate text for seminary students and for professionals in the field of moral theology, it mirrors volume one chapter for chapter, discusses the same major topics, and summarizes the main lines of its argument. So, while the chapters have been reorganized *internally*, teachers who use this volume and other readers who wish to dig more deeply into a topic will find it easy to locate the corresponding treatment in the larger work.

To the extent that this book oversimplifies its source, that is an unavoidable result of the process of condensation itself; its intent nevertheless is faithfully to summarize the principal elements of the earlier work, presenting these as clearly and simply as possible. It is suitable for college-level courses in theology and for adult education; it should also be helpful to priests and counselors, religious educators, parents, and general readers who wish to know what the Catholic Church teaches about basic questions in moral theology and why.

Then too, the second volume of *The Way of the Lord Jesus* is nearing completion. That volume, *Living a Christian Life*, will treat the specific responsibilities of all or most Catholics—everything from religious duties to responsibilities concerning life and health, property, and sex and marriage. Those who study volume two will need a foundation in the principles, and the present work offers a comparatively easy way of obtaining it.

A: This Book Has Ten Distinct Sections

1. Chapter one, the introduction, stands by itself. It explains what moral theology is, why renewal is needed in it, and how that renewal should be carried out according to the plan of the Second Vatican Council.

2. Chapters two through four discuss the need for directive principles in moral theology. We need them to guide us in making judgments of conscience to direct our free choices. Directive moral principles are not intuitions nor are they rules laid down by the Church or some other authority. They are moral truths.

3. Chapters five through eight deal with the fundamental principles of morality. First we consider basic human goods as elements of our personhood: these "goods," taken together, are what a human person is capable of being. At the present time, however, the moral theory called "proportionalism," which maintains that it is sometimes right to choose and act against human goods, enjoys a certain vogue. We show why it is neither sound nor workable. Next we turn to natural law (a hallowed term, but one frequently misunderstood today), the first principle of morality (integral human fulfillment in human goods), and what are here

called "modes of responsibility" (intermediate principles which lie between the first principle and specific moral norms).

4. Chapters nine through twelve concern the application of principles to actions. We consider the various kinds of voluntariness and the different sorts of responsibility attaching to them; we also explain what commitments are. Moral norms in general are discussed, as is the moral authority of law (a topic treated here mainly because it has been customary to cover it in textbooks on morals). Finally, we take up different kinds of doubts and how they should be resolved.

5. Chapters thirteen through eighteen deal with sin—its nature and its consequences. After explaining what sin is in general, we examine original sin, including contemporary objections to, and accounts of, the dogma. We then go on to discuss distinctions among sins, sins of thought, the distinction between grave and light matter, various theories of fundamental option, sins of weakness, and the "way of sin" which ends in death. This treatment includes the question of hell.

6. Chapters nineteen through twenty-two present the large principles of Christian life in the context of God's saving work in Christ. We consider human fulfillment in Jesus and the contribution which human acts in this life make to the fulfillment of God's plan. This leads to consideration of the relationship between God and humankind and, specifically, revelation and faith. Next we discuss God's redemptive work, especially the old and new covenants and the Incarnation. Finally, we examine the role which Jesus' human life played in God's redemptive work.

7. Chapters twenty-three through twenty-seven explain what Christian life is: how we are united with Jesus' redemptive act, what it means to "follow" Jesus, the crucial role of personal vocation, and the relationship of conscience to the teaching of the Church. We then consider how Christians are God's "children"—that is, our participation in divine life. This leads to examination of Christian love as the principle of Christian life, and to a discussion of the "modes of Christian response," which parallel the modes of responsibility (discussed in chapter eight) but go beyond them. Finally in this section we explain what a life formed by the modes of Christian response is like.

8. Chapters twenty-eight through thirty-three discuss some of the principal elements of every Christian life. First we consider

the practicability of Christian morality, including the organizing role of personal vocation and the indispensable function of hope. We examine prayer, considered as the fundamental category of Christian action, and then take up the sacraments, which are its organizing principles.

9. Chapter thirty-four sums up what has gone before. It sets out our view of authentic humanism and explains how Christians should regard human goods in this life.

10. Chapters thirty-five and thirty-six are a kind of appendix presenting a theological clarification of certain ideas which are basic to this treatment of Christian moral principles. The first of these chapters deals with infallibility in general, the inerrancy of Scripture, the magisterium, the infallibility of moral teachings which are not "defined" doctrines, and the nature and obligation of religious assent to such teachings. The second chapter critiques radical theological dissent, showing the weaknesses of various arguments put forward to support it, and identifying the sources of such dissent and its implications.

B: Key to References in the Text

Because readers of this book can refer to the larger volume on which it is based in order to investigate the sources of various positions and arguments, footnotes have been kept to a minimum and usually only sources of direct quotations are supplied. But more generous references are given in the text itself to the chief sources: Scripture and the teaching of the Catholic Church, especially that contained in the documents of the Second Vatican Council.

Quotations from Scripture, except those within other quotations, are from the New Revised Standard Version of the Bible. References are made by means of the following abbreviations:

Acts	Acts of the Apostles
Col	Colossians
1 Cor	1 Corinthians
2 Cor	2 Corinthians
Dn	Daniel
Dt	Deuteronomy
Eph	Ephesians
Ex	Exodus

Gal	Galatians
Gn	Genesis
Heb	Hebrews
Is	Isaiah
Jas	James
Jb	Job
Jer	Jeremiah
Jn	John (Gospel)
1 Jn	1 John (Epistle)
Jude	Jude
Lk	Luke
Lv	Leviticus
Mk	Mark
Mt	Matthew
Prv	Proverbs
Ps	Psalms
1 Pt	1 Peter
Rom	Romans
Rv	Revelation
Sir	Sirach (Ecclesiasticus)
1 Thes	1 Thessalonians
2 Thes	2 Thessalonians
1 Tm	1 Timothy
2 Tm	2 Timothy

Quotations from the Constitutions, Decrees, and Declarations of the Second Vatican Council, unless otherwise noted, are from *The Documents of Vatican II*, edited by Walter M. Abbott, S.J., and Joseph Gallagher (New York: America Press, 1966). In some cases the Abbott-Gallagher translation has been amended to conform more exactly to the Council's Latin text, and when minor amendments proved inadequate, a fresh translation has been supplied. These facts are indicated with the reference. References to the Vatican II documents use the abbreviations derived from the initial letters of the Latin text of each document and then the numbers of the articles into which the documents were divided by the Council itself.

AA	*Apostolicam Actuositatem* (Laity)
AG	*Ad Gentes* (Missions)

DH   *Dignitatis Humanae* (Religious Liberty)
DV   *Dei Verbum* (Divine Revelation)
GS   *Gaudium et Spes* (Church in the World)
LG   *Lumen Gentium* (On the Church)
NA   *Nostra Aetate* (Non-Christian Religions)
OT   *Optatam Totius* (Priestly Formation)
PO   *Presbyterorum Ordinis* (Priestly Life)
SC   *Sacrosanctum Concilium* (Liturgy)
UR   *Unitatis Redintegratio* (Ecumenism)

Note that in the Abbott-Gallagher edition only the *italicized footnotes* are part of the Council documents. The notes in Roman type were added by the commentator on each document, whose name appears at the end of the essay introducing the document. Because of the added notes, in the Abbott edition the Council's own notes usually have numbers different from those in the official texts.

"DS" refers to Henricus Denzinger—Adolfus Schönmetzer, S.J., *Enchiridion Symbolorum Definitionum et Declarationum de Rebus Fidei et Morum*, ed. 34 (Freiburg im Breisgau: Herder, 1967). This volume, as its title indicates, is a collection of "creeds, definitions, and declarations on matters of faith and morals." Texts are in chronological order. Two sequences of numbers appear in the margins; both are indicated in references in the present text. The lower numbers are found in earlier editions of the handbook and in many publications which used it. Quotations from this collection, unless otherwise noted, are from: *The Church Teaches: Documents of the Church in English Translation*, translated by J. F. Clarkson, S.J., J. H. Edwards, S.J., W. J. Kelly, S.J., and J. J. Welch, S.J. (Rockford, Ill.: Tan Books, 1973). Texts in the translation are arranged topically rather than chronologically; a table (370–75) correlates with DS.

C: How This Volume Came to Be

This book is the product of a collaboration. As was explained above, it is essentially a condensation of volume one of *The Way of the Lord Jesus* by Germain Grisez, a moral theologian who teaches at Mount Saint Mary's College in Emmitsburg, Maryland. It was written by Russell Shaw, Director of Public Information for the Knights of Columbus, who was one of several persons who helped Grisez in the writing of the earlier work. The co-authors have also collaborated on several other projects since the mid-1960s, including *Beyond the New Morality: The Responsibilities of Freedom,* a popular introduction to Grisez's ethical theory (first published by the University of Notre Dame Press in 1974 and currently in its third, revised edition).

In preparing the manuscript, Shaw used both volume one of *The Way of the Lord Jesus* and transcripts of Grisez's class lectures based on volume one. Grisez reviewed and revised Shaw's text, and Shaw then made further improvements in the text as revised by Grisez. While the book thus embodies distinct contributions by the co-authors, readers should be aware that the substantive content reflects Grisez's research and theological reflection, as condensed and restated by Shaw. At the same time, the authors acknowledge shared responsibility for this presentation of the material—both its strengths and its deficiencies—in its totality.

D: Acknowledgments

The acknowledgments section of the "User's Guide and Preface" of the volume on which this book is based explains the origin and sponsorship of Grisez's moral theology project.

Dr. Robert J. Wickenheiser, President of Mount Saint Mary's College, has continued to encourage the work in every possible way.

Rev. Gabriel Brinkman, O.F.M., Managing Director of Franciscan Herald Press, kindly agreed to the publication of this condensed and popularized book based on *The Way of the Lord Jesus: Christian Moral Principles.* Franciscan Herald Press retains all rights to the major work and plans to keep it in print.

Joseph Casey, S.J., John Finnis, Janet Smith, and Michael Carragher, O.P., kindly read the manuscript and made many very helpful suggestions.

Jeannette Grisez carefully did all the necessary secretarial work on this volume.

1. Introduction

This book is written in response to the Second Vatican Council's call for the renewal of moral theology. Other books in the future may also meet the Council's prescription—may, indeed, meet it better. But this work does embody what the Council had in mind and presents fundamental principles of moral theology in a manner faithful to the Catholic tradition while at the same time incorporating the best insights of the present day.

To make clear what we are attempting and why, we shall examine three questions in this introductory chapter: what moral theology is; why renewal in moral theology is needed; and how the renewal ought to be carried out.

A: What Moral Theology Is

Theology in a general sense is thought and talk about God, as well as about everything else insofar as it is related to God. As the word is commonly used, however, "theology" refers to reflection, more or less systematic, on the sources in which the truth of faith is expressed: Scripture, the documents of the ecumenical councils, and so on. Thus, theology is subordinate, not superior, to the normative expressions of the Church's faith. Faith is directed to divinely revealed truths, not to theological propositions. One does not "believe" any theologian—one believes what God has revealed.

Theology, however, has much to contribute to understanding the truths which are the object of faith. "Positive" theology does this by drawing out the meaning of the authoritative sources—Scripture, conciliar documents, and so on—which express these truths, while "systematic" theology seeks to relate truths of faith to other propositions which are not divinely revealed but are certainly true or very well grounded.

Systematic theology has two branches: contemplative and moral. The former, in the past called "dogmatic" theology and today often simply called "systematics," attempts to work out a single, coherent view of reality in light of faith. Truths not part of faith are examined in order to see how everything else is related to faith. Contemplative theology, done correctly, seeks to comprehend all reality in a Christian world view.

Moral theology also reflects upon the truths of faith, but it is less concerned to elaborate a coherent, comprehensive Christian view of reality than to show how one should live in light of Christian faith. Although it has its abstract and theoretical dimension, it is essentially a practical discipline. Its basic question is: What guidance does faith provide for living?

That should not be taken in too narrow a sense. The question is how to live in a way consistent with *all* the truths of faith. Thus, an adequate moral theology must relate matters like the Incarnation and the sacraments to Christian living. Moral theology does not preempt the work of scholars who specialize in these subjects, but it tries to show the bearing which these and all other elements of divine revelation have upon life. Moral theology is interested in the whole of faith but with a specific end in view—to determine how a person of faith should relate faith to life.

The method of systematic theology, including moral theology, is properly called "dialectical." This method begins from and always retains the rich complexity of reality and life, but seeks unifying insights which will help one to "get it all together." Proceeding by dialectical method, we explore the reality of faith from within, trying to understand better that which we already believe and wish to live by.

Dialectical method thus does not involve either questioning the truths of faith or trying to prove them. (Showing the reasonableness of faith is the task of apologetics.) But it does not follow that, as some claim, theology is an exercise in obscurantism. If there is such a thing as divine revelation, there is simply nothing superior to it by which to criticize it or demonstrate its truth. One believes what God has revealed by faith; one seeks to understand it better by the dialectical method of theology.

The Second Vatican Council expresses it this way: "Sacred theology rests on the written word of God, together with sacred tradition, as its primary and perpetual foundation" (*DV* 24). And again: "The task of authentically interpreting the word of God, whether written or handed on, has been entrusted exclusively to the living teaching office of the Church, whose authority is exercised in the name of Jesus Christ" (*DV* 10).

This second statement introduces a new idea—the teaching authority, or magisterium, of the Church. A Catholic does not encounter revelation as an isolated individual; he or she hears God's word in company with others, as a member of the Church, whose competence to hand on and interpret the truths of faith he or she likewise accepts as a truth of faith.

The dialectical method of theology resists attempts to reduce faith to a set of "facts" which can be explained "scientifically." One can speak of theology as a science, and so it is, in the sense that it is careful about facts and logical in reasoning. But it is not a science which stands apart from its subject matter, dominating and controlling it. Catholic theology, we repeat, explores faith from within, not from without.

That suggests an old and rather tired question: Is faith compatible with science? Some who go on raising this question clearly mean to imply either that science has found out something which shows faith to be in error or else that sooner or later it is sure to do so. But this misses the point. "Scientific facts" and logic can no more show truths of faith to be false than they can show them to be true. There is no scientific fact or logical exercise which can either demonstrate or disprove the Trinity or the Incarnation, any more than some chemical test can be devised to show that Jesus is or is not bodily present in the Blessed Sacrament. Truths of faith are not absurd, not contrary to reason; they simply are not susceptible to proof or refutation by "scientific" tools.

Nor does a sound method in moral theology attempt to use psychological or sociological evidence to prove or disprove the Church's moral teaching. While the contemporary experience of the faithful undoubtedly has some relevance for the work of the moral theologian, and even more for those engaged in pastoral ministry, contemporary experience must ultimately be judged by the Church's constant and firm teaching, not vice versa. As the moral philosopher does not alter his judgment that, for example, racial prejudice is wrong, simply because many people are prejudiced, so the Catholic moral theologian does not conclude that the Church's constant and firm moral teaching on some point is wrong simply because, at one time or another, many people refuse to accept it.

This does not exclude pluralism from Catholic moral theology. There is ample room for pluralism, not only of methodologies but of views—including views inconsistent with one another—about the many questions which the Church has not definitely settled.

As we have said, this book presents principles of moral theology. But why do we need to concern ourselves with principles at all? Why not skip the generalities and get down to cases—to specifics like abortion, nuclear deterrence, and issues in bioethics?

The answer is that it is much more important to understand the principles of Christian morality than to solve particular problems. The general understanding—the principles—of how to live in the light of faith provides an orientation which directs the approach to specific issues; and the correct orientation is necessary to ensure that specific issues are correctly addressed. Furthermore, the Church's teaching on very many specific matters is perfectly clear; the problem is not to know what is morally true but to grasp its basis and be able to explain it to others—in other words, to understand the principles.

In unfolding the principles of moral theology, we shall bring into the discussion some ideas, from the field of moral philosophy or ethics, which do not belong to faith itself. This is necessary to clarify certain matters concerning human actions: to understand actions, one must understand human purposes and practical reasoning (the reasoning by which we deliberate about what we ought and ought not to do). We shall not, however, be speaking of obscure theoretical matters, but simply providing clarifications of ordinary language and experience which our subject matter requires even though they are not found anywhere in Scripture or in the teaching of the Church. What are the several different meanings of freedom? What does it mean to make a choice? We shall take up such questions as we go along, because clarity about things like freedom and choice is necessary to an adequate understanding of how we ought to live as Christians.

B: Why Renewal in Moral Theology Is Needed

We have said that this book is a response to the Second Vatican Council's call for renewal in moral theology. But why does it need renewing? Generally speaking, the Church's moral teaching is quite clear. Most people are in no real doubt about where the Church stands on killing the innocent, fornication, stealing, and a great deal else. In calling for renewal, was the Council implying that the Church's teaching on certain questions was mistaken? Or did it have something else in mind?

Evidently it had something else in mind. One learns what that was from a close examination of a brief passage in Vatican II's Decree on Priestly Formation (*OT* 16). There the Council speaks in a manner at once gentle and positive, pointing out what should be done rather than dwelling on what had gone wrong. Yet this positive approach makes clear by implication the deficiencies of moral theology up to then.

The renewal of moral theology, the Council says, requires three things in particular. First, "livelier contact with the mystery of Christ and the history of salvation"—in other words, moral theology should be Christocentric. Second, it should be "more thoroughly nourished by scriptural teaching"—in other words, more grounded in and enriched by sacred Scripture. Third, moral theology should emphasize both the nobility of the Christian calling and the "obligation" of Christians "to bring forth fruit in charity for the life of the world"—in other words, it should stress the peculiar excellence of the calling to heavenly fulfillment while also recognizing that it is just this calling which obliges Christians to strive to make the world better.

Moral theology, as it developed after the sixteenth-century Council of Trent, was deficient in all these respects. Over a period of time, it came to have two great defects.

The first was legalism. Currently, "legalism" is often used merely as a gibe to discredit prescriptions concerning conduct with which one disagrees. Some, for instance, call it "legalistic" to maintain that premarital and extramarital sex are always wrong or to insist that Catholics are bound to worship God at times and in ways specified by the Church. We are not using "legalism" and "legalistic" like that.

By "legalism" we mean thinking about moral norms as if they were simply rules to be obeyed by someone who wants to get along—avoid conflict, be accepted, achieve success—in the society which lays down the rules. In this view, moral norms are not unlike the rules of a private club which requires its members to observe certain niceties of dress and conduct if they are to remain in good standing. While people may obey such rules, they generally do so without supposing that the rules are intrinsically deserving of obedience.

Legalism has two different sources. For one thing, it is a natural stage in a child's development. Children are spontaneous legalists. At the dawn of moral reasoning, when they first advert to the question of how they ought to behave, they typically equate morality—good behavior—with obedience to the rules laid down for them by parents or others on whom they depend, while supposing that bad behavior means disobeying the rules. To be good is to be obedient, to be bad is to disobey.

This childish view of morality frequently persists well beyond childhood—often, throughout the course of a lifetime. This is roughly what Freud meant by superego: in adults, the interiorized, more or less guilt-ridden residue of an infantile view which equates morality with obedience to authority figures. We see no reason to disagree with Freud that what he calls superego is present and operative to some degree in all of us, including even the most morally mature. Nor is it any less true of those who rebel against moral norms. In throwing off the shackles, as they see it, they act the role of naughty children, still viewing moral norms through the fogged lenses of obedience/disobedience.

The second source of legalism lies in the development of moral theology after the sixteenth century. At a certain point it came to seem both reasonable and convenient to view moral teaching as a set of rules to be obeyed.

Indeed it *is* convenient to be able to say, "Here is the rule, and here is what will happen if you disobey it." But the short-term convenience hardly compensates for the long-term harm, both to those who are indoctrinated in this way and to moral theology itself. Among the bad effects are the following.

In focusing on specifics—"Here are the rules"—legalism fails to convey an overall sense of Christian life. For all practical purposes, Christian vocation drops out of the picture. To be sure, a moralist operating in the legalistic mold readily grants that there is such a thing as Christian vocation, but he also takes it for granted that it is the concern of spiritual theology and no concern, professionally speaking, of his.

Legalism also tends to be minimalistic. "How far can I go without breaking the rules?" "When does this stop being a venial sin and start to be mortal sin?" "What is the least I have to do in order to obey the law?" This crabbed approach hardly encourages anyone to live a Christian life as it should be lived—out of love which strives to put to work one's *whole* mind, *whole* heart, *whole* soul, and *whole* strength.

In fact, legalism leaves a kind of morality-neutral zone in a person's life, an area untouched (as the legalistic mindset imagines) by moral considerations. There are many practical questions which cannot be answered by appealing to rules. "Should I marry or become a priest?" "Should I go into this line of work or that?" Legalism has nothing to say on such matters. Thus, it contributes to the impression that such choices have little or no moral significance. "Since I can choose either way without sinning (breaking a rule), my choice has no bearing on morality." This introduces a dichotomy into life, between the area (governed by rules) where morality is operative and the area (to which no rules apply) which lies outside its scope.

Legalism also turns moral teaching and pastoral work into a kind of administrative activity. The job of a teacher of morality is to tell people what to do, to run their lives: "Here are the rules—obey them." The pastor is the local administrator of the same set of rules, and he is likely to imagine that he has the power to excuse from their observance. Thus, legalism very often underlies the "pastoral" idea that one should not impose heavier burdens on people than they can carry ("The Church's teaching on sexual activity is too hard for you to live by, so don't feel that you're obliged to make the effort"). The assumption is that moral norms are not truths but rules, to be enforced or dispensed from as circumstances dictate.

Finally, legalism leads to rebellion. Sooner or later most people with a bit of spunk grow angry at being told, "Here is what the Church requires of you. Obey the rules if you want to get to heaven, disobey and you will go to hell." For a legalistic-minded teacher or pastor, the obvious way of heading off rebellion is to stop harping on the rules, rather like a policeman who turns a blind eye to infractions of the law in order to avoid confrontations with those committing them.

As we said, over a period of time legalism became a characteristic of the classical moral theology which took shape following the Council of Trent. Considering that a great deal of the new moral theology since the Second Vatican Council has been in conscious and self-proclaimed reaction against this classical moral theology, one might suppose that the new moralists would avoid legalistic errors. But that is not the case; for the most part, the new moralists are as legalistic as the old.

Thus, today it is commonly assumed that whatever is not absolutely and certainly forbidden must be permitted: About such matters, people can do whatever they please. Much effort therefore goes into reducing the obligations of Christian life by showing that acts of certain kinds cannot be proven beyond the shadow of a doubt to be always wrong. In that case, performing such an act is called "following one's conscience." Generally rejecting the obligation to assent to the Church's moral teaching, the new moral theology sets the minimum standards of Christian living much lower than the old moral theology did. And it still fails to explain human fulfillment in this life in Christian terms, what the Christian way of life is, and how living as a Christian in this life is intrinsically related to fulfillment in everlasting life.

That points to the other great defect in moral theology as Vatican II found it, one even more profound than legalism. It is failure to understand adequately what a Christian is and what Christian life is. We do not say this patronizingly. The failure in question is analogous to the difficulties experienced by Christians in the Church's early centuries grappling with the fact of the Incarnation. Many early Christological heresies arose because it was hard to see how Jesus could be both fully human and fully divine. Similarly, the failure to understand adequately what a Christian is and what Christian life is arises from the difficulty in properly relating the human and divine (the "natural" and "supernatural") aspects of Christian life. As a result, many thought it necessary to choose between striving to be holy and striving to be fully human. This led to two opposed errors: one stressing fulfillment in heaven while according little importance to life in this world, except as a kind of testing ground; the other emphasizing this life so strongly that heavenly fulfillment seems a vague hypothesis, with little practical importance here and now.

The first mistake was the typical error of classical moral theology. Not infrequently, the idea which came through was *not* that living as a Christian is precisely the way to fulfillment as a human person, but that living a human life and living as a Christian are conflicting alternatives. Naturally enough, Christians—or at least those who aspired to live as they ought—tended to downgrade human goods and human life in this world for the sake, as they understood it, of the supernatural and of the fulfillment to which they looked forward in heaven.

One finds this way of thinking in St. Augustine, a Father of the Church and a great saint, who nevertheless suggests a dichotomy between the city of God and the city of man. It can be expressed as a set of proportions: The city of God is to the city of man as the heavenly is to the earthly and as love of God to the point of contempt for self is to love of self to the point of contempt for God (also see chapters 13:C and 34:A). This plainly puts the human and earthly on the side of moral evil, and makes it seem that Christians cannot love God as they ought unless they despise themselves and earthly goods.

By way of a corrective, much recent work in moral theology rightly emphasizes the importance of human fulfillment and of the Christian obligation to work for the betterment of this world. This is in line with Vatican II's call "to bring forth fruit in charity for the life of the world" (*OT* 16). But there is a problem. Atheistic humanism emerged in modern times partly in reaction to false supernaturalism. It has become a dominant feature of today's world. Under the influence of secular humanism in either its Marxist form or in the consumerist guise which it assumes in Western liberal democracies, some have fallen into the mistake of putting too much emphasis on getting results in this world. All too often today theologians, both in the Third World and the affluent West, argue for solutions to individual or social problems which violate moral norms—for example, the norm which forbids killing the innocent—in order to achieve this-worldly goals they consider important enough to justify such violations.

The Judeo-Christian tradition views moral choices with a sense of ultimate seriousness. By the use we make of our freedom, we implicitly choose life or death. Under the influence of secular humanism, this sense of seriousness tends to disappear in the new moral theology. It supposes that everyone will go to heaven, no matter what choices he or she makes, or that Christians can make individual evil choices yet still retain a fundamentally right moral orientation; or else, despite the orientation of Christian hope to fulfillment in heaven, it silently passes over the whole question of life after death as if it were of no practical importance.

In sum, classical moral theology was too otherworldly—it failed to see the intrinsic and necessary link between human goods and heavenly fulfillment, between life in this world and eternal life; while the new moral theology is too this-worldly—it places so much emphasis on limited fulfillment in this life that it overlooks the Christian hope for complete and eternal fulfillment in the new heavens and new earth which are to come at the end of time.

C: How to Carry Out the Needed Renewal in Moral Theology

Inasmuch as both classical moral theology as it existed up to the time of the Second Vatican Council and much of the new moral theology since the Council err in two fundamental ways— legalism and an inadequate understanding of the complex, divine-human constitution of the Christian and of Christian life—an approach responsive to Vatican II's call for renewal must proceed by avoiding both mistakes. We try to present such an approach in this book.

To avoid legalism, it is necessary to see moral norms as truths, not rules. This view comes into focus when one sees that moral norms are not mere arbitrary decrees, whether of divine or human origin, but are determined by human goods, the fundamental purposes in respect to which our fulfillment is possible. A true moral norm is no more a rule than is, say, a true statement about how to cope with the weather. One person says to another, "It's raining very hard; you ought to take an umbrella!" If it really *is* raining very hard, then the practical advice—"you ought to take an umbrella"—is not a rule but a statement of how one must act in order to survive and flourish in light of reality.

When the Church instructs us regarding a moral truth of which we were not previously aware, we have a clearer grasp of reality than we did before. One can of course ignore reality and act accordingly, but in that case one is frustrating one's own fulfillment and imposing on oneself a kind of mutilation, not only here and now but, potentially, forever. By contrast, acting in a manner which corresponds to the way reality is contributes to one's immediate and lasting fulfillment. This nonlegalistic approach, adopted in this book, is very different from saying either, "Here's what the Church teaches. Obey these rules if you want to go to heaven, disobey them and you will go to hell," or, "Here's what the Church teaches—but it's too hard for you, so you're dispensed."

To avoid falling into the trap presented by an inadequate understanding of the divine-human constitution of the Christian and of Christian life, we need to give an account of the Christian and of Christian life as both fully human and fully divine, on the model of Jesus. Jesus is God but also, by the Incarnation, man; nevertheless, he is not two persons but one. The Christian is a human person by nature but also divine by the grace of the Spirit—God's child by adoption—while yet remaining one person. There is no more conflict in the Christian's being both human and divine than there is in Jesus' being both God and man.

Christian life must be authentically and thoroughly human, but at the same time fully and authentically divine. It is moral theology's task to show that a humanly fulfilling life is one in which fulfillment here and now is at the same time necessarily, intrinsically oriented to the eternal fulfillment of heaven. By distinguishing the human and the divine in the Christian and in Christian life without separating them, such an approach eliminates the apparent need to choose between the two. Thus, it breaks down the unreal separation between the this-worldly and the otherworldly in Christian life that has hobbled so much of moral theology both before and since Vatican II.

The human and the divine are not only present in our lives here and now, but will also be present in heaven. Through our lives we cooperate with God in creating a part of the kingdom which will last forever. In this sense, then, a moral theology responsive to the Council's call for renewal will show in depth what Vatican II meant when it said:

> For after we have obeyed the Lord, and in His Spirit nurtured on earth the values of human dignity, brotherhood and freedom, and indeed all the good fruits of our nature and enterprise, we will find them again, but freed of stain, burnished and transfigured. This will be so when Christ hands over to the Father a kingdom eternal and universal: "a kingdom of truth and life, of holiness and grace, of justice, love, and peace" [Preface of the Feast of Christ the King]. On this earth that kingdom is already present in mystery. When the Lord returns, it will be brought into full flower. (*GS* 39)

2. Free Choice, Self-determination, Community, and Character

Made in the image and likeness of God, human persons are endowed with magnificent powers of understanding and freedom, so that they can consciously live their own lives. To explain how Christian life should be lived, therefore, we begin by discussing free choice and its role in determining the moral identities of individuals and communities.

We address this matter of free choice from four perspectives: that human persons can make free choices; the importance of free choice as a principle of Christian morality; the deeper reality of free choices; and how free choices build up persons and communities.

A: That Human Persons Can Make Free Choices

Faith both presupposes free choice and teaches that human persons can make free choices. In the Old Testament God offers the people his covenant, either to accept or reject. In the New Testament Jesus establishes a new covenant between God and humanity which human beings again are at liberty to accept or refuse. It is up to human persons freely to choose—or to refuse—the relationship of filiation with God.

The Church insists in many contexts on the reality of free choice. In its *Decree on Justification* the Council of Trent specifically rejects the idea that "after Adam's sin man's free will was destroyed and lost" (DS 1555/815). Vatican II in its decree on religious liberty underlines the fact that the act of faith involves a free choice: "The act of faith is of its very nature a free act" (*DH* 10).

Scripture makes the point that when we sin, we do so freely; we, not God, are responsible for our evil choices. The classic formulation of this truth is found in Sirach.

Do not say, "It was the Lord's doing that I fell away";
    for he does not do what he hates.
Do not say, "It was he who led me astray":
    for he has no need of the sinful.
The Lord hates all abominations;
    such things are not loved by those who fear him.
It was he who created humankind in the beginning,
    and he left them in the power of their own free choice.
If you choose, you can keep the commandments,
    and to act faithfully is a matter of your own choice.
He has placed before you fire and water;
    stretch out your hand for whichever you choose.
Before each person are life and death,
    and whichever one chooses will be given.
For great is the wisdom of the Lord;
    he is mighty in power and sees everything;
his eyes are on those who fear him,
    and he knows every human action.
He has not commanded anyone to be wicked,
    and he has not given anyone permission to sin.
(Sir 15:11–20)

Some people nevertheless raise a theological objection to free choice: God causes everything, including free choices; but if God causes choices, they can hardly be said to be free. This would be quite true if God's causality were like any other—in that case it would be absurd to say that something is both created and free. But God's causality is *not* like any other. As we do not understand what God is in himself, so we do not understand what it is for him to cause. The seeming contradiction in the fact that choices are created and also free arises from supposing that we understand God's causality, when in fact we do not.

Today, however, the main opposition to the reality of free choices is not theological. Rather, it is conventional educated opinion which rejects the idea that human beings are free. Contemporary psychology and sociology take it for granted that human beings do not make free choices, and except for believing Christians and Jews, this is the view of virtually all those associated with modern scholarship and science. A formidable intellectual array against freedom! If these determinists are correct, there is little or nothing left of Christianity. It would make no sense to speak of the dignity of human beings made in God's image—for God is free, and according to determinism we are not. Similarly, the notion of a covenant with God which we are free to accept or reject would be meaningless.

It hardly needs saying that there is much that is important and worthwhile in contemporary psychology and sociology. Nevertheless, their deterministic premises require that they be approached with a certain caution, even a certain suspicion. Despite the impressive credentials of those who work in these fields, their assumption of the truth of determinism is an ideological position supported by neither evidence nor good arguments.

Certainly freedom has limits. Modern psychology has no difficulty showing that, as a result of one form of conditioning or another, people commonly have fewer options for choice than they imagine. Likewise, it is a simple matter for sociology to demonstrate that particular individuals and groups—the ghetto poor, for example—*cannot* choose and do many desirable things, because they *cannot* see these things as realistic possibilities. But true as all this is, it does not demonstrate that determinism is true.

Three things need to be said in response to determinism. First, any effort to show that there is no such thing as free choice is radically self-defeating. Experience shows that people often make choices which seem to them to be free. So, determinism is not a self-evident truth. Rather, it is a philosophical theory based on arguments. In arguing their case, determinists proceed in various ways but must always say in effect, "It is more reasonable to think people do not make free choices than to think they do. Therefore you ought to accept determinism." Now, this "ought," spoken or implicit, is an appeal to be loyal to the pursuit of truth; and such loyalty, upon which the determinists urge us to act, is impossible if there are no free choices. One can only do as one "ought" in this matter if one is able to make and keep the commitment—which is a choice—to pursue the truth and be reasonable. Therefore, it is impossible to make an argument for determinism which does not implicitly make an appeal which would be pointless if determinism were true. Hence, every argument for determinism is self-defeating.

Second, it is an implicit assumption of virtually every argument for determinism that everything can and must be completely explained by a "sufficient reason" which wholly accounts for it. As a matter of fact, most things can by and large be explained, and it is reasonable to start an inquiry by assuming that something one is concerned with has an explanation. But it does not follow that *everything* has a sufficient reason, and free choices in fact do not. A choice has an adequate cause—the person choosing—but not a sufficient reason, which by definition would have to be able to explain in each case why just *this* choice rather than another was made. In the case of some choices at least, this simply is not possible. Interpersonal love has no sufficient reason: there is no reason, for example, accounting for the fact that God, out of love, has freely chosen to create and redeem us, nor is there a sufficient reason to explain why some human beings do, and others do not, choose to respond in love to God. One may be able to find many reasons leading up to such a choice, but the reasons do not finally account for the choice—to accept or reject an offer of love—because it is free.

Third, as we have seen, determinists are correct in saying that freedom of choice has more limits than we commonly recognize, and that some persons literally cannot choose various things which others regard as desirable for them. People cannot choose what they do not see any way of doing. One might for example exhort a poor, black addict to give up drugs and make something of his life; but if one learned more about him, one might find out that he has already made the effort, failed, and concluded—reasonably, one would have to say—that his poverty, his lack of education, racial prejudice, and other circumstances have so stacked the deck against him that "making something of his life" is not an available option for him.

It does not follow that he has no freedom of choice. Perhaps he recognizes that he is harming his wife and children and preventing them from receiving welfare by continuing to live with them. Seeing that he can either stay (which would be convenient for him) or leave, he chooses to leave. Thus, although there are limits on free choice, free choice remains operative within those limits, and, all things considered, that may be the best choice that occurs to him.

B: The Importance of Free Choice as a Principle of Christian Morality

Free choice has a threefold importance as a principle—that is, as a source—of Christian morality.

First, and most obvious, choice is a source of moral responsibility. We cannot rightly be praised or blamed, held to be morally guilty or deserving of credit, except for what we have freely chosen to do. Persons are responsible in a full sense only when two conditions are met: first, when it is in their power to do what is good; second, when they either do what is good, fail to do it, or do what is bad by their own free choice—by a choice, that is, which really could have been otherwise.

Responsibility in this sense is not the same thing as being held responsible. A cat may be "responsible" for knocking a lamp off a table and breaking it, but the cat is evidently not responsible in the same way as an adult person who dashes a lamp to the floor in a display of spiteful bad temper. The cat does not make free choices; sane people who break lamps out of nastiness do. On the other hand, someone's natural gifts and temperament—cheerful, gloomy, whatever—do not make him or her either praiseworthy or blameworthy, for these traits are not freely chosen. One's temperament and natural gifts may make it easier or harder to make good choices, but it is still the choices and what follows from them for which one has responsibility.

Free choices are important because they make one's actions *one's own*, one's life *one's own*, one's moral identity *one's own*. Actions, life, and moral identity are all the responsibility of the one who has shaped them as they are by his or her own free choices. Free choice is a principle of responsibility because our freely chosen acts are ours in a unique and especially strong way. Many things in life only happen to us, but our choices are fully ours. They come from us and they constitute us as the kind of persons we are.

Second, as we noted earlier, free choice is important as a principle of Christian morality because of its relationship to the act of faith. Choice is essential to this act; lacking freedom, one could not accept the personal relationship which is at the heart of faith and give oneself in that relationship.

Freedom is essential to every intimate personal relationship. The relationship between two people who somehow came together by accident and stayed together out of habit and convenience would simply not have the same meaning and value as the relationship between a husband and wife who freely chose to give themselves to each other. The freedom of the self-giving is what gives this relationship its special character. So also with the relationship of faith between individuals and God. God offers us communion with himself—not by making us incapable of choosing otherwise, but precisely by making it possible for us to choose. He wants us, evidently, not to be slaves, puppets, or robots, but real friends, who give ourselves to him as freely as he gives himself to us. This places morality and responsibility in a light profoundly different from that cast by legalism and its narrow concern with what a person will be held responsible for.

Finally, and related to this, free choice is important because it is the basis of human personal dignity. "Dignity" is used these days in various loose and sometimes questionable senses (for example, "death with dignity"), but as the Second Vatican Council uses it, dignity has a specific and altogether serious sense: it is the status which persons have because they are like God. "Authentic freedom," the Council says, "is an exceptional sign of the divine image within man" (*GS* 17).

Human dignity thus essentially arises from and resides in the capacity for free choice. But freedom and dignity carry with them obligations.

> It is in accordance with their dignity as persons—that is, beings endowed with reason and free will and therefore privileged to bear personal responsibility—that all men should be at once impelled by nature and also bound by a moral obligation to seek the truth, especially religious truth. They are also bound to adhere to the truth, once it is known, and to order their whole lives in accord with the demands of truth. (*DH* 2)

God has made us free, but through the exercise of freedom we are also self-makers in a very real sense, constituting our moral identities by our choices. Through choice we can enter into communion with God; through choice also we can reject God's offer of friendship and communion.

C: The Deeper Reality of Free Choices

We have seen that there is such a thing as free choice. We have also seen why free choice is important as a principle of Christian morality. But what *is* free choice?

First of all, we need to distinguish the freedom involved in free choice from "freedom" in several other senses.

One of these is physical freedom—the lack of physical obstacles or physical coercion. In this sense, physics speaks of free-falling bodies, those which fall according to the law of gravity. Similarly, animals in the wild are physically free to move about and behave as their instincts and conditioning dictate. Physical freedom is only relative, however, not absolute. Free-falling bodies can only fall "down," not "up"; animals in the zoo are at once physically free *within* their enclosures and confined *by* the enclosures.

There is also freedom from authority. This is the freedom people enjoy when they are free to do as they please; no one else is setting rules which they must obey. Adolescents like this kind of freedom, and not only adolescents. We all like to be free from demands imposed by somebody else, at liberty to do whatever we like in pursuit of whatever we want. Even so, this doing-as-one-pleases is not free choice either. For one can make free choices even in situations where one is *not* free to do as one pleases: the choice to defy and resist those in power, and also the choice to obey. Conversely, small children, who cannot yet make free choices, enjoy freedom to do as they please within the limits set by grown-ups' discipline.

Freedom has a third sense which is very important in theology: the freedom of the children of God. This is freedom from sin and sin's consequences—the liberty we receive in Jesus, by the grace of God. This freedom of the children of God presupposes free choice but is not itself free choice: we share in the freedom of the children of God through the free choice of faith. The freedom of the children of God is always good, however, while free choices can be bad as well as good. Evil people also make free choices but they do not enjoy the freedom of God's children, which is liberation from evil. As this suggests, too, the freedom of God's children is not freedom to do as one pleases. The New Testament makes this clear (see Gal 5:13; 1 Pt 2:16–17).

What, then, is free choice? As we have seen, the answer can be stated rather simply: Free choice is making up one's own mind to do this rather than that, or to do this rather than not doing it, when both alternatives are real possibilities for the one making the choice. The actual *experience* of choice, however, requires a closer look.

Sometimes we think of something to do, see no reason for not doing it, and go ahead and do it. There is no choice in such spontaneous behavior, and so no free choice either. Rather, the experience of choice starts with awareness of conflict: One thinks of doing something, feels inclined to do it, finds a reason for doing it, and yet in some way is blocked from going forward. Perhaps one also sees a reason for *not* doing what one has in mind; or perhaps one also sees some other interesting possibility which is incompatible with the first. In any case, finding oneself blocked from acting spontaneously, one hesitates and begins to reflect and deliberate: "I can do this, or I can refrain from doing it. I can choose this, or I can choose that. Which shall it be?"

Sometimes, while this pondering is still going on, a seeming obstacle or alternative simply drops out of the picture. A man would like to see a highly praised new movie on a Saturday afternoon, but he also knows that his grass needs cutting. When Saturday morning rolls around, it is pouring rain. "Much too wet to cut grass today, so I'll go to the movies." There is no choice here (at least, no choice between cutting the grass and going to the movies). A free choice can take place only when the incompatible alternatives continue, as it were, to stand up, when one really can choose to have either "this" or "that" but not both. At that point one confronts intractable reality: "I have to make up my mind."

And one makes it up: "*This* is what I am going to do." Just here is the choice—choice one does not encounter but makes.

It is important to have a clear understanding of this experience surrounding free choice, in order to be able to examine one's own conscience and to help others examine theirs. In the absence of a clear understanding, the temptation is strong to substitute applied psychology, almost certainly with a deterministic underpinning, for genuine moral thinking and serious efforts to form Christian moral character. Applied psychology has its place, but this is not it.

We are now in a position to give a more exact definition of the freedom involved in free choice. A choice is free if that very choosing itself settles which alternative one adopts, which possibility one takes up and pursues. Before the choice, one could act or not act, do this or do that. Choosing itself decides the matter. The possibility which one will seek to make real is determined by the choice, while the other possibility or possibilities drop away and are no longer possible. Before the choice, there was an alternative; now there is only that which has been chosen.

By choosing, too, one places oneself in a new relationship to human goods. ("Good" here need not mean morally good; "good" as we are using it here signifies, roughly, one of the basic, fundamental purposes on behalf of which human beings can act. Human goods in this sense constitute a kind of outline of human personhood—the sum total of what human beings are capable of becoming by their choices and actions.) As a result of one's choice, one has a greater affinity for the good one has chosen than for the other good (or goods) not chosen.

Looking back, with a new orientation to the good chosen which arises from the choice itself, it is easy to think, "I chose that because it was better." Before the choice, though, it did *not* look better than the alternative in every respect; it merely looked different and incompatible, better in some ways but not so good in others. After the choice, however, that which was chosen has become "good for me" in a sense which that not chosen no longer is. It is not the goods which have changed but oneself. Choosing is a kind of self-creation. The self after choosing is not the same as the self before the choice, for in choosing one changes the self's relationship to the goods at stake. (The change, of course, is not always a reversal. If one chooses in line with previous choices, one only deepens an existing relationship to the relevant goods.)

Choice is distinct from external behavior. Having made a choice, of course, one usually does take steps to carry it out. But the choice and its execution are different things. A man facing a choice between cutting his lawn and going to the movies chooses to cut the lawn—but then it rains before he can carry out his decision. His choice to cut the grass was quite real, even though he could not act upon it. Choosing is an inner orienting of the self, not the outward performance which follows from this new orientation. Morality is indeed in the heart (see Mt 15:10–20, Mk 7:15–23, Lk 6:45); it resides in the goodness or badness of our choices, which are acts of inner self-determination.

As such, furthermore, choices last. One remains what—or who—one has made oneself by an act of self-determination until one determines oneself otherwise by another, contrary choice. Free choices, then, are not just particular events or physical processes, but spiritual realities which persist. The analogy of knowledge helps clarify this. When I learn something, my knowledge persists and I myself am different from what I was before I knew it; the knowledge, moreover, has an effect on my coming to know more by building upon what I already know. It predisposes me to approach the world from a certain vantage point, to observe things in a certain way, to ask certain kinds of questions. Similarly, my choices last: they are acts of self-determination or self-creation which persist and which cause me to look upon new options consistent with them as interesting and appealing, while options of a different sort are more or less lacking in appeal.

This is not to say that, having once chosen and determined oneself in a certain way, one can never change one's mind—never choose differently, never change the self one had previously determined. Change is not impossible (and sometimes is easy), but if one does *not* change, one remains as one has determined oneself— because choices last. A choice can be changed by a contrary choice, but that is what it takes—a contrary choice—to change it.

D: How Free Choices Build up Persons and Communities

Free choices build up persons and communities—morally speaking, that is, choice determines their identity. Several considerations help to explain what this means and why it is so.

In the first place, many choices open up further possibilities requiring more choices. This is particularly clear in the case of large choices of a vocational nature. In deciding, for example, to be a lawyer or to get married, an individual sets out on a path which will demand innumerable implementing choices before he or she reaches its end. But the same also is true of many choices about matters much less important and complex. For instance, in deciding to take a vacation, I place myself in the position of having to make a whole series of additional choices. Where shall I go? Shall I go alone or with somebody else? How shall I pay for the trip? Shall I drive or fly? Where shall I stay? What shall I do when I get there?

This is how we shape our lives. Having made certain large choices, we must follow them up by further choices which have to do with carrying them out. This is clear in the lives of famous figures (Washington agreeing to lead the revolutionary army, Lincoln determining to study the law) but it is no less clear in the lives of the rest of us. We impose patterns and meanings on our lives first by our large choices and then by our lesser choices in implementing them or, for that matter, in failing to follow through.

There is, however, a still more profound way in which choice determines us. In choosing, one both actualizes and limits oneself, and so determines oneself to be the person one comes to be. By choosing, I bring it about that certain goods rather than others will be fulfilling for the self I make myself by choosing. Suppose I choose to marry; as a result, certain goods—those involved in living with my spouse—are fulfilling for this self I have constituted, while others are not. (Having committed myself to marriage, I cannot find fulfillment by living a single life, even though before committing myself to marriage I might have done so.) Through self-determining choices, one establishes one's particular relationship to reality, settling which realities are and which are not to be fulfilling for the self one has constituted. This, too, is true not only of large choices—vocational commitments and the like—but also of the ordinary small choices we are constantly making.

The self-determination in question here is more than just a matter of setting goals. We do, and must, establish many goals for ourselves. But self-determination essentially is concerned, not with *what* we choose, but with the selves we establish in making the choices we make. This is evident from the fact that we cannot really set goals for ourselves without also establishing that certain goods are important to us and therefore worth pursuing in goals which to some degree embody them. True, small children have goals in view even before they make free choices; so, too, do adults who act spontaneously, without choice, in response to their wants and cravings. But in that case they are simply acting on their desires instead of making choices, and reason merely serves passion in pursuit of passion's goals. By contrast, when I choose, I cause myself to be a person of a certain sort—specifically, the sort of person who can adopt this, rather than that, as a goal which suits the person I have constituted myself.

Although choices are central to self-determination, the outward behavior which implements them is also important. The rest of the self, typically, can and will be drawn into the task of carrying out what one chooses: having determined to do something, one thinks about how to do it; having thought out a plan of action, one uses one's body and all one's other capacities in its execution. This may seem a small matter where small choices are concerned, but when it is a matter of a large choice—one's state of life or career—the involvement of the various aspects of the self required to carry out the innumerable implementing choices leads eventually, if one is faithful and consistent, to a very high degree of self-integration in line with the first choice. We express this when we say of someone: "He's a doctor to his fingertips" or "She's a lawyer through-and-through."

It follows that if our large choices and the subsequent implementing choices are good ones and are appropriately carried out, the goodness of the good choices will in time come to characterize the whole of the self. Similarly, if the choices are bad, they will eventually color not only the will or the "moral" self, but the whole self. For good or ill, the whole of a person is implicated in his or her choices.

But what if we make some good choices and some bad, and sometimes act appropriately and other times inappropriately to carry out what we choose? Then, quite naturally, we set up conflicts in ourselves. Everyone does this to some degree, for in this life no one reaches the stage of making only good choices and doing only what is appropriate to carry them out. But the ideal of self-integration and harmony to which we naturally aspire points to the desirability of striving always to choose and act in this way.

Typically, we say of good people that they have good character. "Character" here signifies nothing less than the totality of a person integrated around good choices. And virtues? They are the different aspects of good character. Looking at the matter from one point of view—relationships with other persons—we say that an individual of good character is fair or just; considering the individual from the aspect of sexuality, we say he or she is chaste or modest; from the aspect of response to dangerous situations, that the individual is brave or steadfast; and so on. These virtues, to repeat, are the different facets of a good character, considered in light of different problems and challenges.

As for a bad person, we say that he or she has a bad character, meaning the whole of a person self-integrated around bad choices carried out in action. Vices are the various aspects of bad character—dishonesty, lustfulness, weakness, cruelty, and so forth—although, as we shall see later, bad character cannot be as unified as good character is.

Free choices not only build up persons but constitute communities. The modern individualistic bias, with its impoverished appreciation of community, is an obstacle to seeing this, but its truth becomes clear upon reflection.

Some choices can only be made by two or more people. A marriage, for instance, simply cannot come into existence apart from the joint choice of the two parties. This choice constitutes the community called "our marriage." Similarly, although a political society generally lacks many of the features of true community, to the extent it has the character of a community it is rooted in a common choice. The Preamble to the Constitution of the United States expresses a common commitment to a certain set of goods on the part not only of the Founding Fathers but of many others since—a commitment which bound and still binds together the American people as a coherent political society. Again, a social choice is required when an individual enters an existing community. When, for instance, a person becomes a Christian, he or she makes an act of faith, and the Church administers baptism—two expressions of a common act in which the individual and God enter into the relationship of adopted child and Father.

In any community, some persons are empowered to make choices on behalf of the community as a whole. If these persons act within the limits of their authority, such choices truly implicate and bind the other members of the community. Others can of course reject and resist choices made by the community leaders, but in rebelling against these legitimate community acts, they partly or wholly nullify their membership in the community itself. So, for instance, a teenager who refuses to go along with his or her parents' decision to move to another part of the country ("I'm not going. I'll move in with my friend instead") clearly remains their child but is no less clearly estranged from the family.

A community, like an individual, has a character arising from its common choices and what it does to carry them out. We are not speaking of ethnic stereotypes or anything of that sort. We are simply making the point that an expression like "the American character," although it can be used in vague and dubious senses, expresses something true and meaningful when it refers to those aspects of character which Americans share as a result of their communal choices—for example, their commitment to the proposition that all people enjoy a certain fundamental equality as human beings and the resulting determination (not always acted upon, of course) to treat others fairly.

3. Conscience: Knowledge of Moral Truth

Quite a few strange ideas about conscience are in circulation these days. There is conscience as an inner voice which pipes up saying "Don't!" whenever one is tempted. There is conscience on Freudian lines—an irrational residue of infantile tussles with authority figures. There is conscience on a Promethean model, where one's solitary conscience is the only gauge of right and wrong that matters. And, perhaps especially for some Catholics, there is conscience as rebel: "The Church can't tell *me* what to do."

In what follows we shall see why these and various other notions about conscience fall short of the mark. We shall consider four topics: what conscience is; erroneous conscience; formation of conscience; and the role of the Church's teaching in forming right consciences.

A: What Conscience Is

Lately a good deal of interesting psychological work has been done on development of conscience. It is clear that development does occur and that it makes sense to speak of its successive stages, even though it is far from clear how development takes place and exactly what its stages are.

At the outset of the process, small children begin to acquire a sense of good and bad by learning what is acceptable in the eyes of the powerful persons in their lives, usually their parents. If a child makes mother or father angry, the parent's anger causes the child to experience fear and shame. Pleasing parents evokes responses which make the child feel accepted and at ease. Gradually, it seems, these feelings associated with authority figures on whose approval the child depends—fear and shame, confidence and the sense of being at ease—are interiorized in a stylized, more or less distorted, and perhaps even neurotic (or at least neurosis-inducing) form. These feelings, left over from early childhood and interiorized, are what Freud called "superego" (that which is "over" the conscious "self" or in control of it).

We all have superegos, and for many of us these enduring products of infantile emotion cause problems—not least the problem of dictating behavior contrary to what reason and authentic conscience tell us we should do. For example, responding to the promptings of superego, people not infrequently do compulsive things, whose irrational character they recognize even as they do them, simply to ward off the anxiety which they know they will feel if, contrary to superego, they act rationally. Superego is nonreflective and essentially nonrational. Whatever its role in the lives of particular individuals, it is not conscience.

Nor should conscience be confused with the sense of right and wrong which emerges at a somewhat later stage of development. Then children begin to grasp that they belong to various groups with rules and requirements, and that in order to get along they must go along—observe the rules—for otherwise they are not "good" group members as the group sees things. Thus, at this stage children naturally equate right and wrong with meeting or failing to meet the standards of the groups they identify with: the gang, the class, the team, and so on. As with superego, this too is natural and inevitable. But it is not conscience.

The legalistic notion that morality means conforming to rules is typical of this stage. And usually children *do* conform rather easily—for a while. But then, no less typically, there comes a crisis of resistance and rebellion: "That's what *your* rules say. *I* make my own rules for myself."

This readily evolves into a view of conscience which is in fact very widespread today: conscience is the principle of individual self-assertion against social standards. "Who makes the rules? Those are just rules left over from the past. Nobody takes them seriously today. *I* make my own rules. My conscience is my guide." The rhetoric is libertarian but the attitude is profoundly legalistic, for it assumes that, where morality is concerned, the only alternatives are either to accept and follow rules or to resist and rebel against them. This attitude also tends to confuse the dignity of individual conscience with the absolutizing of individual desires. "I don't care what anybody else says; I want this, and my conscience doesn't bother me in the least when I have it." But this is not conscience either.

What is conscience?

Most fundamentally, conscience is one's awareness of moral truth—of that which is truly right and good to do. Not what superego causes one to feel nervous or at ease about, not what it takes to win and retain approval from a group, not what one happens to crave just now, but what is truly right and good. Confronting reality and one's own possibilities, one perceives what is required for fulfillment. "This is how things are, and this is who I am and what I am capable of being, so *this* is what it will take for me to be fulfilled in the real world as it is, not in some dream world." One makes a judgment about truth which should shape one's choice. This, basically, is conscience.

The forbidden and the permitted are not the basic categories for conscience, nor is mature conscience concerned with how little one must do in order to get by or how far one can go without being called to account. These are the immature preoccupations of legalism. For mature consciences, the fundamental question is: What is the good and wise thing to do? And for mature *Christian* consciences: What is the wise and holy thing to do?

This view of conscience emerges gradually but powerfully within the Judeo-Christian tradition. In the Old Testament, since Hebrew has no special word for conscience, its work in discerning right from wrong often is referred to by a broader term, "heart." The word is not linked, as in English, more or less exclusively to feelings and sentiments, but refers generally to the inner self. It includes the functions of thinking, judging, and willing—all that comes from the self within.

The Old Testament strongly emphasizes that the heart does well in making judgments of right and wrong when, enlightened by God, it is wise. Fools are out of touch with reality; they do themselves harm. It is stupid to turn away from God and serve false gods, for they can do nothing for us. A good heart is a wise heart—it has God's light, it sees reality, and it acts accordingly.

The New Testament similarly speaks of the mind renewed in Christ. But here the word "conscience" also appears. The most important passage is:

> When Gentiles, who do not possess the law, do instinctively what the law requires, these, though not having the law, are a law to themselves. They show that what the law requires is written on their hearts, to which their own conscience also bears witness; and their conflicting thoughts will accuse or perhaps excuse them.
> (Rom 2:14–16)

In other words, pagans can sin, even though they lack the law revealed by God to the Jews, for there is a law of nature, to which conscience testifies, written on every human heart.

The New Testament also makes another very important point about conscience: it can be mistaken. Sometimes it lulls us into a false sense of security. "I am not aware of anything against myself, but I am not thereby acquitted. . . . Therefore do not pronounce judgment before the time, before the Lord comes, who will bring to light the things now hidden in darkness and will disclose the purposes of the heart" (1 Cor 4:4–5). And sometimes conscience is troubled even though God is pleased. "By this we will know that we are from the truth and will reassure our hearts before him whenever our hearts condemn us" (1 Jn 3:19–20).

The Second Vatican Council takes up St. Paul's idea of conscience in its *Pastoral Constitution on the Church in the Modern World*. "In the depths of his conscience, man detects a law which he does not impose upon himself, but which holds him to obedience. . . . For man has in his heart a law written by God. To obey it is the very dignity of man; according to it he will be judged" (*GS* 16). We do not invent this law, we discover it. Rejecting a subjectivist notion of conscience, the Council is insisting that there is an objective norm of morality, which it is conscience's task to discern and conform to. "The more that a correct conscience holds sway, the more persons and groups turn aside from blind choice and strive to be guided by objective norms of morality" (*GS* 16).

In Vatican II's treatment of conscience there is an allusion to St. Thomas Aquinas. This is understandable, for his treatment is used constantly by the magisterium and in theology. Thomas distinguishes among principles of moral thought, moral reasoning, and judgments of what is right and wrong, reserving his own use of the word "conscience" for the latter. In other words, conscience is one's last, best judgment that a course of action is or is not morally correct. Taking this view of conscience, it is self-evident that one ought to follow conscience. There is nothing else against which to measure conscience, for everything else has already been taken into consideration, and one has reached a conclusion: "This is to be done (or not done)." Discerning what one takes to be the truly good—and, for a Christian, holy—thing, one only need make up one's mind to do it.

B: Erroneous Conscience

We ought always to follow our consciences, and we are always wrong if we do not. This is so even if conscience is mistaken, erroneous. For if conscience—one's last, best judgment that something is morally right or wrong—is mistaken, one is in no position to know it, and so one can hardly say, "I don't have to follow my conscience, because it is erroneous." (If one *should* make such a judgment, then it is this second judgment—"I was wrong"—and not the first, which actually counts as one's conscience.) In short, if we violate conscience, we think we are doing wrong. To do what one thinks wrong, however, is always morally wrong. Thus, conscience must be followed even if it is erroneous.

St. Thomas makes this point very strongly. He says, for instance, that a pagan who thinks he or she should not be a Christian would sin by converting. We ought to do what we believe is right even if we are wrong, for in doing what we think wrong we are always morally guilty.[1]

From the perspective of blameworthiness, there are two kinds of error of conscience. The first is blameless. One is mistaken, but one does not know it, and there is nothing one could have done, or can do now, to prevent or correct the situation. Not only should a person follow erroneous conscience in these circumstances, but there is absolutely no guilt in doing so. This, presumably, was by and large the condition of those primitive people who engaged in a practice like human sacrifice, thinking it a fitting religious action. As the example suggests, though, the blameless following of erroneous conscience can and often does produce results at odds with the well-being of human persons. Those who engaged in human sacrifice, believing the gods required it, may have incurred no guilt, but those whom they sacrificed ended up no less dead. Erroneous conscience should be followed, but conscience which sees what is truly good is a great deal better.

There are also blameworthy erroneous consciences. Here the ignorance and error are more or less one's own fault. That may be the case with more of us more often than we care to admit. When it comes to moral truth, we all lean toward evasion and self-deception, for if we saw and acknowledged the truth clearly, it might make demands on us. The ignorance in this case is by no means absolute; one has a vague awareness of the truth, but one suppresses it: "I wonder if what I'm doing is wrong? Oh, well, it's probably okay, and anyway I'm too busy to spend time worrying about it." Typically, as people grow morally and spiritually, they become increasingly aware of such areas of dishonesty and insincerity in their lives and take steps to root them out.

When erroneous conscience is like this (the error is real, but more or less our own fault) we still ought to follow conscience and we do wrong if we act against it. But in following such a conscience, we do not escape guilt. In other words, when conscience errs through our own fault, we do wrong if we act contrary to it, and we also do wrong if we follow it. Are we then caught in a trap? Yes, but of our own making to the extent we have not been honest with ourselves.

Whether and with what difficulty erroneous conscience can be corrected depends on several factors. With the help of good teaching, preaching, counseling, and guidance, many people who are still more or less aware of their error can set it aside and acknowledge moral truth. The case is very different, though, when the error is ingrained and of long standing. Vatican II speaks of conscience which "by degrees grows practically sightless" as a result of a practice of sinning (*GS* 16). In this state of hardness of heart, error virtually defies correcting because the individual is not open to recognizing his or her mistake. Arising from persistence in sin, the condition is a guilty one, yet the person no longer feels guilt or hears the call to repent.

It is no help to tell such people, "You'll be all right if you just do what your conscience tells you." They *are* doing what their now sightless consciences tell them, and they are quite distinctly *not* all right. Perhaps the best time to approach them as they really need to be approached—with the aim of helping them once more recognize and act on moral truth—is when they suffer painful consequences as a result of their evil-doing. Then the message can be, "You're really hurting yourself by what you are doing, and that's stupid."

C: Formation of Conscience

Formation of conscience is only possible for those who wish to live good lives. For a conscience must be docile, teachable, if it is to be formed.

Formation is not a matter of imposing rules and regulations on somebody else. That is simply legalism again. Rather, formation supposes that those who receive it are trying to lead decent lives, and are therefore open to seeing moral truth if it is presented to them clearly and convincingly. Still, human beings are capable of enormous inconsistency; they want to know and do what is right—but not necessarily in all areas and all at once. One is reminded of Augustine's prayer before his conversion, "Lord, make me chaste—but not *now*." The desire to do the right thing makes formation possible; hesitation about doing what is right makes it necessary.

How to go about it? Formation of conscience involves three elements.

The first is the clarification of moral principles comprising that law "written on [our] hearts" of which St. Paul speaks. These can be expressed and presented so that people see their truth. Often, the best approach is dialectical: asking questions and inviting discussion, so that individuals come to state moral truths for themselves. At bottom, people are not ignorant of the law written on their hearts. They simply need help in drawing it out and articulating it. For Catholics, the Church's teaching is an important source of such help.

The second element is to foster awareness of practical possibilities. "Isn't everybody aware of them?" someone might object. To which the truthful answer is, "Yes, everyone is aware of some practical possibilities, but often those—and only those—which contemporary culture emphasizes." In every age and place, conventional wisdom commends unsavory practices—for example, bribery, slavery, abortion—as *the* practical possibilities. People immersed in a particular culture, as we all are, can find it next to impossible to imagine realistic alternatives.

Conscience formation seeks to call attention to alternatives which are practical possibilities for the living of a truly good and humanly fulfilling life. Jesus does this not only by his teaching and preaching but by his example. Indeed, in the fallen human condition, the only truly good way for human beings is the redemptive way of Christ. But it is not easy for people to whom Jesus' way has not been presented as an interesting and attractive option to grasp that. Presenting it as such is part of the task of formation.

Third, conscience formation seeks to show the relevance of moral principles to action. Many decent people are steeped in legalism. They believe that morality is a set of rules, and that, wherever there is no rule, they are free to do as they please. They believe that living a morally good life consists in little more than not committing mortal sins. It is formation's task to show that *every* choice is morally important, and that a good life is one lived *wholly* in the light of moral truth. This often requires challenging the goals and standards which people take for granted. "I'm faithful to my wife, I don't steal from my employer, and I go to church on Sunday—so my moral life is in excellent shape. Of course, I do what it takes to get ahead professionally, including bamboozling clients and running roughshod over colleagues—but that's business, not morality." Conscience formation tries to remove the moral blinders of people who think this way, not least by encouraging them to question their self-righteousness.

The ideal outcome of conscience formation likewise has several elements.

One is that people outgrow immaturity of conscience and put aside legalistic thinking. Anxious feelings, embarrassment, and the approval or disapproval of others no longer rule their lives. They cease supposing that their feelings are a reliable guide to their moral state ("If it doesn't bother me to do that, it must be okay"). More and more they want to do what is truly right, they actually do it, and in doing it they integrate their selves around their choices. The entire personality is increasingly at the service of moral truth and right living.

Practical acceptance of moral truth itself becomes easier. Temptation does not vanish, but it becomes less powerful. People experience growing spontaneity in knowing and doing what is right. The classical name for this is "prudence." Prudent persons are able to think through moral problems for themselves—not necessarily in a highly sophisticated way, but in a way which lets them get to the heart of the matter when they try to explain why something is wrong: "I'm not going to take more than my share because it wouldn't be fair to the others," "I'm not going to pad my expenses because that's stealing from the company."

It is a sign that one has not reached this ideal state of conscience formation if, knowing the relevant facts in a situation, one remains in doubt about whether one may or may not do something. What then? Today it is fairly common for people, particularly persons of a religious bent, to turn to what they call discernment: "I'm going to 'discern' whether this choice would be right, and then follow my conscience." Discernment has an honorable place in the spiritual life, but this is not it. In such cases, "discernment" is simply another name for falling back on one's feelings and doing as they dictate. This way of proceeding easily leads to persistent rationalization in support of a practice of sinning. The appropriate response is further thought and study, along with consulting reliable—that is, authentically prudent—advisers.

D: The Role of the Church's Teaching in Forming Right Consciences

For several reasons, many people think of the Church's moral teaching as the imposition of a set of rules. One reason is rooted in legalism. Often enough, the Church's teaching *has* been presented as a set of rules, and even when it has not, people schooled in legalism suppose that any moral teaching must be an exercise in rule-making. Another reason is rooted in lack of insight into moral truth, a lack which can be on the part of the teacher or those being instructed or both.

Ambivalence also plays a part in this situation. Most of us do not want to be altogether consistent. We want the advantages that come with being Christians, but sometimes we do not want to pay the price. The resurrection is good news, but we would rather not hear about the cross. When someone else points out our responsibilities to us, we are likely to say something like, "You're just trying to impose your rules on me. When it comes to *that*, I'll follow my own conscience." Having said which, we are then also likely to say, "I'm in good faith, I lead a good life, and I deserve the benefits that come from that." Ambivalence. In less abstract terms, we want Jesus to be our friend, but we are not too eager to be his, especially when that involves following his way of the cross.

Moreover, many Christians, including Catholics, seem less than wholehearted in their commitment to the faith they profess. Raised in the faith perhaps, and accustomed to membership in a parish or congregation, they accept the social requirements of "belonging" but not a great deal more. If nobody noticed whether they went to church or not, they might quit going altogether.

It would be asking too much to insist that people not have mixed motives for their membership in the Church. That is how we are. Yet because the motives are mixed, there is an evident need to clarify the requirements of faith and deepen faith itself, both in ourselves and in others. The quality of our religious commitment stands always in need of upgrading. If it is upgraded sufficiently, the things one *must* do as a Christian do not seem like impositions from the outside, but are understood as necessary to living out the commitment consistently and joyfully, even when this means taking up the cross and following Jesus' way.

Persons of wholehearted and mature faith see the Church's teaching not as an imposition but as a precious source of light. They reason along these lines: "God came into the world in the person of Jesus Christ, he founded a Church, and the Spirit is constantly present in that Church today, helping it always to teach what Jesus taught; therefore, I find in the Church's teaching what I need to know about living in a way that is true and holy."

Even so, the Church's moral teaching is not mysterious and impenetrable, something to be taken on faith but not understood. The principles which underlie all of the Church's moral teachings are written in the human heart; as Vatican II expresses it, they "have their origin in human nature itself" (*DH* 14). So, we can see the truth of the moral norms which the Church teaches. When we do not immediately do so, we can take it that the problem is with us, not with the teaching.

The Church's teaching tells us realistically what our situation is; it conveys a great deal of information about the human condition and human possibilities, especially about the fall, redemption, and our vocation to fulfillment in Jesus Christ. Unfortunately, though, actual teaching has not always done this, or done it particularly well. The emphasis has been on normative principles: for example, "You shouldn't commit adultery." Not enough has been said about why people are tempted to commit adultery, and how they harm themselves if they do. This, too, is an expression of legalism.

Since the Church is not a lawmaker in morality, it has no choice—as legalism would suggest—about what to teach. It must teach neither more nor less than what is true. Much of the speculation before Pope Paul VI published the encyclical *Humanae Vitae* in 1968 centered on whether he would "change" the Church's teaching on contraception. Supposing that teaching to be true, however, Pope Paul could no more have "changed" it than some earlier pope could have legislated it into existence. The only real alternatives to teaching moral truth are to teach moral falsehood or not to teach at all. Similarly, pastors do people no favor by "going easy on them"—ignoring or downplaying moral truths, as if they were rules which a pastor has the option of enforcing or not enforcing. The truly "pastoral" thing to do is to help people see the truth and live by it.

This is a very important point, not least because a great deal of popular thinking about pastoral practice today seems to operate on the contrary assumption. To grasp the implications of this, imagine two doctors, one a friendly, sympathetic sort, "good with patients," who hates to upset people, the other a conscientious practitioner whose main concern is treating and curing people if she can. The first physician examines a patient and finds that he has a stomach cancer which requires radical surgery; but the patient is afraid of the surgery, and so the doctor gives him medication for his pains and sends him home. The second doctor also sees a patient with the same kind of cancer; she tells the patient, "I'm sorry, but you've got stomach cancer, and you need to have half your stomach taken out. But I think we've got a good chance of stopping this thing if we get right to it." Which is the better doctor?

Is it so different when the question is: What does it mean to be pastoral? Certainly a good pastor shows sympathy toward those who are in sin and are suffering from its consequences. But he does not stop with sympathy. He tells people the truth, gently but clearly and firmly, and tries to help them escape from their condition of sin. Perhaps he will not succeed. It is certain, though, that a pastor whose "compassion" causes him to shrink from speaking moral truth will not help anyone escape from sin; at best, he will help people avoid feelings of guilt.

4. Some Mistaken Theories of Moral Principles

Tramping through the woods, one has to pause now and then to set aside dead wood and underbrush. That in effect is what we shall be doing in this chapter. Specifically, we shall do three things: examine some theories which deny that morality is a matter of truth; consider two theories, opposed in most ways, which are alike in agreeing that morality *is* a matter of truth but which, unfortunately, are also alike in being wrong; and examine scholastic natural law theory, which, though more nearly right, is still inadequate.

Tedious work. Yet something useful and important will emerge from this exercise: a kind of descriptive outline of an adequate theory of morality, which we shall develop in the chapters that follow.

A: Theories Which Deny That Moral Norms Are Truths

There are three kinds of theories which hold that conscience, whatever it may be, is not an awareness of moral truth.

One is emotivism, whose fundamental tenet is that judgments of conscience are essentially expressions of feelings. To say "That is wrong" amounts to saying "I don't like that"; "It's a sin to lie (or steal or commit fornication or whatever it may be)" is equivalent to "I find lying (or stealing or fornication) offensive." People imbued with emotivism commonly link their moral theory to the idea of superego: moral judgments are simply expressions of the feelings which arise from one's ingrained tastes in matters of behavior.

Like the other theories we shall be examining, emotivism possesses a kernel of truth. Morality does involve feelings, and there are important similarities between some of the feelings we have about moral issues and the feelings we have about matters of taste. If we dislike both lying and hard rock music, our negative feelings about one will be very much like our negative feelings about the other. Moreover, people often use the language of morality to express feelings. Children, for instance, typically say of limitations on their freedom to do as they please, "That's not fair," when all they really mean is that they do not like to be disciplined.

But the difficulties with emotivism are manifest. Ignoring the objective character of morality, this theory is incompatible with Catholic teaching, which holds that conscience can be truly—that is, objectively—correct or mistaken. Emotivism, moreover, makes moral argument as pointless as other arguments about matters of taste. Thus, emotivism trivializes morality and precludes rational reflection on moral questions. But even emotivists, faced with an action they consider gravely unjust—the Nazis' "final solution," say—begin to have second thoughts about their theory. Thus, very often people adopt an emotivist approach in defense of behavior they are partial to ("That's just how *you* feel about it—it makes *me* feel good") while refusing to accept it as a defense for what they consider wrongful behavior by someone else ("That plainly isn't right—and any decent person would *see* it isn't").

A second approach which rejects the idea that conscience is awareness of moral truth is divine command theory, which views moral norms as God's rules for our behavior. Could God have laid down different rules? According to divine command theory, of course he could, but *this* is how he wants things, and it is up to us to obey.

There is a threefold truth in this. Certainly, to be a good person, it is important to obey God's will. And certainly, too, God's will is involved in the structure of moral truth. Moreover, God's will is mysterious; we do not as a matter of fact always understand why he wants us to do what he wants us to do.

Yet the Judeo-Christian tradition insists that God does not merely lay down rules which make things right and wrong. Rather, being wise and good, he directs people to what is *really* good for them. It is not true that a judgment of conscience ("I may not tell this lie under oath") could be reversed ("I should tell this lie under oath") if God "laid down different rules," because the morality of lying under oath is not a matter of rules.

God creates things as they are, and that has natural consequences for the things he creates. Perhaps what is good and fulfilling for human beings is different from what would be good and fulfilling for Martians. No matter. Those things which are good for human beings—and those which would be good for Martians, if God had created any—are not mere impositions, subject to change at God's pleasure, but arise naturally from the fact that God has made us as we are. Divine command theory may impress some good people as a pious approach because it puts so much emphasis on God's will and our duty to obey; but it is ultimately disastrous, since it makes God a tyrant whom free persons can obey only at the price of self-respect while feeling constantly tempted to rebel.

According to still another approach, if God does not make the rules, perhaps individuals do the job for themselves: moral norms come into force for people only if they choose to adopt them. In the account offered by Nietzsche and Sartre, these are the choices by which an individual sets the course of his or her life. The British analytic philosopher R. M. Hare calls his version of this approach "prescriptivism," while according to another version of it such choices are acts of consent to social policies.

This third approach, too, has a certain plausibility. Moral truths do lack practical impact unless somebody accepts them and tries to live by them. Morality is ineffectual if no one cares to live morally. Also, choices often do generate responsibilities: for example, those which arise from one's choice of state of life or career.

However, once real responsibilities arise for a person as a result of his or her choice, they *are* real, and cannot be abolished simply by choosing to repudiate them. For example, having chosen to marry, one has responsibilities toward one's spouse, and no choice one can make will eliminate them. Moreover, not all responsibilities are the product of choice. Children, for instance, do not choose their parents, but have responsibilities toward them. And even if someone violates a moral norm (indeed, even if many people regularly do), the norm remains true, and those who violate it do wrong whether or not they acknowledge it.

Like emotivism, this view overlooks the fact that we are creatures. The real world is not of our creating but God's. Creation possesses meaning and value which he has placed there. We can recognize and live by the meaning and value already existing in created reality, or we can ignore them and act against them. In doing so, we do not change reality but only do battle with it.

B: Two Inadequate Theories of Moral Norms Considered as Truths

There are also theories which, though right in recognizing moral norms as truths, are otherwise mistaken. We consider two.

One is what is called "intuitionism" in philosophy and could be called "inspirationism" in theology. The idea is that judgments of conscience do not proceed from principles, but instead are isolated truths, intuitive insights, messages from God—whatever. One sees a particular moral truth ("I ought to do X") very much as one sees a particular object or situation ("It is raining"). Nothing can be proved or explained by appealing to a principle. Either I see that it is raining or I do not; either I see that I ought to do X or I do not. Some proponents of this view will say that it is possible to generalize from moral intuitions; but because such a generalization is not an independent moral truth—according to this view, only the isolated, concrete insight is that—at best it only points one in the right direction.

This theory tends to be popular with those who believe that God communicates directly with people. "The Spirit speaks to me. When I hear God speaking in my heart, I must obey." One must acknowledge that we sometimes do see a moral truth at the concrete level yet have a hard time explaining why it is true; we seem to have moral intuitions. This view also appears to avoid making morality into an instrument of something else. For if morality is a matter of directly and immediately perceiving what is right, there is no room for ulterior reasons—rewards or punishments—to induce one to conform one's behavior to what one sees to be right.

Nevertheless, in denying human beings their ability to understand moral principles, reason from them, and make judgments based on them, intuitionism and inspirationism take away a great deal of our ability to act humanly. If moral judgments are unique personal insights, groups of people can hardly reason together about their differences in light of shared moral principles. And morality is removed from vast areas of life—those where one receives no guidance from moral "intuitions"—and it is left a mystery how, or even whether, one should act uprightly there.

Inspirationism is also theologically unacceptable. By leaving morality to direct inspiration from God and the immediate promptings of the Holy Spirit one is not crediting more to grace but less. God wishes to raise us by grace to the status of true cooperators in the work of redemption. True cooperators must understand what they are to do so that they can direct their own action. Inspirationism reduces us to the status of slaves or small children, who must be told precisely what to do from moment to moment. It is significant, moreover, that one of the greatest mystics, St. John of the Cross, has little patience with the notion that we should look to divine inspiration to tell us what to do. "There is no necessity for this kind of knowledge," he says, "since a person can get sufficient guidance from natural reason, and the law and doctrine of the gospel."[2]

The second theory which regards moral norms as truths but is otherwise mistaken is cultural relativism. In the most coherent version of this view, moral norms are nothing more than attempts by members of each society to say what behavior is necessary if their society is to survive and flourish.

Here, too, there is truth. Societies plainly do call right and good whatever contributes to their survival and smooth functioning, and condemn as wrong and bad what works against these desired outcomes. Groups of every kind develop rules which help them hang together and do what their members wish to do together. The influence of these conventional moralities is pervasive and often very powerful.

But what societies actually require of their members and what they ought to require are often quite different. A society, after all, is a group of individuals, and just as individuals in isolation can choose and act against the good, so too can individuals organized as a society. A society's conventional morality—the rules it sets for its members—may help it survive and accomplish what it wants (though even that is not assured, as the collapse of societies throughout history attests), but that does not make the conventional morality true and good. Yet cultural relativism leaves one no ground for criticizing the standards accepted in any society—including one's own.

Moreover, as a theory, cultural relativism is self-defeating. In arguing for its truth, its proponents cannot help but say something like, "You ought not to criticize that other society for [whatever practice someone else happens to have been criticizing—human sacrifice, cannibalism, ritual prostitution, institutionalized wife-swapping]." Precisely from the point of view of cultural relativism itself, however, the "ought not" in that sentence makes no sense. If cultural relativism is correct, who is to say that one society "ought not" to criticize another?

But cultural relativism is more than just a self-defeating theory. From the Christian point of view, all cultures and societies in our fallen world are more or less imperfect and, as such, are subject to moral criticism. The repeated imperative of the New Testament is to conform oneself to Christ, not to the world as it is. Christianity does not believe one can find moral truth by looking to and living by the norms of any existing human culture. Rather, Christian standards and norms point toward one ideal (but also real, though not yet fully realized) human community: the kingdom of God. This community must be built up—and not by God's action alone but by ours, too. That requires transcending the limitations, inadequacies, and evil one finds in all other human societies and their conventional moralities.

That is not to say other human societies embody no moral truth. Human beings cannot survive without recognizing at least some truths and, up to a point, living by them: for example, the truths that infants should not be killed but nurtured, that harmless strangers should not be molested, that those who are stronger ought to leave those who are weaker secure in the possession of the necessities of life, that parents and other responsible adults should provide children with instruction in useful skills and wholesome standards of conduct, and so forth. But even though every society accepts norms like these, every society is also more or less infected by sin and, as a result, approves or even requires things which are morally unacceptable: for example, that "defective" or unwanted infants may be killed or abandoned at the pleasure of their parents, that some persons may be enslaved by others, that standards of fair play and honesty which apply in dealings with family members, friends, and neighbors need not apply in dealings with outsiders, that sexual behavior forbidden to women is allowed to men, and so forth.

Christian morality, confronting any culture, cannot simply say, "That is the way this culture is, and it is necessary to accept it as it is, because God wills it so." Recognizing the fallen human condition as it is, Christianity insists on the moral truth of the gospel precisely, though not exclusively, in order to foster real human communion. In this perspective, Christian morality is a morality of liberation and revolution—not the sort of revolution which advocates violence to achieve its ends, but the sort in which the revolutionaries say, "If something is morally wrong, we refuse to do it, and so should everyone else. And if we are made to suffer— martyred—for refusing to do what is wrong, our suffering itself will help to bring about the revolution we envisage." This is the revolutionary message preached and lived by Jesus.

C: Scholastic Natural Law Theory

Scholastic natural law theory comes much closer to the truth than any of the approaches examined so far. It should be noted, though, that its name is something of a misnomer. "Scholastic" associates this theory with Thomas Aquinas and other schoolmen of the late Middle Ages, but the theory was actually developed mainly by Francisco Suarez and others in the sixteenth and seventeenth centuries. Until quite recently it was dominant in Roman Catholic moral thinking.

The theory proceeds along the following lines.

Human nature is a given. It comes from the mind of God the creator, and it makes sense. The patterns of some actions which human beings are capable of performing agree with the intelligible structure of human nature considered in all its essential aspects (bodily, spiritual, and so on) and all its essential relationships (to God, to other people, to self), while patterns of others do not. Those which do are good; those which do not are evil. And what gives obligatory force to the moral norms derived from this kind of analysis? In the final analysis: God's command to do what is in harmony with our nature and refrain from doing what is not.

Scholastic natural law theory has several things to recommend it. In this view, morality is not arbitrary, not something "made up" by individuals or groups. Creation has meaning and value placed there by God; to do what is morally right is to act in accord with the truth about ourselves. Thus, the theory seems consistent with the fact that nature has a certain normative character. By nature, for instance, monkeys thrive on bananas but not on hamburgers; they ought therefore to eat the one and avoid the other. Similarly, it seems plausible to say that, as nature generally sets certain requirements, so human nature sets requirements for what human beings should do and not do. In this view, too, morality is not reduced to a mere adjunct to society and its requirements for survival and smooth functioning, for human nature is more basic than human society.

Furthermore, as we saw earlier, Scripture itself speaks of the "natural law." Although the gentiles lack the revealed law of God, the law written in their hearts testifies to whether they act well or badly. Thus, scholastic natural law theory is not just another philosophical school; its proponents take seriously what Scripture says and the Church teaches. This is a genuine theological account of morality.

All the same, and with due respect to its proponents, this too is an inadequate theory. Indeed, its inadequacies account for, or at least contribute significantly to, a number of the problems of classical moral theology which we examined earlier.

Central to the theory is a logically impermissible leap, from human nature as a given to the way human beings are morally obliged to choose and act. Logically, one cannot derive an "ought" from an "is." How reality is (a fact) does not by itself tell us how to respond to reality (a moral norm). The theory tries to overcome this problem by saying that God commands us to act in accord with nature, but that only pushes the difficulty back a step. Supposing God *does* so command, that by itself is only another fact; it tells us nothing about why we ought to obey God.

The theory, furthermore, misunderstands the normative character of nature, which is *not* the same as the normativity of morality. Morality is concerned with free choices. But that monkeys ought to eat bananas rather than hamburgers, true as it is, has nothing to do with any choice, for monkeys do not make choices. Presented with a banana and a hamburger, a healthy monkey will take the banana, not because it has chosen to but because it is doing what comes naturally. In the absence of choice, the behavior of monkeys and other animals has no moral character even though it is "according to nature." A fundamental confusion must underlie a moral theory which confuses the normativity of nature with the normativity of human practical reasoning.

As that suggests, scholastic natural law theory does not adequately grasp the role of free choice and self-determination. "Here is nature," it says. "You can choose either to act in conformity with it or not." In this perspective, choice merely triggers behavior which is or is not in conformity with nature. The creativity of moral reflection with respect to possibilities and the self-determining—one could almost say self-creating—role of freedom are overlooked.

As a result of such defects, this theory fails to offer convincing arguments concerning concrete moral issues. Its arguments on behalf of specific moral norms are question-begging ones. Why is contraception wrong? Because, the theory replies, it perverts the faculty which is naturally oriented toward procreation. If that is a good argument, then it is also a good argument to say that chewing gum after the sugar is gone is wrong because it perverts the faculty which is naturally oriented toward nutrition or that holding your nose in the presence of a bad odor is wrong because it perverts the faculty which is naturally oriented toward smelling or that using ear plugs is wrong because it perverts the faculty which is naturally oriented toward hearing. Contraception really is always wrong, but chewing gum and holding your nose and using ear plugs are not, and a theory incapable of explaining the difference cannot show that contraception is wrong.

The negativism and minimalism of classical moral theology are to some extent rooted in this theory. For those who equate moral goodness with conformity to nature and moral evil with failure to conform, the emphasis comes to be placed on what does *not* fit the pattern, and these clearly evil acts come to be treated as a moral minimum which tends to become the standard of the morally acceptable: Avoid these things, and it will be enough. As for things which are good but not, in this account, absolutely required—they fall under the heading of "counsels" and moral heroism, admirable for the few but not required of the many.

This approach is inevitably static. For it, given human nature is not a set of goods to be realized; it is as it is. There is no basis here for creativity and innovation. The role of human beings as co-creators and co-redeemers, cooperators with God in bringing about the fullness of the kingdom, gets short shrift. To the extent that this role is acknowledged, it is assigned to extraordinary persons living extraordinary lives; the rest of us, ordinary people doing ordinary things, are held excused.

The intrinsic linkage between human moral life and supernatural life is slighted. If moral goodness is simply conformity to human nature, what does it have to do with being an adopted child of God? Yet Christians are God's children by adoption, and a moral theory adequate to this fact must be able to show how God joins together human and divine life in the Christian without confusing them. This was beyond the reach of classical moral theology. It could only say that people must live morally good lives or else they will lose grace. But why do people lose grace if they do not live morally good lives? Classical moral theology had no real answer.

So much for mistaken theories. Readers familiar with the history of ethics might ask why we have not treated Immanuel Kant's theory in this chapter. Putting aside Kant's complex metaphysics and philosophy of the person, which provide the setting for his treatment of moral principles, his view amounts to a very meager natural law theory. Kant thought immorality can be reduced to inconsistency in practical thinking and willing. As we shall show (in chapter 7:D), one of the requirements of morality—fairness—is close to what he had in mind. His theory is not so much mistaken as grossly inadequate.

Like scholastic natural law theory, Kant's theory fails adequately to ground moral norms in human goods. But unlike scholastic natural law theory, Kant's theory focuses too narrowly on only one aspect of human nature. Also, whereas scholastic natural law theory gave a somewhat plausible account of moral oughtness by saying that God commands creatures to act in accord with their nature, Kant could only say, quite implausibly, that moral oughtness comes from our own reason commanding us to act—as if we were by nature disembodied minds trying to control mindless bodies.

We said earlier that the outline of an adequate moral theory would emerge from criticizing wrong or inadequate theories. It has.

As against emotivism, prescriptivism, and divine command theories, an adequate theory must give an account of moral norms as truths. As against intuitionism and inspirationism, it must help us see moral truths as a framework for organizing life as a whole and as a pattern for life in community with other persons. As against cultural relativism, it must enable us to criticize all existing societies rather than merely accept them as they are. It must, that is, fit the revolutionary character of Christian faith.

An adequate theory must take into account the meaning and value placed in creation by God. A good human life will indeed be in tune with the rest of reality as God has made it. But, as against scholastic natural law theory, an adequate theory will at the same time avoid reducing morality and moral truth to human nature, taken as a given. It will give an account of moral truth which helps us become more than we already are.

Such a theory will help us see moral truth in relation to human good and human flourishing, and to understand human flourishing not simply as consistent conformity to what we already are but as self-constitution, a form of cooperation with God in carrying out his plan—a plan which calls on us to imitate and cooperate with his creative wisdom and free acts of love.

In the next chapter we shall begin to develop a theory such as this.

5. The Goods Which Fulfill Persons

Moral norms are truths which guide us to act in ways that fulfill us, both as individuals and as persons living together in community. But how do they function in this way? If they are both true and guides to fulfillment, their truth must bear on the relationship between human action and the goods which fulfill human beings.

Thus, we shall take up two main topics in this chapter: first, what human goods are; second, what it means to be an integrally good person. Concerning human goods we shall consider four specific questions: what "good" and "bad" mean in general; what they mean in a secondary sense; some false ideas of the good and bad for persons; and human goods as the components of human full being.

A: The Central Idea of Good and Bad

At this stage we are not using "good" and "bad" in a moral sense. For this reason, too, we speak of "bad" rather than "evil," since the word evil tends to be restricted to what is morally bad.

We get some idea of what "good" and "bad" mean in a general sense by starting with mistaken notions. One is that since God creates everything that exists, and since he creates only what is good, nothing that exists is really bad. But some things *seem* bad. It follows that badness is an illusion. Another false idea is that as red is contrary to green, so the bad is a positive reality contrary to the good. Red and green are opposed, positive realities; so are bad and good.

From a theological perspective, neither explanation will do. What is bad cannot be dismissed as illusion. Sin, for example, is both bad and real; Jesus died to conquer sin, and we can hardly suppose he died to conquer an illusion. But neither can the bad be accorded equal status with the good. Otherwise we would have to conclude that God creates what is bad or, if he does not, either that this is the doing of some other creator, more or less on a par with God, or that the world God created has somehow slipped out of his control. People have believed one or another of these things at various times, but none is consistent with Christian faith.

The Christian tradition has developed a better account of the bad. Badness is real, not illusory. It is a real absence in things of what ought to be. This lack is an objective condition, something real, but precisely as a lack it is not a positive reality contrary to the good. Death, for instance, is real, yet it is not another way of being alongside living. It is the absence of life in something which once was alive; it is the lack of something—life—which in some sense ought not to be missing.

" . . . ought not to be missing." That is crucial. Not every lack is bad. To say something is bad means it lacks something it ought to have according to some standard. An absence or lack of this kind is called a "privation."

This account overcomes the theological difficulties already mentioned. Within the Judeo-Christian framework, the bad can be neither an illusion nor the positive counterpart of the good. But it can be, and is, a privation, a lack of something which by some standard should be present.

This way of understanding badness also makes it easy to understand goodness. To be good is for something to be fully, to be all it should be—no lacks, no privations. A good thing has everything it needs to be all it is meant to be.

Nothing which exists is thoroughly bad, since to be "thoroughly" bad a thing would have to be all lacks, all privations—nothing at all. Thus, badness is parasitical: it is a lack in things which are, depriving them of the fullness of being they are meant to have.

But how do we know what things are "meant to have"? Evidently, that depends on what they are. What a thing is determines what counts as its full being. Badness is the lack of some appropriate realization of a thing, not the absence of something one has no right or reason to expect; anything can lack what other kinds of things have and not be bad, as long as it has what is appropriate to the flourishing of the kind of thing it is. We do not call a horse bad if it cannot solve mathematical problems or a man bad if he cannot run as fast as a horse; horses are not meant to reason and human beings are not meant to run like horses. But we do see privations in a human who is not rational and in a horse with only three good legs. Both lack something that humans and horses, respectively, ought to have according to their respective natures.

But there is more to goodness than conforming to nature. The good also has to do with unfolding a thing's possibilities. Take health and sickness. Health is good, sickness bad. Yet sick organisms as well as healthy ones function. Healthy organisms realize possibilities, but so do sick ones—possibilities for sickness. What is the difference? A healthy organism is realizing possibilities in a way that opens it to more and more realization of possibilities. A sick organism is realizing possibilities in a way that tends to block it from further realization of possibilities and, if the condition is serious enough, will eventually keep it from realizing any more possibilities because it will be dead. The good which is health means to be and be more abundantly; the opposite badness means to be less and eventually not to be at all.

This model can be applied in many areas besides health. What is the difference between good and bad thinking (again, not *morally* good but good in the sense of logical and skillful)? Good thinking enables one to keep going—to probe further into the reality of what one is thinking about, understand it better, comprehend it more and more fully; bad thinking separates one from reality, sends investigation down blind alleys, and eventually puts an end to it.

We find the same pattern in fields like art, economics, and technology. The good in every field enables human beings to expand, grow, and be more abundantly; the bad is wasteful, destructive, confining, restrictive. It closes doors instead of opening them, hems people in instead of allowing them to be more fully.

We have not yet arrived at a notion of moral good and evil, but at this point we do have a primary, general notion of the intelligibly good and bad. Good signifies being and more being. Bad leads to being less and less.

B: Secondary Senses of "Good" and "Bad"

"Good" and "bad" are also used in a secondary sense to refer, respectively, to what is sensibly appealing and repugnant. Children say sweets are "good" and sour things are "bad." Good is what they like; bad is what they dislike.

Sensible good and bad really are contraries, just as red and green are. Pain is real and, from the viewpoint of feelings, it is bad; feeling good is also real, and it is sensibly good. And pain and feeling good are positive opposites.

The primary (intelligible) sense of "good" and "bad" and the secondary (sensible) sense have this in common: good and bad in both senses are motives for acting. Pain (a sensible bad) motivates one to remove oneself from the situation in which pain is felt; sickness (privation of health—an intelligible bad) motivates one to take steps to cure it.

Sensible good and bad are easily confused with intelligible good and bad. Because sense experience and the emotions associated with it are so vital to us as bodily beings, we readily suppose that what we *feel* to be good must be really good (in the interests of our full being) while what we *feel* to be bad must be a privation which threatens full being. But what we experience—feel—as good or bad and what is really good or bad for us do not always coincide.

Sometimes sensible and intelligible good do go together, as do sensible and intelligible bad. Sickness is an example. One feels bad, and the bad feeling is a symptom that an intelligible good—"health"—is lacking. Yet the sensible and the intelligible do not always come together so conveniently. Pain, although a sensible bad associated with sickness and other organic ills, is nevertheless an aspect of the well-being and proper functioning of the organism which feels it. Without the experience of pain, an organism would lack an essential warning signal telling it that something is wrong and needs correcting. A person who could not feel pain would be at risk of sawing off fingers, burning hands, ignoring appendicitis, and otherwise doing himself or herself injury without noticing it.

The point is this. Human action is concerned primarily with choice, and choices should be concerned primarily with intelligible goods and bads—the good and the bad that contribute to or take away from full being. We muddy the grounds for choice when, confusing the two senses, we base choices on our feelings of sensible good and bad instead of on our judgments concerning intelligible good and bad—the good and the bad which truly add to or subtract from our full being.

C: False Ideas of the Good and Bad for Persons

Earlier we noted two false notions about good and bad—that badness is an illusion and that good and bad are positive contraries. These mistakes are more than just erroneous theories. Pursued to their logical conclusions, they lead to radically mistaken world views and plans of life.

Take the idea that badness is an illusion. That, roughly, is how Buddhism sees it, and also how Christian Science views a particular kind of badness, sickness. If badness is an illusion, the appropriate response is to see through it—to stop thinking of it as real. Unfortunately, in the case of sickness the "illusion" may kill a person if left untreated, while in the case of other forms of badness scarcely less devastating damage may ensue. In supposing that the bad is an illusion, people who think this way make themselves more vulnerable to it than if they acknowledged its reality.

Those who view badness as a positive reality opposed to the good tend toward the other extreme. If the bad is a positive reality, obviously one should fight and destroy it. This is the approach adopted in different ways by Marxism and Western pragmatism. Both suppose there is a positive set of conditions which constitute the good and another set of conditions which constitute the bad. Marxism's ideal is a secular utopia involving a classless society, and Marxist ideology calls on its adherents to use whatever it takes—the fomenting and manipulation of class conflict, violence—to destroy the present corrupt order for the sake of bringing this utopia closer to reality. Western pragmatism, confusing sensible and intelligible good and bad, takes pain for evil—indeed, tends to reduce evil to pain and what causes it. If pain is the only thing that is inherently evil, the answer to evil is to feel no pain. This way of thinking underlies our sensate culture, whose "solution" to evil is, among other things, to kill those who are perceived as likely to cause suffering (by being born) or likely to feel it (by going on living even after the "quality" of their lives has declined below a certain level).

Just as the understanding of badness as a privation is profoundly different from these two views, so the approach to remedying or removing the bad which arises from this understanding is similarly different. Christianity calls it "redemption."

Redemption does not imagine that sin and its consequences are unreal; it acknowledges sin's full reality and horror. At the same time, it does not consider evil a positive reality, which one must either destroy by force or distance oneself from by whatever is required to feel no pain. Then how does redemption work? Essentially, its strategy is to restore and heal: to overcome privation by making things to be and be more abundantly, to bring what is dead back to life, to liberate and reconcile those who have enslaved themselves by sin. The Judeo-Christian understanding of badness as a privation and goodness as full being thus leads to a world view and plan of life in sharp contrast with the alternatives proposed by zealots, hedonists, and proponents of nirvana.

D: Basic Human Goods—Components of Human Full Being

When we are considering what to do, our deliberation begins with the grounds for making or not making a particular choice. In every case, the grounds for choosing at least one of the alternatives go back to reasons which require no reasons beyond themselves, reasons which point to goods appealing in and for themselves. These are basic intelligible goods for human beings. They are not things outside us which we seek to get and possess; they are aspects of our personhood, elements of the blueprint which tells us what human persons are capable of being, whether as individuals or joined together in community.

The common theme of several basic human goods is harmony. In the world as God made it, all things were initially in harmony—with themselves, with one another, and with God. Sin disrupted this harmony, as the account in Genesis graphically depicts. Now human beings experience conflict within themselves, as well as conflict between their judgments of what is good on the one hand and their choices and behavior on the other; relationships among people are sundered or disturbed; even the relationship between human beings and God is disrupted, so that people feel themselves alienated from the creator and are anxious to restore friendship with him.

These various kinds of disharmony point to the several kinds of harmony or peace which are basic human goods. One is self-integration: the elements of the self are at peace with one another. Another is authenticity: there is harmony among one's abilities, judgments, choices, and behavior—one sees and chooses what is good, and acts appropriately on its behalf. Another is interpersonal harmony: friendship, justice, and so on. And another is harmony with God: the relationship of reverence and friendship which is religion. These harmony goods can be called existential goods because they fulfill persons insofar as they make free choices. The harmony goods can also be called reflexive goods because their very definition includes the making of choices which are harmonious.

But human persons have other aspects besides these. We are bodily beings, we marry and have children, we are intelligent, we interact with the world and transform it. Reflecting on these other aspects, we see other human goods which people can choose and act to realize without having any further purpose in mind.

The account of the fall in Genesis suggests what several of these goods are. Sin leads to suffering and death; the corresponding good is bodily well-being—life, health, and safety. As a result of sin, people are more or less out of touch with reality and truth, and find it harder to appreciate things as they are; the corresponding good lies in having a firm hold on reality, knowing the truth, seeing the world's beauty and enjoying it. Sin makes both work and play more difficult, giving them the character of chores which tax our capabilities; the corresponding good is skillful performance—"work," done not for some other reason but for its own sake, and play, by which the self expands into the world, interacts with it, transforms it, and finds fulfillment in so doing. These goods can be called "substantive" because they can be understood apart from the idea of choice. They stand alone, as it were.

What about marriage and family life? The two accounts of creation in Genesis point out this good. According to the first, man and woman are created *together* in God's image and blessed: "Be fruitful and multiply" (Gn 1:28). According to the second, God first creates the man, observes that it is *not good* for him to be alone, creates the woman from part of man's body, and presents her to him; at once the man recognizes the woman as his appropriate partner, as part of himself (Gn 2:15–23). From this, the sacred writer concludes: "Therefore a man leaves his father and his mother and clings to his wife, and they become one flesh" (Gn 2:24). Thus, the permanent union of man and woman, which normally unfolds into parenthood and family life, is another basic human good. But this good is different from the rest, because it is both substantive and reflexive—substantive insofar as it fulfills the natural capacities of man and woman to complement each other, have children, and bring them up, but reflexive insofar as it includes the free choices by which a man and a woman, in marrying, mutually give themselves and take each other as spouses, and in doing so commit themselves to fulfill all the responsibilities of marriage and family life.[3]

In sum, we find eight basic human goods. Four are existential or reflexive—self-integration, practical reasonableness or authenticity, friendship and justice, religion or holiness. Three are substantive—life and bodily well being, knowledge of truth and appreciation of beauty, and skillful performance and play. The eighth, marriage and family, is complex, and is both substantive and reflexive in its different aspects. Taken together, these eight goods tell us what human persons are capable of being, not only as individuals but in community.

E: What It Is to Be a Good Person

What makes a person good, not just good in one aspect or another but good as a whole? There are several inadequate answers. Typically, they err by focusing on a limited aspect of human full being and taking it for the whole.

One wrong theory holds that a person is made whole by satisfying all desires. Another, Aristotle's, says that because the use of reason is the noblest human activity, the most godlike, the zenith of human fulfillment lies in the life of the mind and the rational shaping of the rest of life. Still another view, that of Nietzsche, emphasizes creativity: people achieve excellence through originality and inventiveness, confronting and surmounting obstacles to self-assertion, making their very lives into cunning and compelling works of art.

None of these views has room for free choice. Proponents of the first two—satisfy desire, live the life of the mind—do talk about choice, but do not appreciate freedom and self-determination, for they take reality as a given: the task is to conform to how things are. The Nietzschean view supplies the missing element of free creativity but takes too little account of reality, which provides the options for choice: the project of a life is arbitrary and individualistic; human beings are self-creators, not cooperators with God. All three views fail by emphasizing substantive goods and neglecting reflexive ones.

There is also a long Christian tradition which errs by emphasizing reflexive goods almost exclusively. Inner peace; harmony among intelligence, choice, and performance; good relationships with other people; friendship with God—here is the prescription for being a good person. In this view, which is St. Augustine's, goodness is virtually reduced to *moral* goodness.

Of course, when we say of someone without qualification, "He or she is a good person," we do mean morally good. We are saying in effect that the reflexive goods are realized in that person's life. According to Augustine, however, peace is a condition to be realized mainly in heaven—in which case it is hard to see what purpose living this present life serves. True, one could amend the theory to give more weight to realizing existential goods in this life; but even so, where would that leave substantive goods, which are just as much aspects of human persons as are reflexive goods? The good life for human beings must include life and health, intellectual and aesthetic satisfaction, working well and playing satisfactorily; for most people it also includes marriage and parenthood.

St. Augustine's emphasis on "peace," though not adequate, is nevertheless suggestive. "Peace" in the Old and New Testaments has a very broad and rich meaning, suggesting the greatest possible fulfillment for human beings in respect to basic human goods. In line with this, an adequate view of human full being must comprehend *both* the reflexive and the substantive goods.

"But," someone might ask, "what about other goods one could think of?" Other goods are either not good in themselves (but only means to sharing in the basic goods), or are only sensible goods such as pleasure, or are particular aspects of—or other names for—basic human goods named here. For instance, someone might ask where political liberty fits in this scheme. But political liberty is not inherently good, an end in itself for human beings. It is an aspect of freedom to do as one pleases, and as such is morally ambiguous—good to the extent that it is part of a just political arrangement and used to pursue basic goods more effectively, not good when part of a system in which some persons take advantage of their political liberty to exploit others. So political liberty, despite its considerable importance, is not a basic human good. Nor are all the many other "goods" one could name which are not on the list of basic goods we have given.

While the "harmony" goods do not exhaust human goodness, they do enjoy superiority over the substantive goods in a person of whom we say that he or she is good without qualification, morally good. People who are at peace with themselves, whose honest judgments, choices, and behavior are in harmony, whose relationships with others are marked by friendship and justice, and whose relationship with God is one of reverence, are saints. Saints get sick and die, they may not be very bright or well-informed, they may lack a lot in the area of the substantive goods; yet they are saints if they are realizing the existential or reflexive goods in an exemplary manner.

The realization of these goods is primarily and essentially *within* persons and groups of persons. Often, of course, there is also appropriate external behavior: harmony between friends is expressed and in many cases deepened by exchanging gifts; the harmony of a reverent relationship with God similarly finds expression and deepening in acts of worship. Yet it is inner reality, not external forms, which is essential, both for good and for ill. What is in the heart is what counts in realizing, or failing to realize, existential goods. "What comes out of the mouth proceeds from the heart, and this is what defiles" (Mt 15:18).

It is different with substantive goods. A good heart does not guarantee their realization. If a woman gives her friend poison by mistake, sincerely believing it is medicine which the friend needs, she is truly expressing friendship—but the friend may die just the same. Health is in a healthy body, not a benevolent will; knowledge is in a well-informed mind, not a kindly heart.

One can act for the sake of substantive goods without having anything else in view: for example, people often exercise just for good health. But no one can act only for the sake of reflexive goods, without further "content" as it were. One cannot be friendly without sharing something in common with one's friend, over and above friendship itself; and this "something in common" will be something—a sport, a hobby, an intellectual or aesthetic pursuit, and so forth—which embodies one or more substantive goods. So, for instance, although interpersonal ties within a family are crucial, still family members must cooperate in regard to the essentials of procreation and survival if their interpersonal relationships are to continue and flourish.

Morally good people may suffer from ill health, poor education, straitened circumstances, and many other woes of the "substantive" domain. But if they intend what is right, if their hearts are sound, they *do* realize reflexive goods. Not that substantive goods are unimportant—they, too, are real human goods. But evils contrary to substantive goods are inevitable in this fallen world, and those most successful at realizing them and those least successful share something in common: sooner or later they will die. Hence, if human "full being" were only the realizing of substantive goods in this world, it would not amount to much.

The object of Christian hope is that those whose hearts are true—people who have cherished all the basic human goods in this life—will rise again to full, glorious, bodily life: a new life in which human goods, both reflexive and substantive, will be perfected. For Christians the ideal of human fulfillment ultimately means the fulfillment of human persons in respect to all the human goods in heavenly communion with one another and with God. Then we shall enjoy again, and more abundantly, all that human beings lost at the beginning by sin.

In general terms, we now have an idea of human well-being and full being, and can develop a theory explaining how they are the basis for the rightness and wrongness of actions. In the next chapter we shall examine a profoundly mistaken theory along those lines. In chapters seven and eight we shall present an acceptable theory.

6. Critique of the Proportionalist Method of Moral Judgment

Moral norms are based on human goods. But *how* are norms derived from goods? We shall spend the next several chapters after this one answering that question.

In this chapter, though, we need to examine and criticize a plausible but mistaken approach to the question, that of the theory called "proportionalism." (It also sometimes goes by the name "consequentialism," since it focuses on the outcomes—the consequences—of choices and actions. But "proportionalism" is the better name because it expresses what proponents claim is its characteristic method, which calls for comparing the relative proportion of good and bad in the alternatives available in a situation of choice.) We will deal with four topics: what proportionalism is and why it is plausible; why the arguments for it fail; what considerations show it to be entirely unacceptable; and the profound reasons why it goes wrong.

There are good grounds for devoting so much attention to proportionalism. Although the flaws which make it an unacceptable system have been out on the table for a long time now and are evidently beyond remedy, many people continue to view it as an attractive, common-sense approach. In particular, some Catholic moral theologians who reject elements of the Church's received moral teaching have adopted proportionalism as their preferred methodology.

A: What Proportionalism Is and Why It Is Plausible

The heart of the method lies in comparing options and judging that the one which promises the greatest benefit (or, when there are no good options, the least harm) is the one to choose. In every choice, whatever is chosen has some negative aspect, at least to the extent that it does not include what is *not* chosen. What is a responsible person to do? "Obviously," the proportionalist says, "choose the greater good or the lesser evil."

There are many varieties of proportionalism. Some proportionalists hold that there are some things which one may absolutely never do—for example, act in a way likely in the long run to undermine the very good to which the act is directed or act against the Golden Rule enjoining us to treat others as we would wish to be treated. Others say proportionalism should be used only in deciding what rules to adopt, not in choosing among particular options. Others would limit it to conflict situations where violating a moral norm would seem to do less damage than observing it. And there are still other variations on the proportionalist theme.

All varieties of proportionalism nevertheless agree in saying that, sometimes at least, one should weigh alternatives in light of their impact on human goods, and choose the one which promises to produce overall the most good or the least harm, even if that means choosing here and now to destroy, damage, or impede some instance of a basic human good.

An example will help make this clearer. The United States currently has a nuclear deterrent strategy. What should be done about this? In very general terms, there seem to be three options, and it is interesting to see how various proportionalists evaluate them. (We are not arguing military strategy here, and someone who thinks we have the facts wrong is welcome to believe that, even though we think we have them right. Either way, the purpose of the example is simply to shed light on the moral questions which are precisely our concern.)

The first option is to keep the deterrent and continue the present policy. What policy? To have at hand a nuclear force sufficient to respond to an enemy attack at virtually any level of ferocity. If worse comes to worst, that means destroying an enemy society, including obliterating cities. The deterrent also includes lesser threats, but it emphatically includes *this* threat and the will to carry it out. Keeping the present deterrent strategy means being constantly able and willing to kill tens or even hundreds of millions of people, the great majority of whom would not be engaged in any hostile activity at the time they were killed.

This has practical drawbacks. Maintaining this kind of deterrent means that a very large nuclear war can take place, conceivably touched off by accident. It is expensive, and likely to become more so as technology grows more complex and sophisticated. At the same time, while retaining the deterrent, we can attempt to negotiate mutual arms reduction or disarmament. So much, then, for the probable or possible effects of keeping the deterrent we have.

The second option is to attempt a change to a counterforce deterrent. The threat is not to obliterate cities but, in response to a nuclear attack, to wipe out the enemy's military forces and military capability; the will to kill huge numbers of noncombatants is not necessarily required. But the cost of a counterforce deterrent would be enormous, since our nuclear forces would have to be able to deliver a devastating retaliatory strike against military objectives even after absorbing an enemy first strike. Moreover, a counterforce strategy means competing in readiness to fight a meaningful war, and so makes it more likely that a nuclear war will be fought.

The third option is to give up the deterrent—not at some point in a utopian future, when there is agreement on enforceable mutual disarmament, but here and now. The drawbacks of this are also obvious. We are certainly not going to fight a nuclear-armed enemy with conventional weapons. Abandoning the deterrent therefore might mean surrendering to hostile domination, with loss of political freedom and much else. It could mean rather widespread loss of life, and very likely would bring religious persecution with it. Nor would the world then be a particularly stable and peaceful place. Even if we abandoned our deterrent, there is no reason to think the Soviets and the Chinese and other nuclear-armed powers would abandon theirs. Perhaps there would be a large scale nuclear war anyway; perhaps that would even be more likely than if we kept our deterrent.

Facing these options, a proportionalist will say, "Although I can see some good in all of them, on balance they're all pretty unappealing. What to do? It will be right to choose the option which on the whole will do the least harm to human goods." But which is that? Proportionalists find themselves unable to agree. Some argue for maintaining the deterrent and the deterrent strategy very much as they are, others urge changing to a counterforce strategy, and still others advocate unilateral disarmament. Those who support each option suggest a way of evaluating the prospective results of all three options, but each way of evaluating results seems inadequate and even arbitrary to proponents of the other options. Right here we begin to suspect that proportionalism, despite its apparent reasonableness, is not quite so workable a method as proponents claim.[4]

Yet when proportionalists are not arguing with one another about the right resolution of a moral issue, proportionalism often does sound plausible. There are several reasons for that.

Proportionalists often examine the same approaches to morality we considered in chapter four and reach the same conclusion: they are inadequate or wrong. Catholic proportionalists in particular are likely to say of conventional natural law theory that it is "formalistic," that its emphasis on conformity to nature involves "biologism," and so forth, whereas proportionalism is concerned with human persons and what is good for them.

Proportionalism also appears self-evident. "Where there is no good option, choose the lesser evil." What else—choose the *greater* evil? It would be outlandish to quarrel with advice to do less harm rather than more.

Proportionalists claim their theory can account for exceptions to rules, while theories which insist on absolute moral norms cannot. An exponent of the latter view might say people should never lie, but many proportionalists will say that lying is sometimes the right thing to do. Why? Typically, they will offer an example along the following lines.

A husband and wife are driving down the highway, when their car is hit by a truck. The man is only shaken up, but the woman suffers a serious head injury. At the hospital the doctors determine that she needs immediate surgery. She is conscious, so, while they are preparing for the operation, they allow the husband to visit her for a few minutes. "But be careful," they warn him. "She can't afford to be upset. If her adrenalin goes up, she may bleed to death on the operating table. Don't tell her how badly off she is."

The husband goes in to see his wife. He tries to be encouraging, but she insists on asking, "Is there a chance that I might die?" He knows what the doctors want him to say—and also the advice which proportionalists probably would give: "Tell her 'No'. Tell her she just needs to rest. Tell her anything except the truth." And the advice of those who believe there is an absolute, exceptionless moral norm which forbids lying? "Don't upset her if you can help it, but since she put you on the spot by asking the question, tell her the truth." Of which counsel a proportionalist is likely to say: "Some morality—kill your wife to avoid telling a white lie!"

Proportionalists also claim their position is rooted in the Christian tradition. Citing classical moral theologians who speak of allowing bad effects for proportionate reasons, they say they are only extending what such theologians did in a more limited way.

Furthermore, proportionalists can point to ordinary experience to support their view. People routinely deliberate, conclude that of two (or more) alternatives one promises more good or less harm, and settle matters on that basis. They also often explain choices which are obviously morally good by speaking of the greater good and the lesser evil. Thus, a woman office worker who refuses her supervisor's sexual advances and soon after loses her job may account for her decision in seemingly proportionalist terms: "Certainly it was bad to be let go, but it would have been a lot worse to act like a prostitute in order to keep working there."

B: Why the Arguments for Proportionalism Fail

Thus, proportionalism makes a rather impressive appearance at first sight. Upon closer examination one finds that the appearance is deceiving.

The fact that many other moral theories are inadequate or false does not make proportionalism adequate and true. While proportionalism may seem a more attractive theory than those which proportionalists and we agree in criticizing, that still leaves open the possibility that proportionalism has radical flaws of its own.

Pointing to the outlandishness of saying, "Choose the greater evil instead of the lesser," would be a sound argument for proportionalism only if we could speak meaningfully of "greater" and "lesser" evils in situations where a choice is necessary—if, that is, we could know which evil is greater and which lesser in the precise context proportionalists are concerned with. However, while we *can* measure goods and bads, we cannot do it in the way proportionalism requires.

Rational deliberation ends if we are in a position to see that something is an unqualifiedly greater good or lesser evil—that is, better or worse overall, not better in some ways and worse in others. (In practice, this can happen only when the deliberation concerns purely technical questions—how to proceed most efficiently.) Then the alternative which promises less good or more evil in every respect becomes rationally uninteresting and drops out of consideration. No need remains for a moral judgment, for there is no choice (unless it be the choice to follow mere feelings against reason). We *cannot* have any reason to choose what we perceive as unqualifiedly less good or more evil, and since we cannot, in such circumstances we have no need for a rational judgment about which option we ought to choose. Proportionalism, however, presents itself as a system for making rational judgments about possible choices, whereas in the situation just described, rational deliberation ends *without* choice. Here neither proportionalism nor any other moral theory is relevant.

What of cases where making an exception to a particular moral norm is obviously the right thing to do? "Keep your promises" is a valid moral norm, but sometimes promises should be broken. The answer is that one need not appeal to proportionalism to account for exceptions to such norms. Rather, the exception is made on the basis of the very principle which underlies the general obligation to act in accord with the norm. (We shall explain this point more fully in chapter 10:C.)

What about the man whose wife might die if he tells her the truth? The norm against lying is very likely absolute—no exceptions allowed. It should be noted, though, that many who are not proportionalists and who hold, contrary to proportionalism, that there are absolute norms, would not include the norm against lying among them; thus, they would argue, without conceding anything to proportionalism, that there are times when lying is the right thing to do. But suppose one holds that the norm against lying *is* exceptionless? For the moment, we shall only say that the example above by no means demonstrates the absurdity of this view, as proportionalists might suppose. Why that is so will emerge before the end of this chapter.

It is true that some classical moral theologians occasionally talk like proportionalists. But none formulated proportionalism as a theory or attempted to defend it as such, and their occasional proportionalist arguments merely reflect the fact that, before proportionalism emerged as a systematic approach and its flaws were exposed, reasonable people could adopt bad proportionalist arguments without seeing clearly what they were doing. In the theological tradition, moreover, when moralists speak of proportionality, this need not be understood in the proportionalist sense. They usually mean that in some situations, besides those moral considerations which first meet the eye, there are further *moral* considerations to take into account; if these do not rule out the choice, "proportionality" is present, but if they do, it is lacking.

Finally, there is no support for proportionalism, which is supposed to be a system for rationally guiding choices, in the everyday experience of deliberation which ends successfully without choice, one alternative having been perceived as a greater good or lesser evil. As for the fact that people often use proportionalist language, that proves nothing. Even though the sexually harassed office worker in the example may speak of losing her job as a "lesser evil" than acting like a prostitute, the structure of her choosing is not proportionalist at all. She could just as well say, "Fornication is always wrong, and I would rather be faithful to my moral standards, to the man I hope to marry some day, and to myself, than do something which is degrading and sinful." However she expresses herself, she has used a prior *moral principle*—fornication is wrong—to establish the "lesser evil." By contrast, proportionalism would have it that the moral evaluation only emerges from weighing and balancing the proportion of good and bad in the options which she faces. Would some proportionalists say she may give in if she *really* needs the job? Perhaps. For if fornication is not *always* wrong, who is to say what price she should regard as sufficient to justify it?

C: The Arguments against Proportionalism

Proportionalism is unacceptable as a theory of moral judgment. Several considerations make this clear.

There is a theological argument against proportionalism, along the following lines. God is all-good, all-powerful, and all-knowing; his loving providence extends to every creature, and nothing happens which he does not at least permit. God permits evil only because he sees how to bring good out of it. But, bearing this in mind, if the key to choosing rightly is proportionalism's "Choose the option which promises the greater good or the lesser evil, on the whole and in the long run," the moral problem would appear to have a very simple solution (which proportionalists themselves have overlooked): Try anything. If one can do it, it must fit into God's provident plan, and God will bring the greater good out of it sooner or later. However, it is patently absurd to regard "Try anything" as a moral norm. Therefore, either proportionalism or divine providence must be rejected. Now, divine providence is a matter of Christian faith. So, proportionalism is inconsistent with Christian faith.

There are also a number of philosophical arguments against proportionalism. The most familiar of them concerns the fact that proportionalist theories assume that moral situations have fixed boundaries, whereas they do not. Plausible as it may sound in a particular situation to cite certain alternatives as if they were the only ones, with a little ingenuity one can usually generate other alternatives besides those a proportionalist wishes to take into account. Does a woman who is subjected to sexual harassment at work really have no choice except the moral equivalent of prostitution or losing her job? If she complained to top management or to the agency responsible for enforcing sex discrimination laws, she might be pleasantly surprised.

Similarly, while it sounds sensible to say, "Look at the likely outcome," just how much is one supposed to include in the "outcome" of one's action? Looked at comprehensively, the consequences of many actions are seen to extend in all directions and virtually forever. What are the consequences, in their totality, of having or not having a particular child, of dropping or not dropping the atomic bomb on Hiroshima, of doing almost anything else of reasonable magnitude and complexity? Who can know? God can; his providence embraces everything. But our human providence cannot begin to extend so far or embrace so much.

And, in looking at consequences—consequences for *whom?* Friends and neighbors, or enemies and strangers, too? Only people now living, or also people who have not yet been born? To make proportionalism work, one would have to answer all these questions, but there is no rational basis in proportionalism (or anywhere else) for answering them.

Another philosophical argument is of particular importance. One might challenge a proportionalist in these terms: "You speak of comparing the goods and bads in likely outcomes, and you say we should choose the alternative which promises the greater good or lesser evil. But where is your scale? How do you propose to add up the relevant goods and bads in these different options, and then measure the results against one another?"

Consider the nuclear deterrence example we looked at earlier. Even if every sort of good and bad at stake were ignored but one—say, life and death—the problem would be unmanageable, for the choice to be made concerns the future, which no one really knows, and must conjure with diverse sorts of risks to the lives of different groups of people. But in reality a number of different values are involved in all of the alternatives—life, the impact on global development, political freedom, the practice of religion, and so on. Plainly there is no way to add up all the morally relevant goods and bads in each scenario and show clearly that one alternative promises greater good or lesser evil than the others.

This is not just a temporary difficulty, which an ingenious proportionalist thinker may solve one day. The problem *cannot* be solved.

Here is why. We have seen that when, deliberating, we come to perceive one alternative as offering unqualifiedly more good or less harm than the rest, it becomes the only rationally viable one, while the others simply drop out of consideration. There remains no choice to make between alternatives supported by reasons, and we make none. Proportionalism, however, would have it that precisely when there is such a choice to make, one alternative does promise unqualifiedly more good or less harm, and we can ascertain which one this is, yet still have a choice to make. Thus, proportionalism's attempted solution to the problem of how to make moral judgments is inconsistent with the facts which create that problem.

The balancing of benefits and harms, therefore, works in situations in which no rationally guided choice is either necessary or possible. But when such choices are necessary, proportionalism is of no help. For all the alternatives have something to be said for them and also against them, but the goods and bads, benefits and harms, of the alternatives cannot be measured against one another. There is no common denominator for judging, as proportionalism would have it, that the good promised by one alternative outweighs that promised by the others. And only where this *is* the case—where we *cannot* really see the "greater good" or the "lesser evil"—do we have a rationally guided choice to make, and so need a moral norm to determine what is ultimately reasonable. At that point proportionalism has nothing useful to say.

Take the case of the man who must choose whether or not to tell his gravely injured wife the truth about her condition just before she goes into surgery. Undoubtedly, many proportionalists would say that the right thing for him to do is lie, in order to avoid upsetting her and endangering her life. (Even this, one might note, is not the sure thing the proportionalist calculus supposes. The woman is no fool, she knows she has been badly injured, and her agitated husband's transparent lies may alarm her more than telling the truth would do.)

If, however, the husband is convinced that the norm against lying is absolute, exceptionless, he is likely to reason as follows: "My wife is entitled to the truth about her condition, so that if she must die, at least she will not be unprepared. Moreover, if I lie now, I will be treating her differently than I ever have before and than she has ever treated me. I will be acting as if survival were the most important thing in our relationship. But it isn't. We are committed to the same things, and being truthful with each other is one of them. We believe that if we remain faithful to each other and to what God wants of us, our faithfulness will be rewarded in the long run. For me—and for her—it is a greater good to do what we believe to be right. But it is a greater *moral* good, determined by *moral* standards, not by trying to calculate selected short-term benefits and harms of particular options which can't really be weighed and measured against one another anyway."

In sum: When the greater good and lesser evil really are clear, there is no real moral problem. When there *is* a real moral problem, that is because the good and bad in the respective alternatives cannot be compared in a way that makes it meaningful to say, prior to moral judgment, "less good," "more bad," "less evil," "more good," and so forth. Instead, the alternatives are better and worse than one another in different respects. Perhaps the same good is at stake but is subject to different and incomparable risks or is at risk in different people—say, oneself and someone whom one cares little for. Perhaps one alternative is morally bad, while another is bad in relation to prospects for physical survival. Where is the common scale for comparing those two things? Unless there is an antecedent moral principle that can yield a morally relevant result, there is no scale. And because there is no scale, when a rationally guided *choice* must be made proportionalism is irrelevant.

Proportionalists try to find ways to do the measuring and weighing their system requires. They suggest, for example, that although individuals disagree on the relative importance to be assigned various mixes of good and bad found in competing alternatives, communally accepted standards can be used to settle the question. But *which* community's standards? A fundamentalist Moslem country? An officially atheistic society like the Soviet Union? Or shall we use the individualistic, consumerist standards of the United States and other Western countries? The standards of the Christian community, insofar as they are those of the gospel, would provide clear and authentic guidance, because they embody genuine moral norms; but if the standards of any other community are employed, they must not be regarded as beyond criticism, for that would lead to cultural relativism.

Proportionalists sometimes speak of solving their problem by adopting a hierarchy of values. But how? The problem was to find a moral standard to settle what we ought to choose; now we are making a choice in order to settle what the moral standard will be. Adopting a hierarchy of values, setting priorities—these are choices. What moral principle should guide us in making them? If, in a proportionalist approach, this is the fundamental moral choice which determines all others, there is nothing in the proportionalist system to guide it; and we have already seen that prescriptivist subjectivism—"My commitments settle what's right and wrong for me"—is not tenable.

Proportionalists sometimes suggest that the calculating their system requires should be guided by moral intuition; Karl Rahner speaks of a "moral instinct of faith."[5] We examined the problems with intuitionism and inspirationism in chapter four. It is true that good people—people who live consistently by sound moral norms—do eventually reach the point of being able, more or less, to judge and act correctly in what looks like an "intuitive" manner; but that is because they have become sensitive to what is and is not in line with moral norms, *not* because of some intuition prior to norms.

This underlines a curious fact. For years, theological proportionalists have objected that the Church's moral teaching on many matters is not supported by good reasons. On behalf of dissenting opinions on contraception, homosexual behavior, abortion, remarriage after divorce, and much else, they propose proportionalism as a reasonable theory which gives a solid underpinning to their views. Yet this supposedly reasonable theory, in order to find a grounding for itself, ends by invoking community standards, opting arbitrarily for a hierarchy of values to guide choices, or appealing to intuition. Proportionalists speak in measured, rational terms about greater goods and lesser evils, but in the final analysis their system, like the judgments it purports to justify, has no rational basis.

D: Theoretical Presuppositions of Proportionalism

What are the profound reasons why proportionalism goes wrong? What theory of morality and of human goods underlies this approach?

Proportionalists accept the idea that there are human goods like life, truth, justice, friendship, religion, and so forth. Christian proportionalists in particular agree that human goods are commended to us by faith and by the Christian tradition. No Catholic theologian, proportionalist or not, agrees with a gross utilitarian like Bentham that the good is pleasure and the bad is pain.

But the use proportionalists wish to make of human goods in their theory affects the way they think about them. To avoid approving evil choices, proportionalists must maintain that the goods which they say can be sacrificed for proportionate reasons have no moral specification; thus, one finds them speaking of human goods as "premoral," "ontic," "physical," and so on.

They must also think of goods in a very concrete way. If the issue in a particular situation is human life, the admonition that all human lives are sacred is not helpful to proportionalists; they want to know *whose* lives are at stake, how their chances of survival are affected by the likely outcomes of particular courses of action, and so forth. These are not foolish questions. But are they the *right* questions?

Proportionalists need to assume that human goods are important only insofar as they exist in specific instances: human life is important only insofar as it is this person's life or that one's. Thus, they make even the substantive human goods more concrete than they are and tend to ignore the reality they have in the wills of those who choose for them—or against them. At the same time, they also psychologize the reflexive goods of "harmony."

Consider the husband and the injured wife. A proportionalist analysis focuses on the probability of the wife's surviving if the husband adopts various courses of action—and her chances of survival *are* morally relevant because life is a human good, a fundamental aspect of her personal reality. But the relationship between husband and wife is also morally relevant. To the extent proportionalists take it into account, they are likely to treat it only as a psychological reality, a certain set of experiences, rather than a real bond between two persons which has a moral character. Yet precisely from this latter point of view it is absurd to tell the husband, as a proportionalist implicitly would in advising him to lie, "A little damage to your faithfulness to each other won't do any harm; it may even help your relationship."

Reflexive goods simply do not fit the proportionalist way of thinking about human good. The proportionalist calculus therefore tends either to psychologize them and treat them as concrete goals to be achieved, or else to ignore them. As for a substantive good like life, the proportionalist attends only to its individual, concrete realizations. However, even substantive goods take on a certain reality in a person's self-determining, free acts which bear on them; and one's fulfillment in respect to substantive goods will come about far more by God's re-creative act than by one's own efforts. Hence, the moral significance of a choice lies not so much in its concrete results as in what one does to oneself in making it: we are obliged to be faithful, not successful.

All this applies also to the communal choices in which many people participate. (Granted, communities do not have minds and wills of their own. But the leaders of a community, acting in their official capacity, make choices, and the members of the community are involved in these willy-nilly. These are the communal choices for which many—perhaps all—community members have moral responsibility.) For example: If the United States or some other nuclear nation maintains a deterrence policy involving the will in certain circumstances to kill millions of people engaged in no hostile activity at the time they are killed, the individuals who make up such a nation make themselves, to the extent they approve and cooperate with the policy, persons with a murderous will. This is so even though the deterrent is never used. We saw earlier that there is no workable proportionalist scale by which to weigh the options revolving around deterrence and say one embodies "lesser evil." But, proportionalism aside, one *can* say that maintaining the deterrent is morally evil because it expresses a will to kill harmless persons.

As this suggests, proportionalists have lost sight of the fundamental reality of moral action—that it is self-determination, making oneself to be a certain sort of person by the choices one makes. They are right to take consequences into account, for the moral evaluation of a choice hinges to a great extent on one's estimate of what will happen if one chooses and acts in that way. But they are wrong to focus almost exclusively on consequences, overlooking the fact that the *moral* character of a choice resides precisely in its being self-determining for the one who makes it.

Inevitably, then, proportionalism undermines the creativity which should characterize moral life. Take an absolute norm like "adultery is always wrong." A legalism which sacrifices persons to rules? That is how proportionalists would have it.

Of course, there is more to marriage than not committing adultery. But once the norm that adultery is always wrong is discarded, what is left of marriage? A proportionalist will sketch out a theory—marriage is sharing in satisfying sexual experience, living real community, and so forth. The proportionalist knows quite clearly what marriage *is*. If one's marriage fits the pattern, it is a worthwhile marriage; if not, it is "dead." That is the argument for divorce. It is also, strange to say, the rationale for celebrating a variety of pairings for which ordinary Christian language at least does not use the word "marriage."

In fact, though, the absolute norm "adultery is always wrong" together with a few other absolute norms are essential to the authenticity of the marital commitment. They do not say what marriage is. They merely say what is excluded, leaving it to each married couple to decide creatively what the positive content of their marital relationship will be. In this view, one marriage need not be like another. Real marriages are alike in excluding whatever is inconsistent with marital commitment, but otherwise they differ according to the partners' creativity and their response to God's grace. Proportionalism says couples must conform to a pattern which predefines marriage. In reality there is no one predefined model which every "good" marriage must resemble.

Nietzsche was an early, strenuous opponent of proportionalism. Wrong in abandoning objective standards and making individuals autonomous in relation to God and one another, he nevertheless was right to insist that creativity is essential to human full being. Hence his critique of proportionalism, which was advocated in his day by British utilitarians and which he called a "shopkeeper's ethics." In our day as in his, proportionalism thinks of upright choices as means to ends, while remaining blind to the fact that the moral life is essentially a process of creative self-determination through choice.

7. Natural Law and the Fundamental Principles of Morality

According to the teaching of the Church which we examined in chapter three, natural law provides the basis for judgments of conscience. But scholastic natural law theory, discussed in chapter four, fails to establish a basis for moral norms in human goods. By contrast, proportionalism, criticized in chapter six, tries to base moral judgments on human goods, but proves unworkable.

With this chapter, we begin laying out a more adequate natural law theory, which gives a central role to human goods. (Incidentally, if the Church did not use the expression "natural law," we very likely would not—not because there is something wrong with it, correctly understood, but because, misunderstood, it can give rise to legalism and lend support to conventional morality, especially to the mistaken idea that specifically Christian moral norms are no more than counsels for the few and impractical ideals for the many.) To begin with, in this chapter we shall cover four points: the Church's idea of natural law; the principles of practical reasoning, presupposed by moral principles; the first principle of morality; and the meaning of what we call modes of responsibility.

A: The Church's Idea of Natural Law

St. Paul, as we saw earlier, speaks of the moral law written in human hearts: Even the Gentiles, who lack revelation, have access to this guide, and will be judged by whether they follow it or not (Rom 2:14–16). This law written in hearts is natural law.

The Second Vatican Council and the popes from Leo XIII on regularly assume the account of natural law given by St. Thomas Aquinas. He begins with what he calls the "eternal law." This is God's wise and loving plan for creation. It is "law" in the sense that it is what God has in mind and wills to bring about in creating.

Human beings are part of creation, but a special part. Other things in our experience—inanimate objects, plants, animals— have no choice except to conform to God's plan; he makes them what he wants them to be. But human beings have intelligence and freedom, and God intends that these gifts be used: we can know something of God's plan for our own fulfillment and freely help to carry out that plan. This knowledge which we naturally have about what is good for us is our share or participation in the eternal law. Thomas calls it "natural law."

"Natural" knowledge of a "natural" law of morality is not inconsistent with the fact that there is also such a thing as "revealed" moral truth. In fact, there is an overlap. St. Paul points out that pagans know without revelation some of what Jews know from divine revelation. For instance, revelation says killing the innocent is wrong, but a person without access to the law of Moses can also know this.

But even though people *can* naturally know a great deal about right and wrong, in the fallen human condition they often have trouble doing so. Thus, God generously reveals a number of moral truths which in principle could be known without revelation in order that, as Vatican Council I says, they can "readily be known by all men with solid certitude and with no trace of error" (DS 3005/1786; translation supplied).

Thus, the Church traditionally has taught that divine revelation includes truths of the natural law—for instance, the Ten Commandments. But suppose someone fails to see the truth of something which the Church teaches belongs to natural law. Does this mean that, the Church notwithstanding, it does not? No—for even apart from personal sin, the human condition, including the institutionalized immorality present to one degree or another in every human culture, can blind people to truth.

Natural law is most perfectly revealed in Jesus. He is the Word, the perfect image of the Father; and the Word became man—a human individual who most perfectly expresses what human beings are called to be. Not that Jesus was or did everything worthwhile and fulfilling; he was not a concert pianist, a parent, a distinguished scholar, an outstanding athlete, and much else. But in relation to the essential human calling to discern, embrace, and live out one's vocation as a child of God in fidelity to the will of the Father and in community with other human persons, he was indeed "perfect man," who, as Vatican II teaches, "fully reveals man to man himself and makes his supreme calling clear" (*GS* 22). In Jesus as a human being—in his words, attitudes, and deeds—we primarily learn what natural law is and how a Christian should live.

B: The Principles of Practical Reasoning as Such

The thinking which underlies human action and guides it is practical reasoning. Even before thinking of what we *should* do, we think about what we *could* do: "What are my options?" (It may be of course that the "options" are so obvious that we are not conscious of this step. Conscious or not, though, it does come first.) We therefore need guidance from principles of practical reasoning before we can even take up a moral question.

Thomas Aquinas likens the most basic practical principle to the principle of noncontradiction which underlies all thinking (the same thing cannot both *be* and *not be* at the same time and in the same respect). He expresses the principle which underlies all practical thinking as: The good is to be done and pursued, the bad is to be avoided. That does not tell us what to do; it merely tells us what is basic to doing anything at all. In thinking about doing something, we *must* think in terms of doing or achieving what is good and avoiding what is bad; otherwise, we would have no reason to act.

The basic human goods give content to this principle. They tell us in very general terms what is to be pursued and what is to be avoided. For example: "Health is a good thing to be protected, sickness is a bad thing to be avoided." Such general determinations of the first principle always are among the starting points of deliberation. Usually, of course, we do not make the specific statement that goods like health and friendship are to be sought while evils like sickness and hostility are to be avoided—that is too obvious to need stating. But even if left unstated, such principles are essential to the process of deliberation and choice; we can only have reasons for regarding possibilities as interesting when we are thinking of some human good to be pursued or some evil which would mutilate such a good and is to be avoided.

This usually is so even when people choose something contrary to a good. We never act for the sake of what is bad precisely as such; rather, except when we give in to merely emotional motivations, we are pursuing a real human good or avoiding an evil opposed to such a good—although we are willing to act against some other good (or some other instantiation of that same good) in order to achieve the objective. Thus, someone who deliberately chooses to commit suicide does not adopt the view that life as such is a bad thing which should be destroyed; rather, he or she has decided to flee some misery and has concluded that death is the only sure way.

Although people always choose for the sake of goods (whether intelligible goods, as is usually the case, or at least emotionally appealing goals), they do not—as the example of suicide shows—always choose in a manner consistent with all of the goods. One can choose what limits, damages, destroys, or impedes human goods, and one can choose to foster the realization of human good in some people at others' expense.

Here the moral problem enters in. There would be no problem if the choices we faced simply involved pursuing real human goods, but life often is a great deal more complicated. We can give in to merely emotional motives, and we also can choose one good at the expense of another, our own good at the expense of someone else's, and so forth. Which is the right choice? We need a moral principle for discrimination.

At this point proportionalism offers its solution to the part of the problem which arises from conflicts among different instances of a real human good or goods. "No matter what we choose, we get mixed results. In conflict situations, we just can't avoid bad results for some human goods and some people. So let's weigh the goods and bads, and choose the greater good or lesser evil." But we have seen that the diverse packages of goods and bads in the options confronting us in a situation of choice are simply not susceptible to the rational weighing and measuring which proportionalism calls for (though they can be, and often are, weighed and measured irrationally, on the basis of feelings). Proportionalism is not the principle we are looking for.

C: The First Principle of Morality

What, then, is the first principle of morality? It must supply an answer to this question: Among the possibilities which I see in a situation of choice, how can I tell which are morally good and which are morally bad?

Scripture offers some help. The most general moral principles found there are the love commands: Love God above all things, and love one's neighbor as oneself. A choice in accord with love of God and neighbor is morally good; a choice contrary to love of God and neighbor is morally bad.

Important as that is (at least, to someone who accepts the truth of the gospel and wishes to live by it), what exactly does it mean? People often say love moves them to do whatever it is they feel like doing, but not everything someone might feel like doing is unambiguously good. Is helping a despondent brother with terminal cancer kill himself a morally good thing to do or is it not? Is it an expression of love—and therefore morally right—for a wife to be faithful to a husband who is unfaithful to her, while spurning a relationship with someone else with whom she has real bonds of sympathy and mutual affection?

Although not even Scripture is entirely clear about what love requires, it does contain some indications. St. Paul, for instance, writes: "Owe no one anything, except to love one another; for the one who loves another has fulfilled the law. The commandments, 'You shall not commit adultery; You shall not murder; You shall not steal; You shall not covet'; and any other commandment, are summed up in this word, 'Love your neighbor as yourself' " (Rom 13:8–9). Love, then, means fulfilling one's responsibilities in the community shaped by the covenant. So it is by no means a mere truism without content to say that the basic principle of morality is love of God and neighbor. Still, natural law is available even to people unaware of the covenant (see Rom 2:14–16). How might one formulate their understanding of the first principle of morality?

Vatican II gives a valuable indication in the *Pastoral Constitution on the Church in the Modern World:* "The norm of human activity is this: that in accord with the divine plan and will, it should harmonize with the genuine good of the human race, and allow men as individuals and as members of society to pursue their total vocation and fulfill it" (*GS* 35).

Morally good human acts are those consistent with the real good of the human family. No individual is responsible for bringing about the total human good for everybody; but each of us is obliged to do his or her own share in light of humankind's divine calling in this world and the next. This means, among other things, that one should avoid choosing what will not fit in his or her Christian life—both those things which fit in *no* Christian's life and those which do not fit one's own particular life understood in relation to one's personal vocation.

But even Vatican II's formulation needs clarifying, to make explicit the principle's bearing on choices and to show how human goods provide standards for practical judgment. Here is a formulation of the basic principle of morality which does this: *In voluntarily acting for human goods and avoiding what is opposed to them, one ought to choose and otherwise will those and only those possibilities whose willing is compatible with a will toward integral human fulfillment.* What does this mean?

"Integral human fulfillment" is the realization in all persons of all the human goods in all the ways they can be realized which are compatible with one another. This is an unfolding of what Vatican II says; for in the passage quoted above, "the human race" refers to the whole human family—past and future as well as those who happen to be living now—and so "the genuine good" to which the Council refers includes the realization of all human possibilities in all persons joined in perfect community.

Integral human fulfillment *is* an ideal and not, as a utopian system like Marxism would have it, an achievable stage in history, to be pursued even at the expense of human goods and human beings now. But it is not just a beautiful ideal with no bearing on real life. On the contrary, it is the most practical of ideals, since a will toward integral human fulfillment—a will, one might precisely say, in love with this ideal—is the standard of morality; whereas, in willing at odds with a will to integral human fulfillment, we are being immoral.

The basic principle of morality calls attention to something very important about human goods. Although not limited to their concrete instances, since they also exist in a morally significant way in the wills of those who love or fail to love them properly, they are not principles of morality apart from human beings. These are the goods of real individuals and communities. "Life" is the life of this or that person who lives or could live if given the opportunity; "friendship" is the relationship between or among these particular individuals.

Yet the human family encompasses billions of persons—alive, dead, not yet living—and so the ideal of integral human fulfillment takes in a vast number of possible realizations of human goods. Moral uprightness is the condition of a will which, in its openness to the fulfillment of persons in human goods, is not limited to some people rather than others, some goods rather than other goods. Moreover, it is committed to human fulfillment rather than to narrower experiences like "enjoying yourself" or "having things." (These may be aspects of fulfillment, but they are not the whole of it.)

The morally good person has an openhearted, generous will toward all human goods and toward the well-being and full being of all human persons. Immorality is a kind of arbitrary selectivity in loving human goods and human persons; moral goodness, rooted in the ideal of integral human fulfillment, means loving every possible instance of every basic human good in every person, just as God does.

D: The Modes of Responsibility

This first principle of morality is very general. It is hard to see how it could be used to analyze and solve particular moral problems. We need intermediate principles, midway between the first principle and specific norms, which make it possible to put the first principle to use, rather as the transmission harnesses and passes along the energy generated in an automobile engine for the purpose of turning the wheels.

These intermediate principles are the modes of responsibility. They do not mention particular acts—do not speak of killing the innocent or of adultery or of any other specific deed—but they do identify ways (modes) of choosing and acting in line with the first principle of morality; they are specifications of the first principle which direct willing along morally right lines. They exclude ways of willing which are not compatible with complete openheartedness and reasonableness, despite the fact that our feelings tempt us in those directions and there are usually *some* reasons to heed their promptings.

As that suggests, morally wrong actions are not totally irrational. There are reasons or emotional motives underlying them, basic human goods or sensible goods are involved, or otherwise we could not choose them at all. Immorality means acting for reasons or with emotional motives (which always can be rationalized) yet not acting in a *fully* reasonable way—that is, with a will consistent with loving *all* realizations of human goods in *everyone*. Acting in this latter way is what the modes of responsibility guide us in doing.

We shall consider the eight modes of responsibility in the chapter that follows. Here we shall use one to clarify some general considerations pertaining to them all.

The familiar Golden Rule is one formulation of a mode of responsibility which concerns fairness or impartiality. There are various ways to express the idea, but all exclude unreasonable partiality toward oneself and those to whom one feels attached, while requiring an attitude of solidarity toward others and readiness to carry it out in appropriate deeds. The Good Samaritan, willing to make everyone his neighbor by treating everyone in a neighborly way, exemplifies the Golden Rule in action.

In stating the Golden Rule, one does not mention any particular kind of act. This principle does not speak of stealing, adultery, killing, or anything else. Instead it says how one's will should be related to human goods and other people, regardless of the specific action in question. (To anticipate a bit—no, this does not imply that one can do anything whatsoever, provided one's will is "related to human goods and other people" in the right way. As we shall see, some deeds cannot be performed with a right will by anyone who knows what he or she is doing.)

There are other famous formulations of the principle of fairness or impartiality besides the Golden Rule. One is Immanuel Kant's principle of universalizability: Act always so that the maxim of your action can be a universal law. Kant observes that whenever we do something, we can offer a reason (either a real reason or a rationalization) for doing it; this he calls a "maxim for action." Suppose, then, that in considering a particular action and one's reason for doing it, one asks oneself: "Would I really and consistently want that reason to be sufficient for everyone else who wanted to do the same thing in the same circumstances?" If so, one is acting in accord with Kant's principle in performing that action for that reason.

Kant works all this out in a highly technical philosophical way, but the principle he enunciates is very close to the Golden Rule. His point is that one cannot reasonably offer a set of reasons for one's own actions and those of the people one cares about, while refusing to let the same reasons govern the actions of people to whom one feels no attachment. It is not reasonable to say, "I have a right to take from others, but nobody has a right to take from me," "My children should get A's for doing C work, but other children shouldn't," "It's all right for my country to swallow up vast quantities of scarce natural resources and pollute the environment, but it isn't right for other countries," and so on. Why people adopt such unreasonable attitudes is plain enough: feelings prompt them. However, if one is reasonable in accepting something as a reason for acting, one will accept it consistently and want it consistently accepted by others as if it were part of a set of general rules to be observed by everyone.

Underlying this mode of responsibility, as we have suggested, is the fact that feelings do indeed incline us to take a preferential attitude toward goods and people we are fond of, while being less concerned about—even hostile to—strangers and enemies. We are tempted to discriminate in our own favor and bend the rules for relatives and friends. But that is not reasonable. When we choose and act this way, our hearts are not set on integral human fulfillment, on the whole community of persons and their fulfillment in all the goods, but on some goods and some persons. Thus, the Golden Rule or principle of impartiality explicitly requires something implicitly required by the first principle of morality and the ideal of integral human fulfillment.

But even though we are less than fully reasonable in choosing to be unfair (or, for that matter, in violating some other mode of responsibility), we are not acting irrationally; unfairness is not a form of insanity. When one faces a choice between acting fairly and unfairly, there are intelligible goods (or, at least, easily rationalized emotional motives) on both sides of the argument; and if one makes a preferential choice favoring oneself or those who are near and dear, certain real human goods will generally be realized which will *not* be realized (or realized in the same way and to the same degree) if one chooses and acts impartially. Thus, morality requires some nonrealization of goods which could be realized through immorality: people who treat others fairly (or in other ways do what is morally right) pay a price.

From the moral point of view, fairness is better than any possible advantage which could be gained by acting unfairly. Still, if we focus instead on simply getting what we want for ourselves and people we care about, we at least are speaking sensibly in saying, "It's all very well to be idealistic, but in the real world you've got to look out for yourself—that's the greater good." Choices reflecting this "realistic" attitude are not in accord with generous openness to human goods and persons; but although it certainly is unreasonable, it is not irrational to be systematically selfish. It is simply another life-style, an immoral one.

We shall formulate this mode of responsibility and the others more precisely in the next chapter. Already, though, we can see how a mode of responsibility serves as a useful moral standard, showing that some choices and acts are wrong. We also see its relationship to the first principle of morality and the ideal of integral human fulfillment. Impartiality, the mode we have been examining here, is one intermediate principle among others which can be deduced from the first principle: it calls our attention to a particular way of choosing and acting contrary to the ideal of integral human fulfillment.

In the Christian tradition, modes of responsibility are generally not proposed as propositions. The Golden Rule is an exception, since it is stated clearly in the Bible. Scripture more often offers examples of good and bad acts, good and bad persons, and so communicates and illustrates moral principles in concrete form. Scripture also speaks often of justice, fairness, mercy, and so on—the various virtues.

What is the connection, if any, between moral principles and virtues? Do we have here two distinct, perhaps even competing, approaches to morality—an ethics of moral truth versus an ethics of virtue? Not at all.

Take the Golden Rule again. One who consistently chooses fairly and works consistently to carry out such choices is a fair person—a person, that is, with the virtue of fairness or justice. A virtue is nothing other than an aspect of the personality of a person integrated through commitments and other choices made in accord with relevant moral norms derived from the relevant mode of responsibility. In other words: living by the standard of fairness makes a person fair. Moral norms and virtues are not separate standards of morality; virtues grow out of norms in the lives of people who consistently live by them; righteousness and holiness are fruits of truth in hearts re-created by God's grace (see Eph 4:24).

Jesus did not teach all the modes of responsibility in so many words. In keeping with his culture, his style of teaching was for the most part concrete rather than abstract. Moreover, he taught especially by the example of his own life. "Learn from me; for I am gentle and humble in heart" (Mt 11:29). He was the truth which he revealed; he knew what is morally right; he chose consistently in line with that knowledge; he put himself entirely into carrying out those good choices. Thus, the various aspects of his character were virtues—meekness, humility, fidelity, fortitude, and so forth—arising from his consistent observance of moral norms. His followers, he tells us, can learn those norms and acquire those virtues by taking him as their model.

8. The Modes of Responsibility Which Specify the First Principle

The first principle of morality tells us that in choosing (and other kinds of willing) one should always will in accord with a will toward integral human fulfillment. One cannot choose "integral human fulfillment" as such, but one can choose in a manner consistent with loving that ideal. Important as it is, however, this principle is too general to tell us what kinds of acts are morally right and wrong. To bridge the gap between the first principle and specific moral norms, intermediate principles are needed.

These intermediate principles, which follow logically from the first principle, we call "modes of responsibility." There are eight. In chapter twenty-six we shall see that they correspond to the Beatitudes, which fulfill and transform them. Here we shall consider the modes in their own right, while also showing, at the end of the chapter, how they orient us toward integral fulfillment.

A: The First Seven Modes of Responsibility

The first mode of responsibility is this: *One should not be deterred by felt inertia from acting for intelligible goods.*

The mode comes into play when one sees something worth doing but feels too lazy or unenthusiastic to do it. There is no good reason for not acting; one simply does not feel in the mood. For instance: You intend to get up on time in order to get an early start on some jobs that need doing, but when the alarm goes off, you just roll over and go back to sleep; you plan to tackle a chore you have been putting off when you get back to your office after lunch, but when you return you find an excuse to do something else, promising yourself, not for the first time, that you will get around to the disagreeable task tomorrow. Although one can choose to behave in this way, often no choice as such is needed or involved.

Obviously there are times when people are too tired or too ill to do worthwhile things. Moreover, some people are psychologically crippled by depression. The mode does not insist that one push oneself beyond one's real limits. It only tells us what love of integral human fulfillment plainly requires—to pull ourselves together when that is possible and do something worth doing when there is no good reason for not doing it. People with this virtuous disposition are called energetic, diligent, industrious, and so forth; people with the opposed vice are said to be lazy, sluggish, procrastinators.

We find support for this mode in revelation. God himself is a model, for he is energetic, active—a creator. Moreover, people sometimes decline to act for the sake of what is worthwhile because they see no meaning to life: "We're all going to die sooner or later—what difference does it make?" Revelation provides a reason to hope and reminds us that *now* is the acceptable time for carrying out God's will.

The second mode is: *One should not be pressed by enthusiasm or impatience to act individualistically for intelligible goods.*

A mother and her seven-year-old daughter are in the kitchen getting dinner. The little girl is rather slow and clumsy. Growing impatient, the mother tells her, "Never mind, dear. Your father will be home soon. I'll do it myself."

A magazine editor finds that he has two veteran copyeditors who are fast and skillful, and two youthful newcomers who are inexperienced and slow. He gives most of the work to the veterans and very little to the youngsters, reasoning that his job is to put out a magazine, not teach beginners their trade.

The second mode, then, comes into play whenever one thinks of encouraging the involvement of other people in one's action or the action of one's group, finds no compelling reason for not doing so, but ends up acting for the sake of results rather than to enable people to share in the good. Instead of enlarging the community, keep things simple and get the job done: "If you want something done right, do it yourself." It is not necessary to make an explicit choice to exclude others; perhaps one simply plunges ahead without caring whether others participate or not.

The mode says more than just "Many hands make light work." It makes the point that, while one should do one's share, one should also let others do theirs—for the sake of team work, shared responsibility, community. Getting jobs done is important, but the ideal of integral human fulfillment also requires that people participate in doing them—that they care about the good, serve it, and grow in doing so while contributing to the growth of the community. People with this attitude are often said to have "team spirit," while those who lack it are typically described as "going it alone."

Revelation makes it clear that humankind shares a common vocation: increase and multiply, fill the earth and subdue it (see Gn 1:28). More than that, the new People of God make up the body of Christ, in which each member has his or her particular function (see Rom 12:3–8; 1 Cor 12:4–26). This is the principle underlying shared responsibility in the Church and collegiality among the bishops and the pope.

The third mode of responsibility is this: *One should not choose to satisfy an emotional desire except as part of one's pursuit and/or attainment of an intelligible good other than the satisfaction of the desire itself.*

You feel like having another drink or another piece of dessert. You do not really need the drink or the dessert; the only reason for having them is to get rid of the discomfort of an unsatisfied desire. Here the mode of responsibility comes into play. But not as a spoilsport. The point is not that one should never take a drink or eat dessert. Often, if one has no reason whatever to the contrary, one acts on desires without having to make a choice, and there is nothing wrong with that. Rather, the point is that without a genuine reason one should not choose (against some rational consideration) to satisfy desires; otherwise one is following passion and making reason its slave. Because sensible goods contribute to integral human fulfillment only insofar as they are subordinate aspects of intelligible goods, the mode says: Act reasonably, not just to satisfy mindless cravings.

Ordinarily, of course, it is not too serious a thing to have a second drink or another piece of dessert (even though it would be healthier not to) without a good reason. But often people violate this mode of responsibility on a far larger scale, devoting much of their lives to essentially meaningless routines performed merely to satisfy cravings and compulsions. One thinks of those driven individuals who work harder and harder, longer and longer hours, in order to enjoy an ever higher standard of living, but whose self-imposed routine leaves them no time to "enjoy" anything except, possibly, such relief from anxiety as the frantic observance of their routine affords them. The virtuous disposition corresponding to the mode is best called self-control; the opposed vice includes aspects of lustfulness, gluttony, greed, jealousy, impetuousness, and so on.

Revelation calls our attention to personal freedom and moral responsibility. Throughout the Bible self-indulgence is viewed as a bad thing, a consequence of sin. Scripture also links it to idolatry. One who worships the true God seeks to use his or her God-given gifts in a fruitful, purposeful way; self-indulgence is a waste of gifts, a waste of life itself.

The fourth mode of responsibility complements the third: *One should not choose to act in accord with an emotional aversion, except when necessary to avoid some intelligible evil other than the inner tension experienced in enduring the aversion.* People violate this mode when they either fail to act or modify a reasonable course of action to avoid some unpleasantness.

A man has put off seeing his dentist for three years; he knows he should make an appointment but keeps delaying because he is afraid the dentist will find cavities. An office manager is aware that one of the stock boys has been coming in half an hour late every day for the last week; she knows she ought to talk the problem through with the young man before the situation gets worse, but she puts it off because she fears the conversation might turn into a messy emotional scene. To both these people the mode says: Take heart—rise above your feelings of repugnance, do what you know you ought to do.

Violations of this mode and the previous one necessarily involve a choice—a choice to act in response to feelings rather than for the sake of the intelligible goods which contribute to integral human fulfillment. The virtuous disposition corresponding to the fourth mode is called by names like courage, fortitude, tenacity, and perseverance; the vice is cowardice, squeamishness, and so on.

In reminding us that we have freedom and responsibility, revelation makes it clear that we should not spend our lives calming our anxiety by avoiding things we do not like, as if that were a good in itself. Revelation also assures us of God's support in our upright endeavors, thus fostering hope which counteracts anxiety.

The fifth mode, whose derivation from the first principle of morality was explained in the last chapter, is: *One should not, in response to different feelings toward different persons, willingly proceed with a preference for anyone unless the preference is required by intelligible goods themselves.*

Sometimes it is. The realization of many of the goods of family life depends on the preferential love of family members for one another. Moreover, if one of your children is musically gifted and the others are not, it makes perfectly good sense to pay for music lessons for the gifted child but not the others. You are treating one child in a manner significantly different from the rest, but you are not acting unfairly.

But differences in treatment are unfair when they have no such intelligible grounding. That is usually the case with discrimination based on nationality or race. There can be exceptions. If, for instance, you were trying to organize an Irish-American cultural society in your town, it would be reasonable to call the people in the phone book with Irish-sounding names and skip the rest—but ordinarily race and nationality provide no reasonable grounds for making distinctions.

Partiality can take the form not only of discrimination against others and selfishness but of excessive sympathy for those one feels emotionally attached to. But whereas people are usually quick to condemn gross selfishness, an individualistic fault, partiality on behalf of others is not only more common but often treated as acceptable. It is easy to favor those who are present to us and making claims on our sympathy, at the expense of others who are absent and not immediately pressing their claims. So, at the time, not many Americans objected to dropping atomic bombs on two Japanese cities in 1945, since this was a way of saving American lives by bringing the war to a rapid conclusion; the fact that it also killed many thousands of noncombatants did not seem too important—after all, *they* were Japanese.

While one can choose to be unfair, usually, as this example suggests, one does not make precisely that choice. Instead, one knowingly and willingly acts unfairly as a more or less incidental by-product of doing something else one wants to do: "Nothing personal, buddy—I'm just looking out for number one." Perhaps one is not even conscious of being unfair; one is just not open-hearted enough to be fair. The mode of responsibility tells us to put ourselves in others' places, to take into consideration how what we do will affect everyone else who will be affected. For they are people, too, just like us and the people whom we care about.

Unfairness is very "normal" in our fallen human condition. Ordinarily we take our cue from conventional morality and assume that, as long as we abide by it, nothing we do can be really wrong. And conventional morality's counsel with regard to fairness is quite simple: "Don't be any more unfair to others than the rules of this particular group permit you to be." Living in this way, we are no doubt conventionally decent people. But Christian morality transcends conventional morality; its standard is not the rules and conventions of particular groups, but moral truth.

Still, this mode of responsibility does not tell us never to consult feelings in deciding how to treat others. Rather, it tells us not to make different feelings toward different people the basis for treating them differently *unless that is required by some intelligible good*. Sometimes it is. Affection is important in any intimate friendship—for example, in marriage. In deciding whether to marry Joe or Tom, Mary acts altogether reasonably in giving much weight to the fact that she feels a great deal of affection for Joe and far less for Tom. Similarly, an executive interviewing applicants for a job as his administrative assistant acts reasonably in hiring the one with whom he feels most at ease (supposing of course that he or she is otherwise qualified) since that will be important to their working well together.

Revelation tells us that we are all children of the same Father. Thus, there is a basic equality—in dignity—among all persons. To this the New Testament adds that we are all redeemed by Christ and called to the same heavenly glory. In this way revelation strongly reinforces the wrongness of any sort of unreasonable partiality.

The sixth mode of responsibility is: *One should not choose on the basis of emotions which bear upon empirical aspects of intelligible goods (or bads) in a way which interferes with a more perfect sharing in the good or avoidance of the bad.* In other words, maintain the priorities which integral human fulfillment sets, and don't sacrifice reality to appearance.

People do that in many ways. Very often we prefer to settle for civility and superficial friendliness instead of taking the possibly painful steps required to resolve problems. Someone who really wants to get to the root of a problem in order to correct it may be regarded as a troublemaker: "Don't rock the boat." For example: Family members seriously at odds with one another find that they can get along—even look to outsiders like a "happy family"—by cultivating tacit evasions and polite pretenses. But the problems remain, obstacles blocking truly loving relationships, despite the appearance of serenity. The advice of conventional morality is likely to be, "Leave well enough alone. Keeping up appearances is what counts. It would be too painful to confront the problems." Sometimes that may even be good advice, if politeness and surface tranquility are really all that is possible. But where it is possible to develop real friendship, authentic community, and people settle for appearances, this mode is being violated.

Violations always involve a choice: to prefer appearances to reality. There is no one word for the virtuous disposition involved, but it goes by such names as sincerity and seriousness; the vice is called superficiality, self-deception, insincerity, frivolousness, and so forth.

Revelation makes it clear that real values lie beyond experience. It is vastly more important to do what is right than to feel good. Acting in light of moral truth, not keeping up appearances, is what counts.

The seventh mode of responsibility is this: *One should not be moved by hostility to freely accept or choose the destruction, damaging, or impeding of any intelligible good.*

This mode may be more widely recognized and accepted than any other; at least, very few people try to defend merely hateful acts of revenge. On the other hand, people do often make a case for "teaching those so-and-so's a lesson they won't forget" and otherwise acting in ways that look very much like revenge. The seventh mode prohibits such behavior, motivated by hostility, which reduces human fulfillment without reason. Its counsel is: Calm down; it doesn't help to hurt people; more injury, violence, or killing will not undo the hurt already done or build community.

One can choose to seek vengeance, but one also can violate this mode without doing that, by allowing side effects which one would not accept except for one's hostile feelings. Irritated at neighbors who partied into the wee hours, a suburbanite mows his lawn first thing in the morning; in a kinder frame of mind, he would be more considerate about not disturbing others' rest.

The person whose virtuous disposition corresponds to this mode is said to be patient, long-suffering, forgiving; the person who has the opposite vice is called vengeful, vindictive, spiteful, and so forth. Revelation tells us repeatedly that God is forgiving. It tells us, too, that it is up to God, not us, to see to it that the scales are righted and justice is done—according to *his* standards—in the long run.

B: The Eighth Mode of Responsibility

The eighth mode is this: *One should not be moved by a stronger desire for one instance of an intelligible good to act for it by choosing to destroy, damage, or impede some other instance of an intelligible good, whether that same one or another.*

This mode comes into play when one is tempted to do evil for the sake of good, adopt bad means to a good end. Proportionalism systematically rejects this mode as a moral principle.

The mode is violated only by choices. For example: This newborn has Down's Syndrome and it will cause a lot of problems for its parents if the baby lives, so instead of treating and feeding it, we shall sedate the infant and let it starve to death. Or: Left to its own devices, some hostile power might be tempted to invade one of our allies, while using nuclear weapons against the United States to prevent it from intervening; so, to prevent that from happening, we shall threaten the hostile power with nuclear retaliation even up to the level of wiping out its society. Such choices are the essence of Machiavellianism: Do what you must to protect your interests.

The mode's message is that we must respect human goods by refusing to act against one for the sake of another. Living this way, we shall not always get what we want; we shall not be able to achieve some goods and avoid some harms. But Christianity has a response to what otherwise might appear to be a dilemma: Be confident in God's providence. Do what is right, but do *not* try to get the best results at any price. We are not responsible for bringing about the greatest good for the whole human race, but only for serving the goods of human persons as best we can. Confronted with the fact that one instance of human good cannot be served without choosing to do injury to another, we acknowledge that our responsibility is not the same as God's and we can trust him.

Obviously one should not make "Trust God" an excuse for acting irresponsibly. The assumption underlying trust in God is that one does the very best one can to carry out one's own responsibilities. But having done this and still finding oneself in a predicament from which escape seems possible only by choosing a "lesser evil," one is entitled to say, "I've done all I can, and now I can only trust in God."

The eighth mode of responsibility is *not* a variation of the Stoic maxim "Let right be done though the heavens fall." True, the same point is at issue—one should not do moral evil to prevent another evil or bring about something good. But the Stoic maxim is wrongheaded for two reasons. One is that it exalts personal moral purity more than it deserves. Reverence for human goods points to moral requirements, but—ultimately—moral requirements, important as they are, are not ultimate; only God is ultimate. Moreover, Christians *do* care whether the heavens fall (literally or only metaphorically), and recognize that they should do their best to keep them from falling. If, however, it appears that one can do so only by doing moral evil, a Christian says, "I can't do that. I must trust God instead. He probably won't let the heavens fall, but even if he does, I believe that finally he will bring into being new heavens and a new earth, far better than the ones I know now." Yet the Christian attitude is not a moralism without concern for human persons, for it emphasizes reverence for the human goods precisely because these are aspects of human persons, made in God's image and called to share in heavenly fulfillment in Christ.

Although the eighth mode tells us never to act against one instance of the good for another's sake, this precept seems to carry a significant qualification in the Old Testament: Never act in this way *unless* divinely authorized to do so. This is most obvious in the case of killing. To understand the situation, one must remember that the Old Testament is the record of a group of people living by a conventional morality of their own; time and again they identify the achieving of their objectives—to escape oppression, to win in battle, to take revenge on an enemy—with God's will. Focusing on obedience to God, they tend to ignore the claims of human goods such as life when respecting those goods would interfere with pursuing their objectives.

A different picture emerges in the New Testament. Here it becomes clear that human fulfillment does not lie in achieving particular earthly objectives. His kingdom, Jesus assures us, is not of this world (Jn 18:36). No longer are a society's requirements for survival equated with the will of God. Indeed, what is required to achieve any earthly objective—even the spreading of the faith or the flourishing of the Church—may in some circumstances be contrary to God's will. It has taken Christians a long time to grasp this. Hence the long, sorry history of religious wars and persecutions carried on by Christians certain they were doing what God wanted.

Similarly, although the eighth mode entirely rules out choices to kill, the Old Testament is often mined to provide religious grounding for killing in war and capital punishment. Plainly, too, a prohibition of every choice to kill is a stricter position than classical moral theology and most of the Christian tradition has held. Still, a development of doctrine in the direction of the stricter position seems both possible and necessary. Not even the Old Testament gives unbridled license to violence. Private feuds are excluded; when the people go to war, there must be a good reason; on the whole it is better to settle disputes peacefully. Beyond that, it seems hardly possible to reconcile choices to kill in war and capital punishment with the words and deeds of Jesus in the New Testament—for example, his teaching to love our enemies, turn the other cheek, do good to those who hate us (Mt 5:38–48). The Church at least has never taught that choices to kill are an obligatory part of Christian life. Even the "just war" theory starts with the assumption that war is unlikely to be just, and lays down conditions whose violation enables one to make this judgment.

To say one may not choose to kill people nevertheless does not mean one may never engage in activity which results in someone else's death. In defending others against violence unjustly directed against them, one may use force to stop the wrongdoing. If, for instance, armed criminals were attacking his family, a man who lacked less forceful means of defense might reasonably respond by opening fire on the criminals with his shotgun; similarly, a country could defend itself against an unprovoked invasion by using military force against the invading army. The choice in such cases is not precisely to kill; rather, it is a choice to use the minimum means necessary to stop those wrongly engaged in using force and violence against others. (Thus, the man in the example may *not* shoot to kill if it is clear that a shotgun blast in the air will scare off the marauders; and a nation may *not* obliterate enemy cities as a way of compelling an invading army to withdraw.)

C. How the Eight Modes Shape Life toward Integral Human Fulfillment

The eight modes of responsibility cover all the areas in which we encounter moral problems. They follow from the fundamental principle of morality—be open to and care about all the human goods in all people—and specific moral norms follow from them. Standing between the fundamental moral principle and specific norms, the modes are extremely important. If one understands them, one is in a position to give a plausible explanation of any particular moral norm (supposing of course that it is true) and also to work out new moral norms for new situations.

The eight modes together shape an individual's life toward the ideal of integral human fulfillment. This ideal calls for service to intelligible human goods, and such service often requires resistance to the urges and aversions of sentient nature as such. In concluding this treatment, it is worth considering how the modes function in this regard.

The message of the third and fourth modes is that one should not simply follow feelings in the hope of avoiding frustration or reducing anxiety, but should act for the sake of reasonable purposes for action. To be sure, feelings are important. It often makes good sense to consult one's feelings in deciding what to do. But it is not reasonable to act on the basis of feelings against reasons rooted in intelligible goods. These modes tell us to follow reasons against feelings whenever the two conflict.

The first mode tells us to overcome laziness and inertia and try to achieve some good. To this the eighth adds an important cautionary note: In acting for the sake of one instance of the good, do not destroy, damage, or impede some other instance or instances. The end does *not* justify such a means, and "lesser evils" (supposing one could really know them) are not to be chosen. So the first and eighth modes together direct us toward acting for the goods of human persons and reverencing them. The sixth mode lends support by directing us toward the real good in its wholeness, rather than the mere experience or appearance of the good in isolation from the reality.

These five modes of responsibility provide us with an orientation to the goods themselves. The others—five, seven, and two—orient us in our interpersonal relations; they tell us how to relate to people.

The fifth mode says: Be fair, treat everybody impartially, recognizing that all are children of God and possess a fundamental equality in dignity. To this the seventh adds: And even if it *is* fair—as it can be—to take revenge, do not do so; do not adopt the ethic of "an eye for an eye." The second mode's message is that, besides treating people impartially and not hurting them to get even, one should enter into cooperation with them. Join with others—and be sure to let them join, too—in pursuit of the good. Build community.

Implied in these eight modes of responsibility is a world view. But it is not the world view of conventional wisdom. The latter amounts to saying one should obey society's rules so as to be accepted as a decent member of society, but, observing that minimum, one is then at liberty to do as one pleases, and nobody else has a right to complain or interfere.

We all encounter and are tempted by that world view. Yet we cannot help having some insight into the world view of the modes of responsibility. There is nothing mysterious or esoteric about them. Anyone who makes a commitment to try to know what is morally true and live by it, even when doing so is difficult, is truly committed to living inspired by the ideal of integral human fulfillment. But how does one make that commitment?

The act of faith is such a commitment for Christians. Included in the commitment to God is a commitment to turn away from the darkness and live in the light of truth. But even a good pagan who does not hear the gospel preached desires to live in the light of moral truth and pursue human goods in an openhearted, generous way—and that also is an implicit act of faith. If such a person later hears and accepts the gospel, his or her commitment to live by the ideal of integral human fulfillment is not repudiated but transformed into the following of Jesus, a way of life which points to fulfillment in heaven as the reality to which, thanks to Jesus, the pursuit of "integral human fulfillment" now leads.

9. The Voluntary: What Moral Norms Bear Upon

Having examined the modes of responsibility, we must consider moral norms, which tell us whether particular acts are right or wrong. But first we must see what human acts *are*. That, essentially, is the subject of this chapter.

The question is more difficult than one might suppose, and also extremely important. The issue is precisely this: What are we morally responsible for, and how responsible are we?

People often think of moral principles as having to do with outward behavior. Taking a norm like "Do not kill," they apply it to any behavior which brings about somebody's death. As we know from the gospel, however, morality is much more a matter of inward attitude than outward behavior: "What comes out of the mouth proceeds from the heart, and this is what defiles" (Mt 15:18). Thus, to understand the morality of human actions, we must examine choices and other kinds of voluntariness and see how moral norms apply to them.

We shall consider six topics: kinds of voluntariness which precede choice; pursuing goals, choosing, and accepting side effects; responsibility in choosing and responsibility in accepting side effects; commitments; kinds of voluntariness which presuppose choice but are not choices; and omissions.

A: Kinds of Voluntariness Which Precede Choice

Two kinds of voluntariness precede choice: simple willing and interest.

"Simple willing" refers to the basic aliveness to human goods which everyone naturally has. Before making a choice, one must be drawn toward the goods involved in the several possibilities in such a way that they can provide reasons for choosing. Lacking this basic thrust toward life, truth, friendship, and the rest, one would never think of doing anything for their sake. Thus, for there to be any choices at all, there must be an underlying willing of goods, by which one is alive to them as general possibilities of human fulfillment. This underlying willing is simple—that is, unqualified—willing.

"Interest" refers to a willing which is more focused than simple willing. One's interest is aroused only as one becomes aware, at least vaguely and remotely, of some range of possible ways in which one might conceivably act for goods. Because interest depends on this further awareness, one's interests develop and vary with experience, knowledge, relationships with other people, and so forth. In particular, because one cannot even begin to consider acting for something unless the purpose is or includes some goal with emotional appeal, the willing we call "interest" always builds upon habits of feeling. Thus, while everyone is alike in being alive to the good of life, people differ in their interests in self-preservation and care for the lives of others, in avoiding disease and preventing accidents, and so on.

Whenever we deliberate, we would (if we could) act for all the intelligible goods promised by all the possibilities under consideration. That "would (if we could)" is interest. It motivates us to make a choice, which is required by our inability to act at once for everything in which we are interested. For unless we choose, we shall satisfy none of the interests at work in that set of alternatives.

Once a choice has been made, the willing which we call "interest" before the choice is given a new name: "intention." It continues to motivate the choice and the subsequent willing involved in its carrying out. Because choices are self-determining, they feed back upon interests, and so modify and develop them. For this reason, most of an adult's interests are not instances of voluntariness which altogether precede choice. Although they do so in the sense that every choice presupposes some already existing interest or interests, they usually depend more or less on past choices. To the extent they do, one is responsible for them.

B: Pursuing Goals, Choosing, and Accepting Side Effects

Pursuing goals, choosing, and accepting side effects are really distinct from one another, although one never chooses without pursuing a goal, and one never accepts side effects without choosing.

Pursuing a goal means acting in view of some definite outcome, either for the sake of an intelligible good in which one is interested or under the impetus of a merely emotional motive. To act under the impetus of a merely emotional motive—and to use reason to shape the action so that it will be effective—often is not a bad thing to do. That is so when there is no *reason* to refrain from the action. For example, a student who goes to the infirmary with a sore throat, moved only by the desire to feel better, does nothing wrong provided there is no reason not to go to the infirmary. In cases like this, one spontaneously does what one feels like doing; no choice is necessary, and so no moral question arises.

But suppose the student cannot possibly get to the infirmary without cutting a class. Now there are conflicting possibilities, with different goods at stake. A choice is required, because there is a reason not to do what the student feels like doing. On reflection, however, a good reason for going to the infirmary also may come to mind: "I normally would not cut that class," the student says to himself, "but I've had this sore throat for three days, and I'm just going to get sicker if I don't do something about it." So he cuts class and goes to the infirmary, pursuing the goal of obtaining treatment by a course of action chosen with the intention of restoring health. Evidently there is a difference between pursuing a goal by merely emotional motivation and pursuing a goal— perhaps the same goal—by choice for the sake of an intended end.

Side effects may also come into play. Although the student has a good reason for choosing to go to the infirmary, he foresees problems if he cuts class. Perhaps he has been having trouble with that course; this is the last lecture before a big exam; the professor is likely to give some helpful hints. In choosing to go to the infirmary, the student does not choose the bad side effects of cutting class, yet he foresees them and, without desiring them, willingly accepts them.

There is more to choosing than simply pursuing goals. A choice is the selection of a line of action from among possibilities or against counterindications. In choosing, one engages in self-determination by adopting a proposal to do something. This is not the same as freely accepting side effects, for a choice, strictly speaking, bears upon the content of the proposal one adopts in making it, not upon side effects which one anticipates and accepts but does not choose. That, for example, is what happens when a deliberative assembly adopts a motion: the content of the motion is precisely what is chosen, even though the assembly may see that other things besides the motion's "content" will come about as side effects of carrying it out.

Sometimes the action we choose immediately realizes the good we intend. A woman decides to play tennis instead of reading a book, just because she intends that good which is inherent in playing tennis. When she does what she decided to do—plays tennis—she realizes the good she has in view without having to make any more choices.

In other cases, though, the good one has in view in choosing a particular action is not realized in performing the action but only later. In taking medicine for a sore throat, one's health is not restored at that very moment but subsequently. In taking the medicine one does what one can to get over the sore throat; but the end one intends—health—only comes about at the end of a causal process over which one does not have total and direct control.

In still other cases, the intended end will only be achieved as a result of some further action (or actions) requiring a further choice (or choices) on one's own part or on the part of some other person or persons. For instance: someone plays tennis not for the sake of the game but in order to make a business deal; the action—playing tennis—is a means to the end intended in making a deal, which is a quite distinct action. Or: one man threatens another, "If you insult my wife again, I'll kill your child." If the threat works, it is effective only because the second man decides not to insult the first's wife again. Thus, a choice is a means when one chooses to do something for the sake of a purpose which will only be realized, if at all, through some other choice or set of choices, one's own or someone else's.

Often, too, one foresees that carrying out a choice will have side effects—an impact, for good or ill, on human goods other than those to which the choice itself is directed. Such side effects are not the same as the content of the proposal one adopts by choice. The student chooses to go to the infirmary for the sake of his health; the problems which may arise from cutting class are neither part of what he has chosen nor are they included in or conducive to what he intends.

On the other hand, one cannot honestly say something is an unintended side effect when it *is* part of a proposal adopted for the sake of an ulterior good. The man who threatens another man's child is not entitled to regard what he threatens to do as an unintended side effect, for the threat is precisely his chosen means of protecting his wife.

But suppose a woman who has decided not to submit without a fight if someone ever sexually attacks her fights off a man who tries to rape her by slashing his throat with his own knife. Unless she deliberately kills the attacker, perhaps for revenge, by using greater violence than necessary to thwart his attack, she can rightly say that his death was not something she chose; it was an unintended side effect of defending herself, rather than part of a proposal which she adopted by choice. In practice this can be a subtle distinction indeed, but it is essential to understanding the morality of complex actions.

C: Responsibility in Choosing and in Accepting Side Effects

We are primarily responsible for what we choose. But we also are responsible, though in a different way, for the side effects of our choices and actions.

Choosing is directly in our power. In choosing, one determines oneself with respect to the goods involved in the proposal one adopts. A woman who chooses to play tennis makes herself a tennis player. A man who chooses to kill another man makes himself a killer. Not that we have no moral responsibility for side effects resulting from our actions (we do) or that such results are not morally important (they are); but moral responsibility lies much more in what one chooses and does to oneself by one's choices than it does in their results.

The point is clearest when something happens so that what is chosen and what results differ drastically. Suppose John chooses to murder Bob, but Bob dies of natural causes before John can act on his choice: John's self-determination in choosing to kill is nevertheless real, and he is morally guilty of murder. Or suppose

Mary chooses to give her sick child medicine, and to her horror the child has a violent allergic reaction and dies: morally speaking, Mary is a caring parent, not a murderer. Certainly, consequences are important—*morally* important if they are included in the proposal one adopts or if one intends them—yet the primary locus of moral responsibility is not in the consequences but in the identity one gives oneself by choosing.

In a morally complex act, where one chooses a means to an ulterior end—tennis for the sake of a business deal, threatening somebody's child for the sake of protecting one's wife—one's responsibility extends not only to the good one ultimately intends but to the means one chooses to reach it. A woman playing tennis to make a business deal makes herself to be both a business-woman *and* a tennis player; a man who threatens a child's life as a way of protecting his wife gives himself the moral identity of a solicitous husband *and* a child-threatener and killer. We are morally responsible for whatever we choose, even if we choose some things only as means to other ends which we "really" have in view.

The nuclear deterrent provides a good example. Of course we do not "really" want to kill millions of small children and old people in a paroxysm of nuclear violence. We want peace and freedom. We are only making this threat (with considerable reluctance and genuine regret) to keep the leaders of unfriendly powers from taking away our liberty and the liberty of our friends. All very true. But in choosing the deterrent, we determine ourselves not only in respect to the goods we intend to protect but in respect to the death of those millions of children and old people under certain conditions. This is a real act of self-determination, and it is beside the point that we feel revulsion at the thought of what we have chosen to do and that we hope the time for doing it never comes. In making this choice, we give ourselves at one and the same time the moral identity of lovers of peace and freedom *and* that of killers of children and old people.

We saw in the last chapter that four of the modes of responsibility (three, four, six, and eight) are concerned only with choosing. Three and four tell us not to choose to follow desires or to be restrained by fears; six tells us not to choose the felt aspect of the good in preference to its fuller reality; and eight tells us not to choose to destroy, damage, or impede any instance of a good for the sake of something else. These four modes, then, are concerned only with choices, not with accepting side effects. But the others (one, two, five, and seven) can come into play in reference to accepting side effects; one may *not* accept side effects when doing so would violate one of these modes.

Suppose there are rats on your property. You want to poison them, but there are also small children in the neighborhood who may get into your backyard and eat the rat poison. You say to yourself, "Nobody asked those kids over here. If they poison themselves, that's their problem." Poisoning children is not part of the proposal you adopt, and, of course, you do not intend to harm the children (in the sense that you have no interest in doing that); but you do foresee the poisoning of children as a possible side effect of your action. You would not risk it if your own child might be poisoned. Thus, the fifth mode of responsibility—treat others as you would want them to treat you—comes into play and tells you, "Don't put rat poison in the backyard." Accepting side effects must be judged in relation to fairness.

Again, suppose you are contemplating a course of action which will produce side effects harmful to someone you hate. You are bidding on a contract, and your competitor will go bankrupt if he does not get it. You might rightly accept this side effect of your successful bidding if you have nothing in view except carrying on your own business. But if you have a grudge against the other fellow and are delighted to underbid him, knowing he will be forced out of business, you are accepting that side effect in a way forbidden by the seventh mode of responsibility: do not act out of hostility.

Similarly, we are not permitted to accept side effects when doing so will violate the first and second modes of responsibility: act for the sake of the good, but do not act for the good individualistically.

D: What Commitments Are

Although the word "commitment" has many different meanings, we use it to refer to certain choices motivated at least partly by the intention of one or more of the reflexive goods—self-integration, practical reasonableness and authenticity, friendship and justice, religion. Commitments typically involve undertaking a relationship with another person or group of persons. So, for example, the act of faith, marital consent, religious vows, and determining to reform one's life are commitments.

Making a commitment is different from setting out in pursuit of some definite goal, even a very large one like becoming famous or ending the arms race. There is nothing wrong with pursuing definite goals—indeed, it is often necessary and morally obligatory—but this is not what is meant by a commitment. For commitments are open-ended and share in the indeterminacy of the interests which give rise to them. One can definitively achieve a goal, but one can never say one has so fully realized the good one intends in making a commitment that no further realization of it is possible.

Making the act of faith, for example, is not simply setting out to achieve certain objectives; it is undertaking a whole way of life, without knowing—without it being *possible* to know—everything one will have to do in the course of a lifetime to live out the commitment. Marrying (if one enters marriage as a commitment) does not mean simply imagining a certain state of affairs and saying, "Sounds pretty good—I think I'll go for it." It means undertaking to cooperate with another person in a common life in a multitude of ways that cannot possibly be anticipated at the beginning. Within the framework of these commitments—the life of faith, married life—one will no doubt pursue many specific goals, but these are not the commitments themselves. Rather, they are more or less appropriate ways of implementing and serving commitments.

Still, large, long-term goals and commitments are at least alike in that they organize people's lives. Setting out to make a million dollars before you are thirty will certainly give a great deal of structure to your life. So will setting out to be a good priest or a good doctor. Within the framework of the latter commitments, however, there is room for a creativity which is not possible within the framework of pursuing a goal like making a million dollars. With a goal in view (and one *should* have goals in mind), all one can do—at best—is adapt one's pursuit of it to changing circumstances and devise more effective ways of reaching it. But in living out a commitment, one is constantly challenged to think of new goals and new projects for serving the good, goals and projects of which no one else may ever before have thought.

Commitments are made freely—that is, by choice. Usually one sees alternative commitments one could make, and always one is aware that if one undertakes *this* commitment, it will entail many responsibilities. One has the choice of saying *yes* or *no*. Having made a commitment, however, one is likely to do many things in carrying it out without choosing each time, since many of the ways in which a commitment is fulfilled tend to become matters of habit which exclude ways of acting incompatible with the commitment even before they come to mind.

For example, a husband and wife for whom their marriage is a commitment may reach a point at which they hardly have to *choose* any more not to be unfaithful—the practice of marital fidelity has become so ingrained that they are scarcely ever tempted even to think about being unfaithful. Still, what is done within the framework of a commitment without having to make additional choices is done freely, with the freedom of the commitment itself. Thus, habitually faithful husbands and wives are not simply plodding along a well-worn rut with blinders on; their fidelity has the freedom and moral significance of their marital commitment. Moreover, even the most faithful person sometimes is tempted to violate (or, at least, omit to fulfill) his or her commitments and must reaffirm and deepen them by choosing to reject the temptation.

E: Sorts of Voluntariness Which Presuppose Choice

Simple willing and interest come before choice. But there are also kinds of voluntariness which come after choice and presuppose it. Although the modes of responsibility do not directly apply, since they bear only on choice and accepting side effects, there is nevertheless a kind of moral responsibility in these cases. Examples will make this clear.

One such instance might be called executive willing. (By "executive" we mean a willing which occurs in the course of *executing* a choice one has made.) Someone makes a choice and, in carrying it out, sees that it has an unforeseen impact on some human goods. Without choosing this impact or accepting it as a side effect, the person simply goes along with it willingly. A mobster setting fire to the store of a shopkeeper who refuses to pay "protection" money discovers that the shopkeeper is inside;

without making any further choice, and so without *choosing* murder, he proceeds, aware that he is causing someone's death and not really caring. No choice, but very real moral responsibility, quite similar to the responsibility one has for accepting the side effects which one foresees in making a choice.

Another sort of voluntariness which presupposes choice is that involved when one's actions have unforeseen consequences which could and should have been foreseen. A woman who gets drunk at a party and then drives home may not think about the possibility of killing someone in an accident, but she could and should do so; even if no accident occurs, she has some moral responsibility for endangering lives. A more conscientious person *would* think of the danger and refrain.

There can also be moral responsibility in readiness to will, as a result of previous choices. Suppose a man repeatedly commits small sins of cheating and dishonesty. When he has the unexpected opportunity to steal something of great value without being observed, he is likely to be in a frame of mind—as a result of previous, repeated choices to do small dishonest deeds—to commit the big crime.

Hence, one can have a moral responsibility for things one is not thinking about or paying attention to, and therefore can hardly be said to "choose." Scripture speaks of unknown faults and sins: even though we examine our consciences carefully, we do not notice them—yet we are not thereby without responsibility, for we *could* have. "I am not aware of anything against myself," Paul says, "but I am not thereby acquitted. It is the Lord who judges me" (1 Cor 4:4). How serious our responsibility in such circumstances may be and whether mortal sin is involved are questions to be considered later (in chapter 15:B).

F: Omissions and Our Responsibility for Them

We are responsible not only for what we do but for what we fail to do, supposing it should be done. But note the latter qualification. We are guilty of an "omission" in a moral sense only when we have a moral responsibility and fail to fulfill it. Forgetting to do something one has no moral responsibility to do is not an omission. Skipping lunch because you are too busy to eat is not an omission, morally speaking—unless, that is, you have a moral obligation to eat lunch.

There are different kinds of omissions. One is a choice precisely not to do something which should be done. A couple have an infant with Down's Syndrome, and they do not want the child. They choose not to feed it so that it will starve to death—that is, they choose to kill it by omitting care which they have an obligation to give.

A more common kind of omission occurs when someone with a moral responsibility does something which conflicts with fulfilling it, knowing it will go unfulfilled. Parents on a vacation find that one of the children has a high fever. It could be something serious, but they put the child to bed with an aspirin because they are enjoying themselves and do not want to take time out for a long drive to the doctor. They have not chosen to neglect their child, yet the omission is a side effect of what they do choose: concentrating on their own fun. Again, students who ought to study for an exam decide to have a party first; they do not exactly choose to omit study, but they know perfectly well that they *will* omit it because they will be too tired to study later.

Omissions also occur when we know we should choose but fail to get around to it. A mother and father see that their little daughter is not well—the child is listless, tires easily, sleeps badly, has poor color. Probably they ought to do something. But then again—maybe it is just a bug. Maybe they can safely wait and see. Maybe. . . . They never do make up their minds. Again: A young woman knows she ought to start examining her conscience carefully as a necessary part of getting her life straightened out, but somehow never does get around to it. There are good intentions—or, more accurately, appropriate interests—in such cases, but the relevant choices are lacking.

Finally, there is the kind of omission which occurs when one never even thinks of doing something one could and should do, but which one *would* think of if one were more responsible. Suppose Bill is aware that his wife has been unusually quiet and withdrawn lately, but he thinks little of it because he is full of his own affairs. One day she attempts suicide. A less self-centered husband would have seen the problem developing and tried to find a way to help. Bill cannot say he has no responsibility.

Thus, we have four different kinds of omissions, each with its own kind of responsibility. Are these distinctions irrelevant hair splitting? Not really. Suppose people feel guilty about some negligence many years earlier—parents, for instance, whose child has turned out badly and who blame themselves. It is no help to such people to tell them, "You didn't *choose* to be neglectful parents, so you didn't commit any sin and you shouldn't feel morally responsible." They know perfectly well that they are somehow responsible, even if they cannot say exactly how. On the other hand, neither is it helpful to say, "You're right—you didn't do your job back then, and you're to blame for what happened." The real service is to show the parents that there are different kinds of responsibility for omissions and to try to help them understand theirs, so that they can take whatever steps may now be appropriate and possible.

10. From Modes of Responsibility to Moral Norms

The modes of responsibility and their corresponding virtues point us in the direction of a morally good life, but they do not by themselves tell us which actions are and are not morally good. "Act impartially" is excellent advice, but it leaves unanswered whether *this* particular way of acting is impartial. So with the rest of the modes: we need moral norms which are more specific in order to know whether particular kinds of action do or do not conform with them.

Such norms either are judgments of conscience or else contribute to their making. This chapter therefore continues and moves beyond the discussion of conscience begun in chapter three. The two chapters that follow round out the discussion. Here we consider six topics: whether all the modes of responsibility have force in the same way; the derivation of norms from the modes of responsibility; why some norms are absolute and others are not; the adequacy of the method of deriving moral norms; rights and duties; and whether moral norms for societies are different from those for individuals.

A: Not All the Modes of Responsibility Have the Same Force

There is a sense in which all the modes of responsibility have normative force in the same way. All express the first principle of morality and require that reason prevail over feelings when feelings would unreasonably constrict love of the goods and of the

people who can share in them. The ideal of integral human fulfillment and the requirement to will in a manner consistent with
it underlie the modes.

Yet not all the modes have the same normative force. Depending on which is violated, one's will is more or less out of line with
integral human fulfillment. It is worse to try to cause serious
bodily harm to somebody one hates (against the seventh mode)
than to practice favoritism in giving or withholding life-
threatening assignments (against the fifth mode), and worse to do
the latter than to let inertia or anxiety keep one from extending
help to someone in a life-threatening situation (against the first or
fourth mode). In all three cases the behavior may lead to someone's death, but the kind of immorality involved is different in
each.

Why? In the first case, someone willing to kill a person he or
she hates has a will set against the good of life and against the
good of community (with that enemy). In the second, a person in
authority who practices favoritism in giving hazardous assignments need not have a will set against life but is displaying partiality in a serious matter. In the third, the will of someone too
fearful or inert to help another person in a desperate situation is
not set against either life or community, but neither is it directed
to the realization of these goods as strongly as it should be.

Because different modes oblige us in different ways, the immorality of violating them varies. This helps explain why people often are aware of some modes but virtually oblivious to others.
The requirement of fairness is obvious to most people, as is the
wrongness of revenge. But many are reluctant to acknowledge that
there is anything wrong with merely neglecting to act for the good
(a violation of the first mode). "I don't say laziness is good, but
don't tell me it's wrong." In fact, laziness *is* wrong, but usually
not so wrong as violating some of the other modes. (In particular
instances, nevertheless, laziness can be more serious than, say,
unfairness if laziness leads one to neglect something serious while
unfairness leads one to be partial in a trivial matter.)

Recognizing some modes but not others gives rise to a variety
of errors. For instance, someone who acknowledges only the fifth
mode may mistakenly suppose that unless something is immoral
in the same way unfairness is, it is not immoral at all; or such a
person may suppose that because something *is* immoral—laziness,

say—therefore it must be immoral in the same way as unfairness. We should neither underestimate nor overestimate the significance of the weaker modes. All of the modes of responsibility *can* generate serious responsibilities, but some are more likely to do so than others.

B: The Derivation of Norms from the Modes of Responsibility

A specific moral norm is a proposition characterizing some kind of act as wrong, good, obligatory, or permissible. In this system, then, there are four moral predicates: wrong, good, obligatory, permissible.

Where do moral norms come from? Usually we do not start by seeing what mode of responsibility is relevant, then reason from it to a norm. Rather, each of us has a store of moral norms ready at hand—principles of conduct learned from parents, teachers, and many other sources. The Christian community hands on moral norms to its members, for the way to follow Jesus is an important part of the gospel. It is not necessary or even possible for each and every individual to establish for himself or herself the precise rational basis for each and every moral norm to which he or she subscribes.

The natural moral law—the law written in hearts—enables us to grasp that on the whole sound moral norms make sense and are true, although we may not be able in every case to say exactly why. Yet people who habitually violate moral norms often reach the point of *not* knowing what is right, because they are likely to resort to rationalization and close their eyes to the truth in order to subdue their guilt feelings without reforming their lives. On the other hand, people who try to live uprightly can usually see the cogency of sound norms without much difficulty; they strive to observe the norms they have received from responsible sources and do their best to hand them on to others.

Sometimes, however, one must proceed in a thoroughly conscious and deliberate way: start with moral principles, derive norms from them, and articulate the process by which this is done. New situations involving new kinds of action arise and must be evaluated. Received norms are questioned, arguments flare up, the established norms must be reexamined and either discarded, refined, or defended. Then one needs a logical way of proceeding from principles to conclusions—that is, from the modes of responsibility to specific norms.

Consider a specific norm: Promise keeping is obligatory. Most people accept the truth of that. But *why* is it true?

To see why, we must keep in mind the first principle of morality—act with a will consistent with love of integral human fulfillment. We must consider how the will is related to human goods in *not* keeping promises. We must reflect on how this particular relationship of will to goods looks in light of the modes of responsibility. Then, based on these steps, we must reach a conclusion: Because the will involved in not keeping promises is inconsistent with fairness to others (after all, *I* want others to keep *their* promises to me), and because unfairness is ruled out by the moral principle which we have called the fifth mode of responsibility, breaking promises is morally wrong. Promise keeping is obligatory.

Consider another moral norm: Contraception is wrong. Considered from a moral perspective, contraception is not simply behaving in such a way that one does not have children; otherwise all those who were able to have children but did not would be contracepting, which is plainly not the case. Rather, the choice to contracept is a choice to prevent the handing-on of human life when, as far as one knows, that might otherwise take place. But this is a choice to impede a certain human good (life), in a particular instance (the coming to be of this particular unwanted baby); and such a choice against an instance of human good is a violation of the eighth mode of responsibility; contraception therefore is wrong.

If no mode of responsibility excludes the ways in which an action relates one's will to relevant human goods, and if the action serves some human good, the action is good, though not necessarily obligatory. For example, giving a friend a birthday present. No mode of responsibility says a will to give the present is wrong; doing so serves the good of friendship; so the action is good.

Thus, actions of some kinds are wrong and actions of other kinds are good, depending on the will toward human goods which they involve. But even actions which are good are not necessarily obligatory. It is good to give a friend a present, yet one may not be obliged to do so in every instance. For instance, a poor man might reasonably conclude that, instead of giving gifts, he should use his limited resources to provide for the education of his children.

An action is obligatory when the only alternative to doing it is to do something wrong. If one has made a promise, and the alternative to keeping the promise is breaking it, and it would be wrong to break the promise—then keeping this promise is obligatory. Or, to take an instance of a softer obligation, suppose you have decided to take a brisk walk for your health every day, but today you skip it just because you feel lazy. That is wrong. Any act of a good kind is obligatory by the first mode of responsibility when one has nothing else as good or better to do.

We should, however, avoid the rigoristic notion that all obligations are equally serious. The first mode, for example, is the softest, least binding of the modes of responsibility, and omitting to do something good when one has nothing else worthwhile in mind is not immoral in the same way as violating some of the other modes. On the other hand, even "soft" obligations are quite real: for example, the obligation to take a healthy walk when one has no reason except laziness for not doing it.

What about the permissible? A permissible action is one of which we cannot say it is either wrong, good, or obligatory, *because it has not been sufficiently defined.* What we know of the action does not sufficiently specify the will's relationship to human goods in choosing it. For instance—being a vegetarian. One might choose a meatless diet for health reasons or religious reasons or simply to show off. "To be a vegetarian" does not identify the reason. So being a vegetarian is "permissible" as long as all one knows about it is that it means not eating meat; yet "permissible" merely signifies that we do not know the relationship to human goods which choosing this kind of action involves in this particular case. Once we do know, the action is no longer merely permissible; it is either wrong or good or obligatory.

C: Why Some Norms Are Absolute and Others Are Not

Most specific moral norms are not absolute. How is this to be explained?

One way is to suppose that actions are simply units of behavior. But then *all* norms seem open to exceptions. Outward performances as such are quite ambiguous; their moral character depends on the intentions of those who perform them. So, it seems, if one performs an action (meaning, a certain pattern of outward behavior) with a "good" intention, it is morally good; and if one performs it with a "bad" intention, it is evil. This, however, is a faulty explanation, for it overlooks the fact that moral actions are essentially acts of the will (which may be carried out by outward behavior) rather than units of external behavior (to which we can attach various "intentions," more or less at will). The moral question is precisely: In choosing this action, what am I *willing?*

The correct explanation lies instead in the fact that, in learning more about a particular action so as to be able to specify it more precisely, one may find that its moral characterization changes— from wrong to good, from good to obligatory, or whatever. This often happens. The first principle of morality, the basic human goods, and the modes of responsibility generate different moral characterizations of different kinds of acts, and more and less specified kinds of acts sometimes are morally different kinds of acts.

Take promise keeping. Keeping promises is obligatory. Joe invites Marjorie to dinner on Friday, and she accepts. In midweek, though, Arthur invites her to a better restaurant, so Marjorie breaks her date with Joe. That is not fair—she would not want someone to do the same to her. The norm stands: she *ought* to have kept her promise.

Suppose, however, that Marjorie wakes up Friday morning with a headache and a fever. Flu. She would not expect or even want anyone who feels as rotten as she does to go out with her. So she calls Joe and breaks their date. She is acting fairly. And since fairness (the fifth mode) is the basis of the norm that promises should be kept, in these more specific circumstances Marjorie is entitled *not* to observe the norm on the very same basis that makes it valid in the first place. Fairness grounds her original obligation to keep her date with Joe, but when additional data— her illness and its unpleasant symptoms—change the specification of this behavior, fairness itself requires a different characterization of this now more highly specified action. The norm stands—promises should be kept—but it is not absolute; promises whose keeping would require one to accept damage which one would not expect others to accept in the same circumstances need not be kept.

Notice that the solution here does not lie in saying it is a "greater good" or "lesser evil" to stay home instead of keeping a date when one is sick. The accurate way of stating the matter is to say that it is usually fair to keep promises and unfair not to keep them; but changed circumstances or new information can also make it fair not to keep a promise. When the specification of an action changes because the circumstances change or we have acquired more information than we had at first, a different norm may come into play.

The obligation to keep promises also has other limits. Suppose I make a promise in good faith, but find out later that keeping it would require me to do something wrong. An acquaintance asks me to keep some antique prints for him, explaining that his apartment is being painted and he will pick them up in a week or so. A few days later I learn that the prints are stolen goods. If I keep my promise and give them back to my acquaintance instead of restoring them to their rightful owner, I am doing something wrong. Obviously I ought not to keep my promise, because of the priority of a moral obligation—not to cooperate in a theft—which existed when I made the promise, even though I was not then aware it applied in this case.

Some negative norms, however, are absolute. They have no exceptions, for they concern actions of such a kind that violation of a mode of responsibility is built into the willingness to perform them. No change of circumstances or additional information can change that.

Take the norm which says that infanticide is wrong. To choose to kill a child involves a will contrary to the good of human life. But might there not be exceptions to the norm? No, for regardless of any further specifications—that it will be burdensome to the parents to have to care for this child, that its life will be short and pain-filled, that the child is unwanted, that there is not enough money to pay for its care—to choose to kill the child still involves a will against life. Further specification can affect the degree of immorality, since circumstances have a bearing on *how* perverse the will to kill is (it would be worse to kill a child because one simply did not want to be bothered with it than because one wished to end its suffering). And almost certainly circumstances of this sort will help those who decide to kill a child to rationalize their deed. But their choice remains morally wrong. The norm which tells us not to kill small children is absolute.

An analogy with diet helps clarify this matter of absolute and nonabsolute norms. Most dietary norms are nonabsolute. Generally speaking, children should have milk in their diets, but some children should not drink milk because they are allergic to it; so the norm which tells us to give children milk is not absolute. The same is true of most negative dietary norms. Do not eat only candy bars and potato chips; but if you are stranded in a wilderness with only potato chips and candy bars—eat them! But there are also negative dietary norms which are absolute. Do not make a meal of cyanide. No matter what the circumstances, there are no exceptions to that.

It is the same with moral norms. Most specific norms, positive and negative alike, are nonabsolute—they admit of exceptions when the action in question is further specified, so that from a moral perspective it is no longer really the same action. But some specific norms, like the norm against infanticide, are absolute. No matter how much more we learn about the circumstances, the additional information cannot alter the fact that the action involves a will set against a basic human good. Just as no circumstances can make it anything but self-destructive to make a meal of cyanide, no circumstances can make killing a small child anything but an act rooted in a will against life. A moral norm like this has no exceptions—it is absolute. And, since life and the other basic human goods are not apart from persons but are aspects of their full being, such absolute moral norms shield every person's inherent dignity.

D: The Adequacy of the Method of Deriving Specific Moral Norms

We need at times to analyze and criticize our judgments of conscience. The method of deriving moral norms described here sometimes is not by itself capable of supplying a conclusive critique of these judgments. But that is so only if a judgment of conscience depends on certain other judgments which defy analysis.

Moral norms are universal, but each judgment of conscience is unique. A norm says some *kind* of action is right or wrong, but a judgment of conscience concerns *this particular* action. While an absolute norm excluding some way of willing and acting holds in every case, judgments of conscience are not concerned exclusively with such matters. Usually they deal with the matter of nonabsolute norms, both negative and affirmative.

If one has a reason for not observing a negative, nonabsolute norm, that is because the action is being further specified, and the same reason will apply in any similar case. For instance, if one has a reason for *not* keeping a promise in these particular circumstances, the same reason will be valid in other cases involving circumstances like these. Thus, nonabsolute negative norms do not defy analysis.

However, there are other factors affecting judgments of conscience which defy analysis in this way. For judgments of conscience not only forbid doing what ought not to be done, but direct doing what ought to be done. In applying affirmative norms to reach such affirmative judgments of conscience, two factors resist analysis.

First, in making a judgment of conscience, one must always ask whether one has taken into account everything which needs to be considered. "Have I looked at all the facts? Have I considered all the implications? Have I weighed all the alternatives to what I am proposing to do?" It is impossible to give a conclusive rational answer to such questions. No deductive method can help, for the requirement of reasonableness varies depending on the context. In matters of life and death, the effort to make sure everything has been taken into account will be far more exhaustive than when, say, the question is keeping or breaking a dinner date.

Although in the nature of things it is impossible to be absolutely certain one has considered everything which should be considered, before moving forward—before, that is, taking the step from "This kind of action is good" to "This is what I should do"—one nevertheless does answer the question. In this nondeductive step, one establishes that the prospective choice is an instance of a certain kind of action: for example, "This is one of those times when I am (am not) obliged to keep my promise." Once that determination has been made, the moral characterization of the action follows from principles, not from unconscious factors or some mysterious intuition.

Second, there is a further role for nondeductive judgment when, as often happens, one confronts two or more good options, none of them obligatory. This is common in vocational choices: "Shall I be a doctor or a lawyer?" "Shall I get married or go into the priesthood?" There is merit in either course of action, and one is more or less drawn to both. And no matter how long and hard one reflects on human goods and modes of responsibility, one will never come to a decision that way. A different kind of judgment is needed.

Here one who is deliberating can legitimately invoke "discernment," in which feelings not only play a role but determine the outcome. But not just the spontaneous feelings of attraction and repulsion with which one may have begun the process. Rather, the feelings in question are those of an authentically prudent person, whose life is consistently oriented to integral human fulfillment and ordered by the modes of responsibility and who, having gone as far as possible by deductive reasoning from moral principles, now pauses in contemplation of two or more good options. (Needless to say, for a Christian, this pause should be filled with prayer for the help of the Holy Spirit, and examination of the options in the light which faith throws on them.) Eventually one option becomes increasingly attractive, while its competitors grow less interesting. Since an option has emerged through discernment, and since one ought to commit oneself to *some* good option, the conclusion is clear: "This is what I ought to do—I really have no other choice (except, of course, the choice, motivated by fear, to procrastinate)."

E: Rights and Duties

From a moral perspective, the question about rights is this: Are they an additional, independent source of morality, standing outside and apart from the principles we have been examining? This is not an idle question. "Your approach is terribly complicated," many people would say. "Isn't there a simpler way of knowing what's right and wrong? Why not just recognize the rights which belong to God and other people? If you respect those rights, surely you're being morally good. And then there's no need to juggle integral human fulfillment, modes of responsibility, specification of norms, and the rest, and try to make them all fit together like the pieces of a jigsaw puzzle."

Unfortunately, there is a problem with this seductively simple approach. It is a conspicuously disputed question whether certain crucial rights exist.

For example: Do the unborn have a right to life? To make the argument that they do, it is necessary to ground their right in a duty not to kill them. But where does the duty come from? Starting with the good of human life, one must establish that this good is really at stake in the case of the unborn, against all the arguments that they are not alive, are not human, or are not persons. One also must consider the kind of will involved in choosing to destroy the life of a human individual: it is a choice to attack an instance of a basic human good. In short, rather than simply saying that the unborn have a right to life, one finds oneself elaborating an argument which relies on principles to defend a specific moral norm. Having done that, one points out that the wrongful harm done to a helpless, innocent, unborn child by killing him or her also is terribly unfair. Now, finally, one can say: "Surely, the unborn have a right to life."

As in this case, so in general, statements about rights are not principles but conclusions. Rights presuppose duties. We can clarify and defend statements about rights only by identifying the duties underlying them and showing where they come from. But to do that we must look to the human goods and the modes of responsibility which ground these obligations. True, it sometimes seems obvious—at least to some people—that certain rights exist. But without proceeding as we have suggested, it is impossible to make an argument in their defense.

Talk about rights is notoriously ambiguous. There is an enormous literature on the subject—qualified rights and unqualified rights, natural rights and ascribed rights, rights created by society, and so on. There are as many kinds of rights as there are duties toward others, and we have already glimpsed the rich variety of duties generated by the eight modes of responsibility, the different kinds of actions, norms which are absolute, and norms which are nonabsolute. To give an adequate account of rights would require making all the distinctions which we have made in regard to these matters.

Most people who talk about rights do not do this. Instead, treating one kind of right as the model for all, they generalize fallaciously. "Certainly the unborn have a right to life. But rights admit of exceptions. I have a right not to be disturbed when I'm resting, but if it's a matter of life and death for somebody else, my right has to give way. Therefore, the right of the unborn to life. . . . " A dandy argument—except that rights are *not* all the same.

If one grasps that rights always depend on duties, and that duties flow from human goods and modes of responsibility, one will find nothing surprising in the fact that not all rights have the same characteristics. Some are absolute and some are not. The right of the unborn not to be killed is absolute because the duty not to kill them is absolute; and the duty is absolute because one can only make a choice to kill the unborn by choosing to destroy an instance of the good of human life, contrary to the eighth mode of responsibility. The right of children to be educated is also a real right, but it is not absolute. There is a duty to educate children, grounded among other things in the fifth mode (fairness). But in any particular case, other circumstances enter the picture: the resources available for education, the other needs which also must be satisfied with the same resources, the child's capacity to benefit from education, and so forth. Further specification of the action by these additional data may rightly lead to the conclusion that the same mode—fairness—requires forgoing the education under consideration in a particular case.

F: Moral Norms for Societies

Many people suppose that "personal" morality is one thing and "social" morality another, and the two are very different. Accordingly, they think that morality for individuals is not the same as morality for societies, and certainly not the same as the moral code (whatever it may be) that governs the conduct of states and those who lead them. This way of thinking is characteristic of Machiavelli. It is profoundly mistaken.

Evidently there is a sense in which the moral norms which apply to societies are different from those which apply to individuals. A political society ought to levy just taxes; individuals, acting as such, do not levy taxes at all. Husbands and wives ought to remember one another's birthdays; the United States is not obliged to remember the birthday of its spouse. There are some kinds of actions which only individuals can perform and some which only societies can perform; and in this sense different norms apply to individuals and to societies.

But there are also many kinds of actions which can be performed by individuals and societies alike. Here the same moral norms apply. Take lying. Lying is wrong for individuals, but is it also wrong for the state? Some people would say, "The government *has* to lie sometimes if the state is to survive. Such lying is in the public interest." But this is simply proportionalism at work, and proportionalism presents the same problems in the case of societies as in the case of individuals. Inherently unworkable, its main function in the social context is to rationalize what people in power choose to do.

A society is people cooperating on behalf of common purposes, and the moral principles which apply to the actions of individuals apply also to the actions of societies. Integral human fulfillment, human goods, modes of responsibility—these principles of individual action are likewise principles of a society's action. If it is wrong for John and Mary and Joe to lie, it is no less wrong for the Church, the Soviet Union, and the political party of your choice to lie.

"But," someone might object, "in social acts, the common good is at stake. And Aristotle says the common good is something greater and more godlike than the good of any individual." But Aristotle's notion of the common good arises from his view of the state as a kind of social organism whose parts are individual citizens. In this scheme, individuals can be treated much as one treats parts of a body—for example, lopped off if that would serve the rest. However, this view of the state is false, and so is the view of the common good arising from it.

True, the good of all the members of a society together is something more than their individual fulfillment *as members* considered separately. But integral human fulfillment remains the fundamental moral principle, and this is the well-being and full being of all persons in all their dimensions. Although their social dimension is an aspect of their human fulfillment, individuals are more than just parts of society. No society short of God's kingdom begins to embrace the whole person; much of every person lies beyond every other society. Thus, it is wrong to subordinate the good of individuals to the good of society and say that individuals can be sacrificed as if they were merely parts of some greater whole.

Machiavelli aside, the idea that the morality appropriate to societies is different from individual morality arises from superego and social convention. Awed by the state, which seems a source of rights and duties and fulfillments with great power to reward and punish, one imagines that it is entitled to do whatever it must in pursuit of its goals. We need to set aside this childish, mythic view, and, while acknowledging and respecting human goods with a social character, to take a realistic view of the state's authority and the limitations imposed on it by moral norms.

11. The Moral Authority of Law

It is a specific norm, not a "moral principle" as such, that one ought to obey laws. Classical treatises on moral principles all nevertheless deal with law, kinds of law, and the obligation to obey laws. We follow their example, since some who use this book will expect it, and the subject of law does raise some important moral questions. We shall consider four main topics: the idea of authority and the grounds for obedience in general; what divine precepts are and why they should be obeyed; the laws of political societies and other human societies, except the Church; and the law of the Church.

A: Authority and Obedience—Their Grounds and Limits

The word "authority" has two quite different meanings.

In one sense authority is the competence to make judgments which reasonable persons of lesser competence will accept as true. Typically, this is the authority of an expert in his or her field—a physicist about physics, an automobile mechanic about cars, and so on. The teaching authority of the Church is something like this, in that it is a competence to make judgments which others who lack the same competence should accept. But the Church's teaching authority is also very different because it is very differently grounded—in God's self-revelation and guarantees rather than in human efforts and attainments.

In another sense, authority is competence to give directions which those who are directed have a duty to obey. One might consult an authority on wines about a good vintage, but one does not have to follow his advice—he has authority only in the first sense. But if a policeman says not to park in this block, one has a duty to obey—not because the policeman has special expertise, but because he has authority in the second sense. It is in this sense that we speak of the "authority" of the law.

Power is not the same thing as authority. Suppose a gang of outlaws overruns a town. The desperadoes have the power to give orders and enforce them; others disobey at their own peril. Still, no one has a *duty* to obey, for the outlaws' power has no moral ground, and, without that, it is not true authority. (One may of course have a duty to stay alive and in that sense may also be obliged to do what the outlaws say or at least not get caught disobeying them; but the obligation here does not come from the authority of the outlaws—they have none—but from the duty to stay alive.)

Not every real obligation to comply with someone else's wishes is an instance of obedience to authority. Suppose the Smiths invite the Thompsons to dinner on a night of their choosing and the Thompsons pick Wednesday; the Smiths are then obliged to have the Thompsons to dinner Wednesday night. But not because the Thompsons have authority and the Smiths are obliged to obey; rather, because the Smiths, like everyone else, are obliged in fairness to keep their promises.

The same kind of relationship is involved wherever there is a contract. If an employer keeps a contract's terms in regard to things like wages and working conditions, an employee should do the work which the contract calls for him or her to do. But this is not because the employer has authority in the sense discussed here. Rather, a contract is a kind of two-way promise, whose fulfillment is a duty in fairness for both parties.

Nevertheless, in some lasting relationships of a contractual nature, something resembling the authority of law does arise, so that it is possible to speak of "managerial authority." Within limits, superiors in such situations have a right to give directions which employees are bound to carry out. But this managerial authority extends only to the work covered by the contract and what is necessary to its performance. Managers have no right to tell employees how to act about matters which fall beyond their terms of employment. That is why a manager must bargain with employees if they are asked to take on additional responsibilities, take a pay cut, or otherwise make adjustments in what they have agreed to.

Real lawmaking authority is the competence of some people to make decisions and give directions which other people are morally obliged to heed and obey, even if they have never undertaken to do so. Such authority arises from two sources—which, however, often overlap.

In one case, people have a moral responsibility to cooperate in regard to something, but some are better equipped than the rest to make decisions about what form the cooperation should take. Since all should seek to fulfill the common obligation to cooperate, fairness requires that those better qualified to make decisions make them and those less qualified obey.

A family—parents and children—provides a typical example. Here the common responsibility is to cooperate in bringing the children from the dependency of childhood to responsible adulthood. Many decisions are required, and, at least initially, children cannot make them. Thus, it is fair that the parents make the decisions and the children obey.

Even as children grow and acquire decision-making capabilities of their own, parents remain responsible for the family as a whole. They therefore continue to have a duty to make decisions for the family while the children continue to have a duty to obey. Yet reasonable parents will gradually adopt a more participatory *process* of family decision making, which takes account of the children's increasing maturity; moreover, as the children grow, parents will also gradually cut back on giving them directions about matters which are their own affair.

Secondly, real authority arises in a case in which people make a commitment to the pursuit of a common good. Communal choices are then required to shape their common life toward the good, and all who share the commitment must submit to those choices and act on them. But how are the choices to be made?

Sometimes they are made by consensus. This is a typical pattern for friendships and for some small private associations. Everyone participates in making decisions, no decision is final unless everyone agrees, and everyone is responsible for carrying out what is decided. Even so, there is an authority-obedience relationship: namely, everyone shares in authority and everyone shares in submission to authority.

Although this arrangement seems ideal to people who do not like authority (unless, of course, they happen to be the ones wielding it), it is workable only in small, more or less intimate groups. It certainly does not apply to a nation, the United States or any other. As a practical matter, it is impossible for millions of people to participate directly in making communal choices. And even if a yet-to-be invented electronic system were somehow to make such participation technologically feasible, the number and complexity of decisions to be made for a society on this scale would remain so staggering that the task would still have to be reserved to a relatively small number—legislators and the like—who could devote full time to it. Other members of society have other roles to play and other contributions to make.

If, then, a political society's common life is to thrive, most of its members can only share in authority in very limited ways—for example, by voting. For a citizen of a country like the United States, to vote is to exercise a governmental office through which one participates in the process of making communal choices and shares in authority. But neither the citizens of a country nor even the members of most smaller societies can participate directly in making most decisions which shape their common life; *their* decision, rather, is to submit to authority and help carry out the decisions which authority makes.

Thus, the second ground of authority is that which underlies decision making for a community based on common commitment. Some make decisions, and all carry them out (including those who make them—authorities are obliged to abide by their own rules and regulations). The moral ground of obedience is the commitment which constitutes the society, while fairness is the relevant moral principle. If the commitment is one which ought to be made, those who make it also ought faithfully to implement it. Fairness requires that they do their respective shares to make the society work and realize the common good. Obedience to authority is a necessary part of this.

Whichever way it is grounded, the duty to obey, although serious, is not absolute. Sometimes the decisions of a genuine authority ought not to be obeyed, since obeying would violate a prior moral obligation. There are three different kinds of cases.

In one, authority directs that something wrong in itself be done. For example, parents instruct a child to deny having anything to do with a fire that resulted from the child's playing with matches. They are telling the child to evade responsibility by lying. The child should not obey. It makes no difference whether the *authority* is in good faith or not; when one is sure that what authority directs one to do is wrong, one should not obey.

In another case, duties conflict. A woman is supposed to report for jury duty at nine o'clock, but when the time comes she is driving her husband, who appears to have had a heart attack, to a hospital emergency room. Her duty to be on time for service on the jury is real, but so is her duty to look after her husband.

In the third case, the legitimate decisions of authority should be set aside, even in the absence of any conflict of duties, because one is sure the authority which made the decision would want it set aside in the circumstances. Plato gives a classic example. A watchman in a fortified city has standing orders not to open the city gates to anyone at night. But one night he sees the city's own army approaching, hard pressed by a pursuing enemy. If the gates stay closed, the city's own soldiers will be massacred. So he opens the gates, reasoning that the city fathers who told him to keep them shut for safety's sake would want him to set aside their instructions in order—for safety's sake—to save the city's army. Such "disobedience" is reasonable and morally right.

B: Why Divine Precepts Should Be Obeyed

Although most people who believe in God have no difficulty accepting the idea that they should obey divine precepts, it is by no means self-evident *why* they should obey. Some seem to reason more or less along these lines: "God is a lot more powerful than I am, and he'll be angry if I don't obey. I guess I'd better." This reduces God's authority to power and makes our relationship with him one of fearful submission. Is it possible to do better than that?

Most of what God reveals about what we should do consists not of laws but of moral norms—truths which God generously helps us see. These norms are not arbitrary decrees, but elements of God's wise plan in whose observance lies our full and authentic well-being. As a result of this divine revelation, we need not spend time in an interminable quest to learn God's plan. God discloses the truth, and the wise person sees it. This theme, expressed in contrasting terms of wisdom and foolishness, runs throughout the Old Testament.

Still, not all of God's precepts are in themselves moral norms. Some are elements of God's specific plan of salvation, which we may understand dimly but whose inner structure and dynamic we cannot hope to grasp. No matter how well one understood what is good for human beings, one would not reason to the truth or necessity of these precepts.

For example, God prescribes that there be a visible human community which is "the Church" and that it be organized hierarchically rather than democratically or in some other way; God prescribes that efficacious signs called "the sacraments" be his channels for bestowing grace on human beings and that these sacraments be received in certain ways and under certain conditions. Why? We can, perhaps, see that these provisions are fitting, but not that they are uniquely so. In the end, we have no better answer than that these are "divine laws." God might have done differently, but this is what he chooses to do, and we must accept his will and cooperate in his redemptive work by carrying out his directions.

But why? "Because," someone might answer, "otherwise you'll go to hell." True enough, but the answer seems to invoke power rather than authority; it supplies no *reason* for obeying except that God will punish us if we do not obey.

Our discussion up to now points to a better reason: God has legitimate authority of the sort we have been describing.

God reveals himself to us as a person who invites us into community, and once he so reveals himself, the human good of religion can be realized by a covenant relationship analogous to a human friendship. One who accepts this friendship by an act of faith enters into a mutual commitment with God, very much like a person entering into a marriage.

In this covenant, God is uniquely situated to make certain decisions for the shaping and development of the relationship. *We* surely are in no position to say how the covenant should be set up and, in general, carried out. Since our relationship with God is one of friendship, and since we are not qualified to make the decisions governing the relationship which he is qualified to make, we have an obligation, grounded in our commitment, to obey his decisions. To refuse would mean that, although we desired the relationship, we supposed ourselves more knowledgeable than God about how to conduct it. When the matter is stated this way, it is evident not only that we ought to obey divine precepts but why.

C: Why the Laws of Political Societies Usually Should Be Obeyed

All associations which are more than contractual and are based, at least partly, on a common commitment have laws, even though they may be called something else. A school may call its laws rules or policies. A labor union or club may call its laws policies or bylaws. Even a family has laws—household rules of some sort—which its members must observe in order to live a common life together. Here we shall speak of the laws of political society, since that is the most obvious case. By analogy, though, what follows applies to other communities and their laws.

There are several different kinds of law in a political society.

Constitutional law—whether written or, as is more often the case, unwritten—specifies the common good for which the society exists, establishes its organization, designates offices, sets limits on authority. But different members of the same political society are related to it in different ways, and this has a bearing on their relationship to its "constituting" law and the procedures it sets forth.

Some—for example, children and those who are mentally incompetent—are not able to participate in the civil process; their relationship to political society resembles that of child to parent, and they must simply accept the decisions which the society makes for them. (This does not mean, of course, that all these decisions are necessarily right or that others do not have a duty to protect the incompetent against decisions contrary to their best interests.)

Others are able to consent to the political society and should be involved in its civil process—"government by the consent of the governed." Their obligation to accept and observe the constitution is grounded in their duty to pursue and protect certain human goods by making and carrying out the commitment to form and sustain such a society. There is an imperative of fairness here: Others are making their contribution; I derive benefits; so I have a duty to do my share. Being a good citizen is a matter of justice.

Civil law provides a public facility for regulating private affairs; it includes the law of property, contracts, and torts (wrong done to one another by private parties which a legal process can correct).

Obligations in civil law arise only if one has some responsibility which requires one to cooperate in using this facility. For example, people with families should probably make use of the civil law of bequests to ensure that their property will be used to care for their survivors if they die. Again, if a man has a new roof put on his house, he and the roofer both make use of the law of contracts in regard to the job. And, assuming it is a fair system, when someone else makes use of the civil law in a way that involves oneself, one ought to cooperate—for instance, by complying with a court summons.

Criminal law properly deals with actions which would be wrong even if the law did not say so. For example, criminal law says in effect, "If someone commits homicide in these circumstances, that is second degree murder." The criminal law does not tell one not to commit murder—that is taken for granted—nor does it make committing murder wrong. It represents a political society's decision about how to deal with something which is wrong quite apart from the law.

Obviously, some misdeeds are only possible because political society itself exists. In its absence, for instance, it would be impossible to commit treason. But given the fact that political society does exist, treason would be morally wrong even if there were no law against it. (Sometimes laws which properly are regulatory, to be discussed next, are put in the criminal code, but that is a more or less serious misclassification.)

People sometimes object to particular criminal laws or proposals for law on the grounds that "you can't legislate morality." As what we have just been saying illustrates, however, criminal law *always* legislates morality: it makes an action which is already wrong a matter of law. Thus, in identifying legal crimes, society must have a clear idea of what is and is not wrong. It also needs to consider which wrong actions should—and should not—be treated as crimes. Not all should. It is wrong for parents to speak sarcastically to their children, but criminalizing such behavior would destroy the privacy of the home and radically undermine the family.

The principal reason for obeying criminal law is the inherent moral character of the actions it concerns. One should not commit a crime because the act in question is morally wrong independently of the fact that it is a matter of law: using cocaine is wrong mainly because it is morally wrong to use cocaine, not because it is a crime.

Regulatory law, the final category, embodies the decisions made by a community to govern its common life, including the activities of the government and its agencies. It takes in everything from traffic laws through the regulation of interstate commerce to the functioning of the armed forces and the public welfare system, and includes the procedural rules and legal sanctions of both civil and criminal law.

The moral obligation to obey regulatory laws arises from the moral ground of the community itself. There is an obligation to share in political society, but the obligation differs for different groups. Some members of a political society, noncompetents, are obliged to obey the law in the same way children are obliged to obey their parents; others who are competent belong to a political society by consent, and both the ground of their commitment and fairness require their consent and obedience.

(Aliens make up a group in society who are neither noncompetent nor consenting members of a society. They are present in a political society like guests whose presence is regulated by a contract. People who voluntarily enter a country which is not their own implicitly contract to obey its laws.)

The duty to obey the laws of political societies is subject to qualifications of two kinds.

First, there can be some defect in a law, or in the way it was arrived at, such that it lacks authority; it represents an attempt at lawmaking, but an unsuccessful one.

Sometimes a law lacks an adequate grounding because the constitution is faulty. The United States Constitution originally contained provisions concerning slavery, but laws requiring that runaway slaves be returned were not morally binding, for slavery is unjust and the Constitution should not have sanctioned it. In other cases a constitution may be just, but it is not the true source of a particular law. If, for instance, lawmakers adopt a law because they have been bribed, that law does not arise from the constitution but from the injustice and corruption of the legislators. It does not have authority and in itself does not require obedience.

The second qualification of the obligation to obey laws concerns the fact that, even though sound, they may be inapplicable.

As we have seen, conflicts of duty can arise in which an otherwise binding law ceases to apply; or perhaps a law simply becomes pointless because the circumstances which originally called it into being no longer exist—for example, a law regulating traffic in ways appropriate to times when roads were poorer and traffic was lighter and slower.

There is also the case, examined earlier, in which one ought to disobey the law's letter in order to obey its spirit. This is called "epikeia," a Greek word with no real English equivalent. If, for instance, I am driving a heart attack victim to the hospital on a road with a fifty-mile speed limit, but it is the middle of the night and safe to go seventy, I ought by all means to go seventy. The purpose of the law which I am technically violating is to save lives, not hinder efforts to save them.

Even though the duty to obey laws is qualified in various ways, one ought to start with the presumption that each and every law should be obeyed to the letter. It is not up to the law to prove itself sound and applicable, but up to one who has doubts to show that the law need not be obeyed. If people were to take the attitude that they need not obey laws whose reasonableness they doubted, everyone would become his or her own lawmaker, his or her own judge of what is reasonable. Disobedience to law is right only when one is morally certain that specifying conditions exist which remove the obligation to obey.

This obligation is in fact quite serious. Someone who does not try to know the law and obey it is immoral. Even though a particular act of disobedience may not be serious in itself, disobedience disrupts the social order and gives bad example. Repeated often enough and on a sufficiently large scale, it reduces society to a collection of individuals who do what they please as long as they can get away with it. Power reigns in place of authority, and relationships among the members of society are poisoned by exploitation, oppression, violence, and a "might makes right" mentality.

D: Why the Laws of the Church Almost Always Should Be Obeyed

The Church's teaching authority is, as we saw above, a competence to judge about truth. This is not a lawmaking authority, since the Church's doctrine is not law but truth. For this reason the Church cannot "change" its teaching, not even teaching which is difficult and may currently be unpopular. For example, it is not

Church legislation but moral truth which rules out remarriage after divorce.

However, as in any human society, there is also lawmaking in the Church. The Church has a pastoral authority which makes law, analogous to the law in political society or any other group. What has been said above about the obligation to obey the laws of political society therefore applies in general to the obligation to obey the laws of the Church.

But the obligation to obey the Church's law is also more serious than the obligation to obey other law because, besides the other grounds which exist in other cases, the governing authority of the Church is itself divinely grounded. Disobedience to Church law is irreverent, with an irreverence much more serious than that involved in disobedience to the law of political society.

The obligation to obey the Church's law binds only its members. Non-Catholics do nothing wrong in not observing this law. But in disregarding the Church's moral teaching, non-Catholics are, whether they know it or not, violating moral truth. Even so, they may be less guilty than Catholics because, not accepting the Church and its teaching, they know less clearly what the truth is.

Those with authority in the Church can, and occasionally do, make changes in its law, but while a law is in force it should be treated with reverence. Nevertheless there are limits—quite narrow ones—to the duty to obey. Conflicts of duties may occur. A law may become inapplicable. Situations may arise in which epikeia can be invoked.

Still, the presumption should be very strongly on the side of the Church's law, since it is most unlikely to be defective. Plainly there can be no defect in the Church's constitution, since it is God-given. Moreover, given the care with which it is composed, the general law of the Church, canon law, is hardly likely to be contrary to its constitution. The chances are somewhat greater that a law made by a particular bishop might be defective—for example, because he has exceeded his authority. But as a practical matter the possibility of there being a defect in the universal law of the Church which legitimizes disobedience can be discounted. This is not to say that it is never possible to think of ways in which Church law could be improved; but the fact that a law could be improved does not make it defective or justify disobeying it.

12. Moral Judgment in Problematic Situations

Although people confident that they know the right thing to do should do it, no one is always so confident. We sometimes have doubts of conscience. We do not know what is right.

Finding it hard to accept what one knows to be right is not doubt of conscience. Neither are hesitations and contrary promptings arising from superego and conventional morality. Again, Catholics unwilling to follow the Church's teaching sometimes seek to dignify their unwillingness by saying, "I have a doubt of conscience about that." Not really. At best, they are confused; at worst, they have a conscience they would rather not have. In either case, their problem concerns assent to Church teaching which is treated in chapters twenty-three and thirty-six.

Here we are concerned with real doubts of conscience. Someone is well disposed, eager to know what is right, and, if a Catholic, willing to follow the Church's teaching if he or she can learn what it is and how to apply it. The individual also is basically well instructed. Yet there is doubt—not the abstract doubt to which a textbook problem can give rise but practical doubt about something here and now: "Is it right for me to do this?"

We shall cover five topics: doubts of conscience in general and their kinds; doubts of fact; doubts about norms; doubts which arise because of real or apparent conflicts of duties; and doubts related to moral absolutes.

A: Doubts of Conscience in General and Their Kinds

What should one do about a doubt of conscience? Evidently— try to find out what is truly right. Right conscience is a matter of knowing moral truth; the basic obligation for anyone in doubt is to try to learn the truth. Generally speaking, people in doubt who do not make a reasonable effort to find out what is truly right are willing to do what is either right *or* wrong—and so are willing to do what is wrong. If they happen to do the right thing (by accident, as it were), they still are morally responsible for doing what is wrong, since, as far as they know, their action could as well be wrong as right.

But what about someone who makes a reasonable effort to find out the truth yet remains in doubt? In general, the answer is: Do what seems to be true. The individual has done what is appropriate to learn the truth and, having done that, need not do more.

People often try to settle doubts of conscience by consulting those who appear to be wiser and better informed—parents (in the case of children), prudent friends, pastors. In acting on such advice, they are not obeying authority. Rather, they consider their advisers' moral judgment likely to be sounder than their own; they trust it as they would some other expert's opinion in his or her area of expertise.

There are several different kinds of doubts of conscience.

One revolves around a doubt of fact. An airliner crashes in the Andes. Would-be rescuers fly over the crash site but cannot tell from the air whether anyone survived. The rescue team's doubt is one of fact: Is there in fact anyone to be rescued? If that doubt were removed, their responsibility would be clear. If there are survivors, the rescuers have a clear duty to try to reach the site as soon as possible; if not, they need not undertake the hard and hazardous trek.

Another kind of doubt concerns norms. An airliner crashes in the Andes. The starving survivors have nothing to eat but the bodies of their dead companions. The survivors know the facts, but they disagree about what is right. Is the resistance of some to eating the dead bodies mere emotional repugnance? Is there really an obligation to eat human flesh to survive? Or is cannibalism ruled out on moral grounds even in these circumstances?

Apparent conflicts are another source of doubts. There are no real conflicts among real moral responsibilities, since all moral norms derive from the basic human goods and from the same first moral principle: willing in line with integral human fulfillment. But there can *seem* to be conflicts among what are genuine responsibilities. In such cases the problem is to resolve the seeming conflicts.

We shall consider separately each of these sources of doubt: uncertainty about facts, problems about norms, and seeming conflicts.

B: Doubts Arising from Uncertainty about Facts

In speaking of doubts about facts, we must distinguish between cases in which the norm relevant to the problem is a legal one and cases in which the relevant norm is a moral one.

In cases of the first kind, the law itself often provides a way of settling doubts of fact. If so, one should make use of it. Sometimes, too, the problem can be dealt with by obtaining a dispensation. This is how Church law provides for certain difficult cases: the law is simply set aside, made nonapplicable, so that it no longer matters what the facts are. If, for example, there is no doubt that a couple could marry validly but an impediment to the legitimacy of their marriage may or may not exist, the Church can dispense them from the Church law forbidding marriage where that impediment is present.

In other cases where it is impossible to settle a doubt of fact and the law appears to apply, one must act on the basis of a reasonable presumption—the most probable judgment one can make as to the facts, given the available evidence and one's ability to evaluate it. In so proceeding, one assumes that to be true which a reasonable person in the same circumstances would think more likely.

The second large category of doubts of fact is that in which the norm to be applied to the facts is a moral one. Cases of two sorts arise.

In one kind, the fact about which there is doubt would make someone's action either less or more wrong. Here one should suppose the worst. Someone unsure whether something was less or more wrong yet willing to do it would obviously be willing to do—and morally responsible for—that which was more wrong.

Suppose Samantha is trying to prevent birth by taking a particular medication. Is it a true contraceptive or does it prevent birth by inducing very early abortion? If Samantha prescribes or takes medication with this doubt in mind, she is willing to do or have an abortion. Again, suppose Punch is willing to take revenge on Judy, without knowing how much harm will result. Punch should suppose that Judy will suffer the worst injury he can anticipate, for if he is willing to inflict injury but is uncertain how much he will hurt her, he is willing to inflict the most damage he can expect.

The situation is different, however, when, on the basis of doubt about facts, one is uncertain whether a mode of responsibility will be violated at all. Then one must simply take the doubt into account as part of the problem and apply the relevant mode.

Suppose Harold is at Jim's isolated house in the country, it is eleven o'clock at night, and Harold has had several drinks. Should he drive home? Ordinarily, invoking the norm of fairness, he would say no. A person driving in this condition threatens other people's safety, and Harold would not want his own safety threatened in this way. Tonight, though, as Harold is preparing to spend the night on the sofa, Jim experiences severe chest pain—a heart attack? There is no ambulance or rescue squad for miles around, and the phone is out of order anyway. Should Jim ask his intoxicated friend to drive him to the hospital, reasoning that it is permissible to take the risk in these circumstances?

The doubt of fact here concerns precisely how much risk is involved. Harold is intoxicated, but Jim believes his friend can probably make it to the hospital without having an accident. If Jim can judge—in fairness—that he would want others who need to reach a hospital to take like risks of involving him and his loved ones in an accident, he may take the risk of asking Harold to drive. But if Jim would not like it if others asked someone as intoxicated as Harold is to drive them to a hospital when he or his loved ones were on the roads, then Jim cannot fairly ask Harold to drive him. Here the doubt about fact is a factor in the problem. The uncertainty is an aspect of what needs deciding, and one applies the modes of responsibility as usual to a problem constituted in part by a doubt.

The same approach will solve the problem posed by the example about the rescue team and the airliner downed in the Andes. Would not every member of the rescue team want others, whose job it is, to risk their lives to rescue himself and his loved ones if they were possible survivors in some disaster situation? Surely, he would. So unless it is virtually certain that there are no survivors, the rescue team must go in.

Another example. Betsy is settling her brother Tom's estate. An acquaintance of Tom's makes a claim: "He owed me a thousand dollars." There is no evidence, but the claim is plausible. A person settling an estate has a moral obligation to pay the debts of the deceased if the estate's assets make that possible; here is a claim which is plausible but unsubstantiated; the doubt of fact is part of the problem about which Betsy must make a moral judgment.

The solution is to fashion a fair rule applicable to any similar case. For instance: Plausible but unsubstantiated claims should not be honored (for if they were, many such claims would be lodged against many estates, quite a few would be fraudulent, and rightful heirs would be cheated). In face of a problem partly constituted by a doubt of fact, one develops a specific norm to supplement the more general norm that debts should be paid.

C: Doubts about Norms

Sometimes doubts of conscience are doubts about norms. One may be unsure whether there is a relevant norm, whether a suggested norm is true, or whether a possibly relevant norm really does apply. Once again it is necessary to distinguish between cases involving legal norms and those involving moral norms.

Where the question is whether a legal norm exists or whether it is applicable, the law usually provides ways of settling the matter. Lawyers are specialists at this. But what if honest and competent lawyers disagree? If the preponderance of expert opinion holds that a norm exists and one is bound by it, one should consider oneself bound. But suppose there is no consensus: the Internal Revenue Service has issued conflicting rulings on a complex tax question, the published regulations offer no clear guidance—what is one to do? Then one is free to judge that the law is not applicable in this case.

In general, having exhausted the possibilities of finding out what the law is and whether it is applicable without getting an

answer, one is not bound by that law in that case. Legal requirements end where the possibility of determining what they are
ends. This is as true of Church law as any other positive law. If
the Church has not made it clear what one's legal obligation is and
if the experts—canon lawyers and the like—cannot say, then one
is entitled to suppose that there is no relevant law applying to the
particular situation one is concerned about.

The situation is very different, however, where moral norms
are at issue. They are truths, not laws, and what has just been
said cannot be applied to the moral domain.

If there is firm Church teaching clearly relevant to a particular
problem, there is no real doubt of conscience for a Catholic about
the moral norm. But what if there is no firm Church teaching or
none which is clearly relevant—for example, with respect to responsibilities in many specific matters of economic justice? Supposing a theological consensus exists, one should say to oneself,
"The people who have studied this question are better situated
than I to reach a sound conclusion, so my judgment is likely to be
in line with truth if I follow their opinion."

And if there is no consensus? Frank stole fifteen thousand dollars twenty-five years ago. Now he wants to make restitution.
How much money does he owe? Fifteen thousand dollars? The
current equivalent of fifteen thousand dollars, making allowance
for a quarter-century of inflation? Fifteen thousand dollars, plus
an additional sum calculated by figuring earnings on fifteen thousand at a reasonable rate of interest over twenty-five years? The
current value of a house which those from whom he stole
the money planned to purchase a quarter-century ago with that
fifteen thousand dollars? No clear Church teaching settles this
kind of problem, and theological opinion is divided. Frank is inclined to repay the fifteen thousand and no more. Is that what he
should do?

The first question to ask in such cases is: If the act in question
turned out to be permissible, would one have a responsibility to
do it? If the answer is no, an upright person will choose to do
something else certainly good. But if the answer is yes—if the act
is permissible, one ought to do it—one should accept the judgment (permissible or impermissible) which seems more likely to
be true.

Frank, for example, should reason along the following lines.
"Assuming it's morally permissible for me to repay the money I

stole without interest, do I have some other responsibility which requires me to do that? I'm married, I'm responsible for my children's education. I'm not sure how far my responsibility for restitution extends, but I know I have obligations to my family. Repaying the fifteen thousand even without any interest is going to impose some real hardships on them. I think the right thing is to pay back the fifteen thousand but not deny the kids an education by paying more."

That is reasonable for Frank, a man of quite limited means. But suppose Ed, confronting a similar question about restitution, has plenty of money and no other clear obligations. Unlike Frank, Ed should pay back not just the fifteen thousand dollars but a far larger sum—say, the greatest of (1) fifteen thousand plus reasonable interest, (2) the inflation-adjusted equivalent of what he stole, and (3) the current value of the house which the victims intended to purchase with the money Ed stole.

What is the difference between Frank and Ed? Frank has a clear duty to provide for his children, but his duty to make restitution over and above fifteen thousand dollars is not clear. Ed has no clear responsibility to use his money for anything except restitution. Thus, in general, those who are in doubt about a moral norm and have no responsibility requiring them *not* to act according to the norm should act according to it, not suppose that their doubt renders the norm nonbinding.

It is easy to apply the same principles to the survivors of the crash in the Andes who are unsure whether they may cannibalize the bodies of those already dead. Provided they have some hope of rescue, they have a grave responsibility to try to stay alive. So, it is clear that they should eat the human flesh if doing so is permissible. Only if doing that is absolutely wrong should they refrain. Someone points out that eating the bodies will in no way harm the dead, since they are beyond help and harm. It seems more likely that cannibalism is not absolutely wrong. Hence, they may do it. (And, in fact, they are right in doing so.)

Some readers may wonder how the foregoing way of dealing with doubts about norms fits into classical moral theology's classification of approaches to this problem.

In that framework, the position adopted here is neither laxist nor rigorist; it falls within the range of what the Church has allowed. The approach to resolving doubts about law is what has been called "equiprobabilism," while the way of resolving doubts about moral norms in some ways resembles "probabiliorism." Still, it is difficult to relate this approach to classical probabilism and its alternatives. These were ways of dealing with doubts of conscience within a legalistic context, where the assumption was that moral norms are like laws. In such a system, having honestly tried but failed to find out what the norm is, one can consider oneself not bound: "A doubtful law does not bind."

As we have said repeatedly, however, moral norms are truths, not laws. Probabilism is not a satisfactory approach for one who is not a legalist. Such a person wants to know what is more likely true; and it is the probable moral truth—not the "safer" opinion nor the one which "favors liberty"—which should prevail. This leads sometimes to a very strict conclusion and sometimes to a very permissive one. No matter. It is not whether the conclusion is strict or permissive that matters, but whether it is more likely to be true.

We should not take the legalistic view that doubt leaves us free to do as we please. Morality is concerned with the service of human goods, and when we encounter what seem to be contrary responsibilities, we should serve the good embodied in the clearer responsibility. If no other responsibility will go unfulfilled by fulfilling an apparent responsibility, fulfill it. If apparent responsibilities and clear responsibilities seem opposed, fulfill those which are clear. The truth about the responsibility and service to the good are determinative.

D: Doubts Which Arise Because of Seeming Conflicts of Duties

Doubts of conscience arising from seeming conflicts of responsibilities can occur in several ways.

First, because of errors about facts and norms. When responsibilities seem to conflict, the first thing to do is check the facts and reflect on the relevant norms. An error may be causing the difficulty.

Second, many apparent conflicts are products of immoral prior commitments. Suppose someone working for the mob feels squeamish at being ordered to commit murder. The obvious and necessary way to resolve the conflict is to give up the commitment to the mob.

Much more subtle instances frequently arise in ordinary life. Excessive regard for conventional morality and "good form" is a ready source of apparent conflicts of responsibilities. By these standards, doing what is morally right may very well mean doing something which is not "nice" or socially acceptable—for example, counselling a young woman not to have an abortion, even though having the baby will disrupt her career and upset her family. If appearances and the opinion of others occupy a place superior to the gospel in a person's life, apparent conflicts of responsibilities are inevitable; but they disappear when immoral commitments and false standards are set aside.

Finally, conflicts can arise between specific duties or between a specific duty and an unspecified obligation. The remainder of this section concerns cases of this sort. Another, most interesting type of case will be treated in the next section: one can *seem* to have a duty to do something which is absolutely wrong.

Here is an example of a conflict between specific duties. A man is supposed to report for work and at the very same time he has to take his wife to the doctor. Obviously he cannot do both. To resolve such problems, one has recourse to fairness and formulates a more specific norm—for example, "If I were in my boss's position, I'd want my employees to attend to important family obligations, even at the expense of taking time off from work."

Sometimes, though, it is difficult to see why one duty rather than another should take preference. Then the solution is to do either, while doing what one can to compensate for not fulfilling the other—for example, "Even though my wife could get to the doctor on her own, we'll both feel better about it if I take her, and I'll make it up to the job by working overtime tomorrow."

Sometimes conflicts arise not between specific duties but between a specific duty and a nonspecified possible responsibility. A student stops a teacher who is hurrying to class and says, "I have an urgent problem, and I need to talk with you right now." Fairness is the operative principle here, too, but the presumption is on the side of the specified duty. Unless it is clear that later will not do, the teacher acts reasonably in replying, "Sorry, I have a class in five minutes, but you can catch me at my office this afternoon."

Even so, the specified duty does not always prevail. A student notices that her roommate is depressed and appears to be in a suicidal state of mind. If she gets involved, she will not be able to fulfill her specific duty to study tonight. But it is obvious that a more specific norm—don't leave potential suicides to their own devices—must prevail.

E: Doubts Related to Moral Absolutes

What about cases where one seems obliged to make a choice which is inconsistent with a moral absolute? The moral absolute holds if the choice would really violate it.

Thomas More and his wife both knew that, if he was sentenced to life in prison and the confiscation of all his property, she and his family would be left in bad straits. "Take the silly little oath," she urged him, "so that you can go free and fulfill your obligations to us." More refused, was punished (ultimately with death on a trumped up charge of treason)—and his family suffered. But there was no real conflict of responsibilities. More had to choose between doing something absolutely wrong (taking a false oath) and doing what would *otherwise* have been his duty. His moral responsibility—and that of anyone facing a similar decision—was to refuse to do the absolutely wrong thing, even though that meant leaving unfulfilled what would otherwise have been his grave responsibility to his wife and children. More was right, and his wife was wrong.

"You're saying," someone might object, "that the morally right thing must be done even though the heavens fall. That is Stoic morality."

We considered this objection earlier in a different context. The same answer applies here. Morality for its own sake is not the be-all and end-all for Christians. We respect moral absolutes out of reverence for human goods, the goods of persons. Thomas More's refusal to take the false oath was a matter of reverence for the human goods of truth and religion, both violated by false oath taking.

Moreover, Christians believe that if human beings do what is morally right, God ensures that the consequences are not ultimately disastrous. They *may* be disastrous in this life, but this life is not all. The operative principle for Christians is not, "Let right be done though the heavens fall"; it is, "God knows how to bring fulfillment out of disaster—he can even raise the dead." (And those who do not believe in the resurrection of the dead are likely not to hesitate at wrongdoing if that is what it takes to bring about—as they see it—the best results possible here and now.)

Sometimes, though, not only does it seem that one must violate a moral absolute, one really ought to do the act which seems— but only *seems*—wrong. In such cases, the appearances are deceiving, for the act has not been analyzed sufficiently to bring to light the moral truth of the matter. Adequate analysis will make it clear that the act does not involve a choice contrary to the moral absolute, but only the accepting of side effects, consistent with that absolute and all other relevant moral norms. Here, the distinction between what is chosen and what is accepted is crucial (see chapter 9:B–C).

For example: it is wrong to choose to kill oneself; and if the word "suicide" is defined simply in terms of behavior, any deliberate act which brings about one's own death will be suicide and therefore morally wrong. The moral act of suicide, however, is not simply behavior of a certain kind. Sometimes people voluntarily do things which bring about their own deaths yet do not choose to kill themselves. Therefore, what they do is not necessarily wrong. Maximilian Kolbe chose to take the place of another prisoner, one condemned to death. Examined closely, it is clear that this was not a choice on Kolbe's part to kill himself, although he foresaw that he surely would die and freely accepted that bad result of what he did. Kolbe saved the other man's life; he did not commit suicide.

It is also wrong to choose to kill an unborn child. But suppose a woman has a tubal pregnancy which is about to rupture, and the doctor removes it. The child dies. Has the doctor performed an abortion? No. He knows that when he cuts the embryo's vital links to his or her mother, the tiny child will die, but he does not choose to kill. Instead, he chooses to correct a pathological condition (without whose correction the embryo's death is certain anyway and the mother's very likely), while accepting the death of the embryo as an anticipated but unintended side effect. Careful moral analysis focuses not on the outward behavior, which does indeed cause the death of an unborn child, but on the choice.

So, to take another instance, one might do something which looks like revenge but which, morally speaking, is not. When a mother slaps her misbehaving son, her behavior looks like tit for tat. And perhaps it is; some mothers at times act like that. But the slap may also be her way of calling the boy's attention to the fact that he is misbehaving—it is education, not revenge. We must look beyond behavior to the underlying will.

Does this mean one can make any atrocious deed morally good, simply by performing it with a good intention? Not at all. Many actions cannot be done with a good will by anyone who understands what the actions are. But, as the examples here illustrate, there are other cases where one can engage in behavior which *looks* as if it violates a moral absolute without willing such a violation—and therefore without engaging in a wrongful *moral* act of that sort.

Finally, a word about cooperation. It is not a separate, complicated problem, but a specification of the problem just discussed.

Cases of cooperation among equals usually pose no special problem. Both (or all) share the same purposes and do the same act together. Both (or all) have the same moral responsibility. Morally speaking, it is as if each were acting alone.

The classical problem of cooperation arises where people acting together are not really doing the same (moral) act, even though they are cooperating in the same (external) behavior. For example, when masters and slaves act together, the masters have purposes the slaves do not share, while the slaves are simply doing what they must to avoid punishment. (Often the situation is not greatly different in the case of employers and employees.)

The relevant question here is: What is one willing? When one person cooperates in another's immoral action, the morality of the cooperator's deed depends on his or her will.

Church documents routinely distinguish between "formal" and "material" cooperation. By formal cooperation, one person makes someone else's immoral action his or her own. A nurse formally cooperates with an abortion at which she is assisting if she wills it, wants it to happen, makes herself fully a party to it. But her action is material cooperation when she does things which help bring about the abortion without making the immoral act her own.

The difference is a matter not of feelings but of voluntariness. An intern may be disgusted by abortion, so firmly disapproving of it that she is sure she will never get one herself, yet take part in an abortion for the sake of completing her training. Since she does not meet the requirement unless the operation really does bring about an abortion, she very reluctantly wills that the operation succeed. Her cooperation is formal. By contrast, a nurse may prepare patients for abortion and even hand over instruments during the operation, without choosing that the unborn be killed. Her cooperation is material.

But even material cooperation can be morally wrong, just as it can be wrong freely to accept bad side effects. If material cooperation would be unfair or give bad example, or if one has a responsibility to testify to the truth by avoiding even this much association with evil—then one should not cooperate materially.

An orderly who considers abortion wrong and is assigned to work in an abortion unit is not formally cooperating, for he does not choose that the unborn be killed. But what light does fairness shed on his situation? If others were killing him or someone he loved, he would be upset not just with those who willed his death but with anyone lending a hand even without choosing or intending the death. He would like everyone to be as uncooperative as possible with the killing. Applying this to his present situation—contributing services necessary for the killing of unborn children—he ought either to take a different assignment if he can get it or leave this hospital and find another job elsewhere. The same is usually true for other people who find themselves cooperating materially in immoral deeds and have another option, even one which will cause them some inconvenience and suffering.

13. What Sin Is and What It Is Not

We have been considering free choices and the norms which direct them toward our individual and communal well-being and fulfillment. Some choices, however, violate moral norms and are morally evil. That is the subject to which we now turn.

Generally speaking, the interest which philosophical ethics takes in evil choices does not require any special treatment of them; knowing what moral goodness is, philosophy knows as much as it needs to know about evil. But moral theology takes a considerably larger interest in evil—in sin—because it considers moral evil in the special context of our relationship with God. Christian life is the fruit of redemption. But redemption from what? From sin. Moreover, Christians do not live in an ideal, sin-free situation, but in a situation of sin, both original and personal. To understand Christian life as a striving for holiness, one must understand what one is striving to overcome as well as what one is striving to reach.

This and the next five chapters therefore treat of sin. In this chapter we consider five topics: what Scripture says about sin; an analytic consideration of sin; how sin offends God; how people are personally involved in sin and how they are involved in social sin; and the explanations nonbelievers give for the phenomena which faith interprets as sin.

A: What Scripture Says about Sin

Scripture says sin is an abuse of free choice. For example:
Do not say, "It was the Lord's doing that I fell away";
   for he does not do what he hates.

Do not say, "It was he who led me astray";
   for he has no need of the sinful.
If you choose, you can keep the commandments,
   and to act faithfully is a matter of your own choice.
                                             (Sir 15:11–12, 15)

Scripture also teaches that because sins are wrong choices, sin is primarily in the heart, not in external behavior: "It is what comes out of a person that defiles. . . . All these evil things come from within, and they defile a person" (Mk 7:20, 23).

Sin has a communal dimension. The community is not as it should be, and individuals, insofar as they conform to community standards which diverge from moral truth, will also not be as they should. Still, one cannot slough off personal responsibility by blaming the community. "All shall die for their own sins" (Jer 31:30).

It is clear in many places in Scripture that one can sin against other people. But every sin is also against God. "Against you, you alone, have I sinned, and done what is evil in your sight" (Ps 51:4). Even so, sinners do not harm God. They harm themselves, and they are fools to do so. "The fear of the Lord is the beginning of knowledge; fools despise wisdom and instruction" (Prv 1:7).

Even though some catechetical materials claim otherwise, Scripture does not limit sin to violations of the covenant relationship with God. True, once the covenant is established, those involved in it violate it by their sins. But sin also precedes the covenant and exists outside it. "All who have sinned apart from the law will also perish apart from the law, and all who have sinned under the law will be judged by the law" (Rom 2:12). All violations of the covenant are sins, but not all sins are violations of the covenant.

Especially in Paul and John, sin is often treated not just as a particular act but as an ongoing condition of alienation from God. The Baptist salutes Jesus as the one who redeems the world from this state of estrangement: "Here is the Lamb of God who takes away the sin of the world!" (Jn 1:29). Closing up the gulf between us and God is reconciliation.

B: An Analysis of Sin

In order to define sin more analytically, it is necessary to begin by recalling the intimate relationship between morality and the reflexive goods of "harmony." In doing what is morally right, one is in harmony with oneself, with one's own principles of action, with other upright people, and with God. All these existential relationships are more or less disrupted by doing what is morally wrong.

And sin? "Sin" is what we call doing what is morally wrong insofar as it is contrary to the basic human good of religion. Moral wrong viewed as causing disharmony with God is "sin." So, to clarify sin, we begin in this section by discussing sin as moral wrongdoing, then go on in the next section to show how such wrongdoing always offends God.

Choices have no moral significance except insofar as one knows what one is doing and is willing to do it. Thus, to sin is to do something one knows one ought not to do, and to do it knowingly and willingly. It follows that sin is not irrational or compulsive (and behavior which is genuinely irrational or compulsive is not sin). In order to do anything willingly, one must have an interesting good in view, something one cares about and deems worth pursuing. A sin is thus an act directed to some real or apparent good.

Yet even though in sinning one acts knowingly and willingly for the sake of some good, still one is not being completely reasonable. The sinner's will is not in line with integral human fulfillment—that is, fulfillment in respect to all the goods in an ideal human community. The sinner settles instead for some more limited good, makes do with what is less. And that is not fully reasonable, since one has as much reason to care about the goods one is not here and now pursuing as about the good one does pursue in making a particular sinful choice. Feelings, not reasons, lead us sinfully to prefer this good to that, my good to yours.

Thus, it can be said that sinners are unreasonable but not that they are sheerly irrational. References to the "mysteriousness" of sin are misleading to the extent they suggest otherwise. Jack wants money and what it can buy; he wants comfort, social status, and power. Where is the mystery in Jack's behavior when he cheats and steals to enrich himself? This is not incomprehensible; it is merely unreasonable—because, among other things, someone who cheats and steals treats others unfairly, and that is less than fully reasonable.

The unreasonableness of sinners also concerns the fact that, instead of choosing in accord with their knowledge of moral truth, they choose against it. They violate conscience. Sally says: "Sure, I know I ought to treat Jane fairly, and if I take credit for the work she has done, I'll be treating her *un*fairly. But that's what it will take to get what I want, so too bad for Jane." The choice does not correspond to the awareness of moral truth. Violation of conscience opens a gap, a lack of correspondence, between choice and conscience.

Just here, primarily, is the privation which is sin's evil. The privation lies in the lack of agreement between the sinner's awareness of moral truth and his or her choice. It is the absence of something which ought to be present: the moral uprightness which consists in correspondence between one's knowledge of what is right and one's choice. Since the privation is evil, the choice it affects is likewise mutilated and evil. The sinful choice and the sinful deed, though positive realities, are colored by the privation of harmony between moral truth (of which conscience is the awareness) and the sinner's will.

People who do moral evil disrupt harmony on every level. There is conflict between their willing of the good which is sinfully sought and their spontaneous willing. Take the dishonest man. While choosing to cheat and steal, Jack, like everyone else, also wants to get along well with other people—wants to be accepted, loved, and so forth. He wants to be in harmony even with those he injures. And so he suffers inner conflict as a result of his sin.

There is also conflict between the sinner's knowledge of moral truth and his or her way of life. Sooner or later Jack starts telling himself: "Basically I'm a decent chap. But I can't really help what I'm doing. I've got to look out for myself. Everybody else does the same thing. You have to be a realist to survive out there in the jungle"—and so on. Self-deception and rationalization are invoked in the effort to screen out the violation of moral truth. Once again—conflict.

Obviously there is also conflict with other people, those whom one injures or is willing to injure in carrying out sinful choices. And there is conflict with God. We shall see more of that below.

Sin is not a passing event. It lasts. Sin is located primarily in choices, and choices are spiritual acts which determine the persons who make them. Our choices cause us to be, in moral terms, the kind of persons we are. Thus our sins persist—not just in external consequences (that may or may not be the case) but in us.

Guilt is the persistence of sin, not a matter of bad feelings. Indeed, it is beside the point whether one feels badly or not. Nor does guilt lie in being at odds with the rules of society or in being held responsible by others or in fearing or incurring punishment. These things have to do with superego and social convention, while guilt is essentially the persistence of sinful self-determination in one who sins. (People also use "guilt" to refer to the sinner's *awareness* of being in sin. Here, though, we are speaking not of the experience of guilt, but of the state of affairs itself.)

Sin lasts, but unless the sinner dies in mortal sin it need not last forever. It lasts until, with God's help, one makes another, incompatible choice which overturns the first, sinful one. Thus, guilt persists until sinners change their minds and hearts—their selves—by repenting.

Repenting means a great deal more than simply not repeating sinful behavior. Jack, who cheats and steals to get ahead, may eventually become so rich and powerful that he decides to stop cheating and stealing. But he does not thereby become just. To be that, a sinner must repent and, in the case of unfairness, undo what was previously done. Until Jack does that, he remains a sinner—and dishonest—even though he may also be a pillar of the community.

Sinful choices have further consequences. As we have seen, there are other kinds of voluntariness besides choice, and the effects of sin spread through them. People who have chosen to do what is wrong find it harder to see what is right. They fail to foresee things they might and should have anticipated. Their duties are less clear to them. Since the truth is not flattering, they begin to make up stories in its place. The more that intelligent individuals systematically engage in this pastime, the more elaborate their stories become. Ordinary people produce fairly simpleminded rationalizations, but subtle and reflective people living sinful lives have been known to spin out a whole metaphysics or theology to keep the truth at bay.

Although the primary locus of sin is in bad will, the "heart," evil extends into the behavior which executes a sinful choice. If one chooses to steal or kill, the sin is primarily in the will, but the actual stealing or killing is also sinful, not morally neutral. Especially in the case of unfairness, carrying out a sinful choice is also destructive of a substantive good: if, for example, Sally acts upon a choice to take credit for Jane's good work, Jane is likely to lose out on a promotion she would have received.

Sin spreads within the self—not just within the psyche, but through the whole self. People cannot persist in doing what they know is morally wrong without suffering repercussions on their feelings and, often, on their physical well-being. Although sin is not sickness, it does ultimately make sinners sick. It also has an impact on human products—on art, technology, even language. It runs through the whole person and, eventually, through society and culture. Sin cannot be kept isolated.

C: How Sins Offend God

It is not difficult to see how certain sins—idolatry, for example—offend God. But all immoral acts offend God. Treating one's neighbor unfairly is an offense against God. But why? How is it that every kind of immorality concerns God?

In considering this question, it is necessary to put aside anthropomorphic notions. God is not offended as we are. He does not get angry in the way we do, his feelings are not hurt, he does not suffer wounded pride. Yet our sins do offend him. How?

We begin by considering our relationship with God in the context of the covenant. God offers us the covenant for our good, for the sake of our human well-being. When we do moral evil, we act against God's good plan for us. In that sense, sin is contrary to his wisdom and love, contrary to his will. Even apart from the covenant, moreover, one who sins sets aside reason and so implicitly sets aside God, the source of meaning and value in creation. Sinners, as it were, declare their independence of anything beyond themselves, including God. In that sense, too, sin is an offense against God.

The sins of Christians have both these aspects. It is—or ought to be—clear to a Christian that God is the creator and source of goods and also that he has established a covenant relationship with his people which requires that they cooperate with him in bringing about their own salvation and fulfillment. Thus, when Christians sin, they know—or at least have every reason to know—that they are setting aside the good will of the good creator, while also betraying the covenant. Their sins are even more offensive to God than the sins of pagans.

The analogy of parent and child sheds light on this. When a child does wrong, parents are offended for reasons having to do with themselves—for example, because they are embarrassed or because they are deprived of the emotional satisfaction they hoped to derive from the good behavior of their offspring. Even the best of parents react in this way. But the best of parents are also offended for another reason. They want their child to be good and do well; they want what is truly best for him or her. And when the child misbehaves, good parents, aware that those who do wrong are hurting themselves, are saddened because what is good *for the child* is being lost. They are offended in that sense—not because of some loss or injury to themselves, but because of the injury and loss which the child whom they love suffers. Their generous and unselfish love is frustrated. And that also is how sin offends God.

St. Augustine's account of sin has profoundly affected the way Christians understand it. He speaks of sin as a turning away from God to creatures, from unchangeable good to things which are changeable, from the heavenly to the earthly, from the infinite to the finite. He also says that sin is an expression of self-love as opposed to love of God.

This reflects the lived experience of a man who was converted from a life of sin to become a great saint, and it is easily understood in light of what we have already said. Sin *is* a turning away from God, since morally wrong choices, which are contrary to one's own good and to the well-being of other persons, violate God's wise and loving plan, contradict his will, and are incompatible with friendship with him. Sin is an expression of self-love rather than love of God, if the "self" in question is the mutilated self constituted by sinful activity rather than a truly fulfilled self.

But St. Augustine's manner of talking about sin, so common in the tradition, raises difficulties. (It was in fact heavily influenced by his neo-Platonic way of thinking, which will be discussed in chapter thirty-four.) Sinning is not choosing creatures in preference to God, for one never has that choice to make. It is only possible for human beings to choose between or among possibilities for human fulfillment. *All* choices, those which are morally good as well as those which are sinful, are choices of human goods. Sin lies in choosing something humanly good in a way detrimental to other goods and/or other persons instead of in a way open to integral human fulfillment.

Moreover, the contrast between loving oneself and loving God can easily be misunderstood as a false opposition. Augustine himself was aware of this problem, for he says that he is referring to *false* self-love; true self-love is not in conflict with love of God; indeed, if one loves oneself properly, one loves God more, and one who loves God above everything loves himself more than those who love only themselves.

D: How Individuals Are Personally Involved in Sin, Including Social Sins

As we have seen, people who sin do not choose evil as such, for no one is interested in evil as such. We always choose some good, something seen as humanly fulfilling. Sinners, however, choose in a way which is not open to all human good; they choose a certain good, and have some reason for choosing it, but they do so in an unreasonable manner.

In the fallen human condition it is easy to do this. Moral goodness is only one kind of goodness, and goods of other kinds can be alternatives to or competitors with it. Someone who makes a sinful choice sees the immorality involved as an evil, but also expects, in or through the immoral act, to accomplish something with a certain appeal. That is precisely why we are tempted to set aside moral goodness. It is not hard in this fallen world to accept its loss if one thereby gets what one wants.

This is especially clear when people are tempted to do evil so that some good may come about. Suppose a general is tempted to kill the innocent in order to terrorize the enemy into surrendering. "It's all very well to reverence life," he reasons, "but sometimes in this world you have to do unpleasant things in order to have what you want and save what can be saved." All arguments for proportionalism run along such lines.

Furthermore, no matter how reasonable people may be, in this fallen world they still find themselves in the midst of evil, and they suffer as a result of it—and that is discouraging. We do our best to do what is morally right, and still things turn out badly. We are still unhappy; we still face the certainty of death at the end of life. Even a genuinely just society would not be heaven on earth. Things still would not always turn out well, people still would suffer, disasters would occur, death would be everyone's fate. It is demoralizing to know that there is not and cannot be a paradise on earth.

And then? Then one is likely to say: "Morality proposes an attractive ideal. But it's *only* an ideal, a dream. The dream will never come true. Meanwhile the world is as it is, and I'd better get what I can from it while I can and however I can." St. Paul put it well: "If the dead are not raised, 'Let us eat and drink, for tomorrow we die' " (1 Cor 15:32).

Perhaps this explains the Church's teaching that, apart from faith and grace, people inevitably commit mortal sins. No doubt it is possible to avoid this sin or that, but without the gifts of faith and grace, which give hope of something beyond the human condition as we experience it in this life, we cannot avoid all grave sin.

As we have seen, when Christians sin they do not choose between God and a human good. Rather, they choose here and now to be unfaithful to their covenant *relationship* with God. When tempted, Christians do not say: "I must either give up what I want or give up God." Instead they say in effect: "This is what I want right now. Excuse me, God—I'll be back later." They experience temptation as an incitement not to reject God entirely but to set aside their relationship with him temporarily. And in a situation of temptation, not even this relationship seems unqualifiedly good.

It is comfortable to suppose that in order *really* to sin one must choose a limited human good over the infinite goodness of God. No one does precisely that—it never happens—and so it is easy for sinning Christians to suppose they never commit sin. But that is an illusion; it is rationalization and self-deception.

Emotion also makes it easy to sin. Emotions are necessary for the attraction we feel toward any option sufficiently interesting that we can even think about choosing it. The emotion inclining one toward a morally excluded option leads one to see in it a certain intelligible good—at the very least, the experience (even if not the reality) of inner harmony. "The best way to get rid of temptation is to give in to it." By giving in, the frustration of wanting something and not having it is overcome. So, surrendering to temptation carries with it at least that appearance of good, which a sinner's rationalization can accept as a plausible counterfeit of the real human good.

Besides its effect on the sinner, sin has an impact on the community. For one thing, choices, including sinful ones, are often made by people choosing to do things together. But even when choices are not communal in this way, they frequently bear upon other persons—for example, by creating situations to which they must respond. The sin of one who treats others unfairly not only injures them directly but tempts them to seek revenge, to be unjust in their turn. One sin foments others.

In this way sin weaves a kind of network or, to change the metaphor, leaves behind it a social residue which goes on having its effect. Sinners may repent, but the social consequences of their wrongdoing persist. Greedy and dishonest people, for example, may mend their ways, but if their sins have helped create an unjust social system or given currency to unjust business practices now widely accepted and imitated, the fact that they reform their lives does not by itself change the economic system or the pattern of sharp practices which they helped bring into being.

Thus "social sin" is a reality. There really are social institutions, structures, arrangements, and practices which are sinful in the sense that they are products of sin, embody sin, and lead to further individual sins. These institutions and structures exist independently of individuals. They are not overcome by individual repentance; they have a kind of life of their own and must themselves be changed or rooted out.

All the same, it is a mistake to think of social evil, any more than evil on the individual level, as a positive reality to be destroyed by the violent overthrow of the institutions which embody it. Evil as such is a privation, to be overcome by repentance, forgiveness, and reconciliation—very likely emerging from redemptive suffering—which heals up the sinner's self-mutilation and fills in the missing content of justice and love.

It is also a mistake to displace individual responsibility onto society. The social dimension of evil does not excuse individuals from trying to do what is right. One may not say: "I didn't create the system, but I have to survive—so I'm not to blame for going along with it." Nor may one say: "The evil is out there in the system, and I intend to change it. But as for changing my own sinful heart—that's small potatoes for a social reformer like me."

To deal with sin rightly, we must repent of our own sins and also do what we can to change the structures and institutions in society which extend sin beyond our individual lives. It is not an either/or situation, as if individual conversion and social reform were alternative options. Christians should have at one and the same time the attitude of the traditionally devout person who examines his or her own conscience and that of the socially conscious person who tries to make a better world. There is more to Christian penance and reconciliation than either individualistic devotionalism or one-dimensional social activism.

E: How Nonbelievers Account for the Phenomena of Sin

Nonbelievers are aware of most of the phenomena which Christians regard as sin or expressions of sin. Indeed, the evidence could hardly be denied. But contemporary nonbelievers by and large do not believe in free choice; they deny that there is any such thing as self-determination. So they offer deterministic accounts of moral evil—according to which, of course, it is something other than *moral* evil.

Such accounts treat moral evil as a kind of immaturity (we are not well adjusted) or as a sickness (we cannot control our abnormally strong drives) or as an imperfect stage in the evolutionary process (we are not so far removed from our subhuman ancestors) or as ignorance (we need more education about the consequences of our behavior). Some nonbelievers—Nietzsche and Heidegger, for instance—take an unconventional view of immorality and see it largely as a lack of creativity (we are stodgy).

To repeat: All these ways of interpreting sin assume that what we call sin is not moral evil, since they assume that people cannot choose freely. Christians must reject this deterministic world view. As we saw in chapter two, free choice is not just a philosophical hypothesis but a principle of faith, divinely revealed, attested in Scripture, defined by the Council of Trent, and fundamental to the Christian world view.

At the same time, we can—and must—admit that determining conditions limit people's options and reduce their ability to know moral truth. Moral responsibility extends only as far as the knowledge of moral truth and the awareness of good alternatives. People often are blamelessly ignorant or mistaken about what they could and should do, and then their freedom is limited. To that extent, deterministic accounts say something true about the human condition. This is not a world where every conceivable good option is available to everyone as a real possibility for choice.

Even so, people often are responsible for some of the limits on their own freedom. Not infrequently, ignorance and psychological illness are more or less the fault of those who suffer from them; and, if not their fault, then someone else's. Moral evil—sin—can lead to psychological problems and to ignorance of moral truth. Moreover, social evil originating in free choices often severely limits people's morally good options, especially the options of the poor and the oppressed. That moral handicap can only be overcome to the extent people make good free choices and work uprightly to liberate society from the slavery imposed by sin.

14. Sin of Adam and Sins of Men and Women

Although dogmatic theology considers original sin, moral theology also needs to deal with it inasmuch as original sin establishes both the context and the basic problem for Christian moral life. Our inability to live consistently good lives without a struggle is to a great extent due to original sin. To be consistently good, our lives must have the peculiar character of Christian life: they must be spent carrying the cross in the effort to overcome evil, both the evil of personal sin and the evil common to humankind which is original sin.

Pope Pius XI gives a compact statement of Catholic teaching on this subject:

> Original sin is the hereditary but impersonal fault of Adam's descendants, who have sinned in him (Rom 5:12). It is the loss of grace, and therefore of eternal life, together with a propensity to evil, which everybody must, with the assistance of grace, penance, resistance and moral effort, repress and conquer. The passion and death of the Son of God has redeemed the world from the hereditary curse of sin and death.[6]

Here we take up five topics: why we should believe in original sin; how it could have been committed by the first human beings; its consequences; how we can be involved in a sin committed before we existed; and some objections and replies.

A: Why We Must Believe in Original Sin

One might of course say, as theologians as diverse as Cardinal Newman and Reinhold Niebuhr have, that one cannot help believing in original sin, or something very much like it, because the empirical evidence is so compelling. Catholics, however, must believe in the doctrine of original sin as it is taught by the Church for two specific reasons: first, it is very closely connected with other essential Christian doctrines; second, it is itself a matter of faith, as the Council of Trent's solemn teaching makes clear.

As to the first point: Even though God creates everything good and is the Lord of creation, still the human condition is profoundly marked by evil. We find ourselves in a situation of conflict, disruption, and sin even before we personally become morally responsible for it. Suffering and death are inevitable and universal. True, someone might say that death is natural. Yet when we think of death for ourselves and those we love, we do not simply shrug resignedly and say, "Animals and plants die, and so do human beings." Deep in our hearts we consider death outrageous. Believing that, we know something is profoundly wrong with the human condition.

But where does what is wrong come from? If one says "from the nature of things," one is either attributing the situation to God, the creator and Lord, or saying that God's providence is inadequate to keep evil from erupting into creation through the activity of some other principle. Neither solution is acceptable to a believer. Hence it is necessary to account for what is fundamentally wrong with the human condition by an abuse of creaturely freedom at the very beginning. The human predicament is somehow the result of collective human fault.

Genesis says as much. Through a narrative rich in symbolic content, it explains how, even though God is good, creator of a good world, and Lord of the world he created, the human situation comes to be flawed: people at the beginning abused their freedom.

This is expressed not only in the story of Adam and Eve, but in all of Genesis up to Abraham—in the story of Cain and Abel, the flood, Babel. Together they present a rich explanation of the misery of the human condition in its various aspects. People committed sin from the beginning, and sin divided people and set them against one another; subsequently, sin was prevalent at all times.

Genesis, however, is not the principal scriptural text on the subject of original sin. That distinction belongs to the fifth chapter of St. Paul's Epistle to the Romans, where he writes:

Just as sin came into the world through one man, and death came through sin, and so death spread to all because all have sinned. . . . If, because of the one man's trespass, death exercised dominion through that one, much more surely will those who receive the abundance of grace and the free gift of righteousness exercise dominion in life through the one man, Jesus Christ. Therefore just as one man's trespass led to condemnation for all, so one man's act of righteousness leads to justification and life for all. (Rom 5:12, 17–18)

The doctrine of original sin and the doctrine of redemption in and through Jesus Christ are intimately, inextricably linked.

Original sin explains the trouble with human life. Redemption explains the remedy and how it becomes effective: through Christ, through participation in his death and resurrection, through our becoming, and indeed the whole world's becoming, a new creation in him. Deny the doctrine of original sin as it has traditionally been understood, and before long one will also deny the doctrine of redemption as traditionally understood.

The Council of Trent clearly defined that through man's (that is, Adam's) sin at the beginning, justice and holiness were lost and the punishment of death was incurred; and that this sin is passed on to all men and women, not by imitation but by propagation. In other words, original sin is something one is born with, not something one personally does. So, according to Trent, infants are involved in original sin even before they can make choices of their own, but the sin is taken away by the merits of Christ. These merits are applied to individuals by baptism, and so it is right and necessary that infants be baptized (see DS 1511–15/788–92).

B: How Original Sin Could Have Been Committed

In regard to original sin, it is important to be clear about what does and does not pertain to faith. One need not believe that the first human beings were endowed with extraordinary knowledge, virtue, power, and so on. Much of the theological tradition, especially that stemming from the Eastern Church Fathers, does suggest a golden age at the beginning, when the human condition was truly wonderful—rich in science, art, virtue, and every human perfection. But God has not revealed this, and the Church does not teach it. It is only theological speculation, which can be dispensed with.

One must, however, accept some things as true about the first human beings who were our ancestors and with whom we are in human solidarity: for example, that they were able to understand right and wrong and make free choices. We also have to suppose, in the words of Vatican II, that God, "planning to make known the way of heavenly salvation . . . went further and from the start manifested himself to our first parents" (*DV* 3). There was a divine revelation to the first human beings; they were aware of their relationship to God and were consciously in friendship with him.

At the same time, one need not think these first human beings understood all that was at stake if they sinned or, specifically, knew that in sinning they were acting to the detriment of those who would come after. They only needed to know right from wrong and to be able to commit sin.

Must one believe there were only one man and one woman at the beginning? Some biologists think evolution theory indicates the need for a substantially larger group at the origin of an organic type as complex as the human. But both Pope Pius XII and Pope Paul VI point out that polygenism, as it is called, appears to be irreconcilable with the Church's teaching.[7] It is not clear, however, that either pope insists that monogenism must therefore be held, since what *appears* irreconcilable with faith might turn out to be reconcilable after all. Hence, one can seek a way to reconcile what the Church teaches with what some hold to be the facts. One such speculation proceeds along the following lines.

It is not hard to imagine that among the first human beings, however large the group was, some sort of struggle arose—perhaps a temptation to settle a disagreement about leadership by an unreasonable resort to violence instead of by peaceful means. When the members of a group disagree about a question of this sort, they easily become polarized. If there were a resort to violence in the circumstances imagined, all the members of the group capable of choosing might well have become involved. One can suppose everyone's doing the wrong thing: choosing up sides and resorting to violence, faction against faction, neighbor against neighbor.

In any human society, however, some person or persons make *the* decision which is decisive for the group. (A simple example: A nation does not go to war unless its ruler so decides, even though elements of its armed forces may engage in battle before the ruler's decision commits the nation.) Where wrongdoing is in question, the group as such only goes wrong when the person or persons primarily responsible for leadership participate in the wrongdoing and give it the seal of authority.

In this way, it is possible to imagine that the first human beings—not just two people, but a clan as large as evolution theory would require—all committed sin; but that the sin became the sin of what was then the whole human race only by reason of the fact that the group's leader assented to it, participated in it, and so made it the sin of the group as such.

This is, we repeat, merely a speculative attempt to reconcile what the Church teaches with what some say science requires. Perhaps there is a better way of doing that. Does the account given here fit the facts? We have no way of knowing. We do know, because it is a matter of faith, that the essential teaching of the Church is true, and we believe that our speculation points to a way in which polygenism could be consistent with that teaching. The key point is that whether humankind at the beginning was two people or a much larger group, the whole of humankind was able to commit a sin provided it was a real community and its leader acted sinfully precisely as the leader of that community.

C: The Consequences of Original Sin

The primary consequence of original sin was that not only the individuals who committed it but human beings as a group were no longer a community in friendship with God. The previously existing, conscious friendship based on revelation was disrupted. But besides this disruption, harmony on every level was damaged. When sin is committed, all the existential goods are affected for the worse. Genesis depicts in a concrete, imaginative way the inner tension, insincerity, and interpersonal conflict—consider Cain and Abel—arising from sin.

Trent, basing its teaching on St. Paul, definitively teaches that death also is a consequence of sin. At first this seems strange. Is not death natural for bodily beings? But there is no contradiction between saying death is natural and saying it was not in God's original plan for human beings.

These bodily creatures, human beings, were created with intelligence and freedom and with the dignity of being made in God's image and called to share in divine life; right from the beginning they enjoyed friendship with God based on revelation. So it is fitting to suppose—and the Church definitively teaches—that God intended to prevent them from having to die. In the absence of original sin, we can imagine that human beings, instead of dying, would have passed directly from earthly life to another life like the resurrection life for which we now hope. (They would not have experienced "resurrection," however, for they would not have died, as we understand death.)

However that may be, as a result of original sin, we have lost the gift of being preserved from what appear to be the natural consequences of our bodily condition. Death, the natural fate of other organisms, is our fate, too. It is not necessary in this view to suppose that God imposes death on us as an arbitrary punishment. Instead, we can suppose that he simply permits that to happen which naturally would happen unless he prevented it by a special intervention. As a result of sin, God lets nature take its course with those who do not cherish his gifts. Many Fathers of the Church explain in this way how death is both a consequence of sin and natural for human beings as organisms.

However one explains it, death's entrance into human affairs as a result of original sin accounts for a great deal about the human condition as it is now.

Human beings are in a more painful situation than are other creatures destined to die. Animals and plants will die, but they do not know it. Even the higher animals, which react instinctively against life-threatening situations, cannot fear death as we do because they are not reflective. But we human beings look ahead and know, with agonized self-awareness, that we and those we love are going to die.

Our emotional lives are profoundly affected by this knowledge. After sin, the human race lives in terror of death. The terror is absent only in small children, who do not yet grasp that they will die and whose emotional reactions therefore have a beautiful spontaneity and lack of affectedness. Perhaps one also sees something of this in very holy people; entirely realistic about death and the terror it gives rise to, they nevertheless have so great a hope of resurrection that they enjoy an inner harmony—a reintegration on the emotional level—lacking in the rest of us. Ordinarily, though, people dread death, and their dread skews the whole of their emotional lives; "all their lives" they are "held in slavery by the fear of death" (Heb 2:15).

One result is a bias toward intense pleasure, sought as a kind of anodyne or escape from pervasive dread. Animals pursue what is gratifying—food and sex—to the extent it is organically necessary and appropriate. But human beings are driven to pursue gratification long after it has stopped making sense. We kill ourselves by eating too much, drinking too much, smoking, taking drugs; we seek meaningless sexual gratification which offers no personal fulfillment and may even be personally destructive to one or both parties. Why do we seek destructive pleasure? To feel a little better even for a little while, to escape pain and anxiety, to avoid confronting the reality which otherwise seems to rule our lives—death.

This state of affairs is "concupiscence." It is not itself sin, but it is a consequence of sin and tends to sin. Here is the real emotional situation of human beings in the condition of fallen nature. One need not think of it as perverse and psychologically deviant. It is the normal psychological state of human beings living in fear of death.

This terror impacts on the world of our experience—a world we now approach simultaneously dreading extinction and craving gratification, a world made up, for us, of threats and allurements. As we experience the world, it is a kind of caricature of itself. In fact, it is hard for us even to *see* the world as it is. For that we turn to the special vision of the artist, who, through long training to *see* what is actually there, glimpses a richer, more multidimensional reality than the rest of us. Most of the time, most of us perceive a world reduced to the dimensions of what is emotionally important to us. And all our emotions are affected by craving for pleasure and fear of death.

Whatever we understand is understood in light of our experience of the world, and since this experience is distorted, so is our basic understanding of all reality. Our grasp of what is good is limited and skewed by a fundamentally faulty perception of how things are. This in turn is reflected in what we do and make—in language, art, science, and technology. Human culture as a whole is affected for the worse. No product of human activity is as it would be without sin.

The cultural consequences of sin set up a kind of vicious circle. Distortion at the cultural level returns to, and reinforces, distortion already existing on the individual psychological level. Think of a child being socialized in a perverse view of reality, a corrupt understanding of what is good, by watching television indiscriminately.

The alternatives for choice which are open to people after sin are not as good as they would have been without sin. Morally right possibilities are not so interesting. Why?

Every choice involves self-limitation: one is *not* fulfilled here and now with respect to the good not chosen. Ideally, community should compensate for this. Although one cannot oneself be everything and have every kind of human fulfillment, a far wider range of experiences and fulfillments is open to the community. "We" together are more than "I" alone. The limitations, the finitude, of individuals find compensation in a community whose members truly love one another and rejoice in one another's fulfillment. That is true in a good family, where parents in many ways set aside their individual desire for fulfillment in favor of their children, grown children in favor of aged parents, one spouse in favor of the other, and so on.

In light of sin, however, the point of self-denial is blurred. Suppose someone accepts the self-limitation involved in doing the right thing: what then? Others cannot be counted on to do their share. Generous people suffer for their generosity by being exploited; forgoing individual fulfillment, they are denied fulfillment in others. So, for example, to the extent children live badly, a generous mother's or father's motivation to be a good parent is reduced. In such circumstances, "looking out for number one" seems to make good sense.

In sum, the human condition after sin is difficult. The alternatives for choice—including, and often especially, the morally good alternatives—are not very appealing. Virtue frequently is its own punishment: "I tried to do the right thing, and look what happened to me as a result!" This is not surprising. Competition is a large part of this life, and the wicked, ready to do what they must in order to get what they want, have a distinct advantage in competing with those who are trying to be morally good.

In light of all this, people see little reason for hope. Death is inevitable; moral goodness is not very rewarding; doing what is wrong seems to offer some immediate pleasure and fulfillment.

This helps explain that "weakening" of the will which is also one of the consequences of original sin.

The will is a spiritual power; it does not grow stronger or weaker as muscles do. Either one makes free choices or one does not; there is no such thing as a choice which is a little bit free. But it makes good sense to speak of weakness of will when morally good options are unappealing and morally bad ones are attractive. Very often that is how things are in the fallen human condition. Our wills are weak because it is hard to see why one should live a morally good life. "If the dead are not raised, 'Let us eat and drink, for tomorrow we die' " (1 Cor 15:32).

D: How We Can Be Involved in a Sin Committed Before We Existed

For people with Christian faith this may be the most difficult question about original sin: How are *we* involved in it? We did not personally commit it; yet the Church does not teach simply that we suffer its bad consequences. On the contrary, the Council of Orange specifically makes the point that, if that *were* the case, it would be unfair—God would be acting unjustly in punishing us for something of which we were not guilty. Somehow therefore we really do participate in this sin. But how?

Evidently not by any personal act of the will, for we come into the world in this state. But is not sin an eminently voluntary, personal thing? That is the problem. The solution proceeds along the following lines.

If man had not sinned at the beginning, humankind would not have been merely the family of Adam; it would have been both a human fellowship and the family of God. Had people at the beginning remained faithful to the revelation they received and had they responded faithfully to God's gifts, then as a human family they would also have been God's family. So, too, would their descendants have been—so would we be—simply by coming to be as members of the human race.

However, at the beginning humankind fell short of its common responsibility. Not only did many (or even all) individuals as individuals fall into sins of one sort or another, but humankind as a community, by the action of its leadership, committed a communal sin. Thus, the human family did not respond to God's gifts, did not remain in friendship with him. As matters now stand, we come to be in a natural human community, without coming to be in friendship with God. To be born a human being does *not* mean being born a child of God, since the human race *as such* is not God's family.

It is quite true that original sin in us is not a personal choice— no one can inherit a choice—and therefore is not a personal sin. What we do inherit, however, is human nature within a human race which *as such* is alienated from God and whose members are in conflict, including religious conflict, with one another. In this way original sin accompanies our human nature and is transmitted by propagation, not by imitation. We come to be in the human community of Cain and Abel, whose common nature did not unite them in friendship with God, and for whom the issue of friendship with God itself became divisive to the point of deadly conflict.

Sin is an evil, and evil is a privation. Where is the privation which constitutes original sin? To put it concretely: What does a new human being lack which he or she ought to have? The answer of course is grace. That means at least the following.

In coming into existence, each new human person ought—according to God's original plan—to come to be within a community in friendship with God. But humankind lost that friendship with God by original sin, so that human beings now do *not* come to be in such a community; a new human person is *not* in friendship with God. That lack—of friendship with God—is the absence of something which should be present, because it was part of God's plan at the beginning. In short, as a result of original sin, human nature commences in each human person without grace, grace which each new person would have had if the first human beings had accepted and lived by God's original plan. This lack of grace is the central privation constituting the evil of original sin.

Moreover, this lack really has the character of sin for us. Humankind as a whole has not developed as a single community; in divided humankind, there neither has been nor is a common, universal will to genuine religious community. Rather, there is the privation of such a will toward friendship with God. This privation is the lack of a social act which should exist but does not. One cannot, simply by being human, share in a social act of friendship toward God, for there is no such social act of humankind as a whole to share in. This is the defect in voluntariness—in will—which makes privation of grace be original sin in us. Thus, original sin is inherited inasmuch as each new human being is involved by nature in a communal omission, the failure to share in a common commitment to friendship with God.

Still, some people will say: "God is harsh to allow us to inherit a human nature and be born into a human community lacking what ought to be there, just because people at the beginning sinned." But how harsh is God, really? He has not abandoned the human race; his offer of friendship still stands. Only now, humankind collectively having rejected his offer, it is up to human persons individually to accept it.

Humankind's leadership at the beginning abused its role by committing a communal sin, with the result that humankind became so divided that no ordinary man could lead it in a common act of repentance back to friendship with God. But Jesus, sent by God, assumes the role of leadership in order to establish and head the community in friendship with God that we are invited to join—the community of the new covenant, which is Jesus' Church. God's family is now a permanent society in the world, open to all human beings who choose to join it. By making this choice and seeking baptism into the Church—or, for someone who has not heard the gospel preached, by looking for God's community of redemption or hoping for it—every human individual can accept God's offer of friendship.

In sum, as a result of original sin, we do not come into existence as members of God's family. But membership is still offered to us. Although we are not members by nature, we become so by the commitment of faith. God has not abandoned us. He has simply given us a different way—a better way—of being in friendship with him.

E: Some Objections and Replies

It is said that modern Scripture scholarship undermines the doctrine of original sin.

Familiarity with sound modern Scripture scholarship and with the actual teaching of the Church provides the best answer to this objection. Modern scholarship does make it clear that the Bible asserts far less about original sin than many people once supposed and some still do; it undermines any reading of Genesis which treats the text as a straightforward report of humankind's early history.

But such a reading is not part of Catholic doctrine about original sin. For example, the picturesque details included in the first few chapters of Genesis are not part of the Church's teaching (nor is the idea that the transmission of original sin is due to sexual passion). So, sound modern Scripture scholarship, while showing that the Genesis account is not history, does not undermine the Catholic doctrine of original sin. Nothing in such scholarship undermines Genesis as an account of the human condition or contradicts any of the relevant truths of faith defined by Trent.

Moreover, as we noted earlier, the doctrinally more important scriptural text about original sin is not Genesis but Romans 5, where St. Paul discusses the sin of man and the redemptive work of Christ. Modern scholarship shows that some have read more into this text than is actually there, but that does not undermine the teaching of Trent. And Trent's understanding of St. Paul is a matter of the first importance, not so much for the sake of the doctrine on original sin, but because rejection or radical revision of that doctrine entails the rejection or radical revision of the far more important doctrine of redemption.

A second objection arises from the fact that many people believe evolution theory has somehow undermined the traditional doctrine on original sin.

Although different theories of evolution conflict with one another in their details, it does appear necessary to accept the general biological theory of evolution. However, evolution theory concerns organic life only, while intelligence and free choice are spiritual capacities which cannot be explained by organic principles. Human beings, in other words, have capacities which evolution cannot account for.

Granting the truth of biological evolution theory, then, one must acknowledge a transformation at some point which can only be explained by a special divine intervention. Some organisms ceased being mere animals and were made into human persons—images and likenesses of God. That is so whether one supposes that at the beginning there were only two such persons or whether one supposes a much larger number. In either case, there had to be a radical change—from animals to persons—brought about by a special creative act of God. To be logical about it, everyone who denies this must end by denying that there are human persons. Of course, they will not deny that there are human beings, but they will deny that any human being can make a free choice—as human persons in fact do.

In relation to the doctrine of original sin, there is no reason not to suppose that the first human persons were, by our standards, very primitive. One need not believe they enjoyed extraordinary gifts or lived in a golden age; they may have been primitive hunters and inhabited caves. All the doctrine of original sin requires is that these human beings knew themselves to be in a special relationship with God, were capable of choosing freely, and somehow constituted a single community. Nor, to the extent the speculation above about how original sin occurred may be correct, does it matter how large the first group of human persons was, provided it was a true society capable of committing itself as a group, morally speaking, by its leader's participating in, and thus ratifying, the immoral choices of the other members.

15. Distinctions among Sins; Sins of Thought

So far we have considered sin in general and original sin. Now we turn to the sin *we* actually commit, personal sin.

This chapter takes up two different topics: the distinction among sins based on their seriousness, and sins of thought. We consider five questions: how sins differ in seriousness; what mortal sin is; how individuals can commit mortal sin by involvement in the sinful activities of groups; and, turning to sins of thought, why they are so important and what exactly they are. The next two chapters will treat the conditions for mortal sin at greater length.

A: How Sins Differ in Seriousness

Almost everyone who does philosophical ethics recognizes that not all moral evil is equally grave, and ordinary people intuitively grasp the same thing.

To begin with, subjective factors can affect the degree of immorality. How aware is the individual of doing wrong? Has he or she actually made a wrong choice? How appealing are the morally acceptable alternatives? The degree of immorality can vary depending on whether the agent is more or less clear about how wrong something is, on whether he or she does or does not make a choice, and on whether the alternatives are appealing or repugnant.

There can also be differences in the seriousness of *what* is done—in the mode of responsibility which is violated, in the human good which is damaged, in the extent to which the wrong action does harm. We saw in chapter ten, for instance, that even though the result—in the example, someone's death—may be the same, it is more serious to try to kill somebody one hates (a violation of the seventh mode) than to practice favoritism in giving and withholding life-threatening assignments (a violation of the fifth mode), and more serious to do the latter than to contribute to someone's death by withholding help because of laziness or anxiety (a violation of the first or fourth mode). Similarly, it is worse, other things being equal, to kill someone than to injure him or her, and more serious to cause someone to sin than to do the person bodily harm.

All this is clear to reason. But faith introduces a further sharp distinction: that between mortal sin and venial sin. It is found neither in philosophy nor in most religious traditions, but it has been an element of faith throughout Christian history. Evidently the distinction—according to which the least serious mortal sin is radically different from, and far more serious than, the most serious venial sin—is essentially linked to revelation. The sharp break, the radical difference, between mortal and venial sin will be examined in the next chapter; here we shall only indicate what it consists in.

The Old Testament—for example, Leviticus in many places—distinguishes between faults, for which expiation is possible, and crimes against the covenant community and its God, which cannot be expiated. Everyone commits faults, but not everyone commits crimes. The latter are punishable by death or exclusion from the covenant community: for example, "Any of the people of Israel, or of the aliens who reside in Israel, who give any of their offspring to Molech shall be put to death" (Lv 20:2). Crimes include idolatry, murder, adultery, false witness in a capital case, and so on. Such deeds are so serious that they deserve the punishment of death or being cut off from the community. (To be sure, not everyone who committed crimes was in fact punished this way; but deeds like these were believed to deserve such punishment.)

Although the Old Testament does not speak of sins as mortal and venial, these ideas underlie the distinction between crimes and faults. "Venial" means pardonable. It signifies that which can be expiated, forgiven, wiped away. A crime, however, cannot be expiated; it deserves the punishment of death, either physical death or the social death of exclusion from the community, and so is "mortal."

The New Testament does not use the words "mortal" and "venial" either, but it makes the same distinction even more clearly. Jesus tells his disciples to ask the Father's forgiveness for their daily trespasses (Mt 6:12; Lk 11:4); but he warns that other transgressions lead to everlasting punishment (Mt 23:33) and seems to speak of some sins as unforgivable: for example, "Therefore I tell you, people will be forgiven for every sin and blasphemy, but blasphemy against the Spirit will not be forgiven" (Mt 12:31).

These ideas became explicit very early in Christian teaching. There are slight transgressions, which even the upright commit daily, and these can be forgiven. But there are also grave sins, which are capable of excluding one forever from the kingdom. Idolatry, adultery, and homicide are among the first sins recognized as mortal. The continuity with the Old Testament is clear.

The Church's teaching insists on the distinction between mortal and venial sins. For example, the Council of Trent teaches that not all sins take away grace—some are venial; it also teaches that each and every mortal sin must be confessed and absolved. In sum, although reason alone cannot fully explain the distinction, it is found in Scripture and in the Church's teaching. It is an essential part of Christian faith.

B: What Mortal Sin Is

By definition, mortal sin is incompatible with sharing in divine life. Someone who commits mortal sin and remains in it is excluded from the kingdom. Christians who commit mortal sin thereby make themselves incapable of full participation in the life of the Church, especially in the Eucharist, since the Eucharist expresses and nourishes the Church's living unity. A person who is not living in unity with the Church by sharing in divine life should not receive Communion, for that would be like an unfaithful spouse asking for marital intercourse. Exclusion from full participation in the Eucharist on account of mortal sin is not an arbitrary punishment; rather, there is an intrinsic connection.

Mortal sin is defined by three familiar conditions: grave matter, sufficient reflection, and full consent. These conditions are intrinsic to the idea of mortal sin. Sin, after all, involves a conflict between a judgment of conscience and a choice. Where there is no judgment that something is or may be wrong, there is no conflict in choosing it. Evidently, then, sin in its primary meaning requires both sufficient reflection (to see that something is or may be wrong) and full consent (to choose it). Furthermore, even if we choose to do what we see to be wrong, we commit only venial sin unless we realize that the wrong is or may be grave matter.

But what is "grave matter"? Some kinds of acts—things like idle talk and lack of attention in prayer—are obviously light matter in themselves. Other kinds of acts are either self-evidently grave matter in and of themselves or else firmly established as such in the tradition: killing the innocent, adultery, lying, theft, and so on. But some of these acts which are grave in themselves are *in particular cases* less serious than acts of that sort usually are. There is no such thing as a small murder or a little bit of adultery, but there are small acts of theft and lying, which infringe only marginally on someone else's rights.

If the wrong is so marginal that the act is not a typical instance of its kind, we have a case of parvity (smallness) of matter: telling a white lie or taking one peanut from a vendor's stand without paying for it. We call such deeds lying and theft because they do not fit any other categories of wrongdoing. But even though one is dealing with a category of action recognized as grave in Christian teaching, particular instances may be so trivial that they are only borderline cases of the wrongful kind of act, and so are not grave. Here we have parvity of matter. Nevertheless, one begins with the presumption of gravity. The burden of proof is with those who believe there is smallness of matter in a particular case.

If someone thinks something is or may be grave matter yet chooses it, that is enough for mortal sin. But even someone who thinks something is not grave matter, and so lacks the sufficient reflection necessary for mortal sin here and now, may not be entirely blameless in choosing it. Perhaps it is really grave and the individual should have known that: he or she is responsible for not knowing. (That responsibility may be only venial, or it may go back to a previous, unrepented mortal sin.) Again, even without knowing or intending it, people may do grave harm—to others or to themselves—which they will have a serious responsibility to remedy later.

"Sufficient reflection" means one must actually be aware of the grave wrong (or, at least, be aware of being in doubt about that) at the time of choosing. There is no conflict with conscience, and so no sufficient reflection, if someone chooses something that is in fact gravely wrong without knowing or suspecting it to be such at the time. Finding out later that it was gravely wrong does not make the earlier choice mortally sinful. Moreover, people who ordinarily know something to be gravely wrong can nevertheless choose it without sufficient reflection if distraction, intense emotion, fatigue, or some other factor prevents them from attending to the fact that *this* is an instance.

Sufficient reflection does not require that one think explicitly, "This is gravely wrong, but I choose to do it." It is possible, after all, to be quite aware of something without reflecting on the fact that one is aware of it. Someone who knows that acts of a certain kind are or may be seriously wrong, and is aware of that when tempted, commits mortal sin in freely choosing to act contrary to the awareness, even though it is only in the back of his or her mind just then. On the other hand, as we have seen, those so distracted, distraught, or exhausted that an act's seriousness escapes their awareness at the time they choose it, do not have sufficient reflection.

It is not necessary for sufficient reflection to know why something is wrong or to think of it as an offense against God. People who have been taught that a certain kind of act is seriously wrong can have sufficient reflection if they believe what they learned even without knowing why. So can people who do not believe in God; for they can still be aware that some things are seriously wrong, and if they deliberately choose to do such things, they commit grave sins. Without thinking about God, even believers, especially those who have not been well instructed or whose consciences have been dulled by previous sins, can commit mortal sins by choosing to do things which they are aware are gravely wrong.

"Full consent" is a definite choice of what one knows one ought not to do. No external performance is necessary; one need not put the choice into action. The choice alone is enough for mortal sin.

Someone who has made a mortally sinful choice and not repented can commit further mortal sins by extending the choice through executive willing. Suppose Lou freely joins the mob, knowing this to be gravely wrong. Later he may find himself involved in many forms of immorality—murder, prostitution, pornography, drugs—as part of his daily routine. He may even reach the point where he no longer makes choices about these matters—they are just part of the job. Yet Lou continues to be aware of what he is doing, he is willing to do it, and he has not repented the gravely wrong choice that began his career in crime. Each new gravely wrong act is a new mortal sin committed in carrying out his original sinful choice.

Apart from such cases, however, people do not commit mortal sins without making choices. Thus, there cannot be mortal sin in the kinds of voluntariness in which there is no choice—for example, failing (without making any choice) to pull oneself together so as to do something which should be done. Also, even though unconscious faults may very well be sins of a sort, they cannot be mortal sins unless they are the carrying out of a previous immoral choice by executive willing. For example, a husband who habitually neglects his wife and family while immersing himself in television or a hobby or some other self-centered activity is guilty of wrongdoing, but it is not mortal sin if he has simply drifted into this pattern of behavior without adverting to the fact that habitual neglect of family obligations is seriously wrong.

In sum, to commit a mortal sin one must both be aware that one has a serious responsibility and choose contrary to it. If someone does this and does not repent, other immoral acts performed in voluntarily following through on the original immoral choice can be additional mortal sins. But there is no mortal sin without, initially at least, awareness that something is or might well be gravely wrong and a choice to do it despite that awareness.

C: How Individuals Sin Mortally by Involvement in Sinful Group Activities

The conditions for mortal sin apply also to mortal sin committed by involvement in a group. Members of a group engaged in some gravely immoral activity are guilty of mortal sin only insofar as they personally choose contrary to conscience in a matter they personally recognize as grave. One cannot be gravely guilty of anything by involvement in a group without *personally* being gravely guilty of something. Thus, simply working for a company engaged in gravely immoral business practices or being a citizen of a country which pursues immoral policies does not—in and of itself—make one guilty of grave wrongdoing.

However, someone aware that a group to which he or she belongs is doing grave evil has a duty to try to rectify the group's action—to get the company to stop cheating its customers, the country to stop engaging in genocidal warfare. But this duty is not absolute. So, for instance, a citizen has only a limited duty to try to get his or her country to mend its ways. Often in fact there is little or nothing the individual citizen, especially a citizen of a totalitarian country, can do. Moreover, those whose lives are already organized by good vocational commitments, and whose time and energy are taken up fulfilling them, generally have little scope for this kind of activity. Thus, it is unreasonable to expect the mother of a large family or a contemplative nun to engage in direct action to halt an unjust war, clean up the environment, or right any number of other social wrongs.

On the other hand, people whose lives are not organized by vocational commitments and who spend a great deal of time on self-gratifying amusements may very well have an obligation, even a grave one, to become involved in trying to correct the unjust policies of their society. In some cases, too, the organizing commitment of a person's life may indeed be one which involves direct action for justice. This is a noble calling for those who have it—provided, of course, their program of action against oppression does not include adopting the tactics of the oppressors and committing crimes of their own in the name of liberation and justice.

Regardless of one's personal situation, one may never do anything which contributes directly to the wrongdoing of a society or group to which one belongs and of itself does nothing else. If, for example, a man thinks his country is waging an unjust war, he may not participate in the killing on the excuse that this is his obligation as a citizen or that he only wants to avoid the penalty imposed on draft evaders. At the same time, one *may* do things which are legitimate and worthwhile in themselves even though they contribute to the wrongdoing of a group to which one belongs. Thus, citizens can pay taxes, even though they go in part to pay for deterrence and abortion, or serve as noncombatant chaplains or medics in their country's unjust war. However, as in any case of accepting bad side effects resulting from material co-operation in wrongdoing, there are limits to what citizens may do. (This issue was treated at the end of chapter twelve.)

D: Why Sins of Thought Are Important

We turn now to the second major topic of this chapter, sins of thought.

We need not look beyond the Ten Commandments to see that there are serious sins of thought, for the last two commandments are concerned with coveting. And, as we have seen, Jesus teaches that morality is in the heart, not merely in external behavior. St. Augustine speaks of "sin in the heart [which is] known to God, though actually it may remain unknown to man."[8] Furthermore, the Council of Trent, in its treatment of the sacrament of penance, teaches explicitly that even sins which are entirely interior can be mortal sins, and sometimes worse than sins committed openly.

Why worse? Because one may think of and consent in one's heart to things far worse than any one would do in the open. Suppose Judy delights in thinking of ways of harming Punch, knowing that this taking delight is gravely wrong yet choosing to indulge in it; that can be a worse sin than anything she might actually do, since fear of consequences prevents her from *actually* doing anything more than a little petty nastiness. She would *like* to kill Punch, but that would be too costly—for her.

As this suggests, what makes sins of thought important is bad will. Sin, after all, is primarily just that—bad will. It is willing against moral truth. And it should be clear that "thought" in "sins of thought" does not mean speculative thinking; it means practical thinking, together with the willing essential to moral guilt. Sins of thought are so important because "thought" in this sense is primarily and essentially where sin is. To be sure, if one not only commits a sin of thought but acts it out, the performance makes matters worse; but even so the sin is primarily in the evil will.

In practice, someone who refrains from overtly evil deeds while indulging in grave sins of thought is hypocritical. This way of acting betrays a legalistic view of morality. The outward conformity to moral standards arises from shame or fear of being caught and punished, not from respect for moral truth and appreciation of the self-determining effects of choice. It is precisely true that someone who wills grave harm to others while presenting a benevolent face to those he or she hates can "smile, and smile, and be a villain." Outward expressions of friendliness and affection by those who harbor malice in their hearts add up to hypocrisy.

In sum, sins of thought are in some ways more important than external behavior. Without sufficient reflection, external behavior can be dreadful without being seriously sinful, but in deliberately choosing to think something gravely wrong, we are really guilty of grave sin.

E: What Sins of Thought Are

Sins of thought are not spontaneous feelings and ideas. We can have any number of spontaneous feelings which are not as they should be, any number of wrong ideas, yet still only experience temptation, because we have not yet made a choice.

Nor need it be a sin of thought to deliberate about doing something wrong. Working during the Christmas rush in an upscale boutique, and badly wanting a fur coat which she cannot afford, Pauline might find herself deliberating about the best way to commit the theft, although she knows that it would be a grave sin. Even so, she does not commit a sin until she realizes she should terminate this deliberation but chooses to go on with it. Deliberation about how to do things, bad as well as good, comes to us spontaneously, but there is no sin without choice.

This point has practical importance, since people who become aware that they are deliberating about how to do things which are gravely wrong may think they have *already* committed mortal sin. That is dangerous, for a person may then reason, "Since I've already committed a mortal sin, I might as well enjoy it"—and proceed to sin in fact. We should not be too quick to suppose we have committed mortal sins of thought. Unless someone makes a choice contrary to a judgment along the lines of, "I should not be thinking this," he or she has not sinned. That is so even though the individual deliberates for a long time before realizing "I could and should stop thinking of this" and thus being in a position to choose to stop.

The sin in a sin of thought is *not* a choice of outward behavior. It is a choice to indulge in the thought itself. Suppose Mac is deliberating about how to steal a valuable book. After a while, it occurs to him that he should not be doing this. But he chooses to continue deliberating. He concludes that it would be too risky to try to steal the book, and so never chooses to do so. But he has committed a mortal sin. Or suppose Maggie is thinking with satisfaction about doing serious injury to Jiggs. There is no mortal sin yet. Then it strikes her that she should not be thinking about hurting him. But Maggie chooses to continue—for the pleasure it gives her—without actually intending to do what she is thinking about. She has sinned mortally.

At the same time, what was said earlier about executive willing holds also in the case of sins of thought. Suppose George chooses to subscribe to a pornographic magazine ("Everybody reads it. After all, this isn't the Victorian age"). If despite his rationalization he knows that this is gravely wrong, he commits a mortal sin in so choosing. Not only that, he commits another mortal sin every time he indulges in thoughts of fornication or adultery as he peruses each issue of the magazine, even though he does not make a new choice on each occasion. Similarly, someone who knows that he or she ought not to give evil thoughts free rein but decides to do so is guilty of a new mortal sin, though without a new choice, every time this occurs, until he or she repents.

However, people who know what choice is, who can identify their own choices, and who are *not* aware of having made a choice contrary to conscience about grave matter in thought, have probably not committed a mortal sin. Thus, when we realize that we are dealing with grave matter in our thoughts, we need to ask ourselves, "Have I chosen?" If the answer is, "It isn't clear that I have," it is safe to assume that there has been no choice and no mortal sin.

Although this analysis is sound in general, still one can hardly tell a child or an unreflective adult who has never given any real thought to choice, "You haven't committed a mortal sin unless you're aware of having made a choice." For someone who is seldom if ever aware of making choices, yet who certainly does make them, this is simply false reassurance. The first thing to do with such people is instruct them about choices, so that they can recognize a choice when they make one. Then they can be instructed about sin, including sins of thought.

"Why do that?" someone might object. "Why not leave people ignorant and innocent?" In the first place because, although such people may be ignorant, they are not necessarily innocent; even though they lack the sophistication to recognize their choices, they do make choices and they may be committing mortal sins. Proper instruction can help them stop. And, in the second place, even if such people are innocent of mortal sin in respect to their thoughts, they hardly are likely to maintain mastery over acts which involve outward deeds if they make no effort to restrain their thoughts.

Sins of thought can be committed in planning to do a sinful deed even before one does it, in choosing to omit something which should be done, in choosing to keep on thinking about something which should not be thought about, in approving and enjoying thoughts about actions, whether our own or others', which we know are wrong. But, apart from cases in which a sin of thought follows by executive willing from a prior, unrepented mortal sin, we cannot commit grave sins of thought without both being aware that it is gravely wrong to think, deliberate, feel, plan, approve, or dwell on something, and choosing to do so any-way—or choosing *not* to do our grave duty in such circumstances, namely, turn our attention to something else.

16. The Distinction between Grave and Light Matter

As we saw in the last chapter, the Church teaches that there is a radical distinction between mortal and venial sin. Intrinsic to it is the distinction between grave and light matter. But what is the difference?

St. Thomas Aquinas gives one answer, while a contemporary fundamental option theory gives a very different one. Although each has something in its favor, neither is entirely satisfactory. Our answer is that grave matter is anything at odds with the real fundamental option of Christian life, the commitment of faith; light matter is the matter of immoral acts which nevertheless are incompatible neither with faith itself nor with that commitment's specific requirements.

We take up four questions: the problem of grave and light matter, how a sound theory of the fundamental option of Christian life solves the problem, the unsound theory of fundamental option which is widespread today, and what is wrong with that theory.

A: The Problem of Grave and Light Matter

Mortal sins and venial sins are utterly different in kind. Even the worst venial sins do not deprive the sinner of friendship with God, but the very least mortal sin (if one can speak that way) does. All mortal sins are deadly; unrepented, they lead to hell.

The problem at issue here will be understood most easily by focusing on venial sins. Every human good participates in the goodness of God, and someone who loves God should love every human good to the full extent of its goodness. But *any* immoral act—including a venial sin—is in conflict with this. Not only mortal sin but venial sin as well conflicts with perfect love of God. If the Church's teaching is true, however, a venial sin is somehow compatible with loving God. Unlike a mortal sinner, someone who commits venial sin still enjoys friendship with God. How can that be?

Perhaps it is not so hard to see in the case of sins which are venial because of lack of reflection or full consent. "I was distracted. I hardly noticed what I was doing. I was under a lot of pressure at the time. I know I did the wrong thing, but I didn't think I was doing something seriously wrong." One can accept the idea that people who are honest in making such statements have done something wrong but still are in friendship with God.

But what about somebody who commits a fully deliberate venial sin? Sam wants a newspaper, but he is out of change and does not want to bother getting any. Spying a vending machine with its door ajar, he glances around to make sure nobody is watching, then reaches in and slips out a paper. Sam knows exactly what he is doing, knows it is wrong, and deliberately chooses to do it.

Still, no one would say stealing a newspaper in this way is, in and of itself, a mortal sin. It is a venial sin because it involves light matter. Sam, like all the rest of us, ought to love God wholeheartedly, and his deliberate venial sin is not consistent with that. But even so, as a venial sin it does not separate him from the love of God. Why not? That is the problem.

There is also a subordinate problem: Why is the line drawn just where it is? It might not be so mysterious if the only grave matters were, say, idolatry, adultery, and homicide. But what about things which do not obviously conflict with one's relationship with God and/or other people—suicide, say, or the mere thought of fornicating? It is clear that the tradition treats these as grave matters, but not so clear why. Moreover, some acts which clearly *are* in conflict with a harmonious relationship with God or other people—skipping morning prayers, say, or honking your horn at a driver who is maddeningly slow making a turn—are just as clearly *not* the matter of mortal sins.

The best attempt in the tradition to deal with these questions is that of St. Thomas Aquinas. He says in some places that mortal sins are against love of God and neighbor, incompatible with the harmony of these relationships; blasphemy, idolatry, homicide, adultery, and theft are examples. Venial sins, on the other hand, are not against love of God and neighbor; they involve disorder in the relationships but are not totally incompatible with them.

Evidently he means that mortal sins violate religion or justice, while venial sins do not. But the problem with this explanation is simply that many grave matters do *not* obviously violate religion and justice.

St. Thomas also says grave sins are contrary to our ultimate end, heaven, while venial sins only interfere with means to that end. That could be so. But sins of the kind he considers mortal also interfere with means; while even small matters like stealing a newspaper are contrary to integral human fulfillment—consistent love of all the human goods—and so, it would seem, inconsistent with wholehearted love of the divine goodness, in which particular human goods are participations.

Popularizations of Thomas's account sometimes put it this way: "We are on a journey to heaven. Mortal sin means abandoning the journey, venial sin is dawdling on the way." Unfortunately, this attractive metaphor explains nothing. Dawdling can be as inconsistent with making a journey as abandoning it (dawdle enough, and you may well die before you get where you are going). Besides, people often commit mortal sins and promptly repent. They, too, might be said to be dawdling rather than quitting the journey.

St. Thomas's account is helpful in calling attention to the fact that mortal sins violate the commands to love God and neighbor while venial sins do not. But it leaves our problem unresolved. How can deliberate venial sins be compatible with love of God?

B: Fundamental Option Solves the Problem of Grave and Light Matter

We saw in chapter eight that people who reach moral maturity make a basic commitment which, supposing they wish to do the right thing, implies submission to moral truth as they understand it. We also discussed commitments in chapter nine, and saw that they are large choices which organize people's lives and relate them to other persons. Vocational choices are typical large commitments. They take in large sections of a person's life.

People gradually grasp the idea of morality as they grow up. Over a period of time, good commitments generally come to shape and direct the lives of those who want to live uprightly. If they marry, they want to have good marriages and raise their children as decent people—and that organizes much of their lives. If they have jobs, they want to do honest work at an honest trade or profession—and that also serves to organize their lives. Their lives as a whole are attempts at moral uprightness as they understand it.

People like this may eventually reach the point where, much of the time, they have very few choices of much moral significance to make. Good mothers or conscientious religious, for example, may find that what needs doing is perfectly clear for days or even weeks on end, for the routine of their lives reflects and expresses their basic commitments. Such people may even have few important temptations. Character does form; people trying to live upright lives which carry out good commitments can and do succeed with the help of God's grace.

There is a great difference between people who on the whole are trying to live morally upright lives and people who on the whole are not. The former want to know what is morally true and will generally try to follow it. But the latter see morality as simply somebody else's set of rules, one more limitation, alongside others, placed on their freedom to do as they please and get what they want. They have no real interest in living morally good lives; one might say they have not even opted into the moral game.

The foregoing is true of the living out of commitments in general. But what is the most basic commitment for Christians precisely *as Christians?* It is the act of faith. Of course, Christians can and do make other commitments besides this one. But faith is the commitment by which, precisely, a person able to make a choice about it becomes and remains a Christian.

Considered as a commitment, the act of faith is a choice to accept God's revelation in Jesus. In making that choice, one also commits oneself to moral uprightness, in recognition of the fact that leading a good life is God's will. As the baptismal liturgy expresses it, one renounces Satan and all his works. Thus, it is part of the commitment of faith and its living out to recognize that, because God wants us to be good, we ought to seek moral truth and try to live by it.

Christian faith, moreover, is not simply a general orientation toward God or moral goodness, but the act, crucial to justification, of turning away from sin and seeking the righteousness of God in Christ. It is a commitment to Jesus which means trying to live according to his model: to follow him and be like him.

The act of faith is a specific commitment, which brings those who make it into a relationship with certain other persons. One commits oneself first to Jesus and then to others as brothers and sisters in him. One makes a commitment to the community of faith, the Church, and to certain definite goods: the truth of the gospel and the religious bond constituted by Jesus' redemptive act and expressed and nourished by the worship of the Christian community, the liturgy, and especially the Eucharist.

Obviously, people can and do make the act of faith while also committing themselves—or *not* committing themselves—to other humanly good things which are perfectly compatible with the act of faith itself. For example, a person can be a good Christian while marrying or not marrying, while pursuing or not pursuing one or another particular career. But what of things which are *not* perfectly compatible with faith? Here we get to the heart of our answer about the question of grave matter: It is every sort of act that is at odds with the specific responsibilities of making, maintaining, and carrying out the commitment of faith, including the responsibility of spreading the faith. Light matter is everything else which, though morally wrong, is not in one way or another at odds with faith or some responsibility consequent upon it.

We are not saying that only "sins against faith"—doubting a religious truth, for example—involve grave matter. They do. But so do sins of any kind which are incompatible with living as an active, effective member of the faith community, the Church.

Acts of some kinds are incompatible with being a faithful member of any community whatsoever. Murder and adultery, for example. The community of faith cannot tolerate such acts either. Thus, not only do things like idolatry and denial of religious truth violate the life of faith; so do all those kinds of acts which no decent human community can accept on the part of its members. These also are grave matters.

At the same time, the Church is not just *any* decent human community. It is a specific community, concerned with the truth of the gospel, the bond with God in Jesus, and the spreading of faith. Some acts which another community could tolerate in its members cannot be tolerated by the community of faith. A political society, for instance, cannot legislate against every kind of scandal, every way in which some people lead others into sin, but to lead others into *any* kind of grave sin is disruptive of what the Church is and is meant to do. The United States, as a pluralistic democracy, cannot adopt laws against misleading people about the truth of the gospel, but from the point of view of the community of faith, misleading people about the truth of the gospel is a very grave matter.

To anticipate a possible misunderstanding: No, we are not saying, contrary to what we said earlier, that only members of the Church can commit grave sins, nor are we saying that all those who are *not* members of the Church are *ipso facto* grave sinners. Recall that we are discussing the *matter* of grave sin. Other conditions—freedom and sufficient reflection—must also be met for particular choices to be gravely sinful. On the one hand, then, many people who are not and never will visibly and self-consciously be members of the community of faith—for example, the proverbial "good pagans"—are not guilty of grave sin by reason of that estrangement, on the assumption that choosing membership was never a realistic possibility for them. But on the other hand, people who "in good faith" are outside the community of faith can and do commit grave sins if they deliberately choose acts which they realize are of a kind incompatible with membership in any decent community.

Christians do many things which have no direct relationship with faith and the life of faith. Ideally, nevertheless, they will eventually be related to faith.

Suppose Margaret chooses a career as a singer. Suppose, too, that she deliberately chooses to perform music of poor quality rather than music of good quality, in the belief that she will make more money that way. This might be an artistic "sin," but it is not a mortal sin, since her commitment to music is not—yet—integrally related to the commitment of faith.

Ideally, though, it should be. Perhaps over a period of time Margaret comes to see her singing career in just these terms—as part of her following of Jesus and her service to his kingdom. She comes, in short, to see singing as a vocational commitment. Once she does, her performance of music she judges to be of poor quality could constitute a serious violation of that commitment, and so might be grave matter.

Still, Christians can do many things which are inconsistent with complete openness to integral human fulfillment—things like taking newspapers from vending machines without paying—and which are therefore immoral, but which are not at odds with faith. Such acts are inconsistent with perfect love of God and are at war with the self-integration of those who do them, yet they are light matter. They are wrong, but they are not excluded by the commitment of faith or by any of its specific requirements. These things are venial sins.

By contrast, mortal sin does violate the commitment of faith in some way—either the requirements of faith itself, or the specific requirements of membership in the community of faith, or the requirements of membership in any decent human community, of which the community of faith is one. A person who commits a mortal sin may accept all the truths of faith, believe everything the Church teaches; yet he or she is willing to violate the duties of the life of faith. In effect, the mortal sinner says, "I know this is incompatible with living out my commitment of faith, but I want it and therefore I am going to do it." That is mortal sin.

The Church does not arbitrarily declare some kinds of acts grave matter. Either by experience or by revelation, the Church knows such acts cannot be tolerated in Christian life: they undermine the individual's faith, disrupt the Christian community, or subvert the community's effectiveness in witnessing to Christ and spreading the gospel. Light matters, by contrast, are those which the Church knows do not subvert faith. Such acts are wrong; someone who loved God perfectly would not do them; yet doing them is compatible with keeping and spreading the faith.

Even so, not everyone may find it obvious why some grave matters are subversive of faith. That is certainly the case today with certain kinds of sexual sins. "What's so wrong with doing that?" many people ask. "No one is harmed by it. Even when I do such things, I still love Jesus in my heart."

Since the Church's teaching that something is grave matter—at odds with faith—is based either on experience or revelation, that is a sufficient response to someone who objects "*I* don't see it." But it is also true that when a member of the Church deliberately chooses to do what the Church teaches is grave matter, he or she is being seriously unfaithful. Even when one does not understand why something is gravely wrong, willingness to do it despite the Church's teaching is willingness to set aside the Church and what it teaches. That is incompatible with being a faithful member of the Church.

Granted, confusion and the effects of bad advice and bad example play a significant role in the behavior of many people who take this attitude. Yet willing disregard of the Church's teaching that something is grave matter is itself grave matter—incompatible with faithfulness to the community of faith—whether or not a particular individual grasps that fact.

The analogy with acts inconsistent with the commitment of marriage—"infidelity" in a broad sense—sheds light on mortal sin.

The Bible often speaks of the relationship to God as being something like a marriage. Many acts inconsistent with the ideal of married love are nevertheless not radically disruptive of the relationship: little deeds of selfishness and bad humor like deliberately staying in the shower an extra couple of minutes when your wife wants to use the bathroom or knowingly playing the television louder than necessary when your husband is trying to take a nap. People who loved each other perfectly would not act like that.

Still, these petty deeds are not at odds with the marriage relationship as are a wife's adultery with an old flame or a husband's beating his wife to settle an argument about money. There are wrongs which the relationship can stand and wrongs it cannot stand. Indeed, this is true of any relationship. Some wrongs fall short of what the relationship ideally ought to be without tending to destroy it; others *are* destructive of the relationship and must be excluded by anyone serious about the commitment. The same is true of the commitment of faith and membership in the community of faith, the Church. Herein lies the distinction between grave and light matter.

C: Another Theory of Fundamental Option Widespread Today

The principal alternative to this understanding of fundamental option is an approach which proceeds along the following lines: Somehow or other, everyone simply and directly opts for or against God; either we choose God or we choose ourselves; and this option decides our moral orientation and moral character. But who is conscious of making such a choice? No one. And since no one is aware of it, evidently the option in question is not a choice. Rather, it must be an exercise of a sort of freedom more fundamental than free choice, a basic freedom. This freedom operates outside consciousness, which is why we are not aware of our fundamental option when we make it. But even though no one knows when or how, everybody does make this crucial option.

The basis of this theory is found in Kant's metaphysics. He believed that the world of experience is totally ruled by determinism; that world, which includes human psychic activity, is something like a huge machine. Being a decent individual, however, Kant wished to find a place in his system for morality and moral responsibility. If the world of experience is altogether determined, morality and responsibility cannot reside there, since they require freedom. So Kant situated freedom and moral responsibility outside experience.

With all due respect to Kant, this is an incoherent theory, which even philosophers who take Kant seriously and agree with him about many things do not try to defend. Today, nevertheless, the theory has great appeal in moral theology. Offering an alternative to legalism and its concentration on isolated acts, it focuses instead on one's overall relationship with God, a matter of undeniable importance for any religious believer.

Moreover, one must agree with this theory insofar as it does at least introduce the notion of an overarching self-commitment into the consideration of morality. Classical moral theology undoubtedly did place too much stress on isolated actions, on a list of mortal sins to be avoided, and in doing so gave the impression that *this*, and nothing more, was what morality was all about. But the life of faith should clearly be a unified and continuous whole; all that a person of faith does should have its place in his or her life of faith. Classical moral theology is of little help in explaining how this can be so, or even why it ought to be so. The idea that everyone makes a fundamental option for or against God appears to provide the required explanation.

The account given by classical moral theology also raises a problem about charity (of which we shall have more to say in chapter twenty-five). What is charity? It seems implausible that loving God with Christian love is a particular choice. It appears to make more sense to identify it with a fundamental opting for God. As a matter of fact, we shall argue that Christian love of God is neither a choice nor any other sort of opting. But if it *were* some kind of opting, it would be hard to accept the idea that it was a particular choice. Attributing it to a fundamental option appears more reasonable.

Many respectable people sincerely believe in fundamental freedom and the idea of an unconscious option for or against God. We do not mean to belittle them in pointing out that this approach is appealing partly because it allows one to hold that particular immoral choices are not morally determinative of the one who makes them. Thus, someone who commits serious sins can say: "Yes, these *could* be signs of a bad fundamental option. However, I'm pretty sure my fundamental option is for God, and so I'm also confident that these sins of mine don't really count. Admittedly, I sometimes do bad things, but I'm not a bad person."

Of course, someone who became an overtly vicious person by sinning would probably have to be put down as having changed his or her fundamental option, or perhaps as having made a bad option in the first place. But most people who sin—even sin mortally—do not turn into visible monsters of iniquity. Thus, someone who believes in fundamental freedom and the fundamental option arising from it will be inclined to tell a run-of-the-mill sinner: "You probably are not changing your fundamental option when you do those things, so don't worry." This encourages the sinner to go on doing the same things without regarding them as mortal sins, without repenting of them, and without making any effort to stop committing them.

D: What Is Mistaken in This Theory

Even if what we have just said is true, however, it does not show that this theory of fundamental option is wrong. So—what *is* wrong with it?

To begin with, there is no evidence of a fundamental freedom and fundamental option outside consciousness, no evidence of an unconscious, basic choice for or against God. Kant's metaphysics, being incoherent, supplies no grounds for regarding these as realities.

Some Catholic exponents of fundamental option argue that the Council of Trent taught that we cannot know with certitude that we are in the state of grace; since we cannot know that, neither can we know with certitude whether we are *not* in the state of grace; thus, there must be a fundamental option outside consciousness. Karl Rahner proposed this argument in 1955.[9] It does not work.

For one thing, the basic premise is mistaken. Trent taught that we cannot know with the certitude *of faith* that we are in the state of grace; it did not teach that we cannot know this *with certitude*. (Some theologians at the time of Trent held that we can, and the Council did not repudiate their idea.) There is a vast difference between knowing something with certitude and knowing it with the certitude of faith. One knows all sorts of things—for instance, that one is now reading a book—with certitude, but not with the certitude of faith. Whether or not we can really know with certitude that we are in the state of grace, one can take the position that it is possible without denying the teaching of Trent.

But even if we cannot know for certain when we are in the state of grace, we *do* know when we commit mortal sins, and until such time as we repent, we also know that we are *not* in the state of grace. In other words, people may be unable to tell for sure when they are in the state of grace, but they can tell for sure when they are not. There is no contradiction in this. Being in the state of grace is analogous to being healthy: We cannot know with certitude that we are healthy, for a person can feel fine, have a complete physical examination, get a clean bill of health, and drop dead on the way home from the doctor's. Usually, though, we can know with certitude when we are sick; people dying of cancer ordinarily know it beyond the shadow of a doubt. So, not only does Rahner's argument have a false basic premise, but its intermediate conclusion (we cannot know with certitude that we are *not* in the state of grace) does not even follow from that basic premise.

Recall, too, that the problem with which we began was how there can be such a thing as *light* matter. If, however, our fundamental option is simply love of God—a choice to be "for" God—all matter of sin would be grave, since any immorality is at odds with God's goodness and with perfect love for him. Love is not specific; perfect love is wholehearted, unqualified. So, if love were the fundamental option, there could be no light matter. Faith, by contrast, is specific; it is a commitment to Jesus Christ and to certain specific things. But even much of a believer's life is unrelated to faith or related to it only indirectly and remotely. Thus, faith as the fundamental option leaves room for light matter while love does not. But since faith, not love, is the fundamental option, there is light matter.

Moreover, proponents of the fundamental option theory which we are criticizing give no real account of the relationship between fundamental option and particular choices. "There are," they say, "some things which are likely to change a good fundamental option for the worse." But why and how? Why does stealing a newspaper from a vending machine not change one's fundamental option, while doing something else may? To try to explain it, fundamental option literature uses words like "expressing" and "disposing," "central" and "peripheral," "core" and "superficial"; but these are metaphors, pictures in words, not explanations. Indeed, exponents of this theory cannot explain the connection between a religious convert's choice—of faith and baptism—and that person's fundamental option for God. They cannot do so because a convert's choices, including the commitment of faith itself, are *particular* choices, and by their account fundamental option is not a particular choice.

Proponents of this theory never say that any specific kind of act will inevitably destroy a good fundamental option, and so they do not explain how that happens either. If consistent, they believe it impossible to know one is in a state of sin. Apparently, then, we can examine our consciences forever, yet never know when we need to repent. But the conclusion which fundamental option theorists prefer to draw is rather different: "Surely, people willing to go to the trouble of examining their consciences can assume that their fundamental option is in good order." In that case, however, willingness to examine one's conscience will suffice; no one need actually do so, and indeed the exercise will not—cannot—produce any useful information.

As a practical matter, this theory is likely to lead to presumption. For, whatever its proponents' intentions, people are likely to understand them as if they were saying: "Don't worry about these things you do which have traditionally been regarded as mortal sins. God loves you and he is very merciful. Just be careful that your whole life—your fundamental option—isn't sinful. You want to be safe? Along with these problematical things which you keep doing, do some other things which are clearly good. Be charitable; don't be judgmental toward others. That way you can be sure your fundamental option hasn't changed for the worse."

This is pharisaism, a bookkeeping morality. "Keep the right balance in your life. Make sure that what is good outweighs the faults, imperfections, mistakes—sins, if you will. Your fundamental option remains in place."

Thus, the radical distinction between mortal sin and venial sin vanishes. Yet that radical distinction is an essential element of the Church's teaching. On this theory, one never knows whether things the Church has taught are mortal sins really are such. For instance, the Council of Trent solemnly teaches that God's kingdom excludes "not only those without faith, but also those with faith who are fornicators, adulterers, effeminate, sodomites, thieves, covetous, drunkards, evil-tongued, greedy (cf. 1 Cor 6:9)" (DS 1544/808). But on the assumption that there is enough goodness in one's life to indicate the presence of a sound fundamental option, one need not avoid such deeds or repent of them or be absolved when one does them. Why then receive the sacrament of penance, except perhaps, once in a great while, for reassurance and emotional support?

Much rationalization has gone into elaborating and bolstering up this theory of fundamental option, but it has no better support than discredited Kantian metaphysics and a fallacious argument based on a misunderstanding of the teaching of the Council of Trent. Anyone who holds this position is in deep trouble theoretically, and, one fears, those who rely on it may be in deep trouble practically.

17. Sufficient Reflection; Sins of Weakness

When we explained what mortal sin is (in chapter 15:B), we briefly stated its three conditions: grave matter, sufficient reflection, and full consent. Having dealt in chapter sixteen with contemporary problems about grave matter, we now turn to sufficient reflection and full consent. With regard to the former, the question is whether an individual's immaturity or the general confusion about the Church's moral teaching can render sufficient reflection impossible. With regard to the latter, while everyone knows that weakness limits responsibility, the question is whether it can do so to such an extent that what would otherwise be mortal sins are venial. And what is this "weakness" we refer to in speaking of sins of weakness?

We take up five specific topics: exactly what is necessary for sufficient reflection; what weakness of will is; various kinds of sins of weakness; quasi-compulsive sins of weakness; and whether people who commit sins of this latter sort can stop committing them.

A: Exactly What Is Necessary for Sufficient Reflection?

Sufficient reflection is one of the conditions for mortal sin. Not having made a judgment of conscience that something is or may be gravely wrong, one cannot act against such a judgment, and so one cannot commit a mortal sin. But since a judgment of conscience is knowledge of moral truth, and since not everyone knows moral truth equally well, how fully must one understand the grave immorality of an act for one's conscience to have met the condition of sufficient reflection?

Nobody doubts that the condition is met in those who really know, in the light of faith, why an act is sinful—who grasp the inherent value of being morally good, understand why they should follow conscience both in general and in the particular case, see the goods at stake here and their relevance to divine goodness, and perceive the connection between human fulfillment in general and fulfillment in Christ.

While this may sound like a lot, many people who are not philosophers or theologians do have this kind of knowledge about many kinds of acts. Most Christians, for example, have no trouble seeing not only that it is wrong to kill in cold blood but why: This is not loving one's neighbor, and if we do not love our neighbor, how can we claim to love God whom we do not see?

Someone who does not grasp even this much about a sinful act nevertheless can have *adequate* sufficient reflection. This is the case, for instance, with people who do not have faith yet grasp the moral truth that it would be seriously wrong to make a certain choice. It is also the case with people of faith who do not see why an action is gravely wrong, but who know that this is what the Church teaches and who believe that, because the Church teaches in Jesus' name, they ought to heed its teaching and try to live by it. Sufficient reflection is present even if such a person supposes, legalistically, that the Church's teaching is simply a rule and wishes the Church would change it ("I wish the Church would lift its ban on birth control"). If this individual believes the Church's "rules" truly ought to be obeyed (because these "rules" are backed up by Jesus himself, who, being God, really deserves our obedience), he or she has adequate sufficient reflection despite the legalistic framework.

But suppose someone grasps neither the seriousness of the matter in itself nor any real moral obligation to accept and follow the Church's moral teaching? Then he or she lacks sufficient reflection. This very likely is the case with some Catholics today on some of the Church's moral teachings, especially in the area of sexual morality. Living in a society in which the vast majority of people seem to have accepted a "new morality," they do not see why acts which are wrong in themselves are wrong, and, on top of that, they have been misled into thinking that the Church's teaching on such matters need not be followed. There are also immature Catholics, raised in the faith but not well instructed, who tend to think of membership in the Church more or less as they think of membership in a social club. They belong for the advantages they perceive in belonging, but they do not consider that membership entails accepting a body of moral truth and trying to live by it. They, too, may lack sufficient reflection with regard to certain kinds of acts.

It does not follow, however, that confused or immature Catholics lack sufficient reflection with regard to every kind of act. Someone confused about sexual morality to the point of lacking sufficient reflection in that area may nevertheless see why it is intrinsically wrong to do serious injustice to others. It is quite possible, for instance, that an individual who thinks there is nothing wrong with fornication (provided nobody gets hurt) does grasp that abortion is killing, and killing is seriously wrong.

Thus, our conclusion is not that confusion about the Church's moral teaching and religious immaturity excuse all the confused and immature people from all moral responsibility. The point is merely that in certain areas, and notably in the area of sexual morality, some Catholics today seem to lack sufficient reflection. Yet even they may feel ashamed of their immoral acts because of superego or may experience a certain uneasiness, on the level of conventional morality, concerning the fact that they are breaking the Church's "rules" by doing things which the Church calls mortal sins. Hence, if such Catholics lack sufficient reflection about certain matters, their guilt feelings are not an accurate gauge of their actual moral state.

B: What Weakness of Will Is

What is weakness of will? We have seen that the will, as a spiritual power, does not grow weak as muscles do, through neglect or abuse. So, how can a spiritual power be said to be weak or, for that matter, strong?

Someone might reply that emotion can get the better of will. But how? Emotion and will do not directly interact. The will determines itself on the basis of intellectual judgment: it is not directly affected by emotion, nor does it affect emotion directly.

Emotions do not compel choices, for we can, and sometimes do, choose contrary to strong emotion. Similarly, willing cannot change how we feel. An angry individual who wants not to be angry is angry just the same.

The will, however, can act indirectly on emotion by affecting attention and action. We imply as much in telling someone with troublesome feelings, "Don't keep stewing over it." If Jack is angry at Fred, he may be able to conquer his anger by deliberately dwelling on Fred's good points instead of whatever it is about Fred that annoys him. He can also choose—contrary to feelings—to do Fred a good turn, literally or metaphorically extending the hand of friendship, and in this way also get the better of his anger.

Emotions, for their part, similarly affect the will indirectly, by focusing attention and influencing our perception of the good. This is how ordinary and not particularly strong emotion leads to action even without willing, provided there is no conflicting inclination. For example: you begin to feel tired; it occurs to you that a brisk walk would perk you up; emotional desire to take the walk arises; you see no reason against it; and so you put aside what you are doing and take the walk. This is intelligently guided action: one knowingly does something emotionally attractive, but does it without choosing because there is no inclination *not* to do it (and therefore no need to make a choice).

Emotion also indirectly affects the will when we choose, by bringing various options to our attention. We only need to make choices because conflicting emotional drives and impulses make us aware of different attractive possibilities. Thus, before choice, emotion stirs up reflection and leads to the consideration of certain possibilities, which are then understood as embodiments of intelligible goods. Without emotion, we would never have any conflicting possibilities to consider, evaluate, and make choices about.

Even after a choice has been made, strong emotion can continue to have an effect by recalling rejected possibilities to mind. Jack is angry at Kate and feels like doing something nasty to her. "I shouldn't do that," Jack tells himself, and puts it out of his mind—for a while. But anger causes the idea to come back, so that Jack finds himself deliberating again about something he rejected earlier.

This can happen over and over. It is like a deliberative assembly where a stubborn minority which has lost a vote keeps bringing up the same proposal again and again. Eventually the assembly's other members may be tempted to give in just to end the harassment. Similarly, Jack may be tempted to give in and do his bit of nastiness to Kate just—as he supposes—to put his mind at rest. This insistent proposing of possibilities is one way in which strong emotion influences deliberation.

Another is by drawing attention to certain possibilities' attractive features while distracting it from their unattractive ones. This trick that strong emotion has—of highlighting certain aspects of alternatives about which one is deliberating while concealing others—can change the character of a choice. Once more, anger can be used to illustrate the point.

We all know we should not lash out in anger. Among other reasons, people who act out anger may themselves get hurt. But emotion can blind those who ordinarily know better to such simple facts. Sybil is cut off at an intersection by another driver. Furious, she sets out after the offender at high speed, leaning on her horn. In different circumstances, she would realize that, morality aside, this is stupid because she is risking an accident. Enraged as she is, however, she thinks of nothing but the anticipated pleasure of doing to the other driver as the other driver did to her, while overlooking the fact that she may kill herself in the process.

Thus, we see how sins of weakness come about. While emotion does not "weaken" the will directly, it works indirectly, bringing possibilities to our attention, oftentimes repeatedly, and urging us to see their positive aspects while overlooking their negative ones.

C: Various Kinds of Sins of Weakness

For the rest of this chapter, what we say about sins of weakness assumes that grave matter is involved. Of course there are sins of weakness in light matter, too, but if one understands what is said here about sins of weakness involving grave matter, it will not be difficult to apply it as required to those which involve light matter.

Before considering various kinds of sins of weakness, we first set aside two kinds of behavior which are not sins of weakness but can be confused with them.

In the first case, circumstances mitigate guilt. Zack, whose family is in desperate straits, steals from another poor man. That is morally wrong, and it could be a serious sin of theft. But it is not as wrong as it would be if Zack were well-to-do. His poverty is a circumstance which mitigates his guilt. It does not make it right for him to steal from another poor man, but it makes his theft less wrong than it would otherwise be.

In the second case, behavior which would be morally wrong if it were chosen is done without choice. This is not a sin of weakness because, being involuntary, it is not a sin at all. Think of Lucy, tortured or terrified to the point of no longer being able to choose but only to react. What she may do is not a sin—and, specifically, not a sin of weakness—because it is not even her own act in any morally relevant sense.

What, then, are real sins of weakness? To begin with, there are three kinds which pose no special problems.

First, emotion sometimes keeps a person from making a choice which should be made: there is a voluntary but choiceless omission in grave matter. Philip knows he ought to urge his eighteen-year-old daughter not to date a divorced man of thirty, but he dreads having a scene with the girl, and so he never gets around to choosing either to do it or not to do it. This is a sin of weakness; anxiety keeps Philip from making a choice to do his duty; but as long as he does not *choose* to neglect it, he does not commit a mortal sin.

(Lest this sound like an easy loophole for avoiding duty in a serious matter without doing anything seriously wrong, we should add that people sometimes engage purposely in a form of mental gymnastics which might be called choosing not to choose: they deliberately avoid confronting something painful which they know they ought to confront. The choice not to choose may be as wrong as a direct choice not to do one's duty.)

Second, someone recognizes that something is gravely evil and chooses to do it, but emotion distracts the person from the gravity of the evil at the time of the choice. Earlier, he or she was fully aware: "That would be a mortal sin if I did it." But when the time actually comes to make a choice, emotion blots out awareness of the sinful character of the act while highlighting other, appealing aspects. Factors like illness, intoxication, and fatigue often play a role. Emotion makes reflection which had been sufficient no longer sufficient. There is a sin of weakness, but not a mortal sin.

In the third case, strong emotion is a factor in an isolated sinful act in which all the conditions for mortal sin are met. The act is one the individual usually would not do, but, under the influence of the emotion, he or she does it on this particular occasion. Linda, who is customarily honest and responsible about doing her work, panics at the prospect of failing an important course and, though considering it seriously wrong, cheats to get a good grade on the final exam. People who behave as Linda does commit mortal sins of weakness.

Such sins can occur in matters of all sorts and under the influence of every sort of emotion. King David's sin of adultery, along with his associated sin in causing the death of Uriah, is an instance from the Old Testament. Although sins of this sort are indeed sins "of weakness," that does not make them venial sins; there is no reason to suppose them anything but mortal sins when the three conditions for mortal sin are met.

D: Quasi-compulsive Sins of Weakness

As we have said, these three kinds of sins of weakness pose no special problems. But what we here call "quasi-compulsive" sins of weakness do. (Note the qualifier "quasi." Behavior which is genuinely compulsive is not sinful—indeed, is not morally relevant in itself.)

Sins of this kind can concern matters of various sorts—sex, drinking, and drugs, of course, but also, not uncommonly, matters relating to hostility. Some people sin repetitively through weakness in matters having to do with anger and hatred. Whatever the particular subject matter, this kind of sin meets the usual conditions for mortal sin, yet it is part of a pattern: temptation, struggle, sin, repentance—and then, after an interval, the fresh onset of temptation and a renewal of the cycle.

Three factors define this kind of sin. First, the individual always recognizes its gravity and most of the time wants to avoid it. Second, when temptation arises, there is a real struggle, because there is a real will to avoid sin. Third, although emotion does not distract the person from the gravity of the act, it does impoverish his or her awareness of alternatives, to such a point that the individual may say in effect, "I can either keep struggling with this temptation forever, or else I can give in, perform the act, regain my normal state of mind, and then repent." And, so reasoning, he or she commits the sin, aware that it is seriously wrong but imagining that the alternative to giving in is to be forever robbed by temptation of peace of mind.

It might well be helpful to explore the psychological factors underlying this sort of situation, but that is not our concern here. The question, rather, is this: Are these quasi-compulsive sins of weakness really mortal sins?

This question has real practical relevance. For much of this century, and even before the theological dissent which began in the 1960s, pastoral practice has taken an increasingly mild view of such sins. Even some bishops who uphold received Catholic moral teaching have given pastoral directives (for example, with regard to couples who practice contraception) which make sense only if quasi-compulsive sins of weakness are not mortal sins. The advice amounts to saying: "You should try to get the better of this, to stop doing what you're doing, but as long as you are struggling, don't regard it as mortal sin."

There are, however, two theological reasons for thinking that quasi-compulsive sins of weakness which meet the usual three conditions for mortal sin really are mortal sins.

One is that this view was clearly part of the Church's teaching and pastoral practice for centuries about which we have solid information—that is, for the centuries, up to this one, since the Council of Trent. (It may very well also have been the Church's teaching and practice in the centuries *before* Trent. But the historical record—seminary education, textbooks, questions submitted to the Holy Office and its replies, and so on—is crystal clear from the sixteen hundreds on.) Catholics throughout the world were consistently told: "These are grave sins. To choose to do them, knowing that, is mortally sinful." Pastoral practice followed logically on this view: "If you sin in this way, you must go to confession before you receive Communion."

Why is this a theological reason for believing that quasi-compulsive sins of weakness are mortal sins? In chapter thirty-five we shall see that, when the whole Church teaches something as binding on consciences, even in the absence of a solemn definition, it is as binding as if it were defined. This does not mean that everything the Church does and says is absolutely unchangeable. But, as we shall argue later, when the Church teaches in *this* way, it cannot be mistaken. And—relevant to the question here at issue—this seems clearly to have been how, during the centuries after the Council of Trent, the Church taught that quasi-compulsive sins of weakness are mortal sins.

The second theological reason is that the Church's teaching on this point has been reaffirmed precisely in the context of the theological dissent since the Second Vatican Council. In 1975 the Congregation for the Doctrine of the Faith published a *Declaration on Certain Questions Concerning Sexual Ethics* stating, among other things, that when an act appears to meet the usual conditions for mortal sin—grave matter, sufficient reflection, consent—it must be presumed in general that mortal sin is committed.[10] (This, naturally, was not well received by dissenting theologians, but that is another problem, to be considered in chapter thirty-six.)

Earlier, Pope Pius XII had made the same point, in a discourse on forming the consciences of the young which Vatican II cited (see *DH* 14) and thus incorporated as part of its own teaching: "We reject . . . as erroneous the claim of those who consider inevitable the failings of the age of puberty, considered by them of no great import and almost as if they were not a grave fault, because, they add, passion cancels the liberty which is required to make a person morally responsible for an act."[11]

We do not suggest that guilt cannot be mitigated. The Congregation for the Doctrine of the Faith in its *Declaration* specifically makes the point that it can, by factors like immaturity, psychological imbalance, and habit. We have already seen how this can happen in the case of immaturity, which, along with a legalistic mentality, can prevent a person from seeing that Christian moral norms—say, concerning sex—are truths rather than rules. Psychological imbalance and habit can distract a person from the gravity of what he or she is doing; sometimes it can even lead to behavior which does not really arise from a free choice. But even so, our central point—and the Congregation's—remains: If in the case of what seems to be a quasi-compulsive sin of weakness the three conditions for mortal sin are really met, then it is really a mortal sin.

This argument, based on the Church's authority, is confirmed when one considers what mortal sin and free choice are. A mortal sin is a self-determining choice—free and knowing—not to live up to the requirements set by faith. The state of mind of a Christian confronting, with sufficient reflection, a choice which concerns grave matter is: "If I do this, I am not living up to the requirements of Christian life." If, nevertheless, this person, out of weakness, makes the wrongful choice, it is as if he or she were taking a break from living in union with Christ: "Of course I'll repent and return, but right now. . . . "

Choices, however, really are effective; we are really morally responsible for what we choose. If one supposes otherwise, one is in the position of saying, "I chose that, but I didn't *really* choose it—I chose something else." But what? Perhaps thinking this way makes some people feel better; but it undermines the reality of free choice and moral responsibility, while not altering the fact that what people choose is really what they choose and are responsible for.

The only alternative is to posit something like the mysterious fundamental option, by which some sort of unconscious act, not the choices one knowingly makes, is what determines one's moral self. But we already have seen why such a theory is unacceptable. Thus, quasi-compulsive sinners should be presumed to be sinning mortally.

"But in some cases," someone might object, "I just don't believe they are. I mean cases when people struggle heroically against their temptation and are truly anguished when they fall." Even here, of course, it is fair to ask how anyone can *know* that such people do not commit mortal sins. But we also concede that what appears, to an observer, to be a pattern of quasi-compulsive sins of weakness may actually be something else. It may be behavior which is genuinely compulsive or otherwise psychologically pathological. Or it may be that an individual lacks sufficient reflection. An adolescent boy may have heard that masturbation is a mortal sin, yet not grasp the truth of that moral norm, while lacking insight at the level of moral truth concerning his responsibility to try to live the Christian life, at least in this particular matter. (Bad religious instruction and conscience formation may contribute to such confusion.) In short, some people who seem to be sinning mortally by committing quasi-compulsive sins of weakness may not really be doing so, either because they are not making choices or because they do not have sufficient reflection.

But if people see that they ought to accept what the Church teaches (even though they do not see the intrinsic reasons), that they ought to try to live up to it, and that *this* is what the Church teaches about this particular matter, they have sufficient reflection. And if they freely choose to perform the action in question despite what they know, they commit mortal sins. By all means, let us make all possible allowance for confused adolescents and persons with disabling psychological conditions: the rest of us, however, do not have these excuses.

E: Can People Who Commit Sins of This Sort Stop Committing Them?

Since we must suppose that quasi-compulsive sins of weakness are mortal sins, they should be confessed. But in confessing mortal sin, real contrition is required, and real contrition requires a real purpose of amendment. This raises an obvious question: *Can* people who commit quasi-compulsive sins of weakness—with all their patterned, repetitive character—simply stop sinning?

The answer must be yes. Someone who commits a mortal sin is morally responsible for it; and that is to say he or she freely chooses to commit it. But someone who makes a free choice to commit sin also can pray for God's grace and with its help make a free choice not to sin.

As for someone who does seek God's help but really cannot stop committing what look like quasi-compulsive sins of weakness: if he or she *cannot* choose to stop sinning, neither is he or she sinning by choice, so what seem to be quasi-compulsive sins of weakness are not. (Even so, someone who acts in the throes of genuine compulsion may be able to do something to conquer the compulsive behavior in the intervals when the compulsion is not acute. A kleptomaniac can seek psychotherapy; a compulsive drinker can turn to Alcoholics Anonymous. People with problems like these have a real obligation to take such steps when they can. If they fail to do so, they are wrongfully failing to do their duty.)

It may also be that someone committing what appear to be quasi-compulsive sins of weakness does not see, in the way required for sufficient reflection, that the act in question is seriously wrong; and, not seeing that it is wrong, he or she may continue to choose to do it, and be unable to choose *not* to do it, because it is very appealing. (This also is how venial sin has a certain inevitability for all of us who are not well advanced in virtue. Practically speaking, we are unable always to choose the right thing when faced with sinful—but "only" venially sinful—alternatives. There is no absolute necessity that we commit venial sin, but there is a practical inevitability, given the appeal of the sinful alternative, the seeming unimportance of venial sin, and our human capacity for rationalizing.)

But if people really do have sufficient reflection, and really do freely choose to do what they know is wrong, then with God's help they could also choose not to do it. Otherwise one is in the position of saying that such people are free (to choose to do what is wrong) and at the same time not free (to choose not to do it), which makes no sense.

That people who commit quasi-compulsive sins of weakness can stop committing them does *not* mean that they can stop without God's help. Grace is necessary, and its availability and sufficiency are taught very clearly and firmly by the Church. Paul quotes his Lord and ours: "My grace is sufficient for you" (2 Cor 12:9). The Fathers of the Church insist that God gives sufficient grace. "A man, helped by God, can, if he will, be without sin," declares St. Augustine.[12] And the Council of Trent teaches definitively that God gives sufficient grace so that mortal sin can be entirely avoided (see DS 1536/804, 1568/828).

Humanly speaking, however, a person must not only ask God for his help but, in order to do so, believe that he or she can stop sinning. Someone with the attitude "I can't stop, no matter what I do" almost certainly will not stop. Trust in God's goodness and in the availability of his grace is essential. On this basis, anyone who regularly commits quasi-compulsive sins of weakness can stop committing them.

This solution to the problem of quasi-compulsive sins of weakness is rendered a practical impossibility by pastoral counseling which tells people, "Nobody expects you just to stop. All that's required is that you work at it. As long as you're trying, you can be sure that what you're doing is a venial sin at most."

As a formal position, this latter approach is sometimes called "gradualism." The idea is that the moral requirements of Christian life are ideals which many people cannot live up to all at once but only little by little; although violations of the ideals are not desirable, still for people generally striving in the right direction they are not mortal sins.

Some participants in the 1980 Synod of Bishops suggested this view. It was rejected by Pope John Paul II at the end of the Synod and later in the apostolic exhortation *Familiaris Consortio*.[13] It is not acceptable, he said, to speak of gradualism as if different people had different obligations, as they would if there were a gradualism of the moral requirement itself. Everyone is obliged to accept the whole moral truth which a Christian life requires and try to live up to it now, not eventually and little by little. It is true that Christian life is a gradual growth in, or toward, holiness, and that sin and repentance are part of the process. But mortal sins do not have to be part of it, and, where they are, they do not become venial for that reason.

18. The Way of Sin to Death

To complete our discussion of sin, we need to consider the stages of a sinful life, beginning with imperfection, which is not sin, and ending with hell.

There is in this progression a certain dynamic, with a kind of inner logic, but no necessity. The steps are not taken automatically. The entire process depends on free choice. Moreover, a sinner can bypass particular stages in the downward path or, with the help of grace, can reverse direction and speed heavenward.

We consider five topics: how imperfection opens the way to temptation; how venial sins lead to mortal sins; how persistence in mortal sin leads to final impenitence; why impenitent sinners end in hell; and whether God can be said to "send" sinners to hell.

A: How Imperfection Opens the Way to Temptation

Imperfection is the lack of holiness in a person insofar as his or her life is not integrated with living faith. Even good and mature Christians are less than perfectly integrated. They have faith and, probably, they generally try to live as faith would have them do; yet some aspects of their lives are not related to—they stand outside and apart from—the commitment of faith.

There are two kinds of imperfection. The first, which is inevitable, is the imperfection of immaturity. Human beings must develop to a certain point before they can exercise their freedom of self-determination, and only by doing so can they set themselves toward moral goodness. As children, even Jesus and Mary were subject to the imperfection of moral immaturity; they grew morally, from the indeterminacy of childhood innocence to the

211

maturity of total self-commitment. Obviously, there is nothing sinful about this unavoidable kind of imperfection.

The second kind of imperfection is the imperfection of disintegrity. *Except* for Jesus and Mary, it too is universal in fallen humankind. Its elements are similarly not sinful, but they can be obstacles to integration. Suppose a child likes physical comfort. All children—all human beings—do, and there is nothing wrong with that. But love of comfort, associated with the more or less disordered human emotional makeup arising from original sin, makes it difficult for the child, and later for the adult, to practice the self-discipline and restraint necessary for self-mastery and growth in holiness. It complicates the task of putting creature comforts and the desire for them in their place—that is, at the service of faith. It inclines one to self-indulgence and cowardice, which give rise to temptations that lead to sin.

The desire for admiration provides another example. Everyone wants to be admired, and there is nothing sinful in that. This desire can be a motive for people to do good and important things. Yet this craving is susceptible to corruption by a sinful culture which places exaggerated emphasis on competition and status. Against this cultural background it is difficult for people to integrate the desire for admiration with faith.

Because of imperfection of both sorts, our emotions are in different ways and degrees *not* integrated with faith. Emotions call our attention to possibilities inconsistent with the commitment of faith, and often enough these possibilities are appealing. This is temptation. Here, then, we have many inevitable temptations to venial sin.

Emotional urges to choose things which should not be chosen come from various sources. Some arise from self-centered desires. Others come from desires generated by relationships with other people. These may take the form of sympathy (the desire to approve what our friends are doing and to go along with them) or fear (the desire not to suffer injury at the hands of others, which leads us to give in to social pressure). Our self-centered desires and our sympathy with others or fear of them incline us to choose and do unreasonable things, things not consistent with the commitment of faith. Not everyone is strongly inclined toward mortal sin, but these urges are universal and make it virtually impossible to avoid venial sin.

Once we have sinned, even venially, we are tempted to integrate our whole self with the sinful self. If we do not repent of our venial sins, we want at least to be comfortable with them. But that requires rationalization. "There's nothing wrong with telling white lies." "Taking something that small isn't stealing." "I've got to have a little fun once in a while."

We may also begin to rationalize for the sake of maintaining good relationships with others. Social pressure then becomes a kind of moral principle to which we give undeserved status. "My buddies would think I was buttering up the boss if I never goofed off on company time." "Everybody at the party will have a new outfit; I can't wear any of these old rags!" Thus, we begin to make our own an outlook, a way of evaluating situations and behavior, embodying a view of reality and of moral values which is an alternative to the one proposed by faith.

Venial sin also leads people to modify their relationship with God, distorting it in ways which are not authentically religious. This can take different forms. Some turn to legalistic minimalism: "Since these sins are only venial, I can commit them and not go to hell." Others take up self-righteousness and fanaticism—the crusade against more serious evil in *other* people. In either case, the image of God will be distorted according to the sinfulness of the sinner.

B: How Venial Sins Lead to Mortal Sin

How does venial sin lead to mortal sin? Certainly not by accumulation—commit enough venial sins, and eventually they add up to a mortal sin. Nor is it true, in any simplistic sense, that the more venial sins one commits, the greater the chances become that sooner or later one will commit mortal sin. Venial sin does not lead to mortal sin by anything like a process of wear and tear. There is no law of nature about it.

Yet there *is* a dynamic relationship between the two things. If we regularly commit deliberate venial sins, sin seems less horrible and intimacy with God less desirable. Moreover, by committing venial sins, we come to have different options than if the sins had not been committed—bad options which very likely would not have existed without the sins. At the same time, the appeal of the bad options we had before can be enhanced. Insofar as venial sin

sets up a new option for committing mortal sin or a stronger reason for doing so, it leads to mortal sin. This can happen in several
ways.

Sometimes venial sins bring people into occasions for committing mortal sins. An adolescent, Jim, commits a sin of disobedience by going to a forbidden place where there are opportunities
to experiment with drugs and sex. He is tempted. If he had
obeyed and not gone there, the temptation would not have arisen.
Or: Jim's dad acquires excess wealth by committing venial sins,
and thereby acquires the means of committing various grave sins
which would otherwise have been beyond his reach.

Venial sins can also put a person in a bind from which it is
tempting to escape by committing mortal sin. Backing her car out
of a space in a shopping mall parking lot while trying to tune the
radio (a venial sin of carelessness), Gladys backs it into a parked
car. She can see at a glance that she has dented the other car to
the tune of several hundred dollars worth of body work. Now
Gladys faces a choice—and a temptation to serious sin: either
identify herself as the guilty party (and pay up) or drive off (and
commit mortal sin). The temptation would not have arisen if she
had not been sinfully careless.

Venial sins also generate objectives which one is tempted to
pursue by committing mortal sins. Not uncommonly, people
make career choices without integrating them with faith but just
for the sake of status seeking (venial sin); then they are tempted
to pursue their careers, and the status they crave—by gravely immoral means. Helen has some acting talent and she likes the lime-
light, so she decides to go on the stage. After a while she finds
out that other actresses get better parts by sleeping with produc-
ers, and she is tempted. Nothing against the theater: something
similar crops up in virtually every line of work—a temptation,
gross or subtle as the case may be, to get ahead by doing what is
seriously wrong. If we sin venially by failing to integrate our
choices with faith, the venial sinning will create a situation in
which we have objectives which, to be satisfied, will require committing mortal sin. Then we must either sin mortally or give up
the objectives. And by now, of course, we are very attached to
them.

These are ways in which venial sins lead to mortal sin. We repeat: there is no necessity about it. But venial sins place us in a position where we have different options and greater incentives to sin mortally than if we had not committed them.

C: How Persistence in Mortal Sin Leads to Final Impenitence

There is a traditional list, drawn from the works of St. Augustine, of sins against the Holy Spirit: impenitence, obduracy, presumption, despair, rejection of the known truth, and envy of the grace others enjoy. "Impenitence" can be understood in different ways, and we distinguish between initial impenitence and final impenitence. Taken together, the other sins on the list constitute a certain progression whose natural, though not inevitable, outcome is final impenitence.

The Church teaches very firmly that nothing is absolutely unforgivable except final impenitence, which means dying in sin. In passing through these several stages, however, the sinner becomes increasingly less likely to escape because increasingly less likely to repent. The options change as one proceeds through the stages of a sinful life.

After mortal sins of weakness, which one means soon to repent, the next step is to commit a mortal sin in which one means to remain. This is initial impenitence. Mike and Betty establish an immoral relationship on a more or less permanent basis. Paul, a used car salesman, defrauds his customers with no intention of making restitution. While not having it in mind to remain guilty forever, such people are willing to remain guilty for an indefinite period.

Next comes obduracy, that hardening of heart of which Scripture often speaks. Although these sinners entered into sin with no plan to repent, it sometimes occurs to them that they ought to do so. But they thrust the idea aside, almost as if it were a temptation.

Presumption follows. Deliberate refusal to repent creates an obvious problem: How can *that* be squared with faith? So it becomes necessary to dwell on the mercy of God and similar comforting thoughts. "God wouldn't send me to hell. I'm sure he'll give me time to repent at the end. And maybe there really isn't any hell. I'm not a bad person—I'm sure my fundamental option

is okay. I needn't repent, because I'm going to be saved anyway."
Presumption means supposing that one will be saved without cooperating with the grace of repentance. And now repentance is
harder than before, because it does not seem necessary.

Next, despair. The false confidence of presumption seeps away.
Perhaps the sinner experiments a bit with insincere repentance,
and finds that it does nothing for him or her psychologically: the
sense of guilt is the same as ever. So the previously presumptuous
sinner now reasons, "I'm no longer able to repent. God has cut
me off from grace. There's no hope for me."

If the sinner still has faith, he or she now confronts a horrify-
ing prospect. "I believe in God but I despair of being reconciled
with him. I'm facing hell." That insupportable tension is relieved
by rejection of the known truth—by ceasing to believe. "This
heaven and hell business isn't for real. It's just the carrot and the
stick the Church uses to manipulate people." (Indeed, the under-
mining of faith began much earlier. There is tension between faith
and sin all along the way we are tracing out. But at the point of
despair, it becomes virtually impossible to hold on to faith.)

Even so, a kind of residue of faith and Christian life remains, a
painful memory of what the sinner once enjoyed, and it makes
him or her ill at ease with unbelief. The tendency, therefore, is to
resent people who still have faith and seek to live by it. This is
what is meant by envy of the grace others enjoy. At this stage, a
sinner may even become militantly antireligious and strive to lead
others into sin by writing books which attack the Church's teaching or campaigning for an immoral cause like legal abortion.
(This partly explains why our secularized culture, reflected in the
mass media, is far from neutral toward Christian faith and Christian moral principles: people who have abandoned faith often turn
to trying to destroy the faith of others and corrupt them.)

And so the sinner comes to final impenitence. When "desire
has conceived, it gives birth to sin, and that sin, when it is fully
grown, gives birth to death" (Jas 1:15). The way of sin ends in
hell.

D: Why Impenitent Sinners End in Hell

Or does it? Not everyone cares to accept the conclusion that
impenitent sinners go to hell. There are several ways of arguing
the contrary.

One is to say that at the moment of death everyone has a final option, an opportunity like that of the angels to submit to God or reject him for all eternity. If so, everyone has a last chance to repent, and it can be assumed that even those furthest gone in sin, facing the immediate prospect of hell, are likely to exercise their option and repent. This idea has been advocated especially by Ladislaus Boros, S.J.[14]

But on what grounds? In the nature of things, there is and can be no direct evidence of a final option at death. Of course people can commend themselves to God before they die, but this theory assumes that in the moment of death itself people face something like a clear, straightforward choice between heaven and hell. Given that choice, who would choose hell?

Unlike angels, however, human beings make choices throughout a lifetime, and this way of thinking belittles the self-determining character of all these free choices. According to it, living a life has no ultimate seriousness, for, whatever one does here and now, one can count on opting successfully for heaven at the end. There is nothing in Scripture to support this view and a great deal against it. "See, *now* is the acceptable time; see, *now* is the day of salvation!" (2 Cor 6:2; emphasis added).

A second way of setting aside the idea that impenitent sinners go to hell is to posit an empty hell. Proponents of this view do not unequivocally deny hell's existence; they merely describe it as a real possibility which might never be realized. Hell is permanent alienation from God, and perhaps no one will ever be permanently alienated. However, this also seems inconsistent with Scripture and the teaching of the Church. The Church has taught solemnly—in a statement of the Fourth Lateran Council—that someone *is* in hell: the devil. One can of course deny the reality of angels and devils, but then one is abandoning Catholic faith. One can also dismiss what the New Testament says about hell by calling it "threat discourse," but then one is making God out to be bluffing, using the inspired words of Scripture to manipulate us with scare-talk.

Some few, finally, will suggest that everyone gets a chance to repent after death. But there is no evidence of this in experience or in revelation, and the Church has always taught that after death it is too late for repentance. Even Boros recognizes this, which is why he speaks of opting in the moment of death, not after.

What, then, does happen to impenitent sinners? Does God make them go to heaven in spite of themselves? If so, freedom is pointless. God offers human beings the choice of joining in heavenly communion with him and one another, but he offers that choice by offering them the chance to enter into the communion of the new covenant and live its law of love here and now. And if they choose not to, he does not overwhelm their freedom by somehow herding them after death into a communion they previously rejected. Does God then annihilate such people? It seems impossible to reconcile annihilation with the Church's teaching that hell is eternal. Moreover, we believe that God creates things good, and they cannot completely corrupt themselves. Whatever exists is good at least insofar as it exists; thus, if God annihilates sinners, he is annihilating creatures still in large part good, which hardly seems consistent with his role as creator.

As a practical matter, final option, empty hell, and the rest are part of a contemporary trend which encourages presumption. This trend places an unbalanced emphasis on God's mercy, while also misconstruing it. Certainly God is merciful. He does all he can to encourage us to repent. He sent his only Son to redeem us. But that only makes clear how perilous our human condition really is. If everyone has a final option or if hell actually is empty, Jesus need hardly have gone through what he did. We said earlier that these theories trivialize our lives; they also trivialize the life and death of Jesus.

What is hell? Essentially, it is existing apart from communion with God and those who are his friends. In other words, it is nothing else than unrepented mortal sin. Free choices last; in making sinful choices, we determine ourselves as sinners. Guilt is not something added on; it is being the sinner one is until one repents. And as mortal sin involves willing acceptance of alienation from God, so hell is the irreversibility of that state of affairs. A person who dies in mortal sin stays in mortal sin, and that is hell.

The Church also teaches that hell is a painful experience. That only makes sense, for human beings are unified wholes, and for such beings their situation, whatever it may be, necessarily has an impact on their experience. Scripture and Church teaching speak of the "fire" of hell. This is a symbol for the painful experience of eternal alienation from God, a sort of suffering we cannot imagine. We must believe that the fire of hell is real, in the sense that hell is a painful experience, but we need not take the scriptural images literally or identify the suffering of hell with poets' and artists' imaginative renderings. Sinners rising in their own bodies in a state of eternal separation from God will suffer that state as it truly is: a thoroughly wretched experience in body and soul. Whatever exactly the experience will consist in, that is the fire of hell.

Within this framework, we are free to add our own imaginative renderings of the experience of hellfire. Perhaps it is the undesired perception by the damned of the splendid new heavens and new earth, overflowing with the triumph of God's love, from which they have cut themselves off irrevocably. Perhaps it is the experience of committing one's favorite sin and doing nothing else—doing that and only that, over and over again, eternally. Perhaps it is like the self-inflicted anguish of a child who spitefully refuses to come to a birthday party, then has to listen to the other children playing in the yard next door without ever being able to give in and join them.

E: Whether God Sends Sinners to Hell

In speaking of punishment it is necessary to make a distinction.

One kind of punishment is educative or medicinal. God punishes people in this sense inasmuch as he lets them experience the reality of bad situations they are in so that they can take remedial action. For example, he allows people to die, and the fact of death tells us that there is something radically wrong with the human situation. But hell is not this kind of punishment, for there is no remedy for the situation of the damned.

Punishment of another kind is imposed by one person (or persons) on another (or others) in response to an offense. Albert is caught breaking and entering and is sent to jail; little Becky is discovered with her hand in the cookie jar and gets sent to her room. That is how we tend to think of punishment. Is hell like this?

Not at all. In thinking of punishment this way, we assume that the offender could be spared. Albert could get a suspended sentence. Becky's parents might laugh off her "crime." Punishment would be fair, but it does not *have* to be imposed.

If, however, the essence of hell is self-imposed alienation from communion with God and God's family, this punishment is not imposed by God at all. God does not alienate sinners from himself. God creates human persons to live in friendship with him, and he empowers them freely to accept his offer of friendship. If we then alienate ourselves from God, our punishment is to be alienated from him; but *we*, not God, do the alienating. This punishment is unavoidable. It is not something added on after the crime. It is the crime itself.

Hell is a man who betrays his friend. Judas and Jesus. No one did anything to Judas after he betrayed Jesus. His punishment was being what he had made himself—a betrayer. Being an unrepentant sinner alienated from God is the punishment for being an unrepentant sinner alienated from God. That is hell.

Thus, God does not send anyone to hell. He creates people and gives them freedom, so that they can choose freely to be his friends and to live in neighborly solidarity with one another. (There is no way of being a friend and neighbor except freely.) God knows that some of those he creates will not make good choices, yet, because they are free, he cannot force them to choose rightly. And if, ultimately, someone chooses to say no to God, God can only accept that answer. We must grasp the fact that God genuinely respects the dignity—the freedom—of his creatures. He does not annihilate those who reject him; he preserves their existence and even the state of rejection they have chosen.

Those who make threats have a choice about whether to carry them out, but hell is not a threat on God's part, not some evil which he adds to the harm which sinners have done to themselves. It is the condition of sinners who have made themselves what they are. For God simply to wipe that out would be for him to undo the self-determined reality of the damned. So, God has no option of saving the damned.

Much of the difficulty people have accepting the idea that unrepentant mortal sinners go to hell arises from a legalistic mentality. They imagine God saying, "Here are the rules. Do as I say if you want to stay out of hell." But God's creation is not legalistic; moral norms are moral truth; and, except that *this* is how he has created us, moral truth is not a matter of choice for God. He does not make arbitrary demands and run us through obedience tests. He invites us to take advantage of a wonderful opportunity, available by reason of our being created in his image and redeemed through Jesus. To take advantage, however, we must freely do our part. And if we freely choose *not* to do that, not even God can do anything about it.

19. Fulfillment in Jesus and Human Fulfillment

So far we have concentrated mainly on common principles of morality—free choice, conscience, natural law, and so on. Now we turn to the principles proper to Christian morality. We begin by considering human fulfillment in the light of faith.

God may be thought of as a family, a community of three divine persons. His aim in creating us is to enlarge his natural family by bringing into being new persons able to choose freely to share in the life of the Trinity. Freedom is our great dignity. God does not compel us to become members of his household. He invites us and enables us to answer his invitation, but he leaves the decision to us.

To be free means we can choose wrongly. If so, we shall suffer the consequences. Self-determination is not a game. Everything is at stake in the use we make of freedom.

Since the time of St. Thomas Aquinas, it has been customary to ask: What is the ultimate end of man? The question implies a sharp contrast between the ultimate end (heaven) and the means to it (life in this world). We take a different question for our starting point: What is God's purpose in creating, and how do we fit into it? As a practical matter, how are human goods to be pursued and human acts performed, so that we play the role God intends for us?

This approach removes the sharp contrast between life in this world and heaven. Thus, it avoids a debilitating either/or—either life in this world is important for itself or heaven alone is important. Instead of having to cope with that false dichotomy, we understand ourselves as agents in a divine plan which gives real importance to this life without assigning it absolute, ultimate significance.

In this chapter we take up three main questions: what God's plan is; how we are united with Jesus now and how, supposing we persevere, we shall be united with him later; and how our acts in this life contribute to the realization of God's plan.

Throughout this and subsequent chapters we are concerned with the moral implications of Christian faith for those who explicitly and consciously accept it. But, as Vatican II teaches, not only Christians but other men and women of good will are called to fulfillment in Christ. For grace is at work in the hearts of all people of good will, and the Holy Spirit, in ways only God knows, offers everyone the opportunity to be saved (*GS* 22). Hence, our effort to help Christians make the most of what they have received should not be misunderstood as belittling the blessings which God offers to others.

A: God's Plan: The Fulfillment of Everything in Jesus

In its document on the Catholic Faith, the First Vatican Council teaches definitively that God creates the world, including ourselves, for his glory. This does not mean he creates us in order to have admirers and adorers. Vatican I also definitively rejects the idea that God creates us to acquire something for himself. He is complete, perfect, in himself; he does not need created things, and he does not benefit from being adored.

But then what does it mean to say God creates for his glory? It means he creates simply to express his goodness and, in the case of created persons, to enlarge his initial family, the Trinity, by adopting them into it. His purpose is his own goodness or glory, not in the sense that his goodness is not yet fully realized, but rather insofar as it can be communicated: he creates so as to communicate his goodness to others, and that communication is his glory.

The communication of God's goodness finds its perfection not in this creature or that one but in the sum total of creation, the whole created order. Human fulfillment is only part of that whole, and therefore is not ultimate; it would be wrong to say

God creates everything for the sake of human happiness. But human fulfillment *is* an important part of the self-expression intended by God in creating. Our pursuit of our true happiness does not conflict with God's glory but contributes to it.

In sum, to say we should act for the glory of God means we should recognize that our happiness is not the be-all and end-all of everything but part of a greater reality, the whole created order in community with God. Yet human persons and human lives are not mere means to an extrinsic end. Whatever contributes to the well being of each of us and all of us is an important part of God's plan. Human fulfillment and the glory of God are inseparably linked.

Subpersonal creatures are for persons—all other material things are somehow for our sake. But God creates persons for their own sake. Yet not as isolated individuals. We are meant to be united with one another in a community of friendship.

In the beginning it was like that. Human beings formed a kind of extended family which was also the family of God. Original sin disrupted this state of affairs. And now? Christ offers another way of bringing all human persons into community with one another and with God: by being united to him as sharers in his human life.

Jesus had—and has—a human purpose. As man, he is trying to do something. If we accept his purpose, make it our own, and cooperate in what he is trying to do, we become members of one society, and that society becomes a unifying principle of creation, according to God's plan "to gather up all things in [Christ], things in heaven and things on earth" (Eph 1:10).

Jesus, as God and man, is the center of God's whole plan. As God, he is a member of the original divine family. As man, he is part of creation, other created persons are linked to him, and non-personal creatures are linked to them. In and through Jesus all creation comes into a unity. He gathers it all together and unites it with the Trinity.

Jesus communicates to us his divine life as God. He does this, however, in a way which respects our distinctness and our dignity. We are grafted onto Jesus, become his members, yet we remain always our individual selves. The relationship he offers us is one to which we must freely commit ourselves—and go on committing ourselves throughout our lives. It is for us to accept or reject

Jesus' communication of divine life to us. Communication with Jesus is altogether personal, a matter of choice requiring free cooperation in his acts.

Scripture speaks constantly of community. The idea of the "kingdom" runs throughout the Bible, and in a kingdom, distinction of persons is always maintained. Similarly, the Bible often uses the analogy of marriage to describe the human relationship with God; in the New Testament, the Church is the bride of Christ. But a conjugal relationship is interpersonal and free; there is a real union, yet undiminished distinctness of persons.

Our relationship with Jesus also has another aspect, in which the emphasis on our responsibility is particularly strong. Although Christ is "the firstborn of all creation" in whom "all things in heaven and on earth were created" (Col 1:15–16), he is not himself all creation, but only one creature among many. His humanity is a single created reality, the first but not everything. What is first but not all, the principle but not the whole, must be completed by the rest. Jesus as man is completed and perfected by the rest of creation. To be sure, the human life of Jesus, as an individual, is already fulfilled: God has raised him from the dead. But other creatures are necessary to his fullness as leader and head. What is a leader without followers, a head without a body? In the case of human persons, completing and perfecting Jesus are likewise a matter of individual choice by those who freely enter into the relationship with him which he offers them.

Despite the testimony of Ephesians, Colossians, and other books of the New Testament, some Scripture scholars manifest considerable resistance to this way of speaking—great reluctance to say that anything at all can in any way complete Christ. The reasoning seems to be as follows: Jesus is God; nothing completes God; therefore, nothing can complete Christ. This is true inasmuch as Jesus is God. But Jesus is also man; no man is complete in himself; thus, the cooperation of other human beings is required for the completion of Jesus. It is a matter of taking the Incarnation seriously. The uncreated Word became flesh—a creature, an individual man. But individual creatures do not exist alone; they exist with and are completed by others. In Jesus' case, it is the Church, the community of his friends and followers, "which is his body, the fullness of him who fills all in all" (Eph 1:23).

This point is essential to appreciating the significance of Christian life. In a true sense—though certainly not in an exaggerated or sentimental sense—Jesus needs us, and because this is so, Christians fall short of what is expected of them by living in anything less than the best way they can. The working out of God's plan requires our living out of the Christian life. Our fulfillment is in being united with Jesus—we are his members. As such, we have a subordinate but real part in the fulfillment, the completion, of Jesus as man which is central to God's whole plan. "In my flesh," says St. Paul, "I am completing what is lacking in Christ's afflictions" (Col 1:24). And not only our suffering but *all* we do should carry on his work and complete him.

B: How We Are United with Jesus Now and Hope to Be United with Him Later

Intimately united with Jesus, we are intimately united with God. But we are fulfilled, not absorbed, in that union. God wants us as friends, not puppets, and in the Incarnation he makes himself humanly accessible to us. God is transcendent, but he is also man, one of us, and we are able to relate to him as such. For Christians, religion is primarily a human relationship to and interaction with Jesus, the unique way to God, who says of himself: "I am the way, and the truth, and the life. No one comes to the Father except through me" (Jn 14:6).

Many people find it difficult to appreciate the significance of our human relationship with Jesus because they take for granted the assumptions of mind-body dualism. They suppose that the real self of a human person is consciousness, with a soul hidden somewhere behind it; and if this is true generally, it is also true of Jesus—hidden within his body are a human mind and soul. Having taken this false step, they then take another and suppose that hidden somewhere within Jesus' soul is the Word, his divinity, which is the *real* Jesus. So, any real relationship with God is necessarily operative only on the spiritual, the ghostly, level, while the flesh-and-blood Jesus seems an obstacle rather than the very way to the Father.

The testimony of the New Testament is more realistic—more incarnational—than that. It is testimony concerning "what was from the beginning, what we have heard, what we have seen with our eyes, what we have looked at and touched with our hands . . .

the word of life" (1 Jn 1:1). God is made flesh, so that Jesus can say, "Whoever has seen me has seen the Father" (Jn 14:9).

So we are intimately united with God in Jesus. But how are we united with Jesus? In three ways.

Jesus is God and man, and we are united with him in both aspects of his reality, both his natures; we share in his divine life, and we also share in his humanity. As to sharing in his humanity, this happens in two ways: bodily unity and existential unity (unity in human acts). So the three ways in which we are united with Jesus are in divine life, in bodily life, and in human acts. Let us consider each.

First, unity in divine life. We become children of God, sharers in his nature, through "God's love [which] has been poured into our hearts through the Holy Spirit" (Rom 5:5). This union will be perfected in heaven, when, face to face with God, we "will see him as he is" (1 Jn 3:2).

Influenced by neo-Platonism, the classical theological tradition tended to reduce the beatific vision to an intellectual act by which we shall understand God better than we understand him now or to an aesthetic act like seeing a beautiful sunset. And no doubt our intellects and our aesthetic sensibilities will be satisfied by the vision of God in heaven. But that "vision" should not be understood only in this way. We know, after all, what acts of understanding and aesthetic acts are, but for us to "see" God in heaven will be for us to participate in his inner life, and we do not now understand what that is.

The neo-Platonic idea of gazing on God does not do justice to Scripture's account of seeing God. In the Old Testament God is the king, the people are his subjects, and seeing God is something like being granted an audience by a benevolent monarch. One can talk with him, dine with him, enjoy the benefits of a real relationship. This same realism is found in the New Testament. "See, the home of God is among mortals. He will dwell with them as their God; they will be his peoples, and God himself will be with them" (Rv 21:3). There is an emphasis on the mutuality and intimacy of an interpersonal relationship: "Now we see in a mirror, dimly, but then we will see face to face. Now I know only in part; then I will know fully, even as I have been fully known" (1 Cor 13:12). To see God is to share maturely in his life: "We are God's children now; what we will be has not yet been revealed. What we do know is this: when he is revealed, we will be like him, for we will see him as he is" (1 Jn 3:2).

Second, bodily unity. We are one with Jesus now. "Do you not know that your bodies are members of Christ?" (1 Cor 6:15). This union is sacramental and profoundly mysterious, but no less real on that account; our sacramental unity with Jesus is bodily unity.

Here, too, conventional thinking creates problems. We suppose that organisms are atomistic, isolated, each complete in itself, and cannot have a common life. But this is contradicted in many ways even in our own experience. Consider marriage. Scripture uses it in speaking of the relationship of human persons with Christ. But although husband and wife are distinct for most purposes, for the purpose of begetting children they make up one complex organism which can procreate. This is also the case at the genetic level. Before coming together, the sex cells have only half the genetic material; when they unite, the genetic package is complete.

Jesus' statements in the New Testament leave little doubt concerning the reality of our bodily unity with him. "Just as the branch cannot bear fruit by itself, unless it abides in the vine, neither can you unless you abide in me. I am the vine, you are the branches" (Jn 15:4–5). Is this merely figurative language? "Those who eat my flesh and drink my blood abide in me, and I in them" (Jn 6:56). Metaphor? Jesus did not protest that he had been misunderstood when, taking these words literally, even "many of his disciples turned back and no longer went about with him" (Jn 6:66).

Our bodily unity with Jesus, sacramental now, will be perfected by sharing in his resurrection life. "The one who raised the Lord Jesus will raise us also with Jesus and bring us with you into his presence" (2 Cor 4:14). This risen life, though different from and better than our present life, will also be bodily. "But someone will ask, 'How are the dead raised? With what kind of body do they come?' . . . If there is a physical body, there is also a spiritual body. . . . For this perishable body must put on imperishability, and this mortal body must put on immortality" (1 Cor 15:35, 44, 53).

Third, unity in human acts. We cooperate with Jesus as man. He wishes to build up a fellowship, a community, of human persons. To this end he not only did certain things during his earthly life but still continues to act to build up that community. Now, however, we cooperate with him. By faith we accept what he is doing and make it our own, first only as beneficiaries but then also as his collaborators.

Like other choices, those we make in living out the commitment of faith and our personal vocations will last, and so our unity with Jesus in human acts will last. Living the Christian life means being existentially united with Christ and with other Christians in an inherently lasting way; this is how the community which is to last forever, the eternal kingdom, is brought into being.

Moreover, each and every one of those lasting choices bears upon one or more *human* goods. Thus, heaven is a community of eternal fulfillment in shared human goods. Jesus spoke of it as a wedding feast (see Mt 22:1–14). The Second Vatican Council says:

> For after we have obeyed the Lord, and in his Spirit nurtured on earth the values of human dignity, brotherhood and freedom, and indeed all the good fruits of our nature and enterprise, we will find them again, but freed of stain, burnished and transfigured. . . . On this earth that kingdom is already present in mystery. When the Lord returns, it will be brought into full flower. (*GS* 39)

This will be, as Revelation expresses it, "a new heaven and a new earth" (Rv 21:1).

C: How Our Acts in This Life Contribute to the Fulfillment of God's Plan

Many people hesitate to believe that human activity *does* contribute in any meaningful way to realizing God's plan. Surely God does not need our help? He gives us everything; all that remains for us to do is ask for what we need and be grateful for what we receive.

We do owe everything we have to God. But if this is a relationship in which God only gives and we only receive, it is scarcely a friendship, which requires a certain mutuality, some kind of exchange. Lacking this, we are God's dependents but not his friends. It is essential not only to our dignity but to the relationship itself that we give something to God. This points to the correct answer to the question, "Why must we live the Christian

life?" Not simply because otherwise we shall suffer bad consequences, but rather because, as God's friends, we must not only
acknowledge his gifts but make a real return to him for them.

But how? We cannot give God anything not already his, but
only what he has first given us.

That, however, is precisely what takes place in sacrifice, without which there is no religion. Sacrifice is essentially giving gifts
to God, in love and gratitude returning to him some of what he
has given us. The destruction of the gift in sacrifice does not signify that it is good to destroy things; it is a gesture signifying the
totality and exclusivity of the gift to God, for that which is destroyed in sacrifice is no longer at the disposal of the one who
gives it up to him.

Although the Old Testament prescribes an elaborate ritual of
sacrifice, the prophets criticize the mistaken notion that external
ritual is its essence. It is the gift of self that matters; contrite and
obedient hearts please God.

> For you have no delight in sacrifice;
>> if I were to give a burnt offering, you would not be pleased.
> The sacrifice acceptable to God is a broken spirit;
>> a broken and contrite heart, O God, you will not despise.
>
>   (Ps 51:16–17)

There is a vast difference between a gift meant to manipulate the
recipient and coax favors out of him or her and a wholehearted
gift given because one cares for the one who receives it. In the
latter kind of giving, one gives something of oneself—specifically,
a willingness and readiness to do what the recipient wants within
reasonable bounds. Thus, sincere gift giving expresses a will to
community.

This is also the case with sacrifice. Preeminently it is true of
the sacrifice of Jesus, who "gave himself up for us, a fragrant
offering and sacrifice to God" (Eph 5:2), but it is also true of the
sacrifice of Christians. First of all, when we participate in the
Mass, we participate in the sacrifice of Christ, "offering the Im-
maculate Victim," as Vatican II says, "not only through the hands
of the priest, but also with him" (SC 48). But beyond that, we
also enter into community with Jesus through the sacrifice we offer by living our lives as Christians. St. Paul calls on his fellow
Christians "to present your bodies as a living sacrifice, holy and
acceptable to God, which is your spiritual worship. Do not be

conformed to this world, but be transformed by the renewing of your minds" (Rom 12:1–2). What are we to bring to the Eucharist and join with the sacrifice of Christ? The fulfillment of our vocational responsibilities, by which we do our share to cooperate with Jesus in spreading the gospel and building up the community of faith. Otherwise we have nothing worth offering.

God has his plan. The selves and the community which we bring into being by our acts are part of this plan and contribute to carrying it out. But if we do not live as we ought, God's plan goes unrealized to the extent that it lies with each of us to realize it in his or her life. As the passage from Vatican II quoted above points out, human lives and fulfillment in human goods—"all the good fruits of our nature and enterprise"—are not mere extrinsic means to heaven but its building materials. Moreover, as members of a body whose head is Christ, we continue Jesus' work down through history and in this way complete him.

But how can our human actions be so important? Everything really depends on God's grace: "By grace you have been saved through faith, and this is not your own doing; it is the gift of God—not the result of works, so that no one may boast" (Eph 2:8–9). Yet grace does not replace our actions; rather, it takes shape in our works. The same passage goes on: "For we are what he has made us, created in Christ Jesus for good works, which God prepared beforehand to be our way of life" (Eph 2:10).

By doing the good works God gives us to do, we also cooperate with the Holy Spirit, who carries Jesus' work through to completion by sanctifying. As Vatican II expresses it: "The promised restoration which we are awaiting has already begun in Christ, is carried forward in the mission of the Holy Spirit, and through him continues in the Church" (*LG* 48). How do we cooperate in sanctification? By leading good lives and offering others encouragement and help to do the same.

There is a real communication of our human goods to the divine persons. Somehow, God is pleased by our gifts; they matter personally to him. This seems clear in many places in Scripture, though *how* it is so is mysterious, something we do not, and cannot now, understand. God is not benefited in any way. Yet our relationship with him is a personal one, and when partners in a personal relationship do what they should, the relationship is perfected.

In one sense, redemption is purely God's act: God, and only God, redeems the world in and through Jesus Christ. Protestant theologians, especially Lutherans, emphasize this truth, and they are right to do so. Redemption is already in principle accomplished by the Incarnation, by which God's unity with creation is unbreakable. And the Incarnation is perfected in the resurrection. Evil in principle is overcome; the kingdom is established in the risen Christ.

Yet Christ's humanity is only one creature, and the rest of creation, including our lives, must be completed by being integrated into Jesus. In this way "the creation itself will be set free from its bondage to decay and will obtain the freedom of the glory of the children of God" (Rom 8:21). Human persons must be formed into a community, and its members, together with the rest of creation through them, must be brought into unity with the redemptive reality of Christ.

Moreover, Christians must continue Jesus' work of spreading the gospel. Redemption has been completed in principle, but the resurrected Christ is not the whole redeemed community. The divine truth and life in Jesus must be extended from him to all people in all places and times. He specifically commissions his followers to do this: "Go therefore and make disciples of all nations, baptizing them in the name of the Father and of the Son and of the Holy Spirit, and teaching them to obey everything that I have commanded you" (Mt 28:19–20). People must make the commitment of faith and live the Christian life. The Christian community must be formed, and like any community, it is formed by personal relationships.

The process of sanctification must also continue and be completed in the life of each of us individually. By no means does this happen automatically. "Man is split within himself. As a result, all of human life, whether individual or collective, shows itself to be a dramatic struggle between good and evil" (*GS* 13). Sanctification begins with accepting Christ in faith as Savior and turning away from sin: "One believes with the heart and so is justified" (Rom 10:10). But more than believing in the heart is required: "One confesses with the mouth and so is saved" (Rom 10:10). This is not just lip service—saying, "Jesus is Lord"; we must live integral lives consistent with the profession of faith. Only then are we sanctified.

This is the essence of Christian life in its progress from baptism to sanctity. One joins the community of faith and lives as a member, including communicating the gospel to others in word and deed. To do that, one must integrate one's whole life and self with faith, so that no part remains as it would be without faith. The work of a Christian is to become and to be *entirely* Christian.

20. The Relationship between God and Sinful Humankind

God's revelation initiates the intimate friendship between him and us upon which Christian life is centered. God creates in order to share his goodness, and from the start he communicated with our first parents, who thus enjoyed flawless intimacy with him until they sinned (see *DV* 3). In the first instance, then, revelation and faith had nothing to do with sin. As matters stand, however, this relationship is conditioned by our fallen state and our need for redemption. Revelation is therefore a call to repentance, and the response of faith is conversion from sin.

This way of looking at revelation, faith, and redemption avoids two extremes: on the one hand, the subordination of revelation and faith to redemption found in classical theology and in the popular piety of bygone times; on the other, the present deemphasis of sin and the need for redemption. We shall develop this view by examining three topics: revelation itself; faith and its various aspects; and revelation and faith in the context of sin. The chapter provides a basis for the examination of Jesus Christ and his life in the two chapters immediately following, while in chapter twenty-three we shall begin to consider Christian life, which is essentially the following of Jesus.

A: Revelation Itself

Revelation is God's personal communication to humankind. To be sure, God also manifests himself simply by creating the universe, but this is not "revelation" properly so called. In its very important Dogmatic Constitution on the Catholic Faith, *Dei*

Filius, the First Vatican Council teaches that, besides making some knowledge of himself accessible to our natural reason by creating, God has also chosen "to reveal himself and the eternal decrees of his will to the human race in another and supernatural way, as the Apostle says: 'God, who at sundry times and in diverse manners spoke in times past to the fathers by the prophets, last of all in these days has spoken to us by his Son' (Heb 1:1f.)" (DS 3004/1785). We have an absolute need for such revelation inasmuch as "God, out of his infinite goodness, destined man to a supernatural end, that is, to a participation in the good things of God, which altogether exceed the human mental grasp" (DS 3005/1786). He addresses us personally because he wishes us to enjoy intimate, supernatural communion with him.

In a way, this is not difficult to understand. Many personal relationships begin when one party introduces himself or herself and addresses the other. We are not in a position to initiate a friendship with God, yet he wills that we be in friendship with him. His revelation is therefore necessary in order to begin the relationship. Furthermore, although revelation does include propositional truths—information—and, as we shall see at greater length below, is not simply some kind of ineffable experience, nevertheless it is essentially *personal* communication, God's revelation of *himself.*

Even so, revelation is not God. While God's act of revealing is not really other than he, the act must be distinguished from revelation itself. That is something we receive from God, namely, a communication through a set of created entities—words and deeds. But how can we separate out these particular created entities from other created things in our experience? How can we recognize revelation when we encounter it? The answer is that revelation is accompanied by signs and wonders, miracles and the fulfillment of prophecies. The only explanation which accounts for these phenomena is that we have here a communication from something, or someone, outside the created order of things.

Consider an analogy. Astronomers begin to pick up a new, complex, and repeated pattern with their radio telescopes. At first, several explanations seem possible—it comes from somewhere on earth, it is produced by some unfamiliar emanation of energy from the sun, and so on. But these explanations are gradually eliminated for one reason or another. Meanwhile, after further study, some scientists begin to think the strange new signal is a message. "And," they say, "if we have it right, it's going to be repeated next Tuesday, precisely at noon." Tuesday noon comes— and the signal is repeated! Conclusion: Earth is receiving a message from an intelligent being outside the solar system.

Revelation is something like that. Things happen in the created order for which the created order provides no explanation; but they can be accounted for as a signal from the creator. It is reasonable to take such words and deeds as revelation. They are created entities, but creation itself cannot account for them. Taken as a communication from God, however, they can be seen to form an intelligible, unified whole. Vatican II says:

> This plan of revelation is realized by deeds and words having an inner unity: the deeds wrought by God in the history of salvation manifest and confirm the teaching and realities signified by the words, while the words proclaim the deeds and clarify the mystery contained in them. (DV 2)

Revelation is thus not a mysterious intuition or experience which cannot be put into words. It is a set of utterances, occurrences, and states of affairs—Jesus' debates with scribes, his multiplication of loaves and fishes, the empty tomb—which can be observed and then communicated by human beings. It is events which happened and words which were spoken—both of which, taken together, make sense only on the supposition that God is communicating in this way. It is God's personal self-communication by means of created things sufficient to present us with what we ought reasonably to accept as his personal self-communication.

B: Faith and Its Various Aspects

What does it mean to have faith in God? To answer that, we must first consider what it means to have faith in another human being.

In principle, we could investigate most propositions which we accept "on faith"—the mean distance of the sun from the earth is 92,900,000 miles, William Shakespeare was born in 1564 and died in 1616—and show them to be either true or not true. But that is not the case with the faith which underlies a personal relationship. Faith in someone else concerns that person; it is irreplaceable; experience and information cannot substitute for it.

Still, faith in someone else does involve propositions—what the other person says, explicitly or implicitly, about himself or herself and his or her intentions. Certain propositions are necessary to initiate a relationship. Whether or not one believes them is crucial to whether or not one believes in the person making them. For example: "I want to be your friend." Accept that proposition as true, and one has entered upon a relationship with the person making it which points toward deeper intimacy in the future. A couple planning to marry provide a striking example of this. Each one's faith in the other sets up expectations that he or she will carry out his or her part in the relationship. Mutual trust is leading them to a common life in which each will depend upon the other to keep his or her commitment. Faith always promises and expects performance, and so it leads to hope. It likewise leads to love: one commits oneself to communion and to what is required to bring it about.

Faith in God is likewise the principle of an interpersonal relationship. God obviously is not another human person, yet he deals with us very much as if he were. Even in revealing himself to begin the relationship, he does not present himself in a way altogether strange and outside our experience. Although there are elements of strangeness in God's self-revelation, so that human beings know they are not dealing simply with another human being, God nevertheless uses the modality of human interpersonal relationship and meets its requirements.

Faith in God is the acceptance of his personal self-communication. But suppose one does not accept it? That would be like reacting with disbelief to the statement "I want to be your friend" and refusing the relationship the speaker was offering. One *must* accept God's self-communication if one is to enter into a personal relationship with him. To hear God's word in the preaching of the gospel, to assent to the truth proposed, and to welcome what God is doing: that is faith.

Thus, even though there is more to faith than assenting to revealed truth, assenting to revealed truth is essential to faith. It is not an either/or situation: either faith as personal communion with God or faith as assent to doctrines. That is a false dichotomy. God's self-communication includes certain truths; and unless one trusts his self-communication, no intimate relationship with him is possible. Precisely because God's revelation is personal communication in a human mode leading toward intimacy, propositional content to which we must assent in order to have faith in God is part of it.

What are the revealed truths to which assent is necessary? Vatican I sums it up this way:

> By divine and Catholic faith everything must be believed that is contained in the written word of God or in tradition, and that is proposed by the Church as a divinely revealed object of belief either in a solemn decree or in her ordinary, universal teaching. (DS 3011/1792)

No doubt some revealed truths are more important, more central, than others, but no truth of revelation taught by the Church can be set aside by a person of faith.

The faith involved in an interpersonal relationship also requires that one agree to do what is appropriate in the relationship. As we saw earlier, Christian faith is the fundamental option of Christian life. A person of faith must live it out.

Vatican II gives this succinct summary:

> Therefore the apostles, handing on what they themselves had received, warn the faithful to hold fast to the traditions which they have learned either by word of mouth or by letter (cf. 2 Thes 2:15), and to fight in defense of the faith handed on once and for all (cf. Jude 3). Now what was handed on by the apostles includes everything which contributes to the holiness of life, and the increase in faith of the People of God; and so the Church, in her teaching, life, and worship, perpetuates and hands on to all generations all that she herself is, all that she believes. (*DV* 8)

Catholic faith means adhering to God in the Church by doing three things: assenting to the revealed truths of faith taught by the Church; worshipping according to this belief by participating in the Eucharist and other acts of worship proper to the Church; and trying to live one's whole life according to this belief and worship.

Truths of faith are not self-evident, and there is an alternative to believing: not believing. Thus, faith requires a choice, and this choice is a commitment which shapes and organizes one's life. As with any other commitment, one does not and cannot know in advance all that living it out will require. But the commitment is by no means unreasonable. It is made for the sake of sharing in the human goods of truth and religion. Truths of faith are humanly important and otherwise inaccessible. Moreover, because we owe everything to God and are utterly dependent on him, we should worship him and accept his friendship. That is the essence of religion, and it is of inestimable worth to human beings. No one can be compelled to make the commitment of faith, any more than anyone can be compelled to commit himself or herself to any other relationship. But in rejecting friendship with God, even more than in rejecting human friendship, one condemns oneself to a humanly mutilated life.

Since believing is reasonable, it is unreasonable to refuse to believe once divine revelation is communicated adequately. But to choose to do what is unreasonable is morally evil. If, then, the good news is adequately communicated, refusal to believe is a sin—a sin, moreover, which originates in a preexisting state of sin. Someone open to what is true and good will be predisposed to accept a true and good message when it is presented credibly; but the reaction of someone not open to integral human fulfillment, someone whose attitude is immoral, is likely to be, "I don't *want* to accept that, I don't *want* to change, and so I *won't* believe." As St. John observes, "the light has come into the world, and people loved darkness rather than light because their deeds were evil" (Jn 3:19).

In saying this, we are not judging individuals. Presumably, many people are nonbelievers because the gospel has not been presented to them effectively. Effective or adequate preaching of the good news means presenting it in such a way that people really can see the reasonableness of accepting it as divine revelation. This requires that evangelizers live in such a manner that those they seek to evangelize can say of them, first, that they really believe what they are saying and, second, that they could not live as they do unless their message were true.

Like refusal to believe in the face of adequate preaching of the good news, loss of faith also is a consequence of sin. People do not "lose" faith as they misplace objects—inadvertently, unconsciously, without noticing what they are doing. Vatican I teaches that God "strengthens with his grace those whom he has brought out of darkness into his marvelous light (see 1 Pt 2:9), so that they may remain in this light"; thus, they "can never have any just reason for changing that faith or calling it into question" (DS

3014/1794). However: "By rejecting conscience, certain persons have suffered shipwreck in the faith" (1 Tm 1:19). The process begins in moral fault; there is no true loss of faith without sin.

Here, too, we are not passing judgment on individuals. In particular cases, who besides God really knows what is going on? Perhaps some people who "lose" faith never had it in the first place. Perhaps some who say they have lost their faith are only expressing negative feelings or confused thinking, while their relationship with God remains more or less intact without their understanding it reflectively.

Still, someone who really had faith and really loses it must have committed mortal sin—or, more likely, many mortal sins. For loss of faith is the breaking off of one's personal relationship with God; and that must be either one's own fault or God's. But it cannot be God's, since even "if we are faithless; he remains faithful" (2 Tm 2:13). So, as we saw in chapter eighteen, loss of faith is a stage in a downward process that moves from remaining in sin by choice through presumption to despair.

Although we believe by our own free choice, faith is also God's gift to us. It is a human act *and* a divine gift. The two things are not mutually exclusive.

Certainly, anything and everything salvific comes from God; and anything of a salvific character which *we* do is no less a grace from God. Jesus says: "No one can come to me unless drawn by the Father who sent me" (Jn 6:44). Vatican I teaches that by living faith "with the inspiration and help of God's grace, we believe that what he has revealed is true" (DS 3008/1789). Vatican II teaches that "the grace of God and the interior help of the Holy Spirit must precede and assist" faith, and the Spirit "constantly brings faith to completion by his gifts" (*DV* 5). Yet, as we have seen, we also have a choice to make: to accept grace or reject it, to believe or not to believe. We cannot believe without grace; but neither can we believe without making a free choice to do so— which also is a grace God gives us.

The absolute certitude of faith is likewise a grace; the factors which make belief possible as a free human act cannot account for it. This certitude is a clear but ordinary sign, visible in every believer, of God's work. Of course, there are rational grounds which, humanly speaking, make it reasonable to believe. But a believer's certitude about the content of faith goes beyond these merely rational grounds. There is no need here for special charisms and signs; the certitude itself is a clear sign of the Spirit's work.

For example, no evidence for Jesus' real presence in the Eucharist can adequately account for a believer's certitude about the truth of the real presence; the certitude is itself the evidence that this belief comes from God. Similarly, a Christian's confidence that living the Christian life is both possible and worthwhile, even though it can be very difficult and sometimes even leads to human failure and defeat, is a sign that he or she is moved by the Holy Spirit. And this certitude, produced by the action of God, is part of the experience of every believing Christian, a sign we overlook because it is so familiar.

The very fact that it was not always familiar to them explains why converts who were formerly without faith feel a sense of wonder, usually lacking in lifelong Catholics, about what they have been given. Having always known both certitude about the truths of faith and the meaningfulness of living a Christian life, the lifelong Catholic tends to take these wonderful gifts for granted. But people who once suffered profound uncertainty, experienced life as meaningless, and have seen how incapable fallen humankind is of doing good, receive faith as a wonderful gift.

In the Church's teaching, living faith—faith informed by God's gift of charity—is contrasted with dead faith. Faith is "dead" in one who loses charity through mortal sin but does not lose faith. As Trent teaches, this is true faith, but not living. People in this state have a human relationship with God but not that more-than-human relationship which comes about when the love of God is poured forth in the hearts of human persons and they share in divine life.

C: Revelation and Faith in the Context of Sin

As a result of sin, human persons have a special—indeed, a desperate—need for God's help. Humankind is mutilated. Sin and its effects are privations, the absence of something which ought to be present. Human nature is truly wounded by sin, and this wounding can only be overcome by a restorative act which humankind is absolutely incapable of performing for itself.

People universally recognize the unacceptable misery of the human condition. We live in the shadow of death, we suffer, we die.

In the absence of faith, the effort to live a decent life is frustrating and eventually impossible. The human condition is not as it should be. Even nonbelievers are aware of this. A radical intervention is needed to set things right.

In this situation, revelation comes to humankind in a different form than it would without sin: as an offer of reconciliation, liberation, justification, salvation. It is God's assurance that our condition is not hopeless. It is his offer of reconciliation: even though we are alienated from him, he is willing and able to bridge the gulf. It is his promise of life: he is ready "to give light to those who sit in darkness and in the shadow of death" (Lk 1:79). The acceptance of this revelation, faith, is conversion; friendship with God begins in justification, in God's setting right what is wrong in the sinner's fallen condition.

Because sin is a privation, it cannot be overcome by an act of destruction, nor by ignoring it or wishing it away. It can only be overcome by God's act of re-creation. God must bring something new into being—new hearts in those who were sinners and resurrected bodies raised from death. This is not work we can do. Yet God makes us cooperators in the work by allowing us to help prepare the ground for it and follow up on it.

In the fallen human condition, faith is a matter of accepting God's offer of liberation and reconciliation. But it is also something more. A person of faith says to God: "I accept your offer. Now what must I do?" He or she is like a drowning boy cooperating with a lifeguard by grasping her hand.

Faith is thus a commitment to cooperate with God in redeeming us. God is not like a foolishly indulgent father who spoils his children by constantly intervening to shield them from the natural consequences of their wrongdoing; respecting our dignity, he lets us bear the consequences of our sins. But because he loves us, he offers us redemption, while also offering us the chance to cooperate with him in bringing it about and requiring that we do so. This requirement is not an imposition by God; it, too, is for the sake of our dignity as free and intelligent beings. "For we are what he has made us, created in Christ Jesus for good works, which God prepared beforehand to be our way of life" (Eph 2:10).

Here, too, an analogy helps. Suppose the United States or some other wealthy, industrialized nation decided to make an all-out effort to bring prosperity to a poverty-stricken third world country. How would we go about it? Perhaps economists and social planners would conceptualize a huge program—a five-year plan, an "alliance for progress." Teams of public health workers, engineers, and technicians of all kinds would be sent in to build roads and bridges, set up clinics, teach the people how to practice contraception and abortion. Factories would be established for the manufacture of television sets and transistor radios. If all went well, the lucky country would soon have fast food franchises and an epidemic of stress-related disease.

No doubt the country would also be wealthier than before. But would its people be better off in terms of human dignity? That is debatable. Economic development is a good thing, and the United States and other wealthy nations have a grave moral obligation to help nations which are poor. But development assistance which respects human dignity would refrain from imposing a social and economic structure and a life-style on the people of another country. The strategy instead would be for helpers from outside to work in solidarity with the people of the impoverished land, sharing their life and language, encouraging them to make better use of their resources, to overcome their problems by means suitable to them, and to do so through their own work and ingenuity. If the strategy succeeded, the people would have contributed significantly to improving their own lot. They would have acquired something more than higher incomes and more material possessions. They would have enhanced their dignity as free persons.

It is not our purpose to offer prescriptions for foreign aid and third world development. Our point is that God's approach to dealing with human beings is something like the second strategy sketched above. He redeems us in a way that invites and requires our maximum cooperation, involving us as much as possible in our own salvation.

Jesus really is a human individual—one of us. His human acts are a part of human life, human history, the world in which human beings live. These free human acts of Jesus make a tremendous contribution to the work of renewal which prepares the ground for God's re-creation. The fidelity and obedience to the Father's will with which Jesus lived his human life ennoble all humankind. What can a human individual contribute to redemption? Consider the human life of Jesus. Consider, too, the lives of those who seek to live in union with Jesus and to model their lives on his.

God does not impose redemption on us, for that would deprive us of our dignity. Nor does he simply blot out sin or overlook it. He takes human freedom and dignity seriously, enlisting our co-operation in our own redemption. Revelation is his offer of redemption, and faith is the human acceptance of that offer—an acceptance which must include willingness to cooperate with him.

Christian life is therefore a struggle against sin and its effects. That was the meaning of Jesus' life, and it is the meaning of the lives of those who seek to follow his way. "Not everyone who says to me, 'Lord, Lord,' will enter the kingdom of heaven, but only the one who does the will of my Father in heaven" (Mt 7:21). Only when we have done all we can as best we can, not on our own but with the help of God's grace, does God respond by doing his part: re-creation—a new heaven and a new earth, resurrection from the dead, new life, and new hearts which will remain holy forever.

21. God's Redemptive Work: Covenant and Incarnation

Having examined revelation, faith, and redemption, we now turn to salvation history as it takes shape in the life of God's people and in the lives of individual Christians. In this chapter we consider three topics: what is preparatory and general in God's redemptive activity; how the new covenant perfects the old; and Jesus' complex human-divine makeup and the human-divine makeup of his life.

This last topic is especially important for moral theology. Jesus and his life provide the model for the Christian and Christian life. Thus, by the end of the chapter we shall have begun laying out the plan for the following of Jesus which is Christian life. Chapter twenty-two will examine more closely Jesus' life, including his virtues, to which we shall return in chapter twenty-six.

A: What Is Preparatory and General in God's Redemptive Activity

God urgently desires our good. No sooner was sin first committed in the world than God set about repairing the damage in a way that respects human dignity. "From that time on he ceaselessly kept the human race in his care, in order to give eternal life to those who perseveringly do good in search of salvation" (*DV* 3).

God's redemptive activity has several constant characteristics which are present from the start as well as in the culmination of redemption in Jesus.

God always takes the initiative. Humankind, having violated its original relationship with God, is alienated from him. He therefore acts to reconstitute the relationship. He does this first of all by establishing a genuine personal relationship—for example, with Abraham (cf. *DV* 3)—which in turn leads to the formation of a covenant community in friendship with him.

Always, too, the leader of the covenant community, as God's special friend, acts as an intercessor for others. We find Abraham interceding for Sodom and Gomorrah, and bargaining with God to save his kinsman Lot (cf. Gn 18:16–32).

God's redemption does not involve anyone paying a price to anyone. "Redemption" is a good word, used in Scripture, but it can be understood in a misleading sense, based too closely on ransoming captives or something similar. Drawing out the implications of such a model can be confusing. For God's redemption means liberating people from sin and restoring them to friendship with him. But how can friendship be bought? Nobody pays God anything for his friendship, nor does he pay anybody anything to be his friend. God's redemption is gratuitous. Many false problems are avoided by excluding the commercial aspects of analogies, such as ransoming slaves, in thinking about it.

There is a better model in the reconciliation of a married couple who have been estranged. God loves his people as a faithful husband continues to love his unfaithful wife and seeks to restore their relationship. There is no totting up of injuries and paying of damages; rather, there is simple forgiveness and renewal of intimacy.

God's covenant likewise has a model in a human relationship which existed before he took it up for his purposes: the treaty relationship between a strong ruler and a tribe or other group which he offers to take under his protection. Such a covenant is an offer of permanent friendship on the ruler's part, in return for which the group pledges to be obedient and loyal—to be his people. Precisely this personal character leads the sovereign to stipulate what the respective parties must do to fulfill the terms of the relationship. Similarly, under God's covenant, their past performance is not a condition for his people to enter into the relationship which he offers them; rather, the duties they must fulfill follow necessarily from their free acceptance of the relationship. To be covenant partners with God, they must follow his ways.

Within a human covenant relationship of this sort, it is in the interests of the stronger party that his people live decently and treat one another well, for then he can protect them effectively and call upon them for the services they have pledged. God's covenant is like that. He wants his people to live orderly lives in their relationships with one another—not to kill, commit adultery, steal, and so on—so that they will be a fitting covenant partner. Thus, the Ten Commandments, besides stipulating exclusive loyalty to God, also indicate how the people should deal with one another. No more than the covenant itself is this law a burdensome imposition. It simply prescribes what is intrinsically required for life within the covenant relationship.

It is clear in the Old Testament that life in the covenant has many important consequences for morality.

First, religion becomes a primary end and good which organizes all of human life.

Even outside the covenant, of course, religion is universally recognized as a human good. Its practices offer a way of placating the gods, dealing with the problem of evil, supplying social cohesion, and so forth. Religion is important. But it need not be—and often is not—the most important thing in people's lives.

Under the Old Testament covenant, by contrast, religion becomes primary in moral terms. The whole of human life is oriented toward the relationship with God. All other human goods will be served if this relationship is given primacy. Israel's faithfulness to the covenant comes first. If this requirement is observed, nothing ultimately will turn out wrong, no matter what may happen; if it is not observed, nothing else will be as it should be.

Second, as in a human treaty relationship, in which the weaker party is expected to manifest the virtues of the stronger (for example, bravery in battle), there is a principle of imitation at work in the covenant relationship with God.

Throughout the Old Testament, and on into the New, God's principal characteristics are shown to be mercy and faithfulness— or love and truth: God's "loving kindness" is willingness to care for the weak and needy, to forgive sinners and receive them back as his friends, while "truth" refers primarily to his faithfulness, to the fact that he performs what he promises. For their part,

God's people are to imitate him: "You shall be holy; for I the Lord your God am holy" (Lv 19:2).

A gradual development—a purification and uplifting—of moral standards takes place because God's people are to imitate him. This sheds light on the scriptural stress on mercy. Even though Old Testament morality may strike people today as harsh, it is gentle and humane by comparison with other standards of behavior at the time: one must be lenient with debtors, one may not treat aliens unfairly, and so on. It also illuminates the emerging emphasis in Scripture on faithfulness—for instance, the rejection of adultery and the requirement of fidelity (in the New Testament, absolute indissolubility) in marriage.

Third, within the covenant human goods are clarified. As time goes by, the importance of life and the significance of death as a great evil become ever clearer in the Old Testament. So, too, for other goods like truth. And this unfolding of human possibilities proceeds even further in the New Testament.

Fourth, the covenant provides a perspective for criticizing conventional morality and making progress in the direction of moral truth. Not even the moral rules of Israel are true and good in all respects. But as insight into moral truth grows through the Old Testament, many deficiencies are uncovered and corrected. (This development is particularly noteworthy in the work of the prophets.) Finally, the process of clarification and purification is brought to completion in the New Testament.

B: How the New Covenant Perfects the Old

There is both discontinuity and continuity between the old covenant and the new. On the one hand, the new plainly replaces the old. Scripture leaves no doubt about that. For example, the letter to the Hebrews tells us that Jesus

> has now obtained a more excellent ministry, and to that degree he is the mediator of a better covenant, which has been enacted through better promises. For if that first covenant had been faultless, there would have been no need to look for a second one. (Heb 8:6–7)

The old covenant was a beginning. As such, it was necessarily imperfect. It provides the stock on which the people of the new covenant are grafted (cf. Rom 11:17–24), but, as a stock, it was not and could not be already the family of God in full flower.

Yet the old covenant did prepare the way for the new. It brought about the necessary human context for the Incarnation and for Jesus' life. The Word did not become some sort of generic human; he became a man of that flesh and blood, of that language, and of those customs, which God had prepared from the time of his ancestor, Abraham. Jesus, Mary, Joseph, the Apostles, and the first Christians—all were Jews, formed to play their essential roles by the old covenant relationship and by the human culture and social structure it shaped. The Incarnation was an event in human history for which an appropriate setting had to be prepared. That preparatory work was accomplished by the old covenant.

The replacement of the old covenant by the new does not mean the old was discarded as if it were something bad. God's redemptive work had already begun under the old covenant. It did not have to begin over again. The new covenant replaces the old, but this "replacement" is more in the nature of fulfillment than substitution. Yet the old covenant was also imperfect and temporary. Once the new was in place, the imperfect and impermanent elements of the old had to be stripped away in order to bring to perfection the relationship with the whole of humankind which God has in view.

But what is the fullness of God's redemptive plan? The Incarnation is the key.

As we saw in chapter nineteen, God intends a perfect, everlasting community of divine and human persons sharing their goods with one another. Jesus Christ, divine and human, is at the center of this communion. He relates perfectly and homogeneously to both sides of the relationship. As the Word, the second person of the Trinity, he is the equal of the Father and the Spirit; as a member of the human family, he is our elder brother, our head, our leader. He is the unifying principle of divine-human communion: "For in him all the fullness of God was pleased to dwell, and through him God was pleased to reconcile to himself all things, whether on earth or in heaven, by making peace through the blood of his cross" (Col 1:19–20).

With the Incarnation, then, a far more profound and permanent communion was established between God and humankind than was possible under the old covenant. Although the community of the old covenant had all the features of a real religious community, it was not adequate to overcome sin and all its consequences. The Incarnation was required for that. With this principle of communion once permanently in place, the Spirit is given to the members of the new covenant community, so that they can share consciously in divine life. Now "all who are led by the Spirit of God are children of God" (Rom 8:14).

We have said that the old covenant had certain inevitable limitations. What were these?

To begin with, hope was focused on this-worldly fulfillment. Jesus had to grapple constantly with this mentality, striving to open his hearers' minds to the idea that his kingdom transcends politics and its members' happiness lies elsewhere than in worldly riches and temporal contentment. Even after the resurrection the Apostles ask, "Lord, is this the time when you will restore the kingdom to Israel?" (Acts 1:6). This mindset has deep roots in the old covenant. It is one reason why Jesus' message often fell on deaf ears.

The community of the old covenant was inclined to be exclusivistic. Since there was only one chosen people, its members tended to think of themselves as superior to those not singled out as they had been. Criticism of this attitude emerges in the prophets; there is a dawning awareness that God's people have been chosen precisely to be a vehicle for the salvation of the nations. But this understanding is far from universal even in Jesus' time.

Under the old covenant one also finds the false notion that it is necessary to sacrifice some human goods in order to cultivate the relationship with God. The mentality of the old covenant tended to locate evil somewhere, in something, so that it could be segregated and destroyed. Here, too, one finds criticism of this way of thinking, especially in the prophets, but the mindset nevertheless persisted. It is visible in the resistance which St. Paul encountered, and by no means entirely overcame, in attempting to convince his fellow Jews that nothing in the created world is unclean in itself.

The new covenant overcomes these limitations. Hope is focused elsewhere than on the this-worldly. Jesus' kingdom is not of this world, and the fulfillment of those who identify with him lies in that kingdom, not here. God's liberation is seen as universal in its outreach: "Go into all the world and proclaim the good news to the whole creation" (Mk 16:15). And the very fact that Jesus is both God and man shows that there is no conflict between religion and other human goods. Human fulfillment takes nothing away from God or from the relationship with God.

Under the old covenant, there were many detailed prescriptions for purifications, rituals, sacrifices. By contrast, the new covenant does not primarily consist in rules to be observed or rituals to be performed. Of course, it presupposes the norms of morality, and it is outwardly expressed in the few, simple rituals of the sacraments. But it consists chiefly in the interior gifts of the Holy Spirit and the way of life to which they give rise. "I desire mercy and not sacrifice," Jesus quotes with approval (Mt 12:7). It is the gift of the Spirit which, effecting an inner transformation, makes us God's adopted children and unites us to Jesus as sharers in his divine nature.

The new covenant therefore consists essentially in an intrinsic inner bonding rather than an extrinsic treaty-like arrangement. At the beginning of his ministry Jesus announces the fulfillment of the prophetic hope expressed in Jeremiah and Isaiah—the hope for re-creation by God. Its definitive fulfillment begins with Jesus' resurrection and with the Spirit's coming at Pentecost.

In communion with God through Jesus, human beings now can live and die in Christ and rise in him to everlasting life. The covenant is carried through to its perfection by that process. This does not mean human life is now easy and painless. Faith does not overcome sin by disclosing it to be unreal, but by accepting the new covenant, with its offer of reconciliation. This reconciliation lies in union with Christ, and those united with Christ must die to sin and rise to a holy life. There is nothing easy about that.

Now, however, the Spirit makes it truly possible for men and women, still suffering the consequences of sin, to live holy lives in this world—a world which itself remains permeated with sin and its consequences, including death. We can live in this world as we should. Yet life cannot now be as it would have been had there been no sin. Jesus' life was hard. So will be the lives of those who strive to follow his way.

An easy life, lived in the pretense that sin is not real, is not a good life. It falsifies reality; it assumes a make-believe world. A life which tries to overcome sin by destroying evil is also out of touch with reality, for evil is a privation and, as such, it can only be overcome by healing and re-creation. A good life is a life like

Jesus', and the new covenant makes such a life possible: *possible* but never *easy*, and often, from the world's perspective, unrewarding and painful.

Is such a life joyful? It is. Joyful with Jesus' joy on the cross and with the joy of the martyrs facing death, confident that through it they would gain eternal life. Joyful with the joy that comes from the Holy Spirit. "I am overjoyed," Paul says, "in all our affliction" (2 Cor 7:4). There is no irony in that, nor is the joy of Christians founded on a delusion. The delusion lies elsewhere: in the superficial ease of a life forgetful of heaven and founded on the belief that sin is unreal.

C: Jesus' Human-Divine Makeup and the Makeup of His Life

Jesus is truly divine and human—divine as the Son of God, human as the son of Mary. This is what it means to say he has two natures: he is the same in kind with God and also the same in kind with Mary and other human persons.

In Jesus these two natures are inseparably united yet also distinct and not commingled. He is in these two natures, as the Council of Chalcedon puts it, "without any commingling or change or division or separation." And the Council declares "that the distinction between the natures is in no way removed by their union but rather that the specific character of each nature is preserved and they are united in one person and one hypostasis" (DS 302/148). Divinity and humanity are not somehow blended even though they are united in this one individual, Jesus. Each maintains its reality and integrity. The divine remains divine, the human remains human.

In reflecting on the makeup of Jesus, we must remember that we do not know what the divine nature is in itself. Any attempt to explain *how* one individual can be both divine and human mistakenly assumes otherwise. But "nature" used to refer to the divinity of Jesus simply does not mean precisely what it means when used to refer to his humanity. Created natures exclude one another; no individual can be two kinds of thing at once. The Incarnation is evidence that the divine nature is not exclusive—it can coexist in one individual with human nature. The rest is mystery. We know *that* Jesus is God and man, but *how* this can be so is a question we have no way of answering.

It is also a teaching of faith that Jesus is one person—a divine person, the Word. But to say Jesus is not a human person takes nothing away from the integrity and completeness of his humanity. The point is to deny that his primary reality is his human, creaturely aspect and to insist that his primary reality is divine. Otherwise there would be no Incarnation, for in that case who or what became "incarnate"? But even though Jesus is not a human person, he has the same capacities and engages in the same kinds of acts, except for sin, that human persons have and engage in.

Jesus, then, is fully and perfectly divine and also fully and perfectly human. It follows that there is no conflict in him between divine and human goods. Otherwise, he would have had to choose between the human and the divine; and since, as a divine person, he cannot be alienated from the divine, he would have had to reject the human. But then, what kind of man would he have been?

Good, however, is simply the fullness of a reality's being; for something to be good is for it to be altogether realized, to be fully what it is. But Jesus was fully divine and fully human. The Incarnation thus makes it clear that divine and human goods are not alternatives—there is not and cannot be any choice between being holy—that is, sharing in the perfection proper to God—and being humanly fulfilled. Vatican II, stressing the link between Jesus and us, says:

> Christ, the final Adam, by the revelation of the mystery of the Father and his love, fully reveals man to man himself and makes his supreme calling clear. . . .
>
> He who is "the image of the invisible God" (Col 1:15), is himself the perfect man. . . . Since human nature as he assumed it was not annulled, by that very fact it has been raised up to a divine dignity in our respect too. For by his incarnation the Son of God has united himself in some fashion with every man. He worked with human hands, he thought with a human mind, acted by human choice, and loved with a human heart. Born of the Virgin Mary, he has truly been made one of us, like us in all things except sin. (*GS* 22)

The complexity and unity of Jesus' twofold nature and unique person are present also in his actions. He does many things—for example, works miracles—which cannot be attributed to him only as God or only as man. His actions are both divine and human, without mixing the two. At the same time, however, there is absolute unity in his person and in what he brings about when he acts. Consider the raising of Lazarus from the dead. Jesus weeps as a man weeps, chooses as a man chooses, calls out to Lazarus as a man calls out; but he also acts as God, knowing as God knows, willing as God wills, giving life to a dead man as only God can. Throughout, moreover, he is one person performing an action— the Word, Jesus, raising Lazarus from the dead—while one thing happens: Lazarus is raised.

Jesus' whole life is like this. All of it is divine, and all of it is also human. The two aspects are not confused, commingled. They are united in the life of one person and in bringing about whatever he causes.

But how are the divine and the human both related and distinct in the life of Jesus?

Insofar as he is God, Jesus reveals the Father in the medium of his human life. It is revelatory; it communicates divine truth and love. The Gospel of John makes this very clear: for example, "Whoever has seen me has seen the Father" (Jn 14:9). Jesus is the Word made flesh, and his human life is the life of the Word; it always reveals and communicates the truth and love of the Father.

At the same time, insofar as he is man, Jesus is primarily responding to the Father. He deals with God as a man in this fallen world should do, accepting God's absolute supremacy and being faithful to his will, recognizing and repudiating evil, looking to God for redemption from evil, and so on. He lives the life of a true Israelite, fulfilling the old covenant by perfectly observing it.

The two aspects of Jesus' life are present simultaneously in everything he says and does. It is not as if part of his life were revelatory and part a human response to God. At one and the same time his whole life is both revelatory—the life of the Word lived to communicate God's truth and love—and a human response to God's mercy, a human sacrifice of obedience.

The two aspects, moreover, are mutually inclusive. Part of what the Word incarnate reveals in his human life is how human beings should respond to God; at the same time, his human life is a man's conscious cooperation with God revealing himself and saving humankind. In other words, Jesus' life, considered as revelatory divine action, reveals among other things how every man or woman should live, while part of his human project is living a human life of religious devotion by which he cooperates with God in revealing and redeeming.

This analysis is not of merely theoretical interest. Jesus' life provides the model of how Christian life should be organized. Christian life is cooperation with Christ. The makeup of a Christian must be like the makeup of Jesus, and the life of a Christian must be structured like his, with the same virtues one finds in his life, passion, and death. We shall begin to see what that means in the next chapter, which examines the life of Jesus more closely.

22. God's Redemptive Work in Jesus' Human Life

Christians are to share in Jesus' life by cooperating with him as well as imitating his virtues; but it is impossible fully to cooperate with someone without grasping what he or she is doing. In this chapter we reflect on Jesus' life in order to understand what it is Christians are to cooperate with.

Our source is the New Testament. We assume its historicity, while rejecting both a naive reading and skepticism. Our view is that of Vatican II:

> The sacred authors wrote the four gospels, selecting some things from the many which had been handed on by word of mouth or in writing, reducing some of them to a synthesis, explicating some things in view of the situation of their churches, and preserving the form of proclamation but always in such fashion that they told us the honest truth about Jesus. (*DV* 19)

A: The Large Choices That Shape Jesus' Life

One might suppose that Jesus, being God, had no important choices to make. As we saw in chapter sixteen, the fundamental option of Christian life is the act of faith, by which one turns away from sin and toward God, and renews the relationship with God which sin disrupted. Jesus obviously need not accept friendship with God. He is always in full communion with the Father, and there is no question of his accepting a relationship which he enjoys by reason of who he is. Furthermore, while we can sin by refusing to make the fundamental commitments we should make, Jesus not only does not but cannot sin. On that score, too, it seems that there was no place for a fundamental option in his life.

It does not follow, however, that Jesus faced no large choices. In arguing from his divinity, one must be very careful about excluding anything really human from his life. Certainly that is true of choice. Jesus "acted by human choice" (*GS* 22). He had choices to make, including some large choices.

Jesus is always in communion with the Father, but it is one thing for him always to be in that communion and another for him to act accordingly. His human life must be lived, and that does not happen automatically.

First of all, he must make a commitment to carry out the Father's will as he discerns it. For Jesus, as for us, that basic commitment is his fundamental option, his most inclusive commitment, the choice which organizes the rest of his life. And for him, as for us, no sooner is that fundamental option made than it raises the question: What *is* God's will for me? What is my personal vocation? Jesus surely asked himself that question, found the answer, and committed himself to carry out his heavenly Father's unique will *for him.*

Had Jesus not chosen to seek and fulfill his vocation, he would not have lived a fully human life and been a perfect man. Human, yes, but mutilated and incomplete in his humanity. Since he is really like us in everything but sin, however, we should not deny him something of central importance to a good human life: the discernment and fulfillment of a personal vocation, which embodies the Father's will for him.

The question of Jesus' human knowledge in general and his knowledge of his vocation in particular is interesting mainly for speculative theology. It is enough for our purposes to say that Jesus knew what he needed to know in order to carry out his mission, without supposing he constantly knew as man everything he knew as God. The latter would mean that, as man, he knew literally everything. But if he knew the future, he could not have made human choices, since one can only choose if one does not know in advance which alternative will be chosen and which will not. Simply from this perspective, it is clear that, as a man living a real human life, Jesus could not have known everything at the outset; his human knowledge was limited.

This makes some people uneasy. Anxious to protect Jesus' divinity, they say: "We must not deny to Jesus what belongs to God." Of course that is true. But the next step is *not* true: "Therefore, we must not deny to Jesus *as man* what belongs to God." That is commingling, and it leads to a false understanding of Jesus and his life. If this view were correct, Jesus would have had no human life to live; he would have been God pretending to be a man and merely going through the motions of living a human life—acting the part of Jesus of Nazareth but not really living it.

That would have consequences not only for him but, especially, for us. For then Jesus would not be a human leader with whom we could cooperate and share a common life. We could not really imitate him, except in superficial things, and we would be right to reason: "Jesus was God, and he did everything perfectly. But *I'm* not God, so Jesus is fundamentally irrelevant to the way I live." Either his human life was, in its essentials, the kind of life any other human being can live with the help of grace—a life, that is, within human power and capacity—or it was not really a human life. And were that the case, it would be irrelevant as a model for our imitation and cooperation. Commingling, which undercuts the reality of Jesus' humanity and his human life, is not only a theoretical mistake; practically speaking, it destroys the principle of our Christian lives.

The accounts of Jesus' temptations by the devil point to aspects of his basic commitment (cf. Mt 4:1–11; Mk 1:12–13; Lk 4:1–13). We find three elements: to do the Father's will ("One does not live by bread alone, but by every word that comes from the mouth of God" [Mt 4:4]); to rely completely on the Father's power, without demanding evidence of it beyond that provided in his providential plan ("Do not put the Lord your God to the test" [Mt 4:7]); and to refuse to compromise with evil even for the sake of accomplishing some good end ("Worship the Lord your God, and serve only him" [Mt 4:10]).

This, however, applies to all of us. What precisely was Jesus' unique personal vocation?

It was to be the savior, to establish the new and everlasting covenant, to be the leader of the new people of God. "I came not to judge the world, but to save the world" (Jn 12:47). "I came that they may have life, and have it abundantly" (Jn 10:10). "I have come as light into the world, so that everyone who believes in me should not remain in the darkness" (Jn 12:46). "For this I was born, and for this I came into the world, to testify to the truth" (Jn 18:37). Jesus himself is the mediator of the covenant which he gives us. "I am the way, and the truth, and the life. No one comes to the Father except through me. If you know me, you will know my Father also. From now on you do know him and have seen him" (Jn 14:6–7).

In order to choose this vocation, Jesus had first to work it out clearly in his mind. He found material in several sketches of the redeemer in the Old Testament. Three stand out: the Messiah, "anointed" by God to be Israel's liberator; the Son of Man, in Daniel 7 an otherworldly figure to whom the Father has given kingship and the judgment of the world; and, in Isaiah, the Suffering Servant, God's prophet and representative to Israel, who will save not alone the Jews but all humankind.

Jesus carries out these roles, but not according to preconceived notions. The anticipations of the Old Testament were helpful but not fully adequate; his vocation, as he came to understand it, transcended them all. Thus, he disappointed the expectations of many people. They looked for a redeemer according to a certain model; he did not correspond to the model they had in mind. He fulfilled the anticipations of the Old Testament in a way which went beyond any and all of them.

B: How Jesus Lived out Those Choices

Begin with the obvious: he prayed. Large choices must be implemented by smaller ones. In order to be guided in making his implementing choices, Jesus must constantly bring to bear his grasp of God's plan on the facts of his immediate situation. He does so in prayer—for that is what personal prayer essentially does. It translates God's general word to humankind into his particular word here and now for oneself; it is the individual appropriation of revelation, communication with God as personal communication. So, as the gospels, especially Luke's Gospel, often tell us, Jesus prayed. That is how he learned precisely what he should do.

He also preached and taught; he announced the kingdom. "Now after John was arrested, Jesus came into Galilee, preaching the gospel of God, and saying, 'The time is fulfilled, and the kingdom of God has come near; repent, and believe in the good news' " (Mk 1:14). Moreover, unlike the typical rabbi, he taught with authority (cf. Mt 7:28–29; Lk 4:32), not simply repeating what had been revealed earlier or transmitting a tradition, but bringing revelation to fulfillment and perfection:

> Long ago God spoke to our ancestors in many and various ways by the prophets, but in these last days he has spoken to us by a Son, whom he appointed heir of all things, through whom he also created the worlds. (Heb 1:1–2)

His life is revelatory in an original and unique way, and this is the source of the authority with which he speaks; he really communicates divine truth.

He directly attacks sin and its consequences. He forgives sinners, casts out demons, heals the sick and the crippled, raises the dead, thereby both eliciting faith and confirming it. He also begins to form the nucleus of the new covenant community. In one sense, there is continuity between God's people of the old and new covenants: we are Abraham's children, and our faith fulfills his. But in another sense there is a new foundation, in that Jesus transforms God's people of the old covenant into a new people. He starts with the apostles and disciples, who are to continue and build up his new covenant community.

In doing all these things, Jesus stirred up conflict. It was bound to happen. Many people of his day, members of the establishment, not only took for granted the limitations of the old covenant, but considered them necessary. They neither looked for nor wanted something different. But Jesus' authentic fulfillment of the old covenant challenged cherished assumptions. Conflict was inevitable; although certainly it is true, as Vatican II observes, that "what happened in his passion cannot be blamed upon all the Jews then living, without distinction, nor upon the Jews of today" (NA 4).

What was the root of the problem? It seems to have turned upon conflicting conceptions of evil and what to do about it.

The Pharisees, typically, externalized evil; they viewed it as something localized and objective—out there—from which those who wished to be pure must keep themselves apart. Their legalism promised security in exchange for behavioral exactness. One who minutely observes the code embodied in the law—rituals and purifications and the rest—is safe.

Jesus constitutes a challenge to this mentality. He does not regard evil as something which can be segregated and shunned, but as a privation which cuts across reality and is harbored in the human heart (see Mt 15:1–20; Mk 7:1–23). Evil cannot simply be evaded or avoided. It must be overcome by healing love. Some of the Pharisees were shocked and scandalized by this attitude. The conflict came to a head over the cures which Jesus worked on the sabbath. Jesus, in the Pharisees' view, was breaking the rules for dealing with evil. Wasn't he even seen regularly mixing with sinners? Indeed, he was. "Those who are well," he explained, "have no need of a physician, but those who are sick. Go and learn what this means, 'I desire mercy, not sacrifice.' For I have come to call not the righteous but sinners" (Mt 9:12–13).

Jesus' attitude and way of behaving are hardly less unsettling to another group, the zealots. They also tended to externalize evil, placing the emphasis on the political context. The Roman domination of Israel was profoundly offensive to them. Their preferred response was violence: Wipe out the enemy!

Jesus rejects this solution also. Violence destroys good along with evil. "Put your sword back into its place; for all who take the sword will perish by the sword" (Mt 26:52). Swords and violence only do more damage to the mutilated human situation. The answer to evil is healing love. It is not an answer acceptable to zealotry.

Jesus also comes into conflict with the leaders of the priestly caste. Having compromised with the Romans, they do not have clean hands and clean hearts. They are defenders of the status quo, anxious to maintain their position. This troublesome layman from Galilee threatens the stability which suits them. He must be gotten rid of.

In sum, Jesus is a challenge and a threat to those with power. Their response is typical of powerful people who feel threatened. They set out to kill him. It is important, too, that he die in a way which thoroughly discredits him: not merely the death of a social outcast, but a death which makes it clear that God has abandoned him. Crucifixion fills this prescription (as Gal 3:13 observes, "Cursed is everyone who hangs on a tree"); and for that, he must be turned over to the Roman oppressors themselves.

C: How Living out His Vocation Led to Jesus' Death and How His Death Was Redemptive

Jesus' death is a direct result of how he lives; it grows out of his seeing his vocation and carrying it out. Death does not cut short his life prematurely, before he can accomplish what he set out to do; rather, his death in some sense is itself the culmination of his life, the carrying out of his basic commitment, the fulfillment of his vocation. This is quite explicit in John's Gospel.

> After this, when Jesus knew that all was now finished, he said (in order to fulfill the scripture), "I am thirsty." A jar full of sour wine was standing there. So they put a sponge full of the wine on a branch of hyssop and held it to his mouth. When Jesus had received the wine, he said, "It is finished." Then he bowed his head and gave up his spirit. (Jn 19:28–30)

Somehow in this act of giving up his life he accomplishes that to which he had committed his life. How?

At the start of his public career, things went well. He and his message were received almost everywhere with enthusiasm and high expectations. Very soon, however, one begins to glimpse bad reactions here and there, even in his own home town, where "his friends" dismiss him with the caustic comment, "He has gone out of his mind" (Mk 3:21). Even where he is well received, people overlook or misunderstand what he is really saying, for they are expecting something quite different.

Of course, his preaching does not go entirely unheeded, and his miracles evoke feverish excitement. But the excitement of one miracle wears off quickly, and then people demand another. The crowds do not welcome redemption as Jesus proposes it, do not see that evil must be overcome as it really is. They want dazzling religious experiences. They want their needs met as they conceive of them. They do not recognize that their needs are shaped by sin and supported by rationalization. Jesus grasps the situation all too well. "Then he began to reproach the cities in which most of his deeds of power had been done, because they did not repent" (Mt 11:20).

On the whole, Jesus' career must have been frustrating for him. Still, he remains faithful to his vocation. There is no compromise, no watering down his message to make it popular. He is endlessly inventive and innovative; he teaches through brilliant parables; he works signs which dramatically underline his teaching. But he offers his fickle listeners, his opponents, and his followers no concessions which distort the message.

When even "many of his disciples" pronounce his teaching regarding the bread of life a hard saying, he responds without compromise: "The words that I have spoken to you are spirit and life" (Jn 6:63). When Peter remonstrates with Jesus over his prediction of his death, he replies: "Get behind me, Satan! You are a stumbling block to me; for you are setting your mind not on divine things but on human things" (Mt 16:23). He rejects the thought of not carrying out his vocation to the end, of backing off, making things easier for himself. For then he would have been silenced, neutralized.

Perhaps he could have survived by working miracles. Even when the crowd came to take him captive in the garden, he might have worked a miracle and slipped away. But what if he had? If Jesus had saved himself by miracles, even though this might have made it possible for him to continue his ministry—what kind of human life would that have been for us to imitate and cooperate in? He would have solved the problem of living in a fallen world by a use of divine power which ordinarily is inaccessible to us. In doing that, he would have rendered absurd the very idea of a redemptive Incarnation.

Instead, he continues to live out his vocation as a man—fulfilling the covenant but doing so in a way which goes beyond his hearers' expectations. For this he will be killed.

The specific choice which leads to his death is his choice to go up to Jerusalem to preach in the temple and celebrate the Passover. Aware that his enemies are seeking his life, he nevertheless persists. For his vocation requires that he call even his enemies, the leaders among the Pharisees and the priests, to repent. Most likely few if any of them will, but that does not mean he can neglect them. So he sets out to confront the religious and social establishment in Jerusalem, intending to present the truth to them in a way which could cause them to rally to him, yet knowing what instead will happen: "The Son of man is going to be betrayed into human hands, and they will kill him, and on the third day he will be raised" (Mt 17:22–23).

Jesus does not choose to be killed; he chooses to be faithful to his vocation. True, he anticipates and freely accepts death, consequent upon that choice; his death is therefore voluntary. But this is a case of something we have seen before: the free acceptance of a particular result as a side effect, rather than the willing of it as a means to an end. Jesus does not choose to kill himself; he is not a suicide. Rather, out of fidelity to the vocation he has received from his Father, he freely chooses a course of action which he knows will carry suffering and death along with it.

By itself, merely dying has no particular value. But accepting death out of fidelity is of value. In laying down his life as he does, Jesus, like martyrs generally, offers a gift, a sacrifice, to the Father.

Consequently, one of the inspired writers portrays Christ as saying at the moment of his coming into the world:

"Sacrifices and offerings you have not desired,

but a body you have prepared for me;

in burnt offerings and sin offerings you have taken no pleasure.

Then I said, 'See, God, I have come to do your will, O God,'

(in the scroll of the book it is written of me)."

When he said above, "You have neither desired nor taken pleasure in sacrifices and offerings and burnt offerings and sin offerings" (these are offered according to the law), then he added, "See, I have come to do your will." He abolishes the first in order to establish the second. And it is by God's will that we have been sanctified through the offering of the body of Jesus Christ once for all. (Heb 10:5–10)

As that makes clear ("*we* have been sanctified"), Jesus does not make his gift to the Father simply for his own sake. He understands himself as a leader, the man raised up by God to inaugurate the new covenant. As the New Testament's accounts of Jesus' institution of the Eucharist make clear, his free acceptance of death is a sacrifice which he offers in priestly fashion on behalf of his followers—both his followers then and his followers for all time to come. It is the human act which, on the human side, establishes the new covenant relationship: "This is my body which is given for you. . . . This cup that is poured out for you is the new covenant in my blood" (Lk 22:19–20).

God on his side accepts the gift and performs the substance of redemption, actually overcoming sin and its consequences. This is clearly marked out in Jesus' resurrection, which is the sign of God's acceptance of the gift. The resurrection is the divine act which, along with Jesus' human act of laying down his life, constitutes a permanent bond of human-divine cooperation. This *is* the new covenant. As the old covenant was sealed in blood (see Ex 24), for blood is life, so Jesus' blood seals the new and living bond between God and his people—his new people united with Jesus.

Divine acceptance of Jesus' gift also constitutes a community inasmuch as the Spirit is sent. Since Jesus is God, the new covenant really contains divine life; he communicates that life to the members of the covenant community by sending the Spirit at Pentecost and subsequently. Divine life is really available to Jesus' followers. The new covenant, unlike the old, is a relationship within which divine life is actually communicated. The anticipations of the prophets are fulfilled, who looked forward to a time when "a spirit from on high is poured out on us, and the wilderness becomes a fruitful field" (Is 32:15).

All this—Jesus' human act of offering his life, the Father's acceptance, the resurrection, the enlivening of the new covenant community by the sending of the Spirit—is sometimes called "objective redemption." There is no difficulty with that, provided it is clear what "objective" means here. Redemption is not a mechanical process or a tangible entity. It is a relational reality based on two acts: Jesus' human act of laying down his life and God's act of accepting that gift. Through the bond thus established, divine life is communicated to members of the covenant community. Thus, "objective" redemption signifies what God does with Jesus' human cooperation. This, as we shall see later, is important to understanding the sacraments, which are cooperative acts that make the covenant relationship present for us to participate in.

By our unity with Jesus, we are included in his covenant community and enjoy the benefit of his redemptive act; this benefit to us is what is called "subjective" redemption. But how, in fact, do *we* become involved in *Jesus'* act?

First, Jesus' death gives us a motive for loving God which we would not otherwise have: "God proves his love for us in that while we still were sinners Christ died for us" (Rom 5:8). One who accepts and understands this with faith is moved to reconsider his or her sinful life and ask a fundamental question: Will I join Christ or reject him? It is with us as it was with the two thieves crucified with Jesus; we can side with his enemies and join them in rejecting, mocking, and killing him; or we can side with Jesus and receive the fruit of that choice: "Today you will be with me in Paradise" (Lk 23:43).

Second, we can join in and cooperate with his action. The next chapter will treat this point at length, but we can summarize it here. Jesus does not live and die simply as an isolated individual. He is a leader with a mission: the establishment and extension of the new covenant community. But this work of his must be continued through history by those who come after him as his followers. By believing the gospel, seeking baptism, and participating in the Eucharist, we join in Jesus' sacrifice: in doing in his memory what he told us to do, we are united with his redemptive act. Moreover, to be a follower of Jesus means being his collaborator, carrying on his work of redemption in one's own particular way. The call to conversion is thus a call to apostleship; the two things are inseparable. In this way, too, we are involved in his act.

Finally, Jesus' example provides us with grounds for hope, and hope enables us to undertake living the Christian life and to persevere in it. In Jesus one finds the answer to the question: What will happen to me if I really try to live this way? It is that, even if such a life is frustrating and a failure by worldly standards, it is ultimately meaningful and worthwhile. The resurrection is God's pledge of that. The suffering which comes with trying to live a good life in a fallen world, building up the relationships with God and human beings that one should, and the crushing defeat of death which faces every human being—these things are bad but not final. The resurrection of Jesus grounds our hope that God's promise of re-creation will be realized in his followers, too: "For if we have been united with him in a death like his, we will certainly be united with him in a resurrection like his" (Rom 6:5).

23. God's Redemptive Work in the Lives of Christians

In this chapter we reach the heart of our treatment of Christian moral principles. What is central to Christian life? Jesus, whom we follow, and his work, with which we cooperate.

Jesus established the new covenant, the everlasting and unbreakable communion between the divine persons and human persons. But how do we enter into that community and share in it? Here we offer an overview of the answer; particular aspects will be examined in the chapters which follow, up through chapter thirty-three.

We cover four topics here: our unity with Jesus' redemptive act; what following Jesus involves; personal vocation; and why following Jesus requires conforming one's conscience to the teaching of the Church.

A: Our Unity with Jesus' Redemptive Act

God offers sinful humankind a new option in Jesus. Human beings, having sinned, are alienated from God, and although a covenant community exists in the Old Testament, the old covenant is not perfect and unbreakable. Jesus changes that. Unlike even the greatest figures of the Old Testament, he is not and cannot be unfaithful. In him, God brings about a perfect covenant, a permanent covenant community, and a new option for us.

This new option is communion with God in Jesus, which the gospel offers and the Holy Spirit gives in baptism. One accepts the gift, as we saw in chapter twenty, through the act of Christian faith. In being baptized and making that act of faith, one receives a share in Jesus' divine life by the gift of his Spirit and undertakes, by the Spirit's power, to do the Father's will as Jesus did.

In undertaking to do the Father's will, one also enters into cooperation with Jesus' redemptive act. He does a great deal more than give us a good example: he performs a social act—forms a community meant to last. Its chief work is to communicate divine truth and love and to confront evil and deal with it as it should be dealt with in a sinful, fallen world.

In sum, by the act of Christian faith a person accepts God's offer of friendship extended in Jesus, receives the gift of divine life, and undertakes to cooperate with Jesus' redemptive act.

But how do we cooperate? One could answer in several ways—for example, by focusing on incorporation in Christ, brought about preeminently by the Eucharist, and on the spiritual dynamic whereby Jesus' "members" become God's dwelling place in the world. The following answer, however, is developed in terms of human acts, the subject matter of moral theology.

We begin with a point made many times before: choices are not passing events but spiritual realities which last. When Jesus commits himself to do the Father's will, when he accepts his personal vocation, and when ultimately he freely lays down his life, these three choices make him who he is, and they remain. His human reality still exists, and, because he has not retracted or changed them, so do his self-determining choices.

We saw in the last chapter that Jesus' redemptive act is essentially his choice to go to Jerusalem and eat the Passover there with the apostles. Although he knows he will be killed, he freely accepts that side effect and persists in his plan out of faithfulness to his vocation. Thus, the Last Supper and the sacrifice of the cross are intrinsically linked, for the same inward human act of Jesus ties together the two outwardly distinct events.

At the Last Supper, Jesus told the apostles: "Do this in remembrance of me" (1 Cor 11:24). Even though they were not entirely clear about the significance of what he was doing and what they were to do, simply by sharing in that Passover they were cooperating with him in carrying out what was, in fact, his redemptive act, and so they were sharers in that act. Plainly, however, his directive—"Do this in remembrance of me"—was intended not just for them but extended to all who would come after them. So, Jesus' commandment to repeat his Eucharistic action establishes a real relationship between, on the one hand, his choice to go to Jerusalem and his free acceptance of death there, and, on the other, the act of every priest who consecrates in the Mass. Thus, the Mass continues to carry out Jesus' choice to celebrate the Last Supper and so it continues—and is— his redemptive act. As the Second Vatican Council expresses it: "At the Last Supper . . . our Savior instituted the Eucharistic Sacrifice of his Body and Blood. He did this in order to perpetuate the sacrifice of the Cross" (*SC* 47). Calvary and the Mass "are one and the same, differing only in the manner of offering."[15]

For the people of the Old Testament, renewing their part in the covenant meant recalling its terms and re-committing themselves to it. But to do in the Mass what Jesus does, "in remembrance of" him, is vastly more. It is to maintain the reality of what he does, keep it alive, and cooperate in it by an outward performance which expresses his lasting commitment. "Do this in remembrance of me" means: Carry out this performance and join in the commitment it expresses.

The apostles at the Last Supper and we at Mass today are not just imitating Jesus' act but taking part in it. Though interrupted in its performance, the first Eucharist never ends; the sacrifice of the cross and the repeated celebrations of the Mass are different outward aspects of one long, continuing human act: Jesus' community-forming, redemptive commitment, in which we join by doing what he told us to do. Individual celebrations of the Mass are of course many acts inasmuch as they are many different performances, but they are also outward expressions of one and the same act—Jesus' redemptive act—which he did as a social act in order to form the new covenant community.

If Christian life is cooperation with Jesus, this makes it clear why the Eucharist is a principle of Christian life. As we shall see in greater detail in chapter thirty-three, everything a follower of Jesus does ought properly to lead up to or follow from the Eucharist. Vatican II says:

Through his very flesh, made vital and vitalizing by the Holy Spirit, he offers life to men. They are thereby invited and led to offer themselves, their labors, and all created things together with him. . . . So priests must instruct [the faithful] to offer to God the Father the

divine Victim in the sacrifice of the Mass, and to join to it the offering of their own lives. (*PO* 5)

Everything a Christian does (except sin, put aside at the beginning of Mass) leads up to the Eucharist by constituting the living
self which the Christian offers with Jesus. From that offering,
which is participation in Jesus' commitment, flows a life which
has redemptive value insofar as it is lived not only in imitation of
Jesus' life but in unity with it. Having committed oneself to share
in his redemptive act and having performed that act outwardly in
the Eucharist, one turns to doing essentially what he did: communicating divine truth and love, confronting evil and dealing
with it in a healing way. At the end of Mass we are told to go
forth to love and serve the Lord, and *this* is loving and serving the
Lord.

B: What Following Jesus Means

People sometimes say, and may more often think, something
along the following lines: "It's all very well to speak of following
Jesus, but how practical is it? He lived two thousand years ago, in
a time and place and culture very different from ours. And he was
God. How can I be expected to 'imitate' him?"

Imitating Jesus does not mean adopting the externals of his behavior and manner of life. Scripture envisages something quite
different.

First of all, one must imitate the Father, the source of all holiness.

> Like obedient children, do not be conformed to the desires that you
> formerly had in ignorance. Instead, as he who called you is holy, be
> holy yourselves in all your conduct; for it is written, "You shall be
> holy, for I am holy." (1 Pt 1:14–16)

It follows that one must love one's neighbor, love enemies, be
compassionate and forgiving. In sum: "Be perfect, therefore, as
your heavenly Father is perfect" (Mt 5:48).

To say the least—a rather large order for a human being. Are
we really to take it seriously? In fact, we are. If someone is in the
state of grace—that is, united with Jesus in such a way that he or
she is in communion with the divine persons and shares in their
life—the prescription to live a life like Jesus' is not impractical or
beyond reasonable expectation. "Those who abide in me and I in
them bear much fruit" (Jn 15:5). Someone who is really a child
of God can live accordingly.

We are therefore called to keep Jesus' commandments. "Those who love me will keep my word, and my Father will love them, and we will come to them and make our home with them. Whoever does not love me does not keep my words" (Jn 14:23–24). Following Jesus means living out faith.

Scripture makes it overwhelmingly clear that loving others is central to following Jesus and keeping his commandments. "This is my commandment, that you love one another as I have loved you" (Jn 15:12). Love in this context is more than good feelings, politeness, and externally friendly behavior, for these can coexist with profound selfishness. Love means voluntarily performing real services. To love someone requires doing good to him or her.

There is nothing wrong with affectionate feelings toward others, but one can have such feelings without the reality of love. Suppose a man truly feels fond of his wife and children yet grossly neglects them—and then feels even fonder because he also feels guilty: Is this love? Love is first of all good will and faithful performance. There is no real love otherwise.

Christians, moreover, are to love others as Jesus loves them. This means helping him redeem them. Here is the vocation common to Christians precisely as Jesus' followers, "Whoever wishes to be first among you must be your slave; just as the Son of Man came not to be served but to serve, and to give his life a ransom for many" (Mt 20:27–28). Redemptive service is not simply giving others what they want; it is trying to help them confront evil and overcome it in reality.

That may not be too difficult with people who are well disposed and basically good, but it will be very difficult in the case of those deep in sin, for they have a perverse sense of what is good for them. Yet someone who really loves them cannot simply leave them as they are, since that means leaving them in sin. God does not simply accept sinners as they are; he accepts them in order to transform them. Only someone who does not take sin seriously can take a complacent view of sinners. But redemptive love does take sin seriously, and it seeks to transform sinners by offering them the opportunity of a new life of holiness.

Obviously, one should not be obnoxious about this, adopt a superior attitude, engage in badgering and browbeating. But, while proceeding prudently and as gently as one can, one must be honest with people about the reality of their situation. Some will be led to conversion, faith, and growth in holiness. Others will react with resentment and hostility. Having been shown, even if only by example, the way of Jesus—a way they do not want to follow—they will find things to condemn in it and in those who do try to live like this. Trying to fulfill Jesus' commandment to love others redemptively unavoidably leads to trouble for one who makes the attempt. Such a person must say no, in deeds and perhaps in words, to things others say yes to; as a result, he or she will encounter criticism, persecution. Christian life means taking up the cross.

"If any want to become my followers, let them deny themselves and take up their cross and follow me" (Mt 16:24). We should suppose that Jesus means what he says. The cross takes different forms in the lives of different people, but it is always present in a redemptive life—an authentically "countercultural" life lived against the grain of worldly standards. People who try to live this way will pay a price. They will be not only provocative but vulnerable, unwilling to protect themselves or retaliate by using the immoral means used against them.

By carrying the cross in this manner, one prepares a sacrifice to bring to the Mass and offer with Jesus' sacrifice. A merely pleasant and easy life does not provide a great deal to offer. Not that one should seek a life which is hard and unpleasant; yet in some way and to some degree, discipleship *will* be unpleasant and hard, because others will make it so. Christian life, as a *costly* discipleship, thus becomes the Christian's own precious contribution to the Eucharist.

This is what active participation in the Eucharist means. It is good for people to sing at Mass, do the readings, perform other roles and functions. Doing these things may even help them and others to participate in a deeper sense. But this deeper active participation is what matters: that in coming to the Eucharist, one really offers one's life—a life lived in a way that makes it worth offering—with Jesus, while joining him in his offering of himself. Without that, no other kind of "active participation" counts for much.

C: The Idea of Personal Vocation

Personal vocation is central to following Jesus. His basic commitment was to do his Father's will, but along with this he also had a personal vocation—a unique role, embodying his grasp on the Father's will for him in particular. He was to be the redeemer and savior, the leader who formed, on the human side, the everlasting community of divine persons and human persons.

Although we are to follow Jesus, we are obviously not meant to do exactly what he did. His task was his, not ours; we cannot do it, and we need not, since in fact he did form this community, it still exists, and he still continues to form it by the unceasing work of the Holy Spirit. There is only one sacrifice in the new covenant; Jesus "offered for all time a single sacrifice for sins" (Heb 10:12). Thus, individual Masses are not additional sacrifices, but different enactments of Jesus' one and only sacrifice. In the New Testament there is, in a sense, only one priest, Jesus (see Heb 7:26–28). The priests who come after him are not priests independently of him but his proxies, doing what he told them to do in his name. The offering in the Mass is really Jesus' act, not the individual act of the ordained person who does it. The ordained priest's personal, individual act is only to serve as a proxy; the priestly act itself belongs to Jesus.

Each of us, however, whether ordained or not, has a combination of gifts and opportunities peculiar to himself or herself. We must examine these for their redemptive potential—the possibilities they offer of communicating God's truth and love, meeting evil, not least in ourselves, and dealing with it as it should be dealt with. Herein lies the personal vocation of each one of us: ability meets opportunity according to God's providential plan. One discerns one's vocation in coming to see one's own particular gifts and opportunities as providential in relation to the needs of the Church and the world.

There is a narrow sense of vocation—the particular calling of certain men and women to the priesthood and religious life—and it is still common for people to speak of and pray for "vocations" as if only a few Christians had them. Certainly it is good to pray that those who have vocations to the priesthood and religious life—and, no less, those who have vocations to marriage and family life—will recognize and accept them. But beyond a vocation to one or another state of life, everyone has his or her unique set of gifts and opportunities, and all Christians should live out their faith according to the gifts and opportunities which are theirs: that is, they should discern, accept, and live their personal vocations.

Vatican II uses "vocation" in several different senses—the human vocation as such (to realize the destiny which God has in mind for human beings), the common vocation of Christians (to follow Jesus and live redemptively), vocation as state of life, the vocation to the priesthood or religious life. The Council also recognizes personal vocation—for example, in urging parents to encourage their children "in the vocation which is proper to each of them" (*LG* 11) or, again, in pointing out that faith itself requires Christians to measure up to their earthly responsibilities, "each according to his proper vocation" (*GS* 43). Pope John Paul II speaks often of personal vocation. For instance:

> For the whole of the community of the People of God and for each member of it what is in question is not just a specific "social membership"; rather, for each and every one what is essential is a particular "vocation." Indeed, the Church as the People of God is also—according to the teaching of St. Paul mentioned above, of which Pius XII reminded us in wonderful terms—"Christ's Mystical Body." Membership in that body has for its source a particular call united with the saving action of grace. Therefore, if we wish to keep in mind this community of the People of God, which is so vast and so extremely differentiated, we must see first and foremost Christ saying in a way to each member of the community: "Follow Me."[16]

All commitments should be made in such a way that they carry out one's faith; they should comprise a unified whole—unified in and by faith itself. Thus, personal vocation is not simply a matter of making the commitment of faith. Rather, all of one's commitments—to marry or not marry, to pursue this particular profession or line of work, and so on—pertain to personal vocation, and should be undertaken for the sake of carrying out one's faith. The unified whole which they come together to form is nothing less than the controlling agenda of the unique Christian life of the one who makes them.

The fulfillment of one's personal vocation accomplishes at least three things.

First, it contributes to the glory of God—that is, the expression of his goodness—insofar as God's glory is manifested in yet another unique and wonderful way. No life is just like another, and every Christian is a special work of God, "created in Christ Jesus for good works" (Eph 2:10). Jesus' humanity is the greatest and most perfect of creatures, but it is limited; our lives and our holiness are needed to complete Jesus and carry on his work.

Second, each Christian is an indispensable member of the body of Christ. The Spirit gives different gifts to each member for the service of the whole body.

> Now there are varieties of gifts, but the same Spirit; and there are varieties of services, but the same Lord; and there are varieties of activities, but it is the same God who activates all of them in everyone. To each is given the manifestation of the Spirit for the common good. (1 Cor 12:4–5; see the whole of 1 Cor 12–14)

The variety of personal vocations is meant to build up the body of Christ as a unified whole which will last forever.

Third, personal vocations are meant to play their role in the process of sanctification. Everything which has suffered injury and alienation as a result of sin—and in some way that takes in the whole created universe (see Rom 8:19–22)—must be purified, healed, and placed at the service of the good. This is the work of the Holy Spirit, but it is carried on through the faithful fulfillment of their personal vocations by countless individual Christians who contribute to redemption precisely insofar as they are gradually sanctified as they do everything—work, family and social life, recreation, and all the rest—in a Christian way. Indeed, by living their personal vocations Christians are meant both to become holy and to redeem the whole culture, uniting it to Jesus and so restoring it to God.

Thus personal vocation is a central principle of Christian life. Children should be introduced to the idea early in their Christian formation, certainly by the time they reach adolescence. At that stage, of course, they have not decided what they mean to do with their lives, but they need to have it firmly in mind that their lives should be lived cooperating with Jesus in his redemptive work.

And if the question of personal vocation is never raised with them? Then, whenever they do come to think about their lives, they are likely to be preoccupied by questions like "Which will best meet my emotional needs—marriage or an alternate lifestyle?" and "Where can I make the most money and enjoy the greatest prestige?" and "What forms of recreation are the most fun?" Meanwhile, few lay people will see their lives in redemptive terms, and the "vocations crisis" in the priesthood and religious life will continue, since few will think of becoming priests and religious.

D: Why One Must Conform One's Conscience to the Church's Teaching

Different roles and responsibilities require different standards and patterns of behavior. In this sense, the variety of personal vocations means real diversity and pluralism. Christian lives are *not* all the same; they *should* be different.

At the same time, moral norms are not rules, customs, or expressions of individual inclination; they are truths. As such, they should be accepted and observed by everyone to whom they apply. Standards of behavior which are specifically relevant to married life do not apply to one who is not married, standards governing priestly ministry do not pertain to those who are not priests, and so on. But all moral standards, as truths, *do* apply to everyone to whom they are relevant.

Furthermore, every Christian is called to apostleship, and apostleship has a prophetic character: more than just receiving and benefiting from God's truth and love, it means communicating these to others. It is not enough simply to receive the gift of justification from God; one must also make it available to others.

Not just priests and religious have the prophetic mission of spreading the faith by bearing witness to God's truth and living it out. Vatican II says Jesus continues his prophetic work

> not only through the hierarchy who teach in his name and with his authority, but also through the laity. For that very purpose he made them his witnesses and gave them understanding of the faith and the grace of speech (cf. Acts 2:17–18; Rv 19:10), so that the power of the gospel might shine forth in their daily social and family life. (*LG* 35)

Elsewhere the Council says that

> the laity, too, share in the priestly, prophetic, and royal office of Christ. . . .
>
> They exercise a genuine apostolate by their activity on behalf of bringing the gospel and holiness to men, and on behalf of penetrating and perfecting the temporal sphere of things through the spirit of the gospel. In this way, their temporal activity can openly bear witness to Christ and promote the salvation of men. (*AA* 2)

Whether one is a cleric, a religious, or a lay person, doing this requires that on appropriate occasions one articulate what one believes. Different people will do this in different ways, depending on their personalities and backgrounds and circumstances— depending, in a word, on their personal vocations. But every Christian, according to the opportunities and the needs, should express what he or she believes in a way suited to him or her, and should live accordingly. The two things together, faith articulated and faith lived, are prophetic.

When someone lives as a Christian and gives an account of his or her life in terms of the gospel, other people are confronted with the reality of God's truth and love. Here is a way of life which is strange by worldly standards. This Christian does not use bad means to reach good ends; eschews many pursuits and gratifications which other people take for granted; refrains from retaliation against enemies and forgives them; and so on. Moreover, an explanation and a rationale underlie this way of life: "We who live this way are following Christ, and it makes sense to do that." As Vatican II says:

> For, wherever they live, all Christians are bound to show forth, by the example of their lives and by the witness of their speech, that new man which they put on at baptism, and that power of the Holy Spirit by whom they were strengthened at confirmation. Thus other men, observing their good works, can glorify the Father (cf. Mt 5:16) and can better perceive the real meaning of human life and the bond which ties the whole community of mankind together. (*AG* 11)

Because the Church's unity is a unity in divine love, modeled and based on the Trinity, Christians should not be in conflict with one another in the way they live their lives. There can, and indeed should, be all the diversity and pluralism required by different personal vocations. But disparity and conflicts are not acceptable in matters that concern all. It will not do to have some Catholics trying to justify their undergoing or performing abortions while others defend the sanctity and inviolability of the lives of the unborn. This is not pluralism; it is the destruction of the Church from within. That is so whenever there is conflict among Catholics on doctrinal and moral issues.

Precisely so that all can give the witness of their diverse lives in a coherent manner for which one and the same gospel can account, the Church's teaching is needed to bring unity of faith into life. It is not a set of rules. It clarifies the truths of faith and the requirements of Christian life.

In sum, our involvement in a common apostolate requires that we receive common moral teaching and follow it. Anticipating that its *Declaration on Religious Freedom* might be misinterpreted in a contrary sense, Vatican II makes this point in that very document.

> In the formation of their consciences, the Christian faithful ought carefully to attend to the sacred and certain doctrine of the Catholic Church. For the Catholic Church is, by the will of Christ, the teacher of the truth. It is her duty to give utterance to, and authoritatively to teach, that Truth which is Christ himself, and also to declare and confirm by her authority those principles of the moral order which have their origin in human nature itself. Furthermore, let Christians walk in wisdom in the face of those outside, "in the Holy Spirit, in unaffected love, in the word of truth" (2 Cor 6:6–7). Let them be about their task of spreading the light of life with all confidence and apostolic courage, even to the shedding of their blood. (*DH* 14; translation amended)

Consciences conformed to the teaching of the Church still have much work to do. To begin with, everyone must find his or her own personal vocation and make a commitment to it; no one can do that for someone else. Then, in living out one's vocation, one constantly encounters opportunities and obstacles; here, too, no one else's conscience can substitute for one's own in determining how to choose among incompatible opportunities (even among duties) and overcome obstacles to faithfulness. Finally, within this context of personal vocation it often is necessary to develop new moral norms in response to new situations and challenges. Accepting the teaching of the Church in every particular thus leaves room for substantial moral creativity.

24. Christians: Human Children of God

We saw in chapter nineteen that Christian life involves unity with Jesus in his divine life, in his human acts, and in his bodily life. Unity in divine life is plainly the most important, and it is to that we now turn. Essentially, we propose to explore the implications of St. Paul's words in the Epistle to the Romans: "God's love has been poured into our hearts through the Holy Spirit that has been given to us" (Rom 5:5).

From the point of view of dogma, this topic belongs to the treatise on grace. But from the point of view of moral theology we need to see how Christian life is the life of one who is a member by adoption of the divine family and how Christian love is such a person's new nature. In this way we shall uncover the meaning of realities which popular religious discourse tends to treat sentimentally or as mere metaphors. Three questions will be considered: what divine life is in us; the relationship between the human act of faith and the love of God poured forth in our hearts; and the human-divine makeup of the Christian.

A: What Divine Life in Us Is

In its deepest meaning, "love" refers to interpersonal communion, a unity of two or more persons which respects and even perfects their uniqueness. But to reach this depth of meaning, it is best to proceed step by step, beginning with a simple grammatical observation. The verb "to love" always has, expressly or tacitly, both a direct and an indirect object: one loves something (direct object) for someone (indirect object).

Love's direct object, the *something* loved, often is confused with the object of desire. But even before one desires a particular good, one must have a positive orientation toward it, and that orientation is love. Again, when desire is satisfied, one enjoys the good one previously desired and continues to love it; love therefore underlies joy as well. Thus, love is a disposition which orients one to the good which fulfills. It presupposes knowledge, since one must be aware of something as potentially fulfilling in order to love it. And because human beings have sentient knowledge and intellectual knowledge, they have both emotional love and volitional love.

Although it is impossible to love anything one does not perceive as promising fulfillment, this does not mean that love's indirect object, the someone loved, is limited to oneself. For where do we find real fulfillment? Not in ourselves in isolation, but only with others, in goods we must share so as to participate in them.

Take love considered as a disposition to fulfillment in the good of human life. Even in its biological aspects, one begins to participate in this good only in a community—parents and child, the family. Again, harmony with others—friendship—is a good which fulfills the individual, but an individual can only participate in the good of friendship with someone else who also shares in it. Thus, while the fulfillment of all love includes one's own good, one is only fulfilled *with* others and, usually, *in* others as well.

Because "love" is an active, transitive verb, we tend to think of loving as an action which one person does to another. "John loves Mary" seems rather like "John hugs Mary." That is a mistake. Even though volitional love is an action and any sort of love is likely to result in outward behavior, love itself is not doing anything to anybody. Loving another is a disposition to the other's fulfillment.

But if love is a disposition toward one's own fulfillment, how is it also a disposition toward someone else's? Because, as we have just said, one's own fulfillment is necessarily bound up with the well-being and full being of others. To be a person is not only to be an individual but to be a member of an interpersonal communion—a member of a family, one of a pair of friends, and so forth. People need one another to be fully themselves. Instinct leads to affection, and affection leads to sympathy; while insight into human goods leads to unselfish interests which make possible benevolence, mutual regard, and commitments to cooperate in community. Love of another is unity with the other. To love one's neighbor means being united with him or her inasmuch as his or her good is one's own good and his or her suffering also is one's own.

This is real unity, but it is not a merging of persons. To love someone else does not mean making him or her one's appendage—or vice versa. Just as individualism is opposed to and destructive of community, so is collectivism at the other extreme. Unity *and* distinction are essential to love.

The Trinity is the preeminent instance of unity and distinction of persons. It is a matter of faith that in God there are three persons who are perfectly distinct but absolutely one. Furthermore, one can think of God, as the words "Father" and "Son" require, in familial terms. Of course, the Trinity is not a family as a human family is; but it is correct, even necessary, to think of God on the model of a family—beginning with "the Father, from whom every family in heaven and on earth takes its name" (Eph 3:14-15).

"God is love" (1 Jn 4:8). We have just said that love is a unity of persons which respects their distinctness. But the very reality of God is to be three in one, one in three—unity in distinctness, distinction in perfect unity. God therefore is love. Love is what God is.

This points to the moral significance of the doctrine of the Trinity, its implications for Christian life. And that is a matter of considerable importance. In one way or another, every Christian doctrine is normative, yet homilies and catechetical materials frequently fail to indicate what doctrines have to do with life. Yet in telling us that God is love—not in a sentimental sense but in reality—the doctrine of the Trinity tells us something of profound practical importance.

Try thinking about the relationship of human beings to God apart from Christianity—apart, that is, from the doctrine of the Trinity: what then?

Then two opposed tendencies emerge. One is to suppose that the misery of the human condition arises from the fact that human beings are not just alienated from God but outside God; the solution then seems to lie in being merged into God (or the absolute or the transcendent or whatever name one prefers to "God"). Much Eastern religion takes this view, and to some extent it has found its way into strains of Christian spirituality which tend to regard prayer, contemplation, and ascetical practice as ways of obliterating one's identity and being absorbed into God. That is not Christian, and it is a mistake. If God creates us to absorb us, there is no point in his creating us in the first place.

The other tendency, which stresses God's otherness, is to suppose there can be no real intimacy between human beings and God. This image of a remote God is found in Aristotle, in Islam, and to some extent even in the Old Testament. In this view, a vast chasm which cannot be bridged separates us from God. A few privileged souls are vouchsafed fleeting glimpses of divinity, but only from afar. Real communion is impossible.

The doctrine of the Trinity tells us something very different: in principle, divine life is *not* incommunicable; but its communication does *not* do away with distinct personhood. The Christian God, the Trinity, is a family. Compared with the ideas of God in other world religions and philosophies, that is startling.

Furthermore, and no less startling, human persons are called to become members of the divine family. The revelation of the Trinity makes it clear that God intends this. "See what love the Father has given us, that we should be called children of God; and that is what we are" (1 Jn 3:1). God calls us to enter into a union with the divine persons similar to their union with one another. "Those who love me will keep my word, and my Father will love them, and we will come to them and make our home with them" (Jn 14:23). "As the Father has loved me, so I have loved you; abide in my love" (Jn 15:9). This language of "abiding in" means the Christian is to be in relationship with the divine persons much as they are with one another; we are to be related to the Father much as Jesus is, though with the differences that distinguish adopted children from a natural son.

This is to say that sharing in divine life means the Christian is divinized. He or she can truly be said to "be God." Strange as this way of speaking sounds to us, it was not strange to the Fathers of the Church. St. Irenaeus says Jesus "became what we are, so that he might bring us to be what he himself is." St. Athanasius says the Word "became man so that we might be made God." St. Basil the Great says that by the Spirit's gift the Christian is "made God." St. Augustine says grace deifies the Christian.[17]

Plainly, Christians "are God" in a special sense; "George is God" does not mean just the same thing as "the Holy Spirit is God." As created persons, Christians are divine only by adoption; nor are they so many independent deities. Yet one can say truly that "George is God, Helen is God, all of us are God if we are in grace" insofar as George, Helen, and all of us share in the one divine reality.

This is not a metaphor. Consider what St. John of the Cross says in *The Living Flame of Love:*

Having been made one with God, the soul is somehow God through participation. Although it is not God as perfectly as it will be in the next life, it is like the shadow of God. Being the shadow of God through this substantial transformation, it performs in this measure in God and through God what he through himself does in it. For the will of the two is one will, and thus God's operation and the soul's is one. Since God gives himself with a free and gracious will, so too the soul (possessing a will the more generous and free the more it is united with God) gives to God, God himself in God; and this is a true and complete gift of the soul to God.[18]

The idea of our divinization is so astonishing, and so different from anything we ordinarily think, that we tend to cast about for ways to weaken its force by giving it an attenuated meaning. That empties Christianity itself of meaning. "But to all who received him, who believed in his name, he gave power to become children of God" (Jn 1:12); "Beloved, we are God's children now; what we will be has not yet been revealed. What we do know is this: when he is revealed, we will be like him, for we will see him as he is" (1 Jn 3:2). Not to believe the reality expressed here, or to interpret it in merely sentimental or metaphorical terms, misses the very heart of Christian revelation.

This also has consequences for Christian life. If one is *not* really a child of God (or if being a "child of God" is a metaphor for some far less intimate relationship), then there is no reason to try to live like a child of God. "Be perfect . . . as your heavenly Father is perfect" (Mt 5:48) only means "Be good." In other words, it is pious talk which no one takes seriously.

But the divinization of the Christian is a central mystery of faith whose profession is implicit each time a believer makes the Sign of the Cross. Three mysteries are signified: the Trinity ("In the name of the *Father* and of the *Son* and of the *Holy Spirit*"); the redemptive Incarnation (it is the Sign of the *Cross*); and our adoption as God's children. For when we say "In the name," we recall that we were baptized *into* the name of the divine persons and so became members of their family; and in blessing *ourselves,* we signify that we possess divine life in such a way that we can really exercise it.

B: The Relationship between Christian Faith and Christian Love of God

Given the reality of sin, our difference from God lies not only in the fact that we are creatures but in our being alienated from him. Christian life does not begin from a neutral position but from this state of alienation. That underlines the absolute gratuitousness of God's way of loving us: almost as if the alienation were his fault, not ours. St. Paul's grasp of this circumstance has the proper note of astonishment: "Indeed, rarely will anyone die for a righteous person. . . . But God proves his love for us in that while we still were sinners Christ died for us" (Rom 5:7–8).

But God does not simply accept sinners as they are, for that would signify either that sin is not real or that God does not care about it. Sin is real, however, and God does care. He accepts sinners in order to change them, convert them—transform them into saints. He calls them to "clothe yourselves with the new self, created according to the likeness of God" (Eph 4:24) and "walk in newness of life" (Rom 6:4).

Nevertheless, God does not impose divine life on human persons. To make us "be God" without involving us would deny us a morally significant role in the most important aspect of our lives. God offers us reconciliation and a share in his own life, but, respecting our dignity, he leaves it to us to accept or reject the offer—to make a choice. We can freely accept God's love, his gift of self, very much as we accept love in human relationships.

One might ask whether the "love of God" is God's love for us or our love for God. In fact, it is both. God communicates divine love to us; we accept it, share in it, return it. There is no sharp distinction. But it is a question how, on our side of the relationship, this happens. Here the act of faith is crucial.

The free choice to believe has human goods in view. Before hearing the gospel, we are in a genuinely bad way: human life is difficult and ends in death; we sin, God's law written in our hearts tells us we sin, and we know our sinning is self-destructive. In itself, the fallen human condition is literally hopeless. A great deal of rationalization and cultivation of illusion are required just to get through life.

Only now there is an alternative: faith. The gospel really is good news for fallen humankind; one cannot imagine any better. The "story" of faith offers a way out of the human predicament. It shows how one can live a morally good life and also that such a life makes sense. And, unlike other world views, faith gives an explanation of life which is plausible.

It is very doubtful whether those who subscribe to certain other world views really could believe in them except to the extent they possess elements common to Judaeo-Christian faith. For example, although Marxism and Western liberal humanism undoubtedly provide people with something around which to organize their lives, these secular creeds offer nothing for a serious person to believe in beyond what they share with faith.

Thus, simply from a human point of view there are good grounds for the act of faith. Desire for redemption from the human predicament and the plausibility of the gospel combine to move us to believe.

But "God's love . . . poured into our hearts through the Holy Spirit" also transforms sinners into God's children. As such, they have more than human good as a reason for believing. God's children accept this relationship offered them by God not just because it makes sense of life and extricates them from a hopeless situation, but because, sharing in God's life, they are disposed to its fullness. Faith is thus transformed by the divine love which faith accepts. The act of living faith is the first act which we do by the love of God poured forth in our hearts by the Holy Spirit. While this act is acceptance of God's offer of salvation, it is also commitment to the divine persons because one is a member of the divine family. Loving them as they love one another is the fruit of faith and charity together.

God is love: divine love is God's reality as one in Trinity; whereas we, in accepting the love of God, remain the persons we are. We do not become the Father or the Son or the Holy Spirit, and there are no other divine persons. The freedom with which God offers his love to us and the freedom with which we accept it remain distinct, and we remain distinct persons. It is not unlike the situation with a husband and a wife: mutual consent unites them in communion even while they remain irreducibly distinct persons.

Yet, we do enter into a real unity with the members of the divine family by accepting divine love. The doctrine of the Trinity reveals the communicability of divine life: through the gift of the Holy Spirit poured forth in our hearts, we become members of the divine family. As the Word became the man, Jesus, while remaining a divine person, so we can become God, while remaining the human persons we are.

C: The Human-Divine Makeup of the Christian

Popular spiritual writing of former times often suggested that loving God means preferring him to created goods, while sin means preferring creatures to God. This view shaped many devout Christians' thinking to such an extent that their very experience of temptation and the struggle for holiness seemed to confirm it. One bad result was that many became convinced that to love God one must regard this-worldly goods as unimportant in themselves, and valuable only as means to communion with God in heaven.

Vatican Council II takes a very different view. It teaches that Christian hope for eternal happiness in heaven "does not lessen the importance of earthly duties, but rather adds new motives for fulfilling them" (*GS* 21; translation supplied). Elsewhere, speaking of the diverse elements which make up the created order of this world, the Council says:

> All of these not only aid in the attainment of man's ultimate goal but also possess their own intrinsic value. This value has been implanted in them by God, whether they are considered in themselves or as parts of the whole temporal order. "God saw all that he had made, and it was very good" (Gn 1:31). This natural goodness of theirs takes on a special dignity as a result of their relation to the human person, for whose service they were created. Last of all, it has pleased

God to unite all things, both natural and supernatural, in Christ Jesus "that in all things he may have the first place" (Col 1:18). This destination, however, not only does not deprive the temporal order of its independence, its proper goals, laws, resources, and significance for human welfare but rather perfects the temporal order in its own intrinsic strength and excellence and raises it to the level of man's total vocation upon earth. (*AA* 7)

In this and other passages, the Council gives its response to modern secular humanism's critique of Christianity.

If loving God requires us to regard human goods as unimportant, it is not hard to see what that critique must be: "Christianity is inhuman—and so much the worse for it." This converges with the defensiveness typical of sinners: "I don't want to believe in Christianity, for then I'd have to adopt the Christian life-style, and I don't wish to change." Take these two things together—the vulnerability of a certain way of presenting the gospel to the charge of being anti-human and the reaction of sinners to the gospel's demands—and it is no surprise that many people find the anti-Christian stance of modern secular humanism plausible and appealing. For it rationalizes sin while emphasizing real human values not always sufficiently appreciated by Christians.

All this leads to our point: there is an important sense in which loving God does not and cannot mean preferring him to any human good. To see the point, imagine a choice between two alternatives: the infinitely good God and some finitely good creature. Loving God would be preferring him in the sense of choosing him over that creature. In fact, we never are presented with these alternatives, and so we simply cannot prefer God in this way. And since it cannot be done, it cannot be what loving God means.

As we saw in speaking of the Incarnation, while for something to be of one finite nature automatically means it cannot be of another finite nature, the Incarnation shows that this limitation is not true of divinity. Divinity does not exclude a person of another nature from sharing in it or prevent a person who is divine from also being of another nature. Jesus is God *and* man. Divinity therefore is not partial and exclusive. God's perfection includes the perfection of everything else; his goodness embraces all good. There is, and can be, no opposition between love of God and genuine love of human goods. Rather, someone who loves God properly will love everything else as he does, and God loves every creature to the full extent of its goodness and moves it toward its fulfillment.

Furthermore, divine goodness as such is not, and cannot be, an object of human choice, since every choice is to do some *human* act in view of some *human* good. This is so even for one who is God's adopted child. True, insofar as such a person chooses to accept this relationship with God, he or she chooses it as an instance of the human good of religion; but insofar as the relationship goes beyond that human good, divine filiation is not realized in and through an act chosen by a Christian but is something given to him or her altogether gratuitously by God.

Nor in sinning can human beings be said precisely to prefer created goods to God. We can only prefer one created good to another. If that is done wrongly, of course, one does not truly love God either, for then one is failing to love the good comprehensively, as he does. Instead, one is opting for human good in an immorally limited way—a way which is self-mutilating because contrary to integral human fulfillment. This can no doubt be called preferring a creature to God, but *not* in the sense that divine goodness and human goods are alternatives for human choice. They are not and cannot be.

How then are the human and the divine related in the Christian? Fundamentally, they are related as they are in Jesus. There is no need for him to choose between human fulfillment and divine goodness. He loves all human goods rightly, for he loves them as God does, to the full extent of their goodness. The relationship between the human and divine in us is like that. As they are in Jesus, humanity and divinity are distinct in us but not opposed, united but not commingled.

A number of problems and errors result if this is not really accepted. Among these is the tendency to suppose that, as human, a Christian is vastly different from Jesus: "He was God, but I am just a human being, and therefore. . ." Thus the principle of Christian life is destroyed: there is no unity between the Christian and Jesus as cooperators in human acts. But if we recognize that the divine and the human are united in us much as they are in him, it will be clear that our likeness to him is such that we can really share in his human life as well as in his divine life and his bodily life.

Another error is to regard the supernatural life of grace as an alternative to human well being. Some formed by the old-fashioned piety mentioned earlier tended to make this mistake: the less human one is, the holier one is. Not only is this false, it gravely hampers the preaching of the gospel today.

Finally, one will be likely to think that the natural as such is incomplete—God's creation is mutilated, less than good. That is hardly compatible with Genesis, according to which God found everything he made "very good" (Gn 1:31). Our condition is not unsatisfactory because we are creatures or human beings, but because of sin. The "restless" human hearts of which St. Augustine speaks are restless not because they are human but because they are the hearts of persons in a condition of sin, to whom only saving grace, which also is deifying, can bring peace.

Sometimes the divinization of Christians is thought of as if it were simply an aspect of human life; grace is treated as something created, something merely human. So someone may say: "What is absolute in Christian life is charity (or grace), and charity means love of neighbor." In a way, of course, that is true. Not just individuals in isolation are called to be children of God but the whole of humankind. We should regard everyone else as either a fellow member of the divine family or potentially one; if someone is a sinner, we should want him or her to repent. Charity *does* mean love of neighbor.

Often enough, however, love of neighbor is taken to mean simply being friendly and generous and getting along with others. Plainly, that should be part of it. But also: "I have not come to bring peace, but a sword. For I have come to set a man against his father, and a daughter against her mother, and a daughter-in-law against her mother-in-law" (Mt 10:34–35). Jesus does not mean to destroy human community and friendship; these are human goods, and nothing in the gospel is contrary to consistent love of human goods. But love of neighbor is not peace at any price, condoning sin, shrinking from fraternal correction, compromising with what is known to be wrong for the sake of getting along with others. Charity is profoundly misunderstood if it is reduced simply to loving one's neighbor and love of neighbor is then trimmed to dimensions which any decent, well-mannered nonbeliever would feel comfortable with.

Charity primarily signifies sharing in divine life. It is the love of God poured forth in our hearts by the gift of the Holy Spirit; it is being a child of God; and it is the disposition to fulfillment in divine life. It also calls one to be authentically human, and therefore to choose and live in view of integral human fulfillment, that is, to be concerned about all genuine human goods.

This requires that one be concerned for the *reality* of community and friendship rather than their appearance. It can mean correcting sinners or those tending toward sin, and that is not a popular thing to do. But Jesus is our model of charity, and he did not bring about a peaceful Jerusalem community celebrating a happy Passover feast.

Finally, of course, it needs emphasizing that we are not exactly like Jesus. He is divine by nature, we by adoption. Divinity in us is a disposition to fulfillment in divine life. Although we are indeed God's children now, what this ultimately will mean has not yet come to light. Only when it does shall we be as fully like God as, through divine action, we are capable of being (see 1 Jn 3:2). Something about our sharing in divine life is still to come—something mysterious because we have yet to experience it. But that is not and never was true of Jesus. His divinity always was complete, total, and absolutely mature.

In no way, however, does the difference between Jesus and us imply that divine love in us is somehow in conflict with human goods. On this account, moreover, not only do human goods retain their integrity but the natural law remains valid and relevant for Christian morality. Being a good human person in this fallen world means cooperating with Jesus, living his kind of human life; but it is a *human* life that we are to live.

At the same time, we look forward to becoming mature children of God. What does that mean? We do not know. "What we will be has not yet been revealed" (1 Jn 3:2). The beatific vision, ultimate intimacy with God, cannot be reduced to a merely human experience or act.

25. Christian Love as the Principle of Christian Life

Christian love—charity—and the pursuit of human goods are not in conflict, not alternatives between which we must choose. Although distinct, both have a place in Christian life. All this was established in the previous chapter.

Now we shall look more closely at the dynamic relationship between charity and the lives of Christians striving to live as they ought. The central question is this: What is the link between charity as a share in divine life and human acts, among which faith is a Christian's first act and fundamental option? We consider three topics in this chapter: the relationship between charity and morally good acts; the love commands of the Old and New Testaments; and the impact of Christian faith and love on natural law morality.

A: The Precise Relationship between Charity and Morally Good Acts

It would seem as if charity were a human act. Scripture contains commands to love God above all things and to love one's neighbor as oneself; charity has traditionally been called a virtue; and lately fundamental option theories have emerged which speak of the fundamental option as if it were between loving God and loving creatures—as if, that is, charity were the act of choosing God over created goods. Considering all this, what else can charity be except a human act?

As we saw in the last chapter, however, love in general is not an act. Ultimately, it is interpersonal communion; at the outset, it is a disposition toward fulfillment in goods—a disposition that underlies both desire and enjoyment. Even though many loving acts flow from loving a person, simply to love is not to do anything to that person.

Moreover, "God's love has been poured into our hearts through the Holy Spirit that has been given to us" (Rom 5:5). What the Holy Spirit primarily confers on us is a share in divine life, adoption as God's children. This is not a human act. Even infants receive charity in baptism and are transformed by it; although they have done nothing themselves, they are no longer in original sin and now are children of God.

Thus, as a disposition to fulfillment in divine life, the love of God is not an act which one is called to perform. The New Testament, especially John's Gospel, suggests as much. For example: "As the Father has loved me, so I have loved you; abide in my love" (Jn 15:9). Charity transforms one; what one should do about it is "abide" in it, remain in it.

Nevertheless, Scripture does contain commands to love. Jesus says: " 'You shall love the Lord your God with all your heart, and with all your soul, and with all your mind.' This is the greatest and first commandment. And a second is like it, 'You shall love your neighbor as yourself' " (Mt 22:37–39). If charity is not a human act, what does this mean?

One way of understanding it is that "Love God above all things" is not, in itself, a command to perform some act; rather, it is a command to be perfect in love of God by integrating one's whole life with charity. Its force is not so much "*Love* God" as it is "Love God with *all* your heart, *all* your soul, *all* your mind, *all* your strength." In other words: Appropriate totally the gift you have received; let charity permeate all you do. There is no specific action alongside others which is "to love." Rather, love is an underlying principle, a disposition toward fulfillment which informs everything one does.

The integration of one's entire life with charity begins with the act of faith. In making the act of faith, one accepts God's self-communication; but God *is* love—charity is the reality of God—so that, in accepting God by the act of faith, one accepts charity. That gift of love of God transforms one's human act of faith. One believes not only out of desire for certain human goods but out of a disposition to fulfillment in divine life. Charity transforms the act of faith in which charity is accepted.

As a disposition to fulfillment, love seeks expression. In the Old Testament, loving God above all things means living as a pious Jew, while loving one's neighbor as oneself similarly means living as a member of the covenant community in a way that promotes the well being of fellow members. In the New Testament, the way to abide in love is to make one's whole life a life of faith in Jesus. He says: "If you keep my commandments, you will abide in my love" (Jn 15:10). Living out the implications of faith is the way to abide and grow in love.

Acts which implement faith according to specifically Christian moral norms (to be discussed below) and certain religious acts are often called "acts of charity." When someone is treated unjustly, bears it peacefully, then goes out of his or her way to do good to the offending party, we say: "That is really an act of charity." And so it is; it is an act by which this person, motivated by charity, lives out Christian faith. Nothing else accounts for such behavior, and so one assumes that its underlying source is Christian faith in which charity is at work. Similarly one calls certain kinds of prayer "acts of charity." The Eucharist in particular is an act of charity—the offering of oneself along with Jesus.

Charity both requires and empowers one to live according to faith. "Those who abide in me and I in them bear much fruit, because apart from me you can do nothing" (Jn 15:5). United with Jesus, we can do whatever is appropriate for us as Christians.

But why exactly does charity require morally good lives? Charity is God's free gift. We do not earn it by moral goodness; we are not justified by good works.

Yet living a good life does follow from charity. One obvious reason is that someone who loves another wants to do what he or she wants. If we love God we want to please him, and we please him by doing what is morally good. This is not a matter of "pleasing" God by simply submitting to him, as if his will were arbitrary. God loves all created goods perfectly, and out of love for him, we try to do the same; but our own fulfillment is among the created goods which God loves, and so we are concerned with it. And where does our genuine fulfillment lie? In living morally good lives.

It is like the situation with parents and children. If parents are good and children really love them, the children will try to live good lives because that is what their parents want—not for their own sakes but for the children's. God is a good Father who wants us to live good lives for our sakes; as children of God, we try to do what he wants.

If one loves God, one also loves those whom he loves. But God loves all his children, and therefore so should we. "Those who say, 'I love God,' and hate their brothers or sisters, are liars; for those who do not love a brother or sister whom they have seen, cannot love God whom they have not seen" (1 Jn 4:20).

To repeat: charity's requirement that we be morally good is not something arbitrarily imposed on us. It is the unfolding of human good. God wants fulfillment for his creatures, and our fulfillment lies in living good lives. That means wanting and working for the good of all creatures, including ourselves, as God does.

This can also be expressed negatively. Someone who does moral evil is not concerned about integral human fulfillment but about some limited aspect of the good (doing evil is a kind of self-mutilation). But a person not fully open to his or her own good is certainly not open to infinite goodness—to divine goodness. Thus, he or she does not have charity. To put it another way, immorality is a closing of oneself not only against one's own good but, all the more, against infinite goodness, in which one's own good is a participation. One who hates the human person made in God's image—the human person fulfilled—surely has no love for the perfection of divine goodness, which is the original on which the image is modeled.

B: The Love Commands of the Old and New Testaments

The love commands of the Old Testament express only partly the moral implications of Christian love. As Jesus says, they do sum up the law and the prophets (see Mt 22:34–40; Mk 12:28–34; Lk 10:25–28), but in fulfilling them, Jesus goes beyond them in important ways. Thus, it is not enough to say that the principle of Christian life is "Love God above all things, and love your neighbor as yourself." There is more to it than that, a content which is only implicit in the commands to love God and neighbor.

The Old Testament love commands formulate the first principle of morality in religious terms. In the context of the covenant, integral human fulfillment lies in friendship with God and peace with the other members of the covenant community. This indicates (but only partially) morality's fundamental orientation toward fulfillment in a perfect community of persons.

Jesus goes further. The parable of the Good Samaritan, appended in Luke's Gospel to Jesus' treatment of the first commandment (see Lk 10:30–37), embodies a crucial widening of the Old Testament's religious horizon, a widening suggested but not fully developed by the prophets (see, for example, Is 49:1–6). The kingdom is not a closed community; potentially, it is all-inclusive. Who is one's neighbor? Whoever is willing to do one good or needs good done to him or her, regardless of preexisting estrangements and hostilities. In short, the New Testament points to a universally inclusive community—a community of the whole human race in friendship with God.

Christian love is also different because it is loving and living in Jesus. He embodies perfect love, and, inasmuch as we are united with him and cooperate with him, we are to love as he does. "As the Father has loved me, so I have loved you; abide in my love" (Jn 15:9). Christian love has the specific character of sharing in Jesus' disposition toward both divine goodness and the good of the human race he has redeemed.

Christian love implies holiness in a way the Old Testament's love commands did not. Jesus not only enjoins holiness but communicates it. One is not simply confronted with the requirements of the covenant relationship but, united with Jesus, is given its fulfillment. Indeed, this is the ground and principle of Christian life: The act of faith in Jesus unites us with him in a dynamic solidarity by which we receive the power of the Spirit so as to fulfill the requirement of love.

Moreover, Christian love transforms the first principle of morality, integral human fulfillment, for it disposes us to heavenly fulfillment, which includes integral fulfillment in all the human goods, and makes it possible for us to realize it. In the light of charity, integral human fulfillment is not just an ideal one attempts to live by, but an object of realistic hope. When in the Creed we profess belief in the resurrection from the dead and everlasting life, we are saying in effect that we look forward to whatever is truly good—we hope for it—in heavenly fulfillment. There no human good will be lacking. Vatican Council II, as we have seen earlier, is quite explicit on this point.

While hope was real in the Old Testament, it was also decidedly limited. It was hope of returning from exile, possessing the land, and other limited fulfillments for the Jewish people. Christian hope is directed to perfect human fulfillment embracing the whole human race and lasting forever. This is indeed ambitious by comparison with any pre-Christian hope.

Contemporary post-Christian secularists, both Marxists and Western liberal humanists, also are quite ambitious. They crave human fulfillment in every respect for all humankind gathered in perfect communion (though they do not hesitate to sacrifice many people in pursuing it); they long for a heaven on earth (but one without God).

Human hearts have truly been restless since Christian hope entered history, unable to settle for anything but perfect fulfillment. The vulnerability of secularism nevertheless lies in the fact that the fulfillment it craves is beyond human capacities and therefore beyond secularism's reach. We all sin and we all shall die. Hope for the realization of integral human fulfillment is absurd apart from the faith which grounds it. Here is the point at which the gospel might yet pierce the resistance of post-Christian secularists, by showing them the only avenue for realizing this ambitious hope of theirs.

C: The Impact of Faith and Love on Natural Law Morality

Grace does not change human nature into something else; Christians are not a new species—we remain what we naturally are. Moreover, since all human choices are among human goods, the moral norms of the natural law oblige Christians as much as anyone else. Thus, there seems to be no place for specifically Christian moral norms which are requirements of Christian love.

On the other hand, it appears that there *are* specifically Christian norms. In the Sermon on the Mount (Mt 5–7) and in many other places, Jesus sets out a body of new moral teaching which goes far beyond anything in the Old Testament or any other religion or world view. Forgive enemies—indeed, love them and pray for them. Give to him who takes from you; go the extra mile with someone who imposes on you. The New Testament is full of such distinctive norms.

Scholars sometimes take them individually, one by one, and try to find precedents or parallels in the Old Testament or some other religious tradition. Having succeeded, they conclude that there is nothing unique in Jesus' moral teaching. But that is a case of not seeing the woods on account of the trees or, to change the metaphor, it is like reducing a human body to its constituent elements in a chemistry lab and then concluding that there is nothing distinctive about the human person. If anything is broken down far enough, one reaches the point at which its distinctiveness disappears.

Taken as a whole, however, the body of moral teaching in the New Testament really is distinctive, even by comparison with the teaching of the Old Testament of which it is the fulfillment. That is precisely the point: the New Testament fulfills the Old. There are links, but there are also great differences; the relationship of Old to New is like the relationship of seed to harvest. Moreover, in comparison with anything else besides the Old Testament, the New Testament is still more distinctive, particularly in its thoroughgoing acceptance of the human. For example, whereas much oriental religion is based on transcending bodily life and escaping from the human condition, Christianity is truly humanistic.

So, the New Testament contains distinctive moral teaching, yet there seems to be no room for specifically Christian norms. How can this apparent contradiction be resolved?

The solution lies in recognizing the reality of the human condition. Humankind is fallen and redeemed. It has been given the power to achieve integral human fulfillment (in the heavenly kingdom) in cooperation with God—in Jesus, to become a perfect community, rejoicing and fulfilled in all the human goods. This state of fulfillment is not, so far as its human aspects are concerned, absolutely outside the potentialities of human nature; yet even in its human aspects, it is truly new. Human life which is not only good but integrally fulfilling—that is, happy in respect to all the human goods for the whole human community: that certainly is new.

The Old Testament clarifies part of our situation. Human beings are fallen and need redemption, but God has not abandoned his people—he brings them into a covenant relationship and promises them a redeemer. The New Testament completes the account. The redeemer has come, redemption is accomplished, and God invites all men and women into a new and efficacious covenant relationship with him, founded on union with Jesus. Integral human fulfillment is no longer simply an ideal but an object of realistic hope.

In these new circumstances, the moral principles of the natural law continue to direct human action to the fulfillment proper to human nature; but now there are also distinctive Christian norms because Christians have specific, distinctive acts to perform. The question is: If human nature is not changed, how can there be a distinctive Christian morality? The answer is: If human beings now have access to a means of being all they can be, someone who lives in light of that fact will be able to do many good things which people otherwise cannot do, and the distinctive Christian norms will be those which concern the doing of such things. Christianity offers options for choice which either would not occur to people apart from faith or would not appeal to them as realistic possibilities apart from hope—or both.

In sum, the message of Christian moral norms, arising from the message of faith, is that we ought to do what is appropriate for people who are not only fallen but redeemed, and not only redeemed but empowered by God to reach human fulfillment in a perfect human community. These norms tell us to live in a way befitting our new, real situation.

An analogy with diet helps clarify this point. A dietitian operates on certain principles, whose most basic is that human diet must suit human beings. There are certain things the human organism as such requires, and others which are not good for it in any circumstances. But a dietitian may have to work out additional norms for a sick person, and in that case the rules of diet become more specific. Perhaps the sick person should eat more of something, or less, than is normally advisable, while foods which ordinarily would be acceptable must be excluded entirely. Thus, the dietitian designs a diet to fit the patient's condition.

Christian life is something like that. Although the human race is in a fallen condition, integral human fulfillment is now a realistic possibility. Because human nature remains as it is, general principles of human morality remain the same. But besides assuming these principles, Christian morality goes further, excluding every act by which fallen humanity is likely to do itself further injury by obstructing its integral fulfillment. Among the acts thus excluded are some which would be acceptable for people not in a fallen condition. Given our disposition to sin, we need to avoid many occasions for sinning which would present no difficulties if we were not fallen. The reality of our situation, fallen but redeemed, makes an enormous difference to what we may and may not do, and calls for specifically Christian norms which do not contradict natural law norms but do go beyond them.

Our situation also makes an enormous difference to how we deal with sin and death, and with the impact which fear of death has on our emotional makeup. Only in this context does Jesus' directive to his followers—deny yourselves, take up your crosses, follow me (see Mt 16:24; Mk 8:34; Lk 9:23)—make sense; otherwise, the only reasonable advice would be to shun the cross and get what one can out of life in the brief time allotted. Similarly, the reality of our situation generates demands that we cooperate with Jesus in building up the kingdom in which humankind's fulfillment is to be realized; we have stringent obligations in this regard which would not otherwise exist.

Thus, Christian morality is distinctive, but its distinctiveness does not lie in distorting human life and human nature. Rather, Christian moral norms reshape the misshapen lives of human beings who lack the promise of integral fulfillment and the realistic hope it engenders. Christian morality *is* at odds with the actual moral standards of societies, including our own, which involve many moral compromises. But instead of overriding the requirements of human good, a Christian life truly fulfills them. Not infrequently, of course, people suppose otherwise, since they equate human good with comfort, and the requirements of Christian morality are by no means always comfortable for fallen human beings. But this tells against inadequate notions of morality, not against the moral implications of the real human condition as faith discloses it.

Even without faith, upright people can and sometimes do arrive at some Christian norms. They realize, for example, that revenge is foolish and self-destructive; thus, a decent pagan like Socrates concludes that it is better to suffer injury than do it. Yet even decent non-Christians do not see the human condition as it really is. For instance, they may suppose that human fulfillment requires escaping bodiliness; but faith promises the resurrection of the body. Paul, not surprisingly, was mocked by the Athenians when he preached the resurrection of the dead (see Acts 17:32). Without faith, not even the best and brightest know the human condition as it is and fully share the way of life suited to that condition.

What is most characteristic of Christian life is that, knowing that the human condition is fallen and that God is working for our redemption, one consciously and gratefully accepts his gifts and seeks to continue Jesus' work by handing on God's truth and love to others. The Christian grasps the meaning of Jesus' words: "I do not call you servants any longer, because the servant does not know what the master is doing; but I have called you friends, because I have made known to you everything that I have heard from my Father" (Jn 15:15). With faith, one can be a conscious collaborator with Jesus; one's whole life can be at once Eucharistic—an offering to God in union with Jesus—and apostolic, while at the same time it is a deliberate effort toward total self-integration with Christian love, that is, toward holiness.

Thus, the Church must be able to guide its members in the following of Jesus. Plainly, however, the New Testament does not answer every moral question. One will look there in vain for teaching on issues like in vitro fertilization and nuclear deterrence. Not infrequently, too, it is difficult to interpret and apply what the New Testament does say. Must one really refrain not just from swearing falsely but from swearing at all (see Mt 5:33–37)? Yet, throughout the tradition, the Church has been able to provide answers to new moral questions and to interpret and apply the moral content of Scripture. Implicit in the Church's work has been a firm grasp on the *principles* of Christian living which are adequately articulated and exemplified in the New Testament.

Although the modes of responsibility generate more specific norms, by themselves they do not generate the specific norms of Christian morality. To that end the modes of responsibility which we considered earlier need to be transformed, fulfilled in light of faith, into modes of Christian response to God's gifts. We find these modes of Christian response operative in the life of Jesus.

Thus, the next chapter will explain how the modes of responsibility are fulfilled in Jesus' life and transformed into modes of Christian response which not only shape his life but can shape our lives, too. His virtues provide the model for Christian character.

But more than that. The Old Testament too gave moral guidance, but it did not empower God's people to follow it. Certainly there are upright people in the Old Testament, but, as St. Paul says, it is their faith which saves them, not the law (see Rom 9:6–33). In the New Testament, matters are vastly different. Jesus and his life, as we have seen, are not simply a model and a guide. United with Jesus, God's people receive the gift of the Holy Spirit; thus, they are empowered to satisfy the requirements of love of God and neighbor—to abide in Jesus and keep his commandments. The gift of the Spirit is the fundamental principle, the very ground, of a life lived in the manner of a child of God.

As a result of sin, all law seems more or less alien to fallen human beings, a burdensome imposition which cannot be fulfilled. This is true even of the natural law, but it is especially true of bad positive law, which is common in human society and genuinely oppressive. The resentment to which bad law gives rise helps color people's attitudes toward morality, to the extent it is viewed in legalistic terms, and reinforces their sin-rooted tendency to resent and resist its legitimate requirements.

The transformation wrought by faith and charity radically changes this situation. As a result of this transformation, Christians are inclined to do what is right and specifically Christian, and find it possible. In modest but real ways, they experience the truth of Jesus' words: "Those who abide in me and I in them bear much fruit" (Jn 15:5). Not that sin and its effects are no longer present in their lives, but grace is also at work, and, insofar as they cooperate with it, their lives change more and more. Among other things, the more they live like Christians, the more they recognize the Church's moral teaching as helpful information, which they might have missed on their own and which spells out how a child of God really ought to live.

Thus, to form conscience from the Christian point of view is to put on "the mind of Christ" (1 Cor 2:16), and for one who has that mind, the specific content of Christian moral teaching is not a burdensome set of demands but something good to know. For this teaching makes it possible for such a person to do consistently what he or she really wants to do, namely, live like a Christian. This is the state of freedom from both sin and law's burdens to which St. Paul refers in speaking of "the freedom of the glory of the children of God" (Rom 8:21).

26. Modes of Christian Response

We have seen that faith and charity transform natural law morality. Now we shall see how, specifically, they transform the modes of responsibility. Uniquely fulfilled in Jesus' teaching and life, these become modes of Christian response.

The chapter has two parts: preliminary and general considerations, followed by a discussion of the eight modes of Christian response. The first part sets out the hypothesis that the Beatitudes, interpreted as transformations of the modes of responsibility, are the key intermediate Christian moral principles. The second part demonstrates this hypothesis.

A: Some Preliminary and General Considerations

Of all the New Testament books, Matthew's Gospel explains most systematically what Christian life should be like. The instruction commences in chapter five with the Sermon on the Mount, and the sermon begins with the eight Beatitudes. Thus, one can reasonably suppose that the Beatitudes express Christian moral principles—normative principles understood in the light of faith. This is how they are treated by the Fathers of the Church, by numerous catechetical works, and by Pope Paul VI in his Credo of the People of God.

Reflection on the Beatitudes supports this view of them. They do not deal with specific kinds of actions but with attitudes or general dispositions. "Blessed are the poor in spirit . . . those who mourn . . . the meek." Still, they have some content and are not all the same—even though the blessing promised *is* the same in each case: everlasting life, perfect fulfillment, variously referred to as being comforted, inheriting the earth, seeing God, and so on.

The first principle of morality, as we saw earlier, is always to will in line with the ideal of integral human fulfillment. Faith and charity transform this into the basic principle of specifically *Christian* morality: to live for the sake of the kingdom, in which all things will find their fulfillment in Jesus. Like the modes of responsibility, which are intermediate principles between the first principle of morality and specific norms, the Beatitudes stand midway between the basic Christian principle—seek first the kingdom—and specific norms of Christian morality. Designating characteristic traits of a Christian, they call those "blessed" who possess such attitudes and act accordingly. For example, a Christian should be poor in spirit—thus, "Blessed are the poor in spirit, for theirs is the kingdom of heaven" (Mt 5:3).

The Beatitudes promise a reward for having the right attitude; the disposition is a condition for receiving the blessing. Evidently, then, a merit relationship exists between attitude and blessing. Yet there is a great deal of scholarly argument about whether this is really so, or whether the Beatitudes instead simply prescribe the gift which God will bestow gratuitously on his children. This debate makes sense in the context of thinking influenced by Lutheran theology, but it is pointless in the context of Catholic theology; indeed, it is contrary to Catholic faith to suggest an absolute opposition between merit and gift.

Against the Reformation, the Council of Trent defined that among God's gifts to us are our good works, which fulfill the requirements of Christian life, and also our merit: merit itself is a gift (DS 1548/810). To respond to God's gift as the Beatitudes tell us (for example, having been forgiven, to forgive others) is to enjoy a grace from God; yet to be merciful is also freely to choose to do what is merciful, and so mercy merits. If one is merciful, one deserves the reward, which is to obtain mercy—that is, to be received into the heavenly kingdom; yet that merit, that deserving, is itself God's gift.

The modes of responsibility are moral truths which set requirements, but they are not self-fulfilling. The fifth mode, for instance, tells us not to be partial, yet people often practice partiality. To fulfill the modes, one must make choices in accord with them. In doing so, one is in that instance a morally good person.

A whole life of morally good choices putting to work all of a person's elements—talents and skills, psychological dispositions, ways of self-expression, feelings, and all the rest—makes one an integrally good person; of such an individual we say that he or she is a person of good character. The different aspects of good character are the virtues. But this process of forming character works the other way, too. If one knows what is morally good, regularly chooses against it, organizes one's life around morally bad choices, puts one's whole self into the service of the life thus organized—then one is a thoroughly immoral person, a person of bad character, whose various aspects are the vices.

Up to a point, the same pattern exists in the sphere of Christian morality. There are Christian modes of response; Catholics know from Scripture and the teaching of the Church what ought to be done. One can choose consistently in accord with this understanding and integrate one's whole self with those choices.

But there are also differences. Understanding how to live a Christian life comes from faith, and faith accepted in baptism carries with it the gift of the Holy Spirit, the gift of charity. As a result, one not only knows what it means to live as a Christian but is disposed to live this way. The moral teaching of the gospel is not received as a set of demands, to which one must conform under pain of punishment, nor even simply as a body of truths, which it would be foolish to disregard, but as the implications of faith and love, which one not only appreciates but is inclined to live out. For this reason, the modes of Christian response are not formulated as commands, "Do this!" but as ways of acting— "To expect, to accept, and so on"—and are expressed by the Beatitudes.

The modes of Christian response fulfill the modes of responsibility. For the fulfillment of Christian life is fulfillment in respect to human goods. Christians have reason to live this kind of life (since hope for the kingdom assures them it has meaning) and they also have the power to live it through the gift of love. To put this another way, the modes of Christian response, expressed in summary fashion in the Beatitudes, are the modes of responsibility transformed by faith (which tells us how to live a good life in a fallen world), by hope (which supplies the confidence in God required to make the effort), and by charity (which gives one the power really to live in this way).

Finally, a word about the gifts of the Holy Spirit (see Is 11:2), traditionally understood to be wisdom, understanding, counsel, fortitude, knowledge, piety, and fear of the Lord. One can trace correspondences between them and the Christian modes enumerated below.

Often, the gifts of the Holy Spirit have been thought of as actuating or supplementing human powers in a manner for which reason enlightened by faith and human love quickened by charity cannot account, as if the Spirit were filling in gaps in our human willingness, ability, and performance. But this view would seem to involve commingling, much as if one were to suppose that Jesus' divinity somehow bridged gaps in his humanity, enabling him to do things which, as man, he could not do. It therefore seems better to identify the gifts of the Holy Spirit with charity, considered as energizing Christian life and the virtues. This avoids commingling and also corrects the tendency to think of the Holy Spirit's gifts as separate, mysterious principles over and above those we have already identified.

With these preliminary and general remarks, we are ready to consider the eight modes of Christian response.

B: The Eight Modes of Christian Response

In each case, we shall begin by simply stating the corresponding mode of responsibility, mode of Christian response, and Beatitude. Then, in a few paragraphs, we shall try to indicate the relationships among the three. Unfortunately, space does not allow a fuller and more satisfying explanation.

The first mode of responsibility is: *One should not be deterred by felt inertia from acting for intelligible goods.* (Put positively: Be energetic and ambitious.) Specified by faith and fulfilled by charity, this becomes the first mode of Christian response: *To expect and accept all good, including the good fruits of one's own work, as God's gift.* (The Christian's energy and ambition must be rooted in humility and trust in God.) That corresponds to the first Beatitude: *Blessed are the poor in spirit, for theirs is the kingdom of heaven* (Mt 5:3).

Tradition and current exegesis agree in identifying the poor in spirit as those who are humble. Thus, the virtue envisaged here is humility. It should not be confused with self-depreciation. Consider Mary's Magnificat: "the Mighty One has done great things for me" (Lk 1:49). Mary is certainly humble, but she is also exultant, and she does not belittle herself. Or consider St. Paul: "By the grace of God I am what I am, and his grace toward me has not been in vain" (1 Cor 15:10). If Paul were to say otherwise, he would be saying God's grace *was* in vain. Humility consists in seeking everything from God, accepting all that he gives, and being fully aware of and grateful for it.

Opposed to humility is an attitude along these lines: "I needn't ask God for anything except what I can't get for myself. I'll accept what I want from God, but not necessarily everything he wishes to give me. Since I deserve his gifts, I needn't be thankful for them. All in all, I'd rather not make a great deal of God's gifts, for receiving gifts puts one in debt, and I don't care to be indebted."

The first mode of responsibility says: Don't be lazy about doing good. Inertia of this sort arises from disillusionment with the fallen world, recognition of one's weakness and limitations, and despair at one's inability to live a good life. Faith and charity transform the first mode of responsibility by conferring the hope and energy needed to live a Christian life—but in cooperation with God, not on one's own. Recognizing not only that all power to do good comes from God but that this power really is available, one seeks it, accepts it, and is grateful.

The mode of Christian response includes the childlike attitude required to enter the kingdom of heaven (see Mt 19:13–15; Mk 10:15; Lk 18:15–17). Small children are totally dependent and realize it, but they do not feel diminished by having to be cared for. Such humility in our relationship with God is commended to us by this mode of response. Indeed, humility is absolutely necessary in order to accept the gift of faith. And with humility, Christian life becomes authentically Eucharistic—a grateful response to God's gift of justification and adoption.

The second mode of responsibility is: *One should not be pressed by enthusiasm or impatience to act individualistically for intelligible goods.* (Put positively: Be a team player.) Specified by faith and fulfilled by charity, this becomes the second mode of Christian response: *To accept one's limited role in the Body of Christ and fulfill it.* (The team player who is a member of Christ's team is always submissive to God's will.) That corresponds to the second Beatitude (or perhaps third—there is a numbering problem here which does not affect our analysis): *Blessed are the meek, for they will inherit the earth* (Mt 5:5).

The meek submit to their lot and accept God's will for them, and God's will for each individual is something both definite and limited. Yet the virtue of meekness does not lie in being merely placid, much less passive. It consists in submitting to a larger whole—God's plan, the imperatives of the kingdom, the requirements of Jesus' Body—embracing one's role in the history of salvation and one's place in the Church, and putting one's best efforts into fulfilling what God wants of one.

What is the "earth" or "land" promised to the meek? In the Old Testament, God's people were constantly hoping to gain or enjoy the possession of their own land. The new covenant discloses a broader horizon: God's plan for a perfect communion bringing all members of the human race into heavenly fulfillment. Blessed, then, are obedient members of the covenant community, who subordinate personal ambitions to the hope of the whole, play their parts in God's plan, and look forward in hope to heavenly fulfillment for themselves and the entire community.

Implicitly present in the act of faith, meekness becomes explicit in one who finds and accepts his or her personal vocation and lives contentedly within its boundaries. To be meek means gladly accepting whatever is given by God: "Not my will but yours be done" (Lk 22:42; cf. Jn 18:11).

Lack of meekness is apparent in one who is frustrated and resentful over the duties and limits of his or her state of life and vocation: "If only I didn't have to do this. If only I could go somewhere else, do something else, associate with other people, have other challenges and opportunities. . . . "

Meekness is also lacking in a Church in which some lay people want to function as if they were priests, some priests as if they were lay people, and some religious women as if they were both. That would appear to be the situation today, as it was in the Christian community to which Paul directed this exhortation: "I say to everyone among you not to think of yourself more highly than you ought to think, but to think with sober judgment, each according to the measure of faith that God has assigned" (Rom 12:3).

The third mode of responsibility is: *One should not choose to satisfy an emotional desire except as part of one's pursuit and/or attainment of an intelligible good other than the satisfaction of the desire itself.* Specified by faith and fulfilled by charity, this becomes the third mode of Christian response: *To put aside or avoid everything which is not necessary or useful in the fulfillment of one's personal vocation.* That corresponds to the third (or second) Beatitude: *Blessed are those who mourn, for they will be comforted* (Mt 5:4).

In order to live out one's personal vocation, it is necessary to set aside incompatible talents and interests one might otherwise have pursued. This is not only a matter of avoiding sin, but of letting go of things which are truly good and potentially satisfying. The virtuous disposition is detachment. In this fallen world, however, no one painlessly and altogether cheerfully puts aside good things. Thus, accepting and living out one's vocation unavoidably involves a measure of sorrow and "mourning."

The third mode of responsibility tells us not to make enjoyment as such a purpose in life. People are inclined to batten on to pleasure and other satisfying experiences, in order to escape the ennui and terror of lives devoid of hope. Faith, however, brings with it the realistic Christian hope of perfect fulfillment in eternal life, while charity empowers one to realize it. Now, along with self-control, detachment—not only from enjoyment as such but from the pursuit of all goods that do not pertain to one's personal vocation—comes into play as something sensible, possible, and necessary. The opposed dispositions are described by such terms as worldliness and anxiety.

Acceptance of vocation and the detachment that goes with it involve recognizing that one's personal vocation, though more or less confining, is part of a larger whole. However insignificant it may seem, it makes an indispensable contribution to the fullness of human life—a fullness which will not come in this world anyway but only in the fulfillment of heaven. Without implying that this world should not be taken seriously, Jesus says: "My kingdom is not from this world" (Jn 18:36). Authentically Christian otherworldliness provides the basis for the detachment and self-control associated with Christian life.

The fourth mode of responsibility, complementary to the third, is: *One should not choose to act in accord with an emotional aversion, except when necessary to avoid some intelligible evil other than the inner tension experienced in enduring the aversion.* Transformed by faith and fulfilled by charity, this becomes the fourth mode of Christian response: *To endure fearlessly whatever is necessary or useful for the fulfillment of one's personal vocation.* That corresponds to the fourth Beatitude: *Blessed are those who hunger and thirst for righteousness, for they will be filled* (Mt 5:6).

People who hunger and thirst for righteousness are ready and willing to do whatever they must to become holy, up to and including suffering martyrdom; they do not let hardships and obstacles keep them from living as Christians. And, in this fallen world, living as a Christian does involve obstacles and hardships: not achieving many things one might have achieved if one had been willing to cut corners, together with ridicule, conflict, and persecution at the hands of those who resent Christian morality as a judgment on their own life-styles.

The mode of responsibility excludes fear of nonmoral evil as a principle of action: Don't let fear of suffering rule your life. The Christian mode of response disposes one not only to endure hardships but to welcome them insofar as they are inseparable from struggling, as part of the following of Jesus, against sin and its consequences. People with this disposition take to heart Jesus' words: "In the world you face persecution. But take courage; I have conquered the world!" (Jn 16:33).

As the fourth mode of responsibility complements the third, so the fourth mode of Christian response complements the third Christian mode. The latter concerns detachment, whose extreme opposite is gross self-indulgence, but self-indulgence generally is accompanied by cowardice, so that a Christian who is not detached usually will not have much courage either. Lack of courage in turn prevents one from pursuing one's vocation in the face of hardship.

By contrast, faith and charity join us closely to Jesus, who has already overcome evil at its root. In doing so, they ground the confidence of Christians in the ultimate success of their struggle. That there is a struggle, however, must never be forgotten. Not only should Christians engage in it with courage; they should joyfully accept the suffering which accompanies it, inasmuch as this suffering unites them with Jesus: "Whenever you face trials of any kind, consider it nothing but joy" (Jas 1:2).

The fifth mode of responsibility is: *One should not, in response to different feelings toward different persons, willingly proceed with a preference for anyone unless the preference is required by intelligible goods themselves.* Transformed by faith and fulfilled by charity, this becomes the fifth mode of Christian response: *To be merciful according to the universal and perfect measure of mercy which God has revealed in Jesus.* That corresponds to the fifth Beatitude: *Blessed are the merciful, for they will receive mercy* (Mt 5:7).

In this fallen world, merely being fair ensures that we will make one another miserable. Fairness is a good thing as far as it goes, but it cannot overcome conflict and division; in the work of building community, justice is necessary but insufficient. The Christian transformation of fairness lies in forgoing rights, setting aside even just claims, and going beyond fairness by being merciful.

The basis for this transformation lies in the fact that we are all members, or at least potential members, of the covenant community established by Jesus. Peter says in Acts: "I truly understand that God shows no partiality, but in every nation anyone who fears him and does what is right is acceptable to him" (Acts 10:34–35). Within this new covenant community, we wish to receive from others the same kind of treatment we receive from God. We wish to be redeemed, forgiven, healed—to enjoy the benefit of God's redemptive work in Jesus.

Wishing mercy for ourselves, we must, as a matter of fairness, extend it to others. In the Christian community, fairness requires mercy: "If you forgive others their trespasses, your heavenly Father will also forgive you; but if you do not forgive others, neither will your Father forgive your trespasses" (Mt 6:14; cf. 18:35; Mk 11:25). But mercy means more than just forgiving others; it means striving generously to do them good, and doing so universally and as perfectly as possible, without calculating the cost to oneself.

Pope John Paul II expresses the limitations of justice without mercy in his encyclical *Dives in Misericordia:*

> A world from which forgiveness was eliminated would be nothing but a world of cold and unfeeling justice, in the name of which each person would claim his or her own rights vis-a-vis others; the various kinds of selfishness latent in man would transform life and human society into a system of oppression of the weak by the strong, or into an arena of permanent strife between one group and another.[19]

This can be seen happening in a variety of social contexts today—for example, in marriages in which husbands and wives try to found their relationship on fairness, turn to asserting their respective rights, and end in conflict, misery, separation, and divorce. Marriage only succeeds when both parties forgo their rights and concentrate on what is good for each other and for the marriage itself.

The sixth mode of responsibility is: *One should not choose on the basis of emotions which bear upon empirical aspects of intelligible goods (or bads) in a way which interferes with a more perfect sharing in the good or avoidance of the bad.* Transformed by faith and fulfilled by charity, this becomes the sixth mode of Christian response: *To strive to conform one's whole self to living faith, and to recognize and purge anything which does not meet this standard.* That corresponds to the sixth Beatitude: *Blessed are the pure in heart, for they will see God* (Mt 5:8).

Chastity is an aspect of purity of heart but not the whole of it. Essentially, the pure of heart are the single-hearted—those who are wholemindedly and wholeheartedly focused on God and his kingdom.

In this fallen world, however, people tend to practice self-deception and pursue illusory goods (which the sixth mode of responsibility enjoins one not to do) largely out of despair at the prospects of achieving anything better. Not surprisingly, this breeds discontent and cynicism: "At heart, everybody looks out for number one. . . . Get past the facade, and you'll find that there's no such thing as a really happy marriage. . . . Society is only a system for allowing the strong to exploit the weak without breaking the law"—and so on.

Christians are called to overcome cynicism not by self-deception and optimistic illusions but by living good lives in Jesus—lives grounded in faith and charity as well as in the realistic hope that living this way makes sense. This means, among other things, that even real human goods should not be sought primarily for the sake of realizing them in this world but insofar as they contribute to heavenly communion. The pure of heart keep all this single-mindedly in view.

But none of us is perfectly pure of heart. Therefore, this mode of Christian response also involves a constant process of conversion—of overcoming sin and seeking to integrate one's whole self with faith and love. We are called to love God with our whole mind and whole heart; and, since we are not whole, the Christian mode involves striving to become so.

The seventh mode of responsibility is: *One should not be moved by hostility to freely accept or choose the destruction, damaging, or impeding of any intelligible human good.* Transformed by faith and fulfilled by charity, this becomes the seventh mode of Christian response: *To respond to evil with good, not with resistance, much less with destructive action.* That corresponds to the seventh Beatitude: *Blessed are the peacemakers, for they will be called children of God* (Mt 5:9).

When people are offended and hurt in this fallen world, they are tempted to get even. The seventh mode of responsibility excludes revenge and acting out of hostility. But even though a decent person may recognize that such behavior is pointless and so forgo it, his or her sense of injury and resentment remains; even without revenge, there is alienation.

The Christian mode goes beyond forgoing revenge and calls for rebuilding damaged relationships. That is how God deals with us, and it is how God's children ought to act: "I say to you, Love your enemies and pray for those who persecute you, so that you may be children of your Father in heaven" (Mt 5:44–45). This is peacemaking—conciliatoriness, overcoming opposition by love. The Christian mode calls for one not to avoid enemies but to do them good, act redemptively toward them, try to help them toward their own true fulfillment. Patient endurance and mildness are aspects of this virtuous disposition.

The duty to make peace is not based on imagining that there are no real enemies, even though one sometimes hears that view expressed: "Everyone is a person of good will at heart; nobody is really anyone else's enemy." Of course, one should give others the benefit of the doubt, but if it were literally true that there are no real enemies, evil would be illusory and Christian life a struggle against illusion. There is no support for this idea in the New Testament or, for that matter, in ordinary experience. Rather, Christian peacemaking means being faithful to Jesus even to the point of sharing in his work of redemption—seeking to make real enemies into real friends forever.

The eighth mode of responsibility is: *One should not be moved by a stronger desire for one instance of an intelligible good to act for it by choosing to destroy, damage, or impede some other instance of an intelligible good.* Transformed by faith and fulfilled by charity, this becomes the eighth mode of Christian response: *To do no evil that good might come of it, but suffer evil together with Jesus in cooperation with God's redeeming love.* That corresponds to the eighth Beatitude: *Blessed are those who are persecuted for righteousness' sake, for theirs is the kingdom of heaven* (Mt 5:10).

Not only do many people in this fallen world have little or no interest in living as Jesus did, but they are irked by the judgment on their way of life implicit in the lives of those who do. Angry and offended, they react negatively against such persons, and this negative reaction, whatever form it may take, constitutes the persecution which is the inevitable lot of those who live Christian lives.

When it is a question of torture and death for the sake of the faith, persecution is a clear-cut matter, painful but generally short-lived. Most Christians suffer nothing that dramatic. Their struggle is simply to go on refusing to compromise in a world in which that makes one unpopular and provokes reprisals; they go through life being mistreated but unable, because of their convictions, to respond in kind or, often, even to defend themselves. The reactions which people who seriously attempt to live like Christians will inevitably encounter thrust the cross upon anyone who makes the attempt. One could argue that this, too, is a kind of martyrdom.

In this fallen world, moreover, it really is impossible in many cases to pursue human goods effectively without making compromises: violate some goods in order to save others and minimize the evil; use bad means to achieve good ends which otherwise will not be achieved.

The eighth mode of responsibility forbids this. The mode of Christian response goes further: Not only must one refrain from using bad means to good ends, one must also do the good which will provoke hatred—and accept the suffering which results—rather than do anything wrong. Refusing to do evil while persisting in fulfilling one's vocation opens a person to being victimized. And a Christian must accept this—accept suffering with Jesus, in order to be raised up with him. This self-oblation does not aim at self-destruction but at true self-fulfillment.

Summing up, then, we see how the Christian modes of response transform the modes of responsibility. Faith sheds a new

314 FULFILLMENT IN CHRIST

and true light on the human condition. The Christian modes supply the pattern for a humanly good way of life in this fallen world, one dictated by the situation we face and by the real requirements of human goodness. There is purpose, meaning, in living this kind of life, for in Jesus' kingdom integral human fulfillment is really possible for all human beings. And we hope for this fulfillment, along with fulfillment in divine life, in heaven. Moreover, having received the gift of the Spirit, we have the power to live holy lives, for those who truly love God are inclined to love themselves and others as God does. Loving that way in the world as it is—fallen but redeemed, broken but called to perfect fulfillment—Christians can respond to both good and evil as Jesus did.

27. Life Formed by the Modes of Christian Response

Having seen what the modes of Christian response are, we turn to life lived according to the modes. This treatment will complete our exposition of the way of Jesus. In chapters twenty-eight through thirty-three we shall consider how one follows that way.

Here we take up three points: that Christian life is fundamentally the same, but Christian lives are diversified according to personal vocation; the derivation of Christian moral norms and the work of Christian conscience; and the demand for perfection—what it does and does not signify. The chapter assumes what is said in chapters ten through twelve about the modes of responsibility and the moral norms of natural law, the moral authority of law, and moral judgment in problematic situations.

A: The Unity of Christian Life and Its Diversity According to Personal Vocation

Although the basic principle of morality—to will in line with the ideal of integral human fulfillment—remains operative in the fallen human condition, people do not, indeed cannot, lead consistently good lives without divine help. Faith is needed to understand the human condition, to live uprightly in these circumstances, and to see the point of doing so. Faith points to the fulfillment of human nature: as revelation makes clear, it is possible to realize the ideal of integral human fulfillment in the context of God's plan for the fulfillment of all things in Jesus.

Given the human condition—that is, the situation we actually face—the way of life marked out by the modes of Christian response is necessary if one is to live as one should and realize human goods. This is the only thoroughly upright way: the way of Jesus. The modes are aspects of Jesus' own central commitments and the acts by which he carried them out.

The pattern is visible above all in the culminating act of Jesus' life. In choosing to go to Jerusalem to celebrate the Passover and thereby lay down his life, Jesus does not rely on his own resources but expects the good he has in view to come about by divine power: this is humility. He accepts the conditions and limitations of his role, and carries it out as the Father wants: meekness. He sets aside everything which would prevent him from doing so: detachment. He faces the evil which one who wishes to redeem must face: faithfulness and courage. He does his best for other people, including those who kill him, whom he forgives: mercy. He presses ahead without illusions or worldly ambitions, acting for the sake of the reality of God's kingdom: purity of heart. He seeks to reconcile fallen humankind with God—to constitute the human dimension of the new covenant: peacemaking. And, for the sake of righteousness, he suffers persecution. Thus, the Beatitudes are summed up and realized in the culminating act of Jesus' life. It is the model of all a Christian life ought to be.

Every genuinely Christian life reveals the same pattern. Its distinctiveness comes from its unity with the redemptive act of Jesus, and the modes of Christian response lie at its heart. These Christian modes are present incipiently—embryonically, one might say—in the act of faith, which is the fundamental option of Christian life. As an embryo grows into a mature person, however, so the Christian modes become ever more differentiated and visibly present in the life of one who accepts and lives out his or her personal vocation.

Hence, the uniform pattern underlying every Christian life. One must look to God, ask him for what one needs, thank him for his gifts, and try to hear what he wishes one to do with them: that is humility. One must obediently accept whatever God calls one to, with all its conditions and limitations: meekness. One must set aside anything not included in one's personal vocation, even though it be something good for other Christians with other vocations: detachment. One must courageously face the evil confronting one: faithfulness. Since cooperation with Jesus in his redemptive work is part of every Christian vocation, one must not only accept God's gifts and forgiveness but extend the same to others: mercy. Recognizing one's superficiality and love of pretense, one must purify oneself through constant conversion: purity of heart. Because any true vocation is a way of overcoming evil, healing disharmony, realizing the existential goods, one must seek peace within one's soul, harmony between Christian insight and behavior, real peace in interpersonal relationships, and the friendship with God which comes in building up the new covenant community: peacemaking. Finally, since in this fallen world one is virtually certain to provoke hostility by living consistently as a Christian, one must suffer evil rather than do it: accept persecution for righteousness' sake.

In sum, all the modes of Christian response must be lived out in every Christian life. But because personal vocations are different, precisely how this is done will differ from individual to individual. There is enormous variety within the common Christian life-style. By using their different gifts to overcome different evils, diverse weak and sinful people become diverse saints—so many splendid, unique works of the Holy Spirit's art.

The Christian modes also account for the diversity of legitimate spiritualities. For example, some people may start by emphasizing mercy and live what might properly be called "lives of mercy." Others stress humility, others detachment, and so on. None of these particular emphases is wrong. For, as we have seen, all of the Christian modes are unified in Jesus' one redemptive act, and, no matter which is taken as a starting point, all the modes—and all the Christian virtues—eventually come into play. If an individual or a "school" of spirituality, stressing a particular mode or aspect of life in Jesus, makes a faithful effort to embrace its reality and follow it out, with constant recourse to the gospel and an obedient attitude toward the teaching of the Church, that individual or school inevitably finds and reproduces the whole model of Jesus' character.

It is necessary, though, to be faithful in following out the logic of the whole of Jesus' way, and it is possible to go wrong. That comes from not only emphasizing one mode but separating it from the total context and so developing a spirituality which is one-sided and, ultimately, not Christian.

Suppose someone focuses too narrowly on mercy. There is a danger that, absolutizing the idea of doing good to others, he or she will end in some form of secular commitment to social reform or revolution. Marxism and a certain sort of secular liberalism both manifest this fixed concentration on mercy in isolation from everything else; neither has humility or the willingness to accept limitations or a spirit of conciliation. The attitude typical of their adherents is: "We will solve all problems and provide goods and services in plenty for everyone. We will destroy bad institutions and those who exploit others. And, if necessary, we will eliminate those who stand in our way."

B: The Work of the Specifically Christian Conscience

We saw in chapter ten that the modes of responsibility can be applied to descriptions of different kinds of acts so as to determine their morality. Because one cannot be a good Christian without being a decent human being, these natural law principles and the norms derived from them are as relevant for Christians as for anyone else. Christian morality does not permit Christians to act contrary to the ideal of integral human fulfillment, to the modes of responsibility, or to natural law norms. But it does make a difference in how Christians view morality and how they try to live.

Although the modes of Christian response correspond to the modes of responsibility, they are not merely principles but already are very general moral norms, for they already have some specific content: "In these various ways, cooperate with Jesus' redemptive act in living out your act of faith and your personal vocation." Applying this content to the different kinds of action which Christian conscience must evaluate, one can derive very specific and specifically Christian moral norms.

It should be emphasized that these norms *are* specifically Christian. Ultimately, of course, natural law morality and Christian morality involve the same principles: human goods and the requirement of unfettered reason to will in line with the ideal of integral fulfillment. But there are specifically Christian norms because there are specifically Christian acts. As a result of faith, it occurs to Christians to do things which do not occur to people who lack faith: primarily, to cooperate in the redemptive act of Christ; secondly, to accept their personal vocations.

Similarly, there are specific ways of falling short, Christian vices, which may not be wrong for other people but are wrong for Christians. A secular humanist, for example, is not "worldly" in the way some Christians are, for the worldliness of the latter is precisely a failure in detachment—a falling-off from a Christian mode of response which itself is meaningless to the secular humanist.

Although the Christian modes do generate specific moral norms, in practice no Christian goes through the exercise of deriving a norm each and every time one is needed. The New Testament and Christian tradition already contain a body of specific Christian norms concerning kinds of acts which are so common that everyone needs to know how to judge them in moral terms. The Church imparts these norms in its moral teaching.

It should not be supposed, however, that the Church teaches morality in just the same way it teaches doctrine. Up to now, for instance, there have been very few dogmatic definitions on moral questions. Yet the Church does propose moral teachings, including specific moral norms, as truths to be held definitively. (We shall have more to say about this in chapter thirty-five.) Moreover, it often has taught moral truth, and continues to teach it, in ways one tends not to think of as "teaching."

The process by which saints are canonized is one such way. In canonizing someone, the Church calls attention to certain aspects of his or her life and commends them to others for imitation. This is moral teaching. Again, in approving the rule of a religious or secular institute, the Church teaches morality by affirming that the way of life embodied in the rule is commendable. Canon law also presupposes a great deal about how Christians should live their lives. Although it is law, not moral teaching, it includes implicit moral teaching (and, before the adoption of the 1917 Code of Canon Law, it also included much explicit teaching, since law and moral teaching had become commingled). The liturgy, too, teaches morality through the choice of readings, the prayers supplied by the Church, and so on.

But despite the availability of this moral instruction, even people who conform their consciences perfectly to the Church's teaching still face the same question faced by everybody else in every concrete situation requiring a choice: "What, positively, should I do?" A faithful Catholic will not do what the Church teaches should *not* be done, but the question at issue is what here and now *should* be done. It can only be answered in light of all the relevant facts and all the alternatives present in the situation. Thus, no specific affirmative Christian moral norm is absolute. Such norms are true, but they cannot be formulated so comprehensively as to take in every conceivable situation and be binding always and everywhere, regardless of other factors in the situation.

Take an affirmative norm such as "Give to others in need." Generally speaking, one should, yet the norm admits of exceptions. If a poor man encounters someone in dire need, should he share the little he has? If he has only himself to care for, very likely he should. But suppose he has children, and he conscientiously judges that the little he has is not enough for them *and* this stranger: Here and now he need not—in fact, should not—heed the norm "Give to others in need."

This indicates where Christian conscience comes into play. In every situation, one must consider the alternatives and one's responsibilities before concluding that one has at hand an affirmative norm which is specific enough to act on. This process of reaching an adequately specified norm is the work of a prudent conscience.

No one else can solve the problem of the man in the example just cited; he must consider the alternatives and understand in the light of faith what is at stake, then make his own judgment. The specific norm which he forms to guide his action may be so specific that it applies *only* here and now, not to any other cases, but that need not be so. If the norm is true and a situation sufficiently like this one arises for someone else, the same norm will apply. However, it may be impractical or even impossible to communicate a true norm about a very unusual or complex situation, because the morally relevant factors are often hard to describe, and so it can be difficult or impossible to determine whether a true norm for one situation really applies to another.

To be able to say in good conscience "This is what I should do here and now," it is necessary, besides understanding the alternatives and one's responsibilities, to have the answers to two other questions which general principles cannot settle: "Have I thought about this matter as much as I should?" and, supposing there is more than one morally acceptable alternative, "Which of these acceptable alternatives is to be preferred?"

The Church's teaching offers valuable assistance here. As to the first question ("Have I given this enough thought?"), it helps by spelling out certain kinds of acts which are grave matter—mortal sins. If someone evaluates the alternatives in a situation in light of the Church's teaching about what is mortally sinful, and concludes that a particular alternative certainly would not be a mortal sin and would be a way of fulfilling his or her Christian vocation, the individual can be prudently confident that he or she has reflected adequately. Perhaps the judgment is not perfect; perhaps something has been overlooked which closer examination would have disclosed. Still, this person can move ahead responsibly, can act, instead of continuing to agonize—as overly conscientious people sometimes do—about what should be done.

As to the second question ("Which of these acceptable alternatives is to be preferred?"), it can only be answered, after one takes care to understand the options, with the help of one's Christian feelings. Even important questions like personal vocation need to be settled in this way. "I could get married or I could become a priest. There would be nothing wrong in doing either. Which should I do?" One must understand the alternatives as well as possible, reflect, pray—and then attend to one's feelings. In due time feelings formed by faith, prayer, and Christian practice will make one or the other of the alternatives seem uninteresting ("That's not for me") while the other becomes clearer and more attractive ("That's it!"). (Even so, one is likely to be tempted to hesitate, and will need to pull oneself together to make the commitment and carry it out.)

Feeling rightly enters into moral judgment not just on large questions but small ones. "Should I go away this weekend with friends, or should I stay home and get ahead on my work?" Assuming no reason rules out either possibility, one should realize that such alternatives embody different goods which are not rationally commensurable; one can only settle the question of which is more suitable to oneself by consulting one's feelings, and comparing the feelings one has about each possibility with one's underlying feelings, connected with faith, about friends and work as elements of one's personal vocation.

As we remarked earlier, the absolute norms of natural law remain absolute for Christians. Christianity does not shunt human nature aside. If, for example, adultery is always wrong for anyone, then it is always wrong for Christians.

However, nonabsolute norms—those usually but not always true—may be reversed in the case of Christians; they can be obliged to do things which it would be wrong for most people to do most of the time. Indeed, considered apart from faith, a Christian life can seem almost scandalous to someone judging by the standards of conventional morality. To violate human laws and set aside all other responsibilities for the sake of faithfulness to Jesus and the Church; to practice severity in self-discipline and the renunciation of human goods; to be provocative and divisive in a society where faith is challenged: such behavior, outrageous in the eyes of many people, can be required of Christians trying to live in unity with the redemptive act of Christ. But even so, the life of a Christian must still be humanly good, and able to be seen as such, if it is to be revelatory.

C: The Universal Call to Perfection and What Perfection Is

Vatican II teaches that all of us are called to perfection: "The Lord Jesus, the divine Teacher and Model of all perfection, preached holiness of life to each and every one of his disciples, regardless of their situation: 'You therefore are to be perfect, even as your heavenly Father is perfect' (Mt 5:48)" (*LG* 40).

Although charity, the love of God poured forth in our hearts by the Holy Spirit, is central to Christian perfection, it is not the whole of it. Perfection requires that one live a human life of faith informed by charity—a life in whose living the whole self becomes integrated with charity. It is indispensable to this project that one's daily life be formed by prayer and the sacraments, and that it include love of neighbor and service of all the human goods. Such a life is not simply a "religious" one; it involves friendship, learning, caring for one's health, the appreciation of what is beautiful, and much else. It is authentically humanistic.

In this fallen world, however, living in view of human goods requires that one not be too intent on getting one's due. That the good be realized takes precedence over the question of precisely *whose* good it is. A Christian should therefore often forgo his or her rights. Unless duties to others intervene, one can give up what is owed oneself without being unfair; indeed, when only one's own good is at stake, it is the Christian way to put it aside and look to the realization of the good in others.

Christians should nevertheless insist on their rights when that is part of their vocational responsibility. A bishop should insist on being allowed to proclaim the gospel freely and publicly without government interference. A parent should insist on monitoring his or her teenage child's social life even though the child complains. It is a failure in vocational duty to let rights like these slip away.

But that is very different from being overly concerned about rights involving only one's own goods. Then it can be a distraction from vocational responsibility to waste time and energy fighting for one's rights. Evil is not healed by demanding justice for oneself, for in this world there is always a gap between what is fair and what fosters reconciliation. There is no community where everyone insists on his or her rights; people only come together when they stop demanding what is due them and meet one another somewhere beyond mere fairness.

It does not follow, however, that Christian perfection means making no distinctions in relationships with others. While "neighbor" for a Christian takes in everyone who needs redemption—that is, everyone without exception—Christian charity is not a humanitarian benevolence which loves everyone in the world equally and alike. Such an attitude is not and cannot be Christian because it overlooks the concrete responsibilities of personal vocation. Who has an obligation to do good to humanity at large? A pope, perhaps; but the rest of us have far more limited roles in salvation, duties to particular persons arising from the vocational commitments which define the particular fields where we are meant to exercise love.

One's particular "field" ought not to be defined too narrowly. For example, the fact that one is married and has a family does not mean one's love should be limited to spouse and children. Everyone has additional social relationships—with people in the neighborhood, people at work, and so on—and specific responsibilities arise from these. Still, at a certain point it is reasonable and necessary to draw the line. Ordinarily, for instance, one simply does not have the same responsibilities to people in a town half a continent away that one has to the people of one's own town. Christian love is preferential, and there is nothing strange or questionable about that.

The reason is not reducible to "You can only do so much," even though that is true and relevant. There is an order of charity among human beings which is grounded in the Trinity. The order of hierarchy of an individual's responsibilities determines the order of charity for him or her. Within this order, furthermore, loving, caring for, and being at one with other members of the Church has a priority for Christians. This point is made repeatedly in the First Epistle of John and elsewhere in the New Testament, for example, Galatians 6:10: "Let us do good to all men, and especially to those who are of the household of faith." The Christian community is a source of charity in this fallen world, and charity *within* the community must therefore be especially intense; the solidarity of the body of Christ is necessary to its apostolic vitality.

We come, next, to what at first seems a real dilemma. The Church has constantly taught that the counsels of perfection—poverty, chastity, obedience—point to a superior way of life. But if that is so, then surely anyone committed to Christian perfection is obliged to follow this way. Yet life according to the counsels cannot be obligatory for all, for then these would not be counsels but commands, and those who obeyed would not be exhibiting generosity but only doing what they are obliged to do.

The problem is not solved by denying the superiority of life according to the counsels. It is a better way of life in at least two respects.

First, secular Christian life is necessarily focused on concerns about goods to be protected and pursued in this world. By contrast, the consecrated life is a systematic effort to live, insofar as can be done in this world, a life suited to the heavenly communion. In heaven there will be no need for marriage and procreation, and consecrated life anticipates this by virginal or celibate chastity; there will be no need to labor for possessions, and this is anticipated by poverty; there will be no need to seek further goals and strive for success, and consecrated life anticipates this by obedience. As Vatican Council II says, life according to the counsels "foretells the resurrected state and the glory of the heavenly kingdom" (*LG* 44).

Second, it is a comparatively easy way to live a genuinely Christian life. Not that Christian life is ever easy, or that consecrated life does not involve hardships. But it is relatively uncomplicated, and the fewer the complications, the fewer are the temptations and the simpler it is to live as a good Christian.

Then why is life according to the counsels not for everyone? For three reasons.

First, as Christianity does not cancel the value of other human goods besides religion, so there are other good ways of life besides the consecrated life. God's original blessing on creation and human beings—"Be fruitful and multiply, and fill the earth and subdue it" (Gn 1:28)—remains operative. Christians still have a mandate, as it were, to cherish the world, make a home in it, contribute to its perfecting. It would not be right for all of them to withdraw from the world.

Second, the Church has a mission to preach the gospel to the whole world, but there are parts of the world which only lay people can reach. This is not a question of geography but of social structures and life-styles. Christians must strive to overcome the evil in the world and restore everything to God in Christ, and many aspects of that work require that committed Christians live active lives in the world.

Third, Jesus and the Church propose the counsels as suggestions, not requirements. They should be taken into account as a kind of advice and allowed to affect one's feelings when one is considering one's personal vocation; but if, in this context, the advice does not prove decisive, one is not treating it as advice in then saying, "There must be something wrong with me." Rather, the appropriate response is: "I have taken this counsel seriously into account and allowed it to work on my feelings, and my inclination is not to follow it. Therefore, I conclude that I should not follow it, and that my vocation lies somewhere else." The counsels, considered as advice, are relevant to vocational discernment before the decision is made, not after; for after a vocation has been discerned, one is simply obliged to accept it and make a commitment to it, whether it be the Christian life of a lay person in the world, a Christian life according to the counsels, or something else.

28. The Practicability of Christian Morality

By now it should be clear what a Christian life is. Essentially, it is a life modeled on the life of Jesus and lived in cooperation with his redemptive act. But is this really possible? Someone who accepts it as a noble ideal still is entitled to—and, indeed, should—ask how a human being can live like this.

Far and away the most important factor in such a life is God's grace. But there is also work for us to do. Personal vocation, prayer, and the sacraments are the elements which pertain to us. We must find and accept our personal vocations, live them out in the context of prayer, and not only receive the sacraments but organize our lives by them.

We shall examine prayer and the sacraments as principles of Christian life in chapters twenty-nine through thirty-three. Here we begin the discussion of how to live this way of life by disposing of the objection that it is impractical or too difficult. We consider four topics: the possibility of living according to Christian morality; how moral progress and growth in holiness are related; the role of personal vocation; and hope as an indispensable dynamic principle.

A: The Possibility of Living According to Christian Morality

People seldom say bluntly that living according to Christian morality is absolutely out of the question. More commonly they say that Christian moral norms are "ideals": in other words, they point to ways of acting which have a certain nobility but are beyond the reach of most people much of the time. Ideally, everyone should live as Jesus did; in reality, mere human beings cannot.

Christian morality does include ideals. Chief among them is the ideal of perfect love of God: to love him with one's whole mind, heart, soul, and strength. This is not done altogether and at once, for it is not a single performance which one can do and, having done it, consider accomplished. Rather, it is the master ideal which guides and directs an entire Christian life.

The case is different, however, with the norms of action derived from Christian modes of response. There are many of these in the gospels—for example, "If anyone strikes you on the right cheek, turn the other also. . . . If any one wants to sue you and take your coat, give your cloak as well" (Mt 5:39–40)—which, although expressed metaphorically, can be reduced to literal statements, as they often are in the epistles. These specifically Christian norms are intended for life in this fallen world. In heaven, after all, no one will have occasion to turn the other cheek or surrender his cloak. Such norms are meant to be observed here and now.

Of course, it is possible to misunderstand them, and then they are likely to seem impossible. "If the same person sins against you seven times a day, and turns back to you seven times and says, 'I repent,' you must forgive" (Lk 17:4). What is forgiveness? Must we feel kindly toward those who wrong us? Most people find it literally impossible to have kindly feelings toward someone who is injuring them. There is, however, no reason to think Jesus requires kindly feelings in these circumstances. Forgiveness is practical. It means that, when others injure us, we choose not to do to them what we feel like doing but to do what we can to control our feelings and then, despite any residual hostility, to treat them as friends.

Viewed in this light, Christian norms can be fulfilled. They are difficult, but they are not mere ideals.

Still, it is often said in a loose sense that the requirements of Christian life are impossible. People generally mean either of two things by this.

Often they mean, "Given my commitments and my objectives, I can't live a Christian life." For example, someone determined to succeed in a line of work where success requires dishonesty undoubtedly finds it impossible to live according to Christian morality. It is not absolutely impossible, but one cannot do it unless one is willing to sacrifice success. Discipleship has a price. That is hardly news.

Again, people often say Christian morality is impossible when they only mean it is difficult. A person struggling against a quasi-compulsive sin of weakness and apparently making no progress may very well say, "This is impossible." If that is not an attempt to evade responsibility for sinful free choices, but only an expression of discouragement, it is an understandable reaction. Indeed, as fallen human beings driven by the fear of death and all it gives rise to, we cannot live decent lives by our own power (see Rom 7:15–25). But what is impossible for us is possible with God (see Council of Trent, DS 1536/804, 1568/828). In situations like this, the first mode of Christian response—humility—is needed.

Sometimes, too, critics of Christian morality reinforce their contention that it is impossible to live this way by suggesting that it is unnatural even to try. And in fact it is "unnatural" for fallen humankind, with a nature crippled by sin. The accepted standards of any existing culture or society include compromises which allow people to get along comfortably within a tolerated range of immoral behavior. Since these social conventions define what most people mean by "natural," Christian life seems unnatural.

But the redemption which God works in and through Jesus has not just left human nature as it was. Jesus' redemptive sacrifice truly renews human nature—makes it the "new nature" of which St. Paul speaks, "created according to the likeness of God in true righteousness and holiness" (Eph 4:24). The gift of the Holy Spirit makes a difference at once radical and profound; the fallen human condition is now, mysteriously, also the redeemed human condition.

Thus, to say, "It would be unnatural and psychologically destructive for me as a fallen human being to live a Christian life," is an evasion, an excuse for not making the effort. For someone united with Jesus and living by the power of the Spirit, this way of life is neither unnatural nor impossible; to receive the help required to live it, one need only ask with faith.

B: How Moral Progress and Sanctification Are Related

The Church makes a clear distinction, based on Scripture and defined by the Council of Trent, between two phases in an individual's redemption or salvation. First comes the initial straightening out called "justification." This is the consequence of conversion from original sin or mortal sin (or both) to the state of friendship with God: a person turns away from sin and is made a child of God.

The second phase is continuing conversion, also called "sanctification." This is the process of gradual growth in holiness culminating in everlasting life. Trent speaks of it as "advancing from virtue to virtue . . . renewed (as the Apostle says) day by day . . . unto sanctification by observing the commandments of God and of the Church" (DS 1535/803).

Justification and sanctification are not separate, but they are distinct. Although no one justifies himself, still, as Trent says, under the impulse of grace even sinners do some things to cooperate in their own justification. Yet there is no merit in that cooperation, for no one not in God's friendship deserves anything from him, and not even cooperation with grace can merit justification. Faith alone justifies. All one can do in this matter is accept God's gift. In that sense, one is saved by faith and not by works. By contrast, sanctification—growth in holiness—involves and requires good works. As St. James says, sanctification is by faith together with works (see Jas 2:14–26). This also is the teaching of the Council of Trent.

But, someone might ask, what do these words of St. Paul mean: "For one believes with the heart and so is justified, and one confesses with the mouth and so is saved" (Rom 10:10)? Do the good works required of us come down to no more than confessing with the mouth? Just say, "Jesus is my Lord and Savior"—and one is saved? That is to misunderstand what St. Paul has in mind. To be sincere, confession with the lips must be carried out consistently; it must be lived. "Let us not grow weary in doing what is right," Paul urges, "for we will reap at harvest-time" (Gal 6:9). Confession with the lips means bearing witness, which leads to salvation because it involves a complete Christian life.

Sanctification, living an apostolic life, and making moral progress are therefore one and the same process. The fundamental reason concerns the fact that charity is central to sanctity.

Charity is the justifying gift which one accepts with faith. It is a share in divine life and love, and, as such, it does not change.

One cannot be more or less an adopted child of God, more or less in God's grace. But there is also a sense in which charity can and should grow and intensify (see 2 Thes 1:3). This happens through the process by which one lives out one's personal vocation and works to share God's love with others; in doing so, one more perfectly conforms one's will to God's will and becomes more fully integrated with God's love, so that the disposition toward divine goodness gradually becomes the motivating force of one's entire life, and love suffuses one's entire personality.

The more perfectly a person is integrated with charity, the more holy he or she is. Furthermore, since faith is the mediating human act by which charity is accepted, charity transforms faith itself. To believe God out of love for him is living faith, and if one's entire life is integrated with faith, then one loves God with one's whole mind, heart, soul, and strength.

One loves God with one's whole heart because all one's desires and interests, choices and actions, are subordinated to living faith and what it entails; one loves God with one's whole mind because all one's ideas, opinions, and judgments are at the service of faith; one loves God with one's entire strength because all one's powers and resources are used in living the life of faith. Everything is integrated in the service of faith living through love. That complete integration is sanctity.

This sketch of the life of faith, with its emphasis on works and merit, should not be rejected on the grounds that everything salvific is the result of God's grace. That is true of course: nothing contributes to our salvation except what God gratuitously gives us. But it is also true that, as Isaiah says, "all that we have done," God has "done for us" (Is 26:12). Although God accomplishes in us the good we do, we nevertheless do it: our upright lives are a grace from God, but we really live them. "For we are what he has made us, created in Christ Jesus for good works, which God prepared beforehand to be our way of life" (Eph 2:10). The Council of Trent expresses the same idea by saying that God "wishes his gifts also to be our merits" (DS 1548/810). The call to live the Christian life, the acceptance of that call, the ability to live that way, and the actual doing of it—these are among God's graces to us, but the life thus lived is one's *own* life, which one personally lives out.

God has made us his children and promised us a full share in his life if we live out the holy life he offers to give us. If therefore we accept his gifts and use them well, we deserve to be treated as his children. That is "merit" for us.

The central point here, in any case, is the distinction between justification and sanctification. It is crucial to Catholic doctrine in this area. Faith alone justifies—that is the Church's teaching. But, once we have received the gift of the love of God poured forth in our hearts by the Holy Spirit, it is no longer justification which is at issue (unless one means that ongoing justification which is continuing conversion) but rather sanctification.

C: The Organizing Role of Personal Vocation

If faith, charity, the modes of Christian response, and Christian moral norms are all readily available principles of a good Christian life, why do the lives of so many Catholics and other Christians apparently fall far short of what one might reasonably expect of lives informed by these principles? We are not speaking of "lapsed" Catholics or hypocritical Christians, but of people who live what are in many respects decent lives but whose growth toward perfection appears to be stunted, stalled at a level where uprightness and sinfulness coexist. What accounts for this?

While there may be different explanations in different cases, the one which applies to many people is that large areas of their lives are ruled by impulses, goals, and even commitments unrelated to faith. Of course, everyone's life includes elements which only gradually become integrated with faith; but with the people we speak of, integration itself seems to have come to a halt, leaving much outside the sphere of faith.

One sees this in young people who have been decently brought up and for whom religion occupies a compartment in their lives. That is the problem: Religion is in a *compartment,* and they have many interests, objectives, and commitments unrelated to it. For them religion signifies a few positive responsibilities, along with the need to avoid mortal sin. The rest of life goes forward uninfluenced by faith.

In a sense, of course, this is the "normal" state of affairs for young people. They are still working at integrating their lives. It becomes a sign of moral immaturity, however, in older persons for whom religion is still compartmentalized.

Moreover, as we saw in chapter eighteen ("The Way of Sin to Death"), even the lives of Christians in grace are riddled with imperfections arising not just from immaturity but from disintegrity. They "naturally" have many spontaneous interests and desires which will lead to sin unless curbed. Many also commit large numbers of venial sins, including some which do great harm to growth in holiness, namely, sins in grave matter which are not mortal sins only because sufficient reflection is lacking. In the lives of such people—shot through with principles of action unintegrated with faith and marked by what would be mortal sins if they reflected sufficiently—living faith may occupy a corner, but much, indeed most, of what they do is done apart from faith and charity. It is scarcely surprising that holiness does not "grow" in such lives.

The way out of this impasse must be by way of personal vocation. Personal vocation is not a single commitment—the decision to be a priest or religious or married person or whatever it may be—but a set of interlocking, integrated commitments which organizes one's whole life in light of faith. Discerning a vocation means considering the sum total of one's abilities and opportunities, weighing the needs of the Church and the world, and then making a harmonious set of commitments which constitute one's life of faith.

But even after one has discerned and accepted one's vocation, there normally are other principles and elements left over, as it were, which do not fit into the pattern of the life thus organized. For example, a married man who is serious about his family obligations, his work, his religion, and his other duties may still retain from earlier days certain interests—friendships, hobbies, recreational pursuits—which, although innocent in themselves, do not fit the life of personal vocation he is now trying to lead in light of faith. Soon enough, conflicts arise and the situation becomes clear to him. Then, if he is consistent and honest with himself, he will either find ways to integrate these carry-overs from the past with the rest of his life or he will eliminate them.

Here Christian modes three, four, and six come into play. Put aside what does not pertain to personal vocation, be faithful and fearless in overcoming obstacles to that vocation, and continually purify oneself of whatever does not meet this standard so that one does God's will in everything. Then growth in holiness can occur.

It is clear in the light of personal vocation what the various Christian modes concretely require for each individual. Either one lives by the modes or, recognizing one's vocational responsibilities, knows that one is falling short and failing those to whom one has duties.

Take the man who would like to be a conscientious husband and father. Suppose he has a circle of friends from bachelor days with whom he plays cards. Unfortunately, they play for fairly high stakes, and, not being a very good card player, he regularly loses money his family needs. If he takes an honest look at the situation, his duty will be clear: Either he must persuade his buddies to play for penny ante stakes or he must stop playing cards with them. (One advantage of marriage as a vocational commitment by comparison with, say, the priesthood is that its duties generally concern others—spouse and children—to whom one is emotionally attached. That makes it somewhat easier to make the sacrifices required to live up to the commitment than if one's duties pertain to people with whom one has weaker emotional bonds.)

A word, finally, about rigorism. Classical moral theology was rightly concerned to avoid this extreme. But do we not fall into rigorism in saying the modes of Christian response generate norms which must be fulfilled—in other words, that a Christian really ought to live this way? Not at all. The process by which sincere Christians go about organizing their lives in light of personal vocation explains why.

One is only obliged to fulfill the Christian modes as their requirements become clear, and no one sees all their requirements all at once. Typically, these emerge gradually, over a period of time. Sometimes, of course, the "period of time" may seem terribly abbreviated—duties surface and converge in a rush—but even so the principle holds true. One lives one's Christian life a day at a time, doing that day's duties as best one understands them and as best one can. That elementary fact removes the curse of rigorism from this view of the modes and the obligation to fulfill them.

Furthermore, the power to live one's vocation and fulfill the modes does not come from oneself but from God, and he gives it as it is needed. Nor, as we have seen, are the Christian modes arbitrary burdens; they specify what must be done to live a morally upright life in this fallen world. Even old-fashioned legalists, concerned to lighten people's burdens and avoid rigorism, in practice recognized the modes. Their advice to the married man gambling away money his family could not afford to lose would have been: "You must avoid that occasion of sin." The language was different, but the requirements of the Christian modes were recognized and expressed.

D: The Indispensability of Hope as a Dynamic Principle

Faith, charity, and hope are related. By faith we accept God's love, offered in a covenant; by that love we are disposed to fulfillment in divine life; by hope we live for the kingdom, counting on God to do what he has promised—to bring us to that fulfillment.

In speaking of God's faithfulness and truth, as it often does, Scripture is not referring to two separate concepts. When he reveals truth about himself, God makes an interpersonal communication, and when such a communication is a promise, as God's revelation is, its truth lies in the faithful keeping of the promise. To believe God's self-revelation, therefore, also means acting on it, expecting him to keep his promises. That is hope.

Thus, hope adds something to faith, namely, a practical disposition of acting with confident trust in God for what we cannot attain by ourselves. As a result, one willingly lets go of those supports and sources of security one would cling to if one did not expect God to keep his promises.

Hope is indispensable as a dynamic principle of Christian life. Without it, we have no other adequate motive to live this way, for not only is it difficult, but, considered only from the perspective of this world and this life, it is not especially fulfilling and almost certainly will lead, to one degree or another, to persecution, suffering, and failure.

That, after all, is the example of Jesus' life: he died a failure. A Christian who tries to follow Jesus and live as he did can expect the same. And despite the successes, satisfactions, and rewards which can and do accompany a Christian life, if there were no hope of resurrection—if one could not count on God to do as he says—consistently living this way would seem pointless. Sometimes at least it would seem to make sense to accept the wisdom of conventional morality and, when need arises, to do evil in order to avoid evil or bring about some good.

True, even without hope a person may be motivated to avoid some evils and do some goods. Many people without hope do.

But one would also find reasons for doing evils—"lesser" evils, to be sure—and omitting goods considered too insignificant to be worth the trouble. As a practical matter, hope makes the difference between a decent non-believer and a sincere Christian.

But, someone might object, surely all this cannot apply to situations in which one is obliged to be concerned with the welfare of others? Here, certainly, Machiavellianism or something like it must be allowed.

May a person really refrain from doing a lesser evil if the result will be that greater evil befalls those for whose well-being he or she is responsible? Cannot—in fact, must not—a father do evil to protect his family? May not a head of state do a lesser evil to prevent his nation from being enslaved or obliterated? Would it not be irresponsible *not* to do evil in such circumstances?

The theoretical answer, as we saw in chapter six, is that goods and bads cannot be commensurated as this objection assumes; the supposedly lesser evil is determined by feeling, not by any rational standard. Practically speaking, however, hope is the Christian answer to the objection. Christian life is not individualistic but communal, and hope similarly has a communal dimension. It is not directed to individualistic salvation but to salvation in a community—the whole community of human and divine persons, sharing in eternal friendship and in fulfillment in human as well as divine goods.

Christians who refrain from doing evil in circumstances like those mentioned above do not hope simply for their own salvation but also for the salvation of those for whom they are responsible. And, in refusing to do evil, they are not sacrificing human possibilities for the sake of divine life, since their hope is precisely confident trust that the human goods of all will be restored and perfected at the resurrection. Christian hope includes human fulfillment, not just for oneself but with and for the others. Living the Christian life even when, by worldly standards, that seems to mean failing in one's social responsibilities is explained and justified by hope. It, too, is foolishness even to decent nonbelievers. Yet it conforms to the definitive model of God's wisdom: Jesus' acceptance of failure in his mission of gathering in the lost sheep of Israel, when he might have "succeeded" by falsifying his mission and becoming the sort of Messiah they wanted (see Lk 13:34–35, 19:41–42, 22:66–67).

29. Prayer: The Fundamental Category of Christian Action

This chapter considers prayer, while the next four are concerned with the sacraments. These chapters are not a dogmatic treatise on spiritual and sacramental theology, and they omit much of great importance on these matters. We consider prayer and the sacraments from the specific perspective of moral theology: as basic principles of Christian life, actions which themselves are central to such a life. As such, prayer and the sacraments clearly pertain to moral theology, even though traditional texts in fundamental moral said little about them.

Prayer's relevance to Christian life arises from the fact that this way of life is fundamentally a communal, interpersonal relationship with the Trinity. Someone who accepts in faith God's self-communication enters into a relationship with him. Prayer sustains and develops this relationship. At the same time, it shapes Christian life by bringing revelation to bear upon it, meditating on how Christian moral norms are to be observed, and thus helping to guide the process of growth toward perfection.

The chapter addresses four topics: what prayer is and why it is necessary; the respective roles of the Holy Spirit and of the Christian in prayer; whether prayer is always answered; and types of prayer (liturgical prayer, sacramentals, devotions, personal prayer), and the relationships among them.

A: What Prayer Is and Why It Is Necessary

While prayer can be described in several ways, the most helpful way to think of it is as conversation with God. St. Francis de Sales writes: "If prayer is a colloquy, a discussion, or a conversation of the soul with God, then by prayer we speak to God and God in turn speaks to us."[20] But more specifically, prayer is our side of this conversation, the complement of listening to God's word in revelation. That makes it clear why the Second Vatican Council links the reading of Sacred Scripture and prayer (see *DV* 25). God speaks; we listen and respond.

Prayer also helps one maintain one's Christian identity. Any serious interpersonal relationship goes a long way to establish the identity of the parties to it, since who one is, in large part, is a matter of one's relationships. To maintain one's identity requires maintaining one's relationships, and maintaining relationships requires communication. As far as the relationship with God is concerned, therefore, prayer—communication with God—is necessary to sustain the relationship and keep up one's identity as a Christian.

Prayer has a practical side. More than just listening to God and accepting what he says, more even than responding intellectually, it involves, as part of the "response" itself, shaping one's life in accord with faith. To respond in this sense is to take into account what one hears and adapt one's plans and actions to the relationship with God. Prayer is thus the link between believing God's word and living the Christian life. That basically is what makes it an important principle of Christian living. Without prayer, faith becomes sterile and isolated from life, lacking its proper expression in good works.

The need for prayer becomes still more apparent when one reflects upon its role in maintaining and building up the relationship which will be perfected in heavenly communion. Acts of prayer are self-constituting human acts. Like other choices, the choices made in praying—to pray, to pray in a certain way, to pray for and about particular things—lastingly determine those who make them. Moreover, prayer shapes the whole person, not only volitionally and spiritually but, insofar as it involves imagination, emotion, and experience, in other aspects of the self as well.

Prayer therefore should not be simply one more activity alongside others—something done when its turn comes, then put aside in favor of the next item on the schedule. Obviously it is important to have a time to pray; that elementary discipline is essential to regularity. But one should strive to integrate prayer with the rest of life, so that it flows into other forms of fruitful activity which express and fulfill personal vocation. Rather than compartmentalizing prayer, one must aim to blend it into the rest of one's life.

B: The Roles of the Holy Spirit and of the Christian in Prayer

St. Paul makes several seemingly obscure statements about the Holy Spirit's role in Christian life. "When we cry, 'Abba! Father!' " he writes, "it is that very Spirit bearing witness with our spirit that we are children of God" (Rom 8:15–16). Again:

> Likewise the Spirit helps us in our weakness; for we do not know how to pray as we ought, but that very Spirit intercedes with sighs too deep for words. And God, who searches the heart, knows what is the mind of the Spirit, because the Spirit intercedes for the saints according to the will of God. (Rom 8:26–27)

What do these statements mean?

They are commonly given a fairly bland interpretation: St. Paul is speaking of the workings of grace; all he means to say is that the Spirit moves us to do certain things—pray in a certain way, desire what we should desire; the only strange thing about these passages is Paul's way of expressing himself.

Perhaps. However, there is no reason not to read his words in a straightforward manner which, though not inconsistent with this interpretation, does go considerably beyond it. Such a reading proceeds along the following lines.

As God's adopted children, we can act in new ways according to the divine nature in which we share by the gift of the Holy Spirit. But such action is not independent of the working of the Spirit. In acting according to the divine nature, we always depend on the Spirit. Acting in this way, and depending on the Spirit, we act toward the Father and the Son as members of the divine family.

In attempting to understand this, we might think of the Christian in this life as being something like an unborn child in the womb. The child is a living human individual, but its life functions depend on the mother. Oxygen and nourishment come through the placenta, waste products are carried away through the mother's system, and so on. The child does things which a living organism does, but it cannot do them apart from its mother.

The Christian's situation resembles this. "We are God's children now," but not yet at a mature stage in our sharing in and exercising divine life; thus, "what we will be has not yet been revealed" (1 Jn 3:2). Meanwhile, in order to act as the children of God we really are, we depend totally on the Holy Spirit. This is the case with our prayer ("that very Spirit intercedes") and with every other aspect of our Christian life insofar as it is a sharing in divinity.

This, however, is not to be confused with our human cooperation with Jesus' redemptive human act—that is, with our Christian moral life of human acts. That also is dependent—on Jesus—but in a way we understand. It depends on him very much as what is done by people engaged in any cause cooperates with and depends upon the activity of the leader whose cause it preeminently is. By contrast, our dependence on the Holy Spirit in activity according to the divine nature is outside human experience and profoundly mysterious. St. Paul would appear to be speaking of it, but we do not know much more about it than he tells us.

Although Christian prayer, considered as involving divine activity, is carried on, as St. Paul suggests, in dependence on the Spirit, prayer in another aspect is simply human action. As such, it should be modeled on Jesus' human action and characterized, like any other moral act, by the Christian modes of response. Its appropriate characteristics are noted many times in the New Testament. Prayer should be humble, for without humility we are not ready to accept God's gifts. It should be Eucharistic—that is, grateful—constantly returning thanks to God for the good he has done us and goes on doing. It should be vigilant and attentive (detachment and fidelity). It should be persevering and confident, sincere and constant.

Still, one might ask whether and in what sense it is possible to pray constantly. Some writers suggest that it is literally possible, or at least that one can maintain a kind of constant prayerful awareness at the edge of consciousness. St. Thomas, however, points out realistically that a person can only attend to one thing at a time, and in trying to pray constantly, one is likely to overlook or botch things which often take priority over prayer.

If continuous prayer is not really possible, however, a certain constancy in prayer remains both possible and necessary. Without always actually being at prayer, one can constantly maintain a prayerful attitude and always be ready to pray. As a member of the Church, too, one can identify oneself by intention with the prayer of other members (somewhere the Mass is always being offered, the Liturgy of the Hours is being recited, and members of religious communities dedicated to perpetual adoration are praying before the Blessed Sacrament). This may not be precisely the same thing as praying constantly, but it deserves to be called constancy in prayer.

Constancy in prayer is attained and powerfully reinforced as one achieves increasing self-integration through faith and charity. In that sense, one's entire life ought to be prayer; it should be formed by prayer in line with the personal vocation discerned as God's particular will for oneself. Then one's life carries out one's prayer, and whatever one does flows from it. One can hardly be said to be setting prayer aside in doing what one has seen in prayer ought to be done. Rather, this is how all of Christian life becomes a life of prayer—a life in which prayer is fulfilled in appropriate action.

C: Whether Prayer Is Always Answered

Prayer of petition raises a special problem. Jesus says in several places in the New Testament that if we ask in prayer, we will receive (see Mt 18:19, 21:22; Mk 11:24; Lk 11:9–10; Jn 15:7, 16:23–24). But everyone who prays has the experience of asking for things and not getting them. One common explanation for this is that we have not prayed long enough. But that is scarcely a satisfactory explanation when things happen which individuals and even the whole Church have prayed would not happen: sickness, the death of loved ones, wars, calamities. To suppose such things occur because prayer to ward them off has not gone on long enough, one must also suppose that God hastens to send us afflictions before we can satisfy his conditions for avoiding them. That is patently absurd.

A traditional solution to this problem holds that God does respond to our prayers. If we ask as we should for the gift of the Spirit, the grace to grow in Christ, our prayer is sure to be answered (see Lk 11:10–13) But if we ask for other things, instead of giving us what we often mistakenly think would be good for us and those we are concerned about, God gives what he knows will really be good. That is a sound answer as far as it goes. Not infrequently, our attitude in prayer resembles that of a teenager who wants a car. Father considers the request, then says, "It wouldn't be good for you." The child replies, "You never listen to me. You don't pay attention to anything I say." Of course, the father did listen; that is why he responded as he did. When we say God does not hear our prayers or answer them, we may be reacting very much like this teenage child.

Frequently, too—and correctly—it is said that our attitude in prayer should mirror that of Jesus: "Yet not what I want but what you want" (Mt 26:39). Our first and fundamental attitude, in other words, should be: "Your will be done" (Mt 6:10). And so it should. But that points to another, deeper difficulty.

If, ultimately, one's prayer should be, "Your will be done," why pray at all? God already knows what we need (see Mt 6:32; Lk 12:30), and we can count on him to give us the best thing to meet our needs in the best possible way. In praying that God's will be done, we are praying for what is sure to happen anyway. So, why pray?

St. Thomas suggests that God not only provides for our needs but wills that what we need should be given to us in answer to our requests. God respects our freedom and our dignity. He does not want simply to give us everything, as if we were absolutely helpless dependents, too feeble and incompetent even to ask for what we need. Even when we can do nothing except ask, he wants us to be active in our own lives at least to that extent.

This view of our role in prayer parallels the view of redemption set out in earlier chapters: God involves us in our redemption because he is trying to foster a personal relationship with us, a two-sided relationship which is real communion. That is why he made us free and why he does not simply wipe out our sin without repentance on our part: if our freedom were not engaged, we would be mere objects. So also with prayer. To be partners in a relationship, we must play our part—do something—and asking is doing something. Moreover, it is a kind of "doing something" by which we prepare ourselves to receive and appreciate God's gifts.

So far so good. But there is a mistake to be avoided here. Part of the truth about God is that he does not know and change as anything we understand knows and changes. So, having excluded from God any kind of knowledge or change which we are capable of understanding, we say: "Very good. God doesn't know as we understand knowing—he knows absolutely everything. And God doesn't change as we understand change—he is absolutely changeless." And then we suppose we understand what it means to know absolutely everything and be absolutely changeless.

That mistake has practical consequences. In supposing we understand what it means for God to be all-knowing and changeless, we make it impossible to relate to him. How can one have a real personal relationship with a God who, in some way one understands, knows everything and is changeless? If God is unchangeable in any way we understand, nothing we say or do will make the least difference to how he deals with us. This more than anything else gives process theology its plausibility and attractiveness; at least it allows us to dispense with the idea that God is unchangeable. But process theology, no less than traditional theology, assumes that we understand God's knowledge and action in our lives when in fact we do not.

To avoid turning God into a merely metaphysical entity, we must bear in mind his utter mysteriousness. While excluding from God ignorance, error, and changeability of sorts which we understand, we must also exclude from him what we understand by the opposite set of concepts. We are left with the fact that God's reality is utterly mysterious. We do not understand what his wisdom, love, eternal life, and divine perfection are.

But how can we relate to a God who is utterly mysterious? The Incarnation provides the answer. (God's visible, audible, tangible manifestations to Abraham, Moses, and others in the Old Testament in a way anticipated and initiated the Incarnation.) We can relate to God in Jesus, and he is by no means utterly mysterious; we relate to him in his humanity as we relate to another human being. In relating to Jesus in his humanity, however, we also relate to the divine Word, the second Person of the Trinity, and through him to the Father and the Holy Spirit. Through the humanity of Jesus we come into contact with God.

> Philip said to him, "Lord, show us the Father, and we will be satisfied." Jesus said to him, "Have I been with you all this time, Philip, and you still do not know me? Whoever has seen me has seen the Father. How can you say, 'Show us the Father'? Do you not believe that I am in the Father and the Father is in me?" (Jn 14:8–10)

Thus, God reveals himself in a way that makes it possible for human beings fully to enter into personal relationship with him.

This religious relationship does not oblige one to have a metaphysical theory of God. In principle there is nothing wrong with having one, provided it is not an erroneous theory which leads people to imagine they comprehend God. Still we must respect, indeed insist on, God's utter mysteriousness so as to avoid entertaining false notions about him—notions which are obstacles to the proper development of Christian life. "Why pray to God? He is unchangeable, and our prayers cannot move him in the least." That is a meaningless objection. God is *not* unchangeable in any way we understand, and the problem thus presented is a false one.

In sum: Are prayers answered? Although it may often seem they are not, they really are. But they are not always answered as we want, since God knows better than we do what is good for us. If the only correct way of praying is, ultimately, "Thy will be done," why bother praying at all? Because we cannot have a personal relationship with God unless we communicate with him, including telling him what we want and think we need. But how can we have a personal relationship with a God who is utterly mysterious? We can have a personal relationship with God through Jesus. He is our mediator and our way.

D: The Liturgy and Other Types of Prayer

While primarily Jesus' action, the liturgy is also the Church's action, insofar as the Church is united with Jesus, and it is our action as individuals, insofar as we are active members of the Church. Since Christian faith and life are cooperation with Jesus, and since the liturgy is the eminent form of such cooperation, the liturgy must be central in our prayer.

The liturgy is a reminder, furthermore, that, as Christianity itself is not an encounter between the individual and God in an ineffable, experiential relationship, so Christian prayer is not individualistic but is carried on in communion. In liturgical worship, above all in the Eucharist, Jesus' redemptive act is made present so that we can participate in it, both as its beneficiaries and as cooperators—co-redeemers—in our own redemption and the redemption of others. Here "grace is channeled into us; and the sanctification of men in Christ and the glorification of God . . . are most powerfully achieved" (*SC* 10).

Sacramentals and devotions, properly understood, are an outgrowth of the liturgy which at the same time lead back to it. Some sacramentals are actually part of the liturgical action surrounding the sacraments: for example, the priest's washing of hands at Mass. Others grow out of the liturgy and, as it were, extend it into everyday life. So, for instance, holy water recalls baptism, the ashes received on Ash Wednesday bring penance to mind. The same thing is true of many devotions—for example, benediction of the Blessed Sacrament is a kind of extension of the Eucharist, the mysteries of the rosary summarize the cycle of the liturgical year, and so on.

The sacramentals and devotions help individuals and groups shape their prayer in a way that focuses on their particular circumstances and needs, and is specifically relevant to their daily lives. By taking differences of age, taste, and cultural background into realistic consideration, they perform a useful and necessary service. As Vatican II says, they dispose people "to receive the chief effect of the sacraments, and the various occasions in life are rendered holy" (*SC* 60).

It is important, however, that they be kept subordinate to the liturgy and always remain oriented to it, rather than competing with the liturgical rites or being allowed to replace them. It is also important to remember that particular sacramentals and devotions are optional. Individuals, families, and groups are free to use those which suit them, but they need not use them all or adopt ones which they do not find helpful.

While the liturgical reform initiated by Vatican II has been a good thing in its own right, one unfortunate side effect has been the widespread abandonment of sacramentals and devotions. As a result, the celebration of the Eucharistic liturgy itself at times is treated as if it were a devotion, and the Mass becomes a setting for forms of devotional expression which suit some in the congregation but not others. When the congregation is composed exclusively of members of a particular group, there is no objection to legitimate adaptations which suit that group; ordinarily, however, a public liturgy for a mixed congregation should be kept fairly unadorned, so that people are not forced to share in (or be alienated by) a devotional style they find repugnant.

Finally, although the liturgy is central, individual prayer is also essential in Christian life. "The spiritual life . . . is not confined to participation in the liturgy. The Christian is assuredly called to pray with his brethren, but he must also enter into his chamber to pray to the Father in secret (cf. Mt 6:6)" (*SC* 12). Everyone must develop his or her own unique relationship with God, a relationship requiring personal prayer as a medium of communication through which revelation is appropriated and applied to life.

Such prayer makes personal for the individual Christian that which is common to all. Far from being mutually exclusive, prayer within the community of the Church and individual prayer are complementary aspects of the process by which people integrate their lives by faith.

30. Sacraments in General and Baptism

In this and the next three chapters we shall consider how the sacraments are organizing principles of Christian life—principles, that is, which shape a life toward perfection in this world and fulfillment in Jesus in heaven. The present chapter treats three topics: the sacraments in general, considered as cooperative acts; the diverse roles involved in sacramental cooperation; and baptism as the basic sacramental principle. We emphasize again that we are not writing a treatise on sacramental theology but simply saying what needs to be said about the sacraments as principles in moral theology.

A: The Sacraments in General Considered as Cooperative Acts

The sacraments are divine-human cooperative acts which involve the action of God, of Jesus as glorified man, of the Church through its minister, and of the recipient. We can begin to understand what this means by considering the Eucharist (and, by association with it, the other sacraments) as the sacramental means by which Jesus' redemptive act is made present for our participation and cooperation.

We saw in chapters twenty-two and twenty-three that, in choosing to eat the Last Supper with his apostles, Jesus freely accepted death and offered himself to the Father. This was the culmination of his redemptive life—a life rooted in his fundamental commitment of obedience to the Father's will, specified by his acceptance of his personal vocation to form the human side of the new covenant, and carried out during his public life in various actions, including finally his choice to go to Jerusalem to eat the Passover, even though he knew he would be arrested and executed.

Jesus' human act of accepting his death and offering it to the Father is a choice which lasts. By Jesus' command, that same act of self-offering is performed in the Mass. Doing what he commanded us to do, we continue and extend the first Eucharist through history and throughout the world.

Evidently, then, the Eucharist is not merely Jesus' unique way of making himself present to us. In instituting the Eucharist he had a larger purpose in view: to make it possible for us to share in his redemptive act. The Eucharist is his act and ours. It is a co-operative act. To be sure, Jesus' part is vastly more important than ours, yet we have a part to play. In the Eucharist, we join him in the cooperative performance of his redemptive act.

This perfectly exemplifies God's general approach to redemption: he does not redeem us without our cooperation. One could imagine God doing everything himself and, as it were, imposing redemption on us, but this is not how he proceeds. Instead he enlists human cooperation. First, of course, there is Jesus' cooperation; the Incarnation ennobles humankind by making the Lord's human life part of our history. But beyond that, God gives us Jesus so that we can cooperate with him. Thus, he greatly increases our dignity by involving us in the work of saving ourselves and others. Considered from this perspective, the sacraments are extensions of the Incarnation. In them, God continues to follow the policy of bringing about human cooperation in his redemptive work—not only Jesus' human cooperation but now ours, too.

In saying this of sacramental cooperation, do we attribute too much to human activity and take something away from God? By no means. Everything salvific, including the human cooperation of which we speak, is a gift from God. "There are varieties of activities, but it is the same God who activates all of them in everyone" (1 Cor 12:6). Human participation in redemption is not a substitute for God's work but a greater work of God which more fully realizes the purpose of creation itself: the expression of divine goodness which we call—and which is—God's "glory."

Because there is this intrinsic connection between the Incarnation and the sacraments, inasmuch as the same principle of divine redemptive action is operative in both, someone who rejects the sacraments is also likely before long to reject the Incarnation.

Such a person will tend to ignore or devalue Jesus' human aspect and become a kind of practical docetist, stressing our Lord's divinity while minimizing the importance of his human acts.

Still, someone confronted with this emphasis on the sacraments as human acts might object that human acts as such cannot justify or sanctify because they cannot overcome sin and communicate divine life. Yet that is what the sacraments do. They can do it because they are not *merely* human acts but involve real cooperation between human beings and God.

An analogy helps. A little girl asks her father to let her drive the car. The father allows the child to turn the ignition key, shift the lever to "drive," hold the steering wheel on a safe stretch of road. When she gets home, the girl tells her mother, "Dad let me drive." She is right—she really did drive the car to some extent, using means which her father provided, cooperating with him, and, of course, leaving everything complicated to him. Divine-human cooperation in the sacraments is something like that.

So, there is in the sacraments the real, four-sided cooperation of which we speak. God the Holy Spirit, Jesus in glory as man, the Church by her minister, and the recipient all cooperate to justify (in baptism and, for mortal sinners, in penance) and to sanctify (in the other sacraments) the recipient.

Sacraments are often said to be signs of a unique sort, and so they are. Often, too, it is said that, as signs, the sacraments suit our human need for the sensible, and that also is true. But it should not be taken to mean that the reality of the sacraments is a purely spiritual encounter, while the external sign has merely instrumental value as a kind of image of what is happening inwardly and invisibly. One finds this sort of thinking in some important recent theological works on the sacraments: The real human-divine interaction occurs in spiritual contact between the soul and God, of which outward performances are only rather insignificant symbols. This, quite simply, is an unacceptable dis-incarnational account.

Rather than being mere symbols of something happening invisibly, the sacraments provide a way for us to cooperate in Jesus' redemptive act. On our side, cooperation in a sacramental act requires understanding and choice, the most significant elements of any act. Our understanding and choosing to do what God gives us to do make a real contribution to the sacramental process. It is like the little girl who drives the car. By doing what her father gives her to do, she really does make a contribution to driving it, even though she does not—and could not—drive the car by herself.

The sacraments therefore are given to us so that we can do something by way of willing cooperation with God's redemptive work in us. The outward performances are not just symbolic; they are the vehicles of our cooperation.

Consider another analogy. A mother decides to make bread. If baking bread were all she had in mind, she would do better to wait until the children were in bed. But because she loves the children and wants them to be involved, she lets them help. One keeps a finger in the recipe book (it would be easier to use a bookmark); another watches the clock to time the baking (easier to use the oven timer); another holds the pans while mother puts the loaves in them (the pans could just as well stay on the counter). Thus, the children really cooperate in making the bread, and when their father comes home, they can say truly, "We helped mother make bread."

It is like that with the sacraments. Certainly God can work in us directly; he does not need our help. And even in enlisting our help, the things he gives us to do and our doing of them are his gifts. All the same, in the sacraments our actions really are our actions. Thus, the sacraments are divine-human cooperative acts.

B: The Four Diverse Roles Involved in Sacramental Cooperation

There are four roles. First, that of the Holy Spirit justifying and sanctifying. Second, the action of the risen Lord Jesus, still operating as a human being inasmuch as his redemptive act has not ceased with his death and resurrection. Third, the action of the Church through her minister, who performs sacramental rites in the Church's name. Fourth, the action of the recipient of the sacrament. (Sometimes, of course, a recipient can do nothing, but ordinarily he or she has a cooperative role.) Let us consider each of these roles.

First, the role of God. Obviously, it is not merely one among others but is all-inclusive, for God creates everything else involved and gives it meaning and value. What is at issue here, however, is the specific role of the Holy Spirit—the Spirit's unique contribution, to which human action contributes nothing.

The Council of Trent teaches definitively that the sacraments contain and confer grace (see DS 1606/849). Grace alone justifies;

only God re-creates and divinizes fallen human persons. Having justified, moreover, grace builds up justice; we grow in holiness through grace. All this comes about, and can only come about, by divine action.

Just as Jesus' humanity does not limit the incarnate God, so the sacraments neither limit nor exhaust God's love. Divine love is infinite. But God has chosen to make himself available to us in sacraments (as he is also available in Scripture and in the incarnate Word) and to act in and through them. The same incarnational principle is present and operative throughout salvation history. By a kind of free self-denial or "condescension," God accepts the conditions of finite media—Jesus' humanity, the human words of the Bible, sacramental acts—in order to communicate with us and involve us in his redemptive action. Indeed, he must do so if we are to cooperate, for we—though certainly not he—require these finite, concrete, tangible means.

As divine acts, the sacraments are also revelatory. While everything Jesus says and does in his life reveals and communicates divine truth and life, the sacraments, as extensions of the Incarnation, are revelatory precisely in that they communicate divine truth and life to us. The sacramental rites make it clear that this is occurring.

Next, the role of the risen Lord Jesus. His redemptive act is a perfect sacrifice, and this human act of his lasts. It is reexpressed or reperformed, made present here and now, in the Eucharist and, in their various ways, in the other sacraments. (Obviously there are differences among the sacraments, but these are not differences in Jesus' redemptive act, which is the same in all of them. Instead the sacraments differ in the way in which the Church and we act in them.)

Jesus acts visibly in the sacraments. The dualistic supposition that what really happens in a sacrament only occurs invisibly and spiritually, while the visible performance is a mere symbol, is a serious error. Anyone who believes in the Real Presence of course accepts the fact that Jesus is substantially but invisibly present in the Eucharist; but the very acceptance of that profoundly mysterious fact might cause one to overlook the other ways in which he is present. Specifically, then, he is also present in the sacramental action, which is carried out as his act. And because that action is visible, he is visibly present.

That in turn points to the role of the Church, acting through the minister. In a sacrament, Jesus' performances are done by the minister, who functions, as it were, as Jesus' proxy. Does this mean Jesus is not really present after all? Certainly not. This is clear if one understands what it means to be a proxy.

A proxy does what is really someone else's act. In a wedding by proxy, for instance, the proxy does not merely stand in for the absent party but performs an action (saying "I do") which is not the proxy's but that other person's. In a sacrament, that is the role of the minister, acting for Jesus.

This role in the sacraments, analogous to that of a proxy in other contexts, belongs first of all to the Church and, through the Church, to her minister. Baptism, confirmation, and holy orders in their different ways make those who receive them participants in Jesus' unique and unending priesthood; orders also makes a priest able to act on Jesus' behalf in the sacraments of the Eucharist, penance, confirmation, and anointing of the sick.

Take the sacrament of penance. The priest does not say, "Jesus absolves you," but, "I absolve you." Acting simply on his own behalf, he can do no such thing. But here he is not acting in his own person but in the person of Jesus. The act of absolving is the Lord's act, performed by the priest. While, in the Catholic view of the sacraments, there is more to the priest's role than this proxy function, the capacity to function *in persona Christi* (as a sort of proxy for Jesus) does make the ordained priesthood different from the priesthood of the faithful in general. Interrelated though they are, the two nevertheless "differ from one another in essence and not only in degree" (*LG* 10).

Thus, the priest does something in the Eucharistic liturgy which only a priest can do: he carries out Jesus' act for him. At the same time, as a member of the Church, the priest is also a recipient of the sacrament along with the rest of the faithful. But his distinctive role is not to be confused with the congregation's, nor is he simply the people's representative. Indeed, the people do not need a representative in order to cooperate with the Lord in his self-offering and in offering themselves. Those things, the most important they do in the Mass, are done by them on their own behalf. And even though the priest does at times act as their representative (for he prays using the plural "we"), this is secondary by comparison with his role as Jesus' proxy.

Finally, then, there is the recipient's role in the sacraments. It is to do something which counts as freely accepting and nurturing divine life in himself or herself. The recipient cooperates in Jesus' redemptive act and offers God suitable worship in doing so. What Jesus does is an act of worship, and one who receives any of the sacraments and so cooperates with Jesus likewise performs an act of worship.

The recipient's actions in the sacraments are also starting points for organizing the rest of his or her Christian life. How this is so will be the subject of the rest of this chapter and the three which follow. But in general terms, insofar as the rest of the recipient's life is grounded in and integrated with what he or she does in receiving the sacraments, it is integrated with faith and love, and so becomes "a living sacrifice" and "spiritual worship" (Rom 12:1). The sacramental acts should be central principles of Christian life to which all other actions in one's life are related as extensions, as it were, of the sacraments themselves.

C: Baptism as the Basic Sacramental Principle of Christian Moral Life

The Church teaches clearly and definitively that to receive baptism, in deed or in desire, is essential for salvation. As Vatican II says: "All must be incorporated into him by baptism, and into the Church which is his body" (*AG* 7). Everything relevant to baptism as a moral principle follows from the fundamental fact that it is personal, human union with Jesus as man. In the case of sincere non-Christians, this incorporation *can* occur without their actually receiving the sacrament, by their will to do what is right, which is what God wills. This constitutes at least an implicit desire for baptism. But the relevant fact here is that incorporation is necessary, and baptism brings it about.

Jesus offers us a new covenant with God; we accept the offer; and baptism seals our relationship with him as a human bond of mutual commitment. In other words, in baptism Jesus brings us into the relationship which is the new covenant. The person being baptized (this is most clear, of course, in the case of an adult) accepts the covenant relationship and makes a commitment to it. That is the act of faith.

The commitments here, of the Lord Jesus and of the recipient of baptism, resemble those of partners in a marriage. One proposes marriage, the other accepts, and their mutual commitment initiates the bond, which is a kind of covenant—that is, the principle of unity which constitutes an open-ended and permanent intimate community. Jesus similarly proposed a covenant relationship in preaching the gospel. He told people to believe in him, spoke of himself as the way to God, and so on. One who hears and accepts Jesus' gospel approaches the Church and asks for baptism. The commitment of faith made in receiving the sacrament marks the person's entry into the new covenant relationship. It is very much as if he or she were married to God through Jesus.

Jesus shares what is his with those united with him. Since he is sinless and enjoys the life of the Spirit as his own, the Christian, in being united with him, is rescued from sin and receives the Spirit. Thus, by baptism he or she becomes a member of God's family and shares in the light and power of the Spirit, which are required to live as a child of God.

Life in the new covenant is life in a community, the Church, whose principle of unity is Jesus. United with Jesus, each baptized person is also united with all the others. We are brothers and sisters "in" Christ. And since the whole of creation is to be restored to God in Christ, those who are united with Jesus receive their places in this restoration or reintegration (described in chapters nineteen and thirty-four) as a result of their relationship with him.

Union with Jesus in baptism also empowers one to participate in the Eucharist (although, of course, one may exercise this power rightly and fruitfully only if one abides in love and holds fast to the faith of the Church). To the baptismal covenant relationship, the Eucharist adds the fulfillment of bodily union (for, as also was explained in chapter nineteen, we are united with Christ not only in human acts and in divine life, but also in bodily union). But Jesus' bodily life now is resurrection life. Through the Eucharist, therefore, one now shares, though not visibly, in Jesus' resurrection life.

In baptism the whole of Christian life is present embryonically, as it were; everything is there in essence. The other sacraments add nothing extrinsic to baptism but only draw out what is intrinsically already there: the fullness of the gift of the Spirit (confirmation), the fullness of union with Jesus (the Eucharist), the fullness of overcoming sin and sin's effects (penance and anointing), the fullness of sharing in Jesus' priesthood (orders), the fullness of the interpersonal communion of members of the Church (matrimony). The other sacraments are in a sense present in baptism and need only to be performed and unfolded.

The rest of Christian life is likewise there, waiting to be developed and lived. Finding, accepting, and living one's personal vocation are implicit in the baptismal commitment of faith, for this is what one is committing oneself to do—live the whole of Christian life by making and carrying out appropriate choices. That is why baptism is a principle for the other sacraments and all of Christian life.

Many problems arise if one fails to grasp this. For example: If confirmation adds something extrinsic to baptism, what is it? What does ordination add to the priesthood of all the faithful into which one enters by being baptized? The answer is that confirmation, orders, and the rest add nothing from the outside; rather, they unfold certain potentialities of being a Christian which are already present in baptism but remain undeveloped in those who are baptized but do not receive these other sacraments. Consider again the analogy of the embryo. Each human embryo has the initial principle of a capacity for marital intercourse, yet that capacity takes a long time to develop, and develops into the different forms of the two sexes. Similarly, baptism creates in the Christian radical potentialities for the other sacramental offices, but these are only realized by those who, in response to their vocations and under the authority of the Church, receive the other sacraments.

Because it unites us with Jesus and involves the fundamental option of faith, baptism has moral implications. One who makes the option of faith accepts Jesus as his or her Lord and leader; such a person's whole life should then be lived in cooperation with him.

To become a Christian but live independently of Jesus would be like marrying someone and then immediately abandoning one's "partner" to live by oneself. Entering into a relationship is pointless unless one means to live with the other person and share in what he or she is trying to do. For one who enters into a relationship with Jesus in baptism, that means living the Christian life.

Even the baptism of John the Baptist, which did not of itself justify, required that those receiving it try to live better lives (see Mt 3:8; Lk 3:8–14). But baptism in the Lord Jesus really transforms its recipients, so that they are called to live the life of Christ. This, moreover, baptism empowers them to do by the gift of the Holy Spirit. To live lives shaped by Christian love is thus not a requirement imposed on Christians but their spontaneous response to what they have received.

Like a good father, who does not invite his small daughter to "drive the car" without providing a way for her really to cooperate in the driving, God gives us a life of good deeds to live along with the means of living it. Through faith, in union with Jesus and by the power of the Holy Spirit, our actions bear real fruit. This is how God deals with us in the sacraments—both inviting our cooperation and making it possible.

31. Confirmation, the Apostolate, and Personal Vocation

Baptism initiates Christian life but does not organize it. That is the work of the other sacraments. In this and the next three chapters we treat confirmation, penance, anointing of the sick, and the Eucharist. (As sacraments to which only some are called, holy orders and matrimony do not organize every Christian's life but only the lives of those who receive them, and so we do not consider them in this volume.)

As we saw in the preceding chapter, the other sacraments add nothing extrinsic to baptism; rather, they unfold and develop to maturity what is already, as it were, embryonically present there. In this chapter we consider how confirmation does this. In brief, as a sacramental principle, confirmation organizes Christian life for apostolate in the way dictated by each one's unique personal vocation. Within that framework, we discuss three topics: confirmation and apostolate; personal vocation as a moral principle; and certain elements of spirituality especially relevant to the apostolate.

A: Confirmation and the Apostolate

The Council of Trent teaches definitively that confirmation is a sacrament distinct from baptism (see DS 1628/871). That does not mean it is extrinsic to baptism, adding something to it from the outside, but that it is a real, specific development of the Christian life initiated in baptism.

In what way? The Council of Florence teaches: "The effect of this sacrament is that the Holy Spirit is given in it for strength just as he was given to the apostles on Pentecost, in order that the Christian may courageously confess the name of Christ" (DS 1319/697). Confirmation is our sharing in the descent of the Holy Spirit at Pentecost, a descent which has never ended. Two contrasting images of the apostles suggest the strength and zeal for witnessing which confirmation is meant to confer: at first they huddle in the upper room in anxious prayer, but then, having received the Spirit, they confront those who killed Jesus, bear witness to him, and call on them to repent.

Vatican II develops these ideas in a passage tracing the transition from baptism to confirmation.

> Reborn as sons of God, [the baptized] must confess before men the faith which they have received from God through the Church. [Note omitted.] Bound more intimately to the Church by the sacrament of confirmation, they are endowed by the Holy Spirit with special strength. Hence they are the more strictly obliged to spread and defend the faith both by word and by deed as true witnesses of Christ. (*LG* 11)

Our lives as apostolic—that is, as sharing in the revelatory work of Jesus—are composed of words and deeds. One must live a Christian life and also give an account of it in terms of faith.

In a note to the passage just quoted, Vatican II cites St. Thomas Aquinas on confirmation's sacramental character, thereby lending its authority to his teaching on this point.[21] Thomas identifies this character as a spiritual power of professing the faith publicly. With regard to God's spiritual gifts, he suggests later, baptism belongs on the "passive" side (in baptism we receive God's gifts for our benefit) and confirmation on the "active" side (it empowers us to exercise God's gifts for the benefit of others).[22]

In confirmation one who has become God's child in baptism is empowered, authorized, and made responsible for sharing in the revelatory work of the divine family. This revelatory work continues Jesus' mission of revealing the truth and life of the Father through human words and deeds to all men and women, in all times and places.

Before Vatican II it was common to take a narrow view of apostolate. It was thought to involve only specifically religious activities, and so to pertain both properly and mainly to priests—indeed, in its fullness, only to bishops as successors of the apostles. Lay people shared in the apostolate only by way of delegation and only to the extent that they could, with hierarchical approval, help clerics do clerical things. The "lay apostolate" was something done with a bishop's mandate to assist priests in work which was properly theirs. Despite the intelligence and good will of those who developed the lay movements of those days, these movements can be seen in retrospect to embody an impoverished concept of apostolate and especially of the laity's role.

Vatican II took a new and more expansive view:

> For this the Church was founded: that by spreading the kingdom of Christ everywhere for the glory of God the Father, she might bring all men to share in Christ's saving redemption; and that through them the whole world might in actual fact be brought into relationship with him. All activity of the Mystical Body directed to the attainment of this goal is called the apostolate, and the Church carries it on in various ways through all her members. For by its very nature the Christian vocation is also a vocation to the apostolate. No part of the structure of a living body is merely passive but each has a share in the functions as well as in the life of the body. So, too, in the body of Christ, which is the Church, the whole body, "according to the functioning in due measure of each single part, derives its increase" (Eph 4:16). (*AA* 2)

A wide variety of activities, not just those of a specifically religious or properly clerical nature, have a role in apostolate. For lay people this includes in particular "the renewal of the temporal order [which is] their own special obligation" (*AA* 7). All sorts of ordinary, honorable activities and occupations in which lay people engage are relevant. "The very testimony of their Christian life, and good works done in a supernatural spirit, have the power to draw men to belief and to God" (*AA* 6).

This assumes that, whatever the personal vocations of particular Christians happen to be, they will, if they do what is morally good, be living out faith, giving witness, engaging in apostolate. That is especially so if, whenever possible and appropriate, they also offer others an account of why they live as Christians. For although much of the time they will act just like everybody else—doing the same jobs, engaging in the same recreations, and so on—sometimes, if they are truly living as Christians, they will behave in ways significantly *un*like what is taken for granted by others, refusing to do some things and insisting on doing yet others which raise questions in the minds of those around them.

Then, if Christians explain their behavior by their commitment to Jesus and to the Christian life, they give witness in a way which unquestionably has an impact. Few people are deeply committed to a cause which transcends them and are willing and able to account forthrightly for what they do on the basis of such a commitment and its requirements. Thus, the gospel is effectively preached to the world by a Christian who really follows Jesus and who does not shirk the responsibility to tell the truth about why he or she refuses to do evil and insists on doing good.

Many people, nevertheless, are better pleased if Christians do shirk this responsibility. For when Christians give a true account of their behavior, they implicitly tell others that they should be living the same way, and that is something many do not care to hear. Jesus' fate at the hands of his enemies shows what can happen then.

Since confirmation gives the power to confess Jesus' name courageously, and since doing so is apostolate, confirmation is the sacrament of the apostolate. Vatican II does not say this in so many words, but what it does say makes it clear that this is a correct way of describing confirmation. For example: "Through their baptism and confirmation, all are commissioned to that apostolate [participation in the saving mission of the Church] by the Lord himself" (*LG* 33). And again: "The laity derive the right and duty with respect to the apostolate from their union with Christ their Head. Incorporated into Christ's Mystical Body through baptism and strengthened by the power of the Holy Spirit through confirmation, they are assigned to the apostolate by the Lord himself" (*AA* 3).

Essentially it makes little difference when one receives the sacrament. (It may make a difference on psychological or pastoral grounds, but these do not touch the heart of the sacrament and what it empowers one to do.) Thus, infants are to be confirmed if they are in danger of death, even though they cannot consciously do anything of an overtly "apostolic" nature either then or for a long time afterwards, and people can participate in apostolic work even before being confirmed, on the strength of the rite they will only receive later.

This is a reminder that the reality of a sacrament extends beyond the performance of the rite itself. The sacrament of penance, for example, begins as soon as one recognizes the need to repent and confess a sin committed after baptism, and it extends as one does the penance which is assigned; the Eucharist is to be extended throughout our entire lives; a catechumen who dies before receiving baptism has, in the view of the Church, already been baptized. And participation in the apostolate can begin before, and ought to extend throughout one's whole life after, one receives the rite of confirmation.

B: Personal Vocation as a Moral Principle

Confirmation involves a commitment by recipients to do the apostolic work which the sacrament empowers them to do, namely, bear witness to Jesus in their entire life of faith. For each Christian personal vocation specifies what this life of faith consists in. Thus, personal vocation is the medium by which confirmation organizes the recipient's life. If someone fails to discern and accept his or her personal vocation, confirmation—the sacrament which strengthens people for the apostolate—has little or nothing to strengthen; the "life of faith" of such an individual remains at best unfocused, random, disorganized.

Of course, not everyone who recognizes and accepts a personal vocation understands and expresses what he or she is doing just that way. That is not necessary. What *is* necessary is that Christians see their lives as the living out of their faith--that they be willing to recognize what God wants of them and try to do it. Far more people do that than speak of themselves as "discerning" a "personal vocation."

No part or element of any Christian's life ought to lie outside the life of faith. As St. Paul says, "Whether you eat or drink, or whatever you do, do everything for the glory of God" (1 Cor 10:31). There are no free areas existing alongside but apart from apostolic responsibility; one is not permitted to live apostolically in certain contexts while living the rest of one's life without reference to Christ. Rather: "Whatever you do, in word or deed, do everything in the name of the Lord Jesus" (Col 3:17).

This does not mean Christians are to be religious fanatics. All human goods, provided they are pursued in an upright manner, can have a place in Christian life. Moreover, each Christian's personal vocation calls for not just one commitment but an integrated set of commitments; thus, the elements of a typical vocation will be expressed in a variety of roles—spouse, parent, worker, friend, neighbor, and so on. The point is that the commitments to these various roles should be consistent and integrated, and, taken together, should cover the whole of a person's life.

What is *not* allowed is such an attitude as this: "Here is my religious life and here is my family life—and these I recognize as the components of my vocation and of my life as a Christian. But over *here* is a whole other area—for example, my work or career—which has nothing to do with my life of faith, and in which I can do as I please." That attitude is an obstacle to growth in holiness which expresses a morally immature personality.

Precisely because every Christian vocation involves suffering and demands fidelity, there is need for the special grace of confirmation, which strengthens one for courageous witnessing. It is not easy to give public witness to faith—derision and criticism often greet those who do. Living consistently as a Christian is likely to lead to difficulties—one will encounter opposition and persecution, without being able to mount an effective defense or respond in kind. Yet one must persevere, even though persevering itself leads to frustration and makes one still more vulnerable. Jesus was faithful, and so must we be.

How does one discern a personal vocation? What is sought is not a moral norm but a fact, the answer to this question: Where do I fit into God's plan?

To begin with, one must open one's eyes to the signs of opportunity and need in the world, while at the same time realistically taking stock of one's abilities and dispositions. Then, one makes a match—between needs and opportunities on the one hand and abilities and dispositions on the other. Discernment is the recognition of this "match."

Often, though, it is more difficult than this suggests. In times past, most people who judged that they were not called to the priesthood or religious life had few options; in many cases their life's work was cut out for them, and even their marriage partners were determined by their parents. But young people in our culture typically confront many alternative possible roles and find it hard to know which embody their vocations. What then?

Then an individual must examine the data in the light of faith, in a spirit of obedience and with the meekness which is readiness to accept whatever God wants; and, having done that, allow his or her feelings (conditioned, as we saw earlier, by faith, by prayer, and by sincere efforts to live the life of faith) to work on the question. Eventually, with respect to each major commitment, certain alternatives will become less interesting and appealing, while one emerges as the "right" choice. Then it is time to accept that possibility as an element in one's vocation, commit oneself to it, and persevere in it faithfully.

This is not a process to engage in only once. It must be repeated whenever one has to make a major commitment, and that can happen at various stages in life, as new needs and opportunities arise and the circumstances of one's life change. Then one must engage again in vocational discernment and make another commitment. Not infrequently, it is a matter of further specifying an earlier commitment, as, for example, when a medical student chooses a field in which to specialize or a priest decides to volunteer for work in the foreign missions. But sometimes entirely new major commitments are needed, for instance, when a man loses his job and must set out on a new career or when a married woman is widowed and must decide whether to entertain the possibility of another marriage.

The question of personal vocation has particular urgency today. There is much talk at present of a "vocations crisis," in the sense that not enough people are entering the priesthood and religious life to replace those leaving by death, retirement, and resignation. But the crisis actually extends far beyond this dearth of new priestly and religious vocations.

Many Catholics entering marriage think of married life and parenthood not as a way of living their faith but in very different terms—perhaps mainly as an avenue to emotional gratification or something of the sort. Indeed, many seem to approach their whole lives simply with the aim of being successful and enjoying themselves. "God is very merciful," they think, "and so I'll surely go to heaven." The idea of sharing in Jesus' apostolic work does not occur to them. *That* is the larger, deeper crisis of vocations.

Undoubtedly, its roots lie partly in the religious education and formation which many children receive—or, more accurately perhaps, fail to receive. Christian life is not presented to them as a life of responsibility and duty in which the cross occupies a central place. That is not a pleasant thought, and so it goes unmentioned.

As they approach adolescence, children should be aware that they will soon face the important responsibility of discerning and accepting their individual places in God's plan. Because the subject has largely been omitted from their religious formation, however, this occurs to relatively few. Instead, in the teenage years most begin to think about making a living, getting married, pursuing various goals and objectives, and doing so in pleasant, satisfying ways. Struggling at the same time with sexual temptation and the emotional confusion of adolescence, they give little or no attention to the question of vocation. Perhaps some will—later. Many will not.

As a result, many Catholics marry without thinking of marriage as a Christian vocation. That, as suggested, could be an even more serious problem than the "vocations crisis" reflected in the shortage of priestly and religious vocations. For if Catholic parents are themselves only halfheartedly (at best) committed to the Christian life, they are not likely to instill a stronger commitment in their children; rather, they are likely to neglect the children's religious formation in whole or in part, including formation which would lead the children to ask themselves what *their* personal vocations are. Thus the cycle—declining religious commitment in general and few new vocations to the priesthood and religious life or anything else—is in danger not only of continuing into another generation but growing even worse.

To break this cycle it is imperative to begin speaking to children in the catechesis after First Communion about personal vocation and the apostolic life, and to go on speaking to them about these matters as they grow older. No one vocation should be pressed on them, although it should be made clear both why Jesus warmly recommends virginity or celibacy for the kingdom's sake and why marriage is unquestionably a vocation and a setting for apostolate along with the others. If children are given the impression that the question of vocation comes down simply to asking "Shall I be a priest? Shall I be a nun?" and if they decide that the answer for them is "No," they are then likely to conclude that they do not have vocations. That is a disastrous mistake.

Moreover, if children do not come to see that other aspects of life, especially their work, should be considered elements of vocation, they are likely to isolate their faith from a large part of their lives. But if they grasp the idea that everyone has a complex personal vocation which must be discerned and accepted, and that each Christian is called to the apostolate in diverse ways, they can eventually make their "vocational" choices (whatever they may be) as true Christian commitments. One result, by no means incidental, is likely to be that many more young people than now will opt for the priesthood and religious life. This emphasis should be a major, integrated element in Catholic schools and religious education as well as in Sunday homilies and, of course, in family discussions.

C: Certain Elements of Spirituality Relevant to the Apostolate

As we saw earlier, prayer shapes Christian life. Certain specific requirements of personal prayer are especially relevant to discerning, accepting, and fulfilling a personal vocation.

One not only must believe the truth of faith that God is provident, but be always aware of his providence at work in one's life. It is necessary to live in God's presence, seeing whatever one has and whatever befalls one as given by him. It is necessary to understand Christian life as cooperation with Jesus and to live it that way. Without this way of looking at life, people will never find their personal vocations. In such a life, of course, there are negative things—things one would rather not encounter and have to deal with—yet a prayerful person will realize that nothing occurs which God does not permit. In prayer one should cultivate the attitude that everything that happens, without exception, embodies some good offered by God.

It is necessary to see Jesus in others—*all* others—and to avoid taking an individualistic, selfish view of life. It is necessary to know moral truth and to have a right understanding of the relationship between this life and everlasting life. These also are attitudes, ways of thinking about things and evaluating them, which one develops in prayer.

It is also necessary to keep clearly in mind the difference between apostolic good results which one hopes to achieve and fidelity. Naturally, in undertaking to do something worthwhile, one should pursue it to the best of one's ability for as long as one can. But ultimately it does not matter whether one succeeds or fails. That is up to God. Our essential task is to be faithful, with grace, regardless of the consequences. Fidelity requires both refusing to do evil for the sake of good results and avoiding the supposedly "prudent" rationalizations which deter people from doing their duty because they anticipate painful consequences. What one does with God's grace and the right intention has lasting good consequences, no matter what the outcome in this life.

An important aspect of the spirituality of an apostolic person is devotion to Mary and the other saints. Solidarity with them builds up lasting communion, and the point of Christian life in this world is precisely to build up the persons and the interpersonal relationships which will last forever. Solidarity with the saints contributes to the fellowship of human and divine persons and so is intrinsically important. Moreover, the saints give us examples of how to live the apostolic life, besides helping us in our common efforts.

Devotion to the saints helps a person maintain the right relationship between this life and everlasting life. People conscious that they truly collaborate with the saints by trying to do in their lives and times the same sorts of things the saints did, keep the lasting significance of their efforts in view.

So, for example, a priest who understands that he is a real collaborator with all the saintly pastors of other times and who takes certain of them as his special models, knows that his ministry is part of something greater than the limited service he can render here and now in this particular parish or apostolic undertaking. He has a true sense of the relationship between what he is doing and the whole apostolate—past, present, and future—considered as a participation in Jesus' saving mission, as well as the relationship of the apostolate to the everlasting kingdom being built up throughout the course of history.

Without such an attitude, one is likely to think: "I'll do what I can, but I have no real obligation either to the past or to the future. And when it comes to the truly intractable problems of the present, there's no point butting my head against brick walls. If God wants them solved, he can solve them himself or find somebody capable of doing it." By contrast, an apostolic person, aware that he or she is a collaborator with the apostles of the past and those yet to come, will recognize his or her responsibilities to the tradition and work hard to lay a solid foundation for the future.

It is true, nevertheless, that what we cannot do ourselves we can do through others. This is Jesus' approach to the apostolate. Instead of trying to do everything himself, he enlists others to cooperate with him. So, the truly apostolic person tries to get other people to accept their Christian responsibilities, too—not least, so that their Christian lives will develop and they will grow in holiness. Part of the lesson of the present shortage of priests and religious may be the need to enlist people in the apostolate who otherwise would not think of becoming involved.

32. Penance, Anointing, and the Life of Self-denial

Vatican II speaks of Christian life, as well as the history of the Church, as a pilgrimage; the "pilgrim" metaphor is among its favorites. Pilgrimages, however, typically involve hardships, and in the pilgrimage of Christian life these are self-inflicted hardships—sins. Of necessity, therefore, Christian life also is a process of continuous conversion or purification, a struggle, as the sixth mode of Christian response (requiring purity of heart) indicates, to make up for past sins, overcome present sin and imperfection, and by self-denial prepare for suffering and death, so that in these experiences one will offer oneself in Christ to God.

From this perspective, the sacraments of penance and anointing of the sick organize all of Christian life. This chapter covers four points: the sacrament of penance considered in itself; how it organizes the whole of Christian life; the three main forms of penance; and the sacrament of the anointing of the sick.

We need to bear in mind the Council of Trent's teaching that Catholics should "keep [God's] severity and judgment in view as well as mercy and goodness" (DS 1549/810). Presently, much preaching and religious writing stress divine mercy while passing lightly over "severity and judgment." But these, too, are realities, and important ones. God is a loving Father, not a careless and permissive one; he requires us to behave uprightly and permits us to suffer the consequences when we do not.

A: The Sacrament of Penance Considered in Itself

The sacrament of penance is necessary for the remission of grave sins committed after baptism. Apart from the sacrament, not even sorrow for sin arising from love of God suffices. True, one *may* receive grace before the sacramental rite is performed. But as Trent teaches: "Although it does sometimes happen that . . . contrition is made perfect through charity and reconciles man to God before the sacrament is actually received, nevertheless the reconciliation must not be attributed to contrition exclusive of the desire for the sacrament included in the contrition" (DS 1677/ 898). There must be some sort of desire, at least implicit, for the sacrament of penance. (Protestants in good faith and, indeed, people of good will in general implicitly desire this sacrament and all the others insofar as, helped by God's grace, they sincerely try to discern what is right and to do it.)

Similarities exist between baptism and penance in that both involve a conversion: the overcoming of sin, the conferring of divine life. Penance also involves a renewal of the baptismal commitment to turn away from sin and follow Jesus. Unlike baptism, however, penance requires that one specifically confess one's sins and make up for them.

In the case of baptism it is sufficient for forgiveness of sins that the recipient sincerely say, "I reject my former life and take up this new one." After all, he or she is entering into the covenant for the first time and beginning a new life in the Lord Jesus. But penance deals with a different situation: Someone already in the covenant has been unfaithful; an existing relationship has been damaged. The sinner must face the facts, acknowledge them to the other parties concerned, that is, to Jesus and the Church, and try to make up for the wrongdoing.

Like baptism, penance also is joyous in its own way, but it can be difficult. That is usually so when someone who has deliberately damaged a relationship repents and seeks to restore it.

Suppose a single man is a playboy; he has had many casual "relationships" but never experienced a real, loving human relationship. Then he meets a good woman, falls in love, and with her help comes to see how exploitative his behavior has been. He proposes and she accepts. But he feels obliged to tell her: "You know, I haven't led a very good life up to now." "That's over and done with," she says. "You've changed." And so he has. His former life can be written off. He need not make up to the woman he loves for being unfaithful to her, since all that belonged to a time before he knew her. This suggests something of the situation as far as baptism is concerned.

But suppose that after five years of happy, faithful married life, this man has an affair. Now he *has* been unfaithful to his wife. He has done real injury, to her and to their relationship, by disappointing her rightful expectations based on their marital commitment. Although he repents and wants to be faithful again, correcting the situation is not so easy now. He has no right to his wife's forgiveness, and even if she does forgive him, he still needs to make up for what he has done by making compensation for his infidelity. Penance is something like that.

Because it involves the confessing and the judging of sins, penance has a judicial character: it is as if the sinner were on trial for a crime. But why not simply confess one's sins in one's heart directly to God? Why is confession to a priest necessary? Basically, the reason lies in the incarnational principle at work in this and the other sacraments—the principle which empowers the priest to act in the person of Christ in absolving while enabling penitents to cooperate in a human way in their own reconciliation with Jesus and the Church. In confessing one's sins to the priest, one confesses to Jesus, who is God, and so one confesses directly to God; but one does this in a human, bodily way, rather than in a purely interior, spiritual way.

As the incarnational principle also suggests, confession of sins is necessary from another perspective. In sinning, a Christian is unfaithful not only to God but to Jesus as man and to the Church. Even mortal sins which someone might consider merely "private" faults—those which may offend God but harm no one else—do injury to the Church at large. For, as we saw in chapter sixteen, every mortal sin is radically incompatible with life within the community of faith which is the Church. As Vatican II says: "Those who approach the sacrament of penance obtain pardon from the mercy of God for offenses committed against him. They are at the same time reconciled with the Church, which they have wounded by their sins, and which by charity, example, and prayer seeks their conversion" (*LG* 11).

The sacrament of penance requires contrition, which ranks, in the words of Trent, "first among [the] acts of the penitent." It consists in "sorrow and detestation for sin committed, with a resolution of sinning no more" (DS 1676/897). Merely being sorry for the past is not enough; one must give up sin now and determine to avoid it in the future.

Genuine contrition also involves a sincere intention to fulfill the other requirements for valid reception of the sacrament, including confessing mortal sins according to their kind and number. This is more or less unpleasant, yet someone unwilling to meet this condition is not really contrite. People who feel badly about their wrongdoing but are not willing to meet the reasonable conditions for setting things right are not really sorry. To return to our earlier example: A wife whose husband has been unfaithful sets a reasonable condition in insisting that he sever the relationship which led to the extramarital affair. If he refuses ("She's really a very nice person, and I'd still like to have her for a friend"), he is not really sorry. In the case of the reconciliation effected through the sacrament of penance, Jesus sets the reasonable condition (reasonable in light of the incarnational principle cited earlier) of confession; either one meets it or one is not really sorry, and if one is not really sorry, there can be no reconciliation.

The specific confession of mortal sins according to kind and number also has other, secondary good results. One concerns the evasiveness and duplicity of human beings in their fallen condition. Unless one must say, "This is what I did, and this is how often I did it," there is a good chance that one will avoid facing the facts and determining to change one's life. Confession of sins makes it more difficult to be evasive. This is a psychological advantage of confession which those who abuse general absolution on "pastoral" grounds seem to overlook.

Trent teaches that, with God's help, people can have humanly good motives for repentance—awareness of the evil of sin and fear of punishment—before being restored to charity. This is what is called "imperfect contrition" or sometimes "attrition" (see DS 1678/898, 1705/915). Very likely it is the kind of sorrow people often bring to the sacrament of penance, where it is adequate for receiving God's forgiveness and, with it, his gift of charity. But what of "perfect contrition," the sorrow for sin out of love for God which secures God's forgiveness even before someone receives the sacrament? Here it is important to realize that the "love" required is charity, the gift which the Spirit pours forth in our hearts, and that charity is not psychologically recognizable. So, one cannot be certain one's contrition is "perfect."

That has practical significance. People aware of having committed a mortal sin should not put off confessing, on the ground that, having made an "act of perfect contrition," they are free to receive the Eucharist and need be in no rush. For they do not, and cannot, *know* they have made an act of contrition motivated by charity.

Of course, someone truly unable to receive the rite of penance here and now should pray to the Holy Spirit for help and try to make an act of perfect contrition (indeed, *anyone* who commits a mortal sin ought to do that), hoping he or she succeeds. But those who can confess should do so as soon as possible, instead of relying on the undemonstrable presumption that their contrition is "perfect." They have no good reason to take the chance of being wrong.

In a general sense, "doing penance" refers to making up for sin. Even after sin is forgiven, it is necessary to repair its consequences. We are not speaking here of repairing tangible, concrete damage (monetary loss, destruction of property, and so on), which one should certainly try to make good to the extent possible, but of existential damage—division within one's self, disruption of one's relationships with other people, alienation from God. Our own inner harmony and integrity need to be reconstituted; our relationships with other people, with the Church, and with God need to be rebuilt.

This is the function of the "penance" assigned to the repentant sinner. But plainly this penance—certain prayers, particular good deeds, whatever it may be—is only a token of the reparation and restoration needed. Beyond this token, a repentant sinner's whole life, especially sufferings accepted and undergone in union with Jesus, can and should serve as the fuller "penance" required to correct the existential damage done by sin.

Take the man who commits adultery. His wife says, "I forgive you," and she really does. Even so, he has a long way to go to set matters right. He must reconstitute himself as a faithful husband. He must strive to undo the harm to his relationship with his wife. He must try to restore his relationships with others who know of his infidelity and are scandalized by it. And, supposing he is a believer who thinks in such terms, he must work to rebuild his friendship with Jesus. So with the consequences of every sin forgiven through the sacrament of penance: One still has the task of "doing penance" in order to restore the integrity and harmony which sin disrupts at every level. Sin is not just a mistake, to be corrected by sincerely saying "I'm sorry"; it is a reality whose consequences persist and need to be set right even after the sin itself is forgiven.

B: How the Sacrament of Penance Organizes Christian Life

While the sacrament of penance is obviously essential to the Christian lives of persons who actually commit mortal sin, that does not make it an organizing principle in the lives of all. However, everyone can be tempted to commit mortal sin, and in various ways the sacrament of penance helps to prevent surrender to such temptations. Not least of these ways is by helping one deal with venial sin, which otherwise could lead to mortal sin. Venial sin is universal and pervasive; to one degree or another, it permeates everyone's life, including even the lives of truly saintly people. Moreover, venial sin really is evil in itself, and Christians are bound to try to overcome it. While this can be done apart from penance, the sacrament is an appropriate instrument in the struggle. This is one reason why it is an organizing principle for the whole of Christian life.

The Council of Trent, Popes Pius XII, John XXIII, and John Paul II, and the Introduction to the New Rite of Penance all commend the use of this sacrament as a way to Christian perfection, which includes overcoming all sin. Here, for example, is Pius XII on the subject:

> But to ensure more rapid progress day by day in the path of virtue, We will that the pious practice of frequent confession, which was introduced into the Church by the inspiration of the Holy Spirit, should be earnestly advocated. By it genuine self-knowledge is increased, Christian humility grows, bad habits are corrected, spiritual neglect and tepidity are resisted, the conscience is purified, the will strengthened, a salutary self-control is attained, and grace is increased in virtue of the Sacrament itself.[23]

As the Introduction to the New Rite remarks, frequent confession of devotion—that is, reception of the sacrament when one only has venial sins to confess—"is not a mere ritual repetition or psychological exercise, but a serious striving to perfect the grace of baptism."[24]

Yet venial sins *can* be dealt with in other ways. Why, then, this emphasis on dealing with them in and through the sacrament of penance? Because, as the passage from Pius XII makes clear, frequenting the sacrament as part of one's struggle to overcome venial sin realistically acknowledges the facts of the human condition and of God's plan for salvation.

To begin with, although the recipient acts in the sacrament of penance (like all the sacraments, it is a cooperative divine-human action), he or she does no more than admit his or her situation and need. That makes it plain that the grace which comes through the sacrament is entirely God's gift. Without grace we can achieve nothing, and not only forgiveness but repentance is God's gift. That is a salutary reminder for someone trying to cultivate humility and gratitude.

Still, we really do cooperate in the sacrament, and our cooperation is conscious and explicit. In line with the incarnational principle which underlies the sacraments, our action is part of the divine-human cooperation which leads to reconciliation. Moreover, the human action in the sacrament is ecclesial in part, that is, action by the Church through its minister, the priest, and this also is something God has in view. It is a good thing to have one's venial sins forgiven on one's own, so to speak, but a better thing to have them forgiven with the help of a friend, for then the friend has the merit of having helped. One of the advantages of the legitimate communal rite of reconciliation lies in dramatizing, as it were, the fact that we bear one another's burdens and help one another overcome our sins.

Because venial sin is pervasive, the struggle to overcome it involves repeatedly reaffirming and strengthening one's commitments of faith and personal vocation. In this way, too, the sacrament organizes one's life. Moreover, the pervasive character of venial sin requires that, over a period of time, someone struggling against it take up every aspect of his or her life and try to root out all the sinful elements. Thus one's whole life comes under scrutiny in the process of ongoing conversion.

The sacrament of penance also organizes Christian life by providing a good reason for not committing mortal sin. That is particularly clear in the case of legalistic individuals who say, "I don't want to commit that mortal sin because I don't want to have to confess it." Certainly there are better, holier motives for avoiding sin, but one should not make the mistake of highmindedly dismissing an acceptable motive which helps some people avoid some sins. Christian life is a journey toward moral maturity and holiness, and on that trip most Christians need all the help they can get.

Avoiding sin also involves avoiding occasions of sin. (We are speaking here primarily of mortal sin, but for the most part what we say also applies to venial sin.) In this respect, too, penance organizes life by giving us a reason to avoid temptation. The lives of people consistently trying to avoid temptation are very different from the lives of those not making the effort.

Avoiding occasions of sin means avoiding situations and actions which lead to or intensify temptation, or else modifying them so that the temptation either does not arise or is less intense. This requires planning, so that good options will be available and bad options less interesting. It requires exercising control over one's life, in order to regulate the situations in which one finds oneself. While no one can anticipate every eventuality, foresight and planning can provide for many.

Sometimes occasions of sin can be avoided entirely. For example, someone with a drinking problem may be able to decline some invitations to social events where alcohol is served. Other times, it is possible to modify situations so that temptation is reduced. If a person with a drinking problem has a good reason for not refusing a particular invitation, he or she can at least explain the situation to the host or hostess beforehand, so as to make sure that there will be no pressure to indulge. Situations can also be modified by placing them in a different context through prayer and reflection. For instance, by considering matters in a wider perspective, people who find certain other individuals excessively annoying can come to see them as brothers and sisters in Christ and in this way master the tendency to get angry at them.

In sum, the effort to avoid occasions of sin means reshaping one's life. Many things not wrong in themselves must be evaluated by the effects they are likely to have on oneself. For example, even though there is nothing wrong in itself with watching television, a Christian should ask, "If I watch this program, what options will it hold out as appealing? Are these among the options I ought to consider? Are there other, better things I could be doing instead?" (If these questions were asked regularly and answered truthfully, there would probably be much less television viewing in Christian households, rectories, and convents.)

Finally, penance organizes life in the sense that one is led to direct one's whole life to the work of making up for sin. Self-denial is involved in every good act. In doing what is right, the wrongful self-assertion and self-love involved in sin are subdued and conquered. Thus, for someone striving to avoid evil and do good, the whole of Christian life assumes a penitential character.

C: The Three Primary Forms of Penance

Still, penance takes certain definite forms, whether it is assigned in the sacrament, prescribed during penitential times, or freely chosen. It is worthwhile to consider why that is so.

In both the Old and New Testaments and throughout the history of the Church, prayer, fasting, and almsgiving have been regarded as the three basic, typical acts of penance. Obviously people can perform these acts hypocritically or in a legalistic spirit, without interior dispositions corresponding to the external behavior. Done in the right spirit, however, they are meritorious, "and your Father who sees in secret will reward you" (Mt 6:4, 6, 18).

To understand the role of prayer, fasting, and almsgiving in Christian life, recall that there are four levels of existential harmony or integration: moral goodness itself (integration of the self at the level of practical reasonableness and free choice), harmony with God, harmony with other people, and harmony among elements of the self which are not themselves involved in moral action but are presupposed by it, for example, emotions and sense experience.

Repentance—sincerely saying "I'm sorry"—corresponds to the first of these levels, namely, moral goodness. That leaves the other three, and it is here that prayer, fasting, and almsgiving come into play.

Take fasting. Commonly thought of only as self-denial in food and drink, it is rightly understood as any voluntary restriction of impulses, desires, and feelings not bad in themselves. Thus, fasting contributes to self-integration at the level of emotions and sense experience.

Almsgiving clearly can be a help to harmony in one's relationships with other people. It can involve giving money, but it can also involve giving one's free time and all sorts of help to others when one is not strictly obliged to give it.

As for prayer, it plainly contributes to friendship and harmony with God. This is especially the case when it takes the form of resignation, the acceptance of hardships and suffering as part of God's will for oneself.

These three practices are related to one another: To overcome evil in oneself, one denies oneself some good; then one freely gives what one has denied oneself to others, while offering the whole of what one has done to God as an act of worship.

The contemporary reaction against prayer, fasting, and almsgiving would have it that they are irrelevant to the lives of serious Christians. If they are understood as isolated and merely external acts, that may be true. Understood from the existential perspective and in relation to one another, however, prayer, fasting, and almsgiving are essential to Christian life. They provide the only way to "make up" for sin by rectifying the existential damage remaining after sin is forgiven.

D: The Sacrament of the Anointing of the Sick

To the sacrament of penance, the Council of Trent links the sacrament of the anointing of the sick; indeed, Trent calls anointing a "culmination not only of penance but of the whole Christian life which itself ought to be a continual penance" (DS 1694/907). Although, if God wishes, the sacrament may lead to the renewal of health and life, basically and specifically it consecrates the recipient for suffering and death with Jesus, a penitential completion of Christian life in this world in the hope of resurrection to eternal life.

The essence of anointing is expressed clearly in the Introduction to the sacrament's new rite:

> This sacrament provides the sick person with the grace of the Holy Spirit by which the whole man is brought to health, trust in God is encouraged, and strength is given to resist the temptations of the Evil One and anxiety about death. Thus the sick person is able not only to bear his suffering bravely, but also to fight against it. A return to physical health may even follow the reception of this sacrament if it will be beneficial to the sick person's salvation. If necessary, the sac-

rament also provides the sick person with the forgiveness of sins and the completion of Christian penance.[25]

Today one sometimes encounters a significantly different view. In its simplest form, it is that anointing is a cure-all for whatever ails people, including psychological as well as physical ills. The sacrament is treated as a healing service. Sometimes, too, because it does not require individual confession of sins, it is used in place of penance.

This has several problems, including the fact that it confuses the effects of anointing with those of other sacraments. It is the Eucharist, after all, which Christ provides as our daily remedy as well as our spiritual food. Moreover, the sacrament of penance, not anointing, is the ordinary source of forgiveness of sins. Penance and the Eucharist are meant to sustain day-to-day Christian life, but anointing has a special purpose; it is for situations in which death is a real, foreseen possibility.

One can easily see how the present confusion came about. Before Vatican Council II, the "last rites" or "extreme unction" was frequently delayed as long as possible—almost to the moment of death, and sometimes beyond. (Not uncommonly, priests found themselves administering the sacrament conditionally to people who seemed already dead.) This putting off of sacramental preparation for death plainly was an abuse. Vatican II sought to correct it by calling the sacrament "the anointing of the sick," a name which makes it clear that it need not—indeed, should not—be delayed until the point of death.

However, Vatican II did not contradict the teaching of the Council of Florence: "This sacrament should not be given except to the sick whose death is feared" (DS 1324/700). Thus, the Introduction to the new rite makes frequent use of the words "danger," "dangerous," and "dangerously" to describe the condition of people who should be anointed. It is not necessary to be scrupulous about this, but neither should it simply be disregarded. Depression, anxiety, routine illnesses, and most chronic conditions do not place people in "danger" of death by any ordinary standards. No less than the preconciliar practice, it is an abuse to administer the sacrament when death is not at all in prospect.

People are in danger of death when they can reasonably regard death as a real prospect because of their illness or weakness. This is the case, for example, with those facing major surgery and with elderly persons with no specific life-threatening illness who nevertheless live with the awareness that death might come at any time. Here anointing is appropriate. But that is not the case for someone no more in "danger of death" than most people are all the time.

As a matter of pastoral practice, it is far better to encourage people to receive the Eucharist and penance frequently than to offer mass anointings. Penance and the Eucharist lead us through Christian life up to its culmination—suffering and death in Christ; in that sense, a Christian should be constantly preparing to receive the sacrament of the anointing of the sick, which consecrates this culminating experience and sees us safely through it.

33. Eucharistic Life as Fulfillment in the Lord Jesus

The Eucharist integrates the other sacraments and indeed the whole of Christian life. It does this by bringing together all the good works of Christian life as the Church's offering in the Mass.

Bread and wine are symbols and instances of our works—fruit of the earth which human hands have made, fruit of the vine and work of human hands, as the offertory prayers express it. They stand for our natural gifts and our work, that is, for all we bring to the Mass. There they are gathered up and offered in Jesus to the Father. Everything in Christian life should prepare for and follow from the Mass.

The Eucharist, moreover, makes real and builds up the everlasting fellowship of fulfillment in Jesus. Throughout our lives God is forming us into the heavenly communion of divine and human persons. We experience success and failure, and finally we are overcome by death, yet whatever good we do in Christ is saved, endures, and forms part of the everlasting divine-human fellowship. The Eucharist makes everything in the life of faith except sin part of the kingdom's building up.

Here we discuss three topics: the complexity and the unity of the Eucharist; the five purposes for which Jesus instituted the Eucharist; and the extension of the Eucharist through daily life by the Liturgy of the Hours and the sacrament of matrimony.

A: The Complexity and the Unity of the Eucharist

The Eucharist is a complex reality. As we shall see at greater length below, Trent distinguishes five purposes for which Jesus instituted it: as a memorial, to keep his sacrifice present; as spiritual food to sustain Christians; as a remedy for and, as it were, an immunization against sin; as a pledge—that is, a down-payment—or anticipation of heaven; and as a sign of the Church's unity, which it also perfects.

Besides this complexity in its purposes, the Mass has two other distinct aspects. On the one hand, it is a revelatory act consisting of words and deeds which communicate divine truth and life. Receiving Jesus bodily in the Eucharist, we share in his divine life and also have his human life as a principle of our lives. At the same time, the Eucharist is a human response to God's revelation. Not only does Jesus offer himself to the Father, but we offer ourselves with him and thank God for his gifts. To put it another way, the Mass is an exchange of gifts: God gives (its revelatory aspect) and we give, in and with Jesus (its aspect as sacrifice or human response).

Despite this complexity, however, the Eucharist is not complicated. It is simple because it has a real principle of unity.

As we saw in chapter nineteen, God is constantly building a marriage of divine and created persons. It is founded and centered on Jesus, a divine person who is also fully a member of the human family. Heavenly communion is the union of the Trinity, inseparable from Jesus as God, with the human community formed by fellowship with this man, Jesus, with whom all human persons are called to be friends.

Being both God and man, Jesus is the bond of fellowship between God and human persons. Just as a man and woman enter marriage by making their wedding vows, so we enter this fellowship by baptism. But just as a married couple's unity must grow gradually as they live together, our Christian lives do not become integrated all at once. As a result of baptism we have faith and are united with Jesus in principle. Yet faith has not yet permeated our lives and our institutions and culture, so that all these exist—as they are meant to do—"in" Christ. How is that to be accomplished? How is everything human, indeed the whole created order, to be restored to God through Christ?

The Eucharist is the answer. It centers upon the carrying-on of Jesus' central act, his offering of himself, which includes his fundamental commitment to give everything to the Father, even to the laying down of his life. This act did not end with Jesus' death. As his self-determining, free choice, it lasts, it continues, and it is outwardly performed again in every Mass. In saying "Do this in memory of me" at the Last Supper, Jesus commissioned not only the apostles but those who would come after them to keep carrying out his act. We do this when we do now what he told us then to do: we do it in the Mass.

This provides us with the way to make our personal contribution to restoring all things to God in Christ. As Vatican II expresses it, speaking of the laity (though it applies not only to them), all human activities, if done in the Spirit,

> become spiritual sacrifices acceptable to God through Jesus Christ (cf. 1 Pt 2:5). During the celebration of the Eucharist, these sacrifices are most lovingly offered to the Father along with the Lord's body. Thus, as worshipers whose every deed is holy, the laity consecrate the world itself to God. (*LG* 34)

In offering these spiritual sacrifices, the faithful as a whole act as a priestly people, and everyone who devoutly participates in the Mass exercises his or her own personal share in Jesus' priesthood (see *PO* 2).

The Mass, moreover, allows us not only to share in Jesus' act but to *experience* the communion we enjoy by sharing in it. For from our perspective it is a fully human act which we ourselves do. And in receiving Holy Communion we experience our union with Jesus and one another much as a husband and wife experience their unity in marital intercourse. Thus, our participation in the Eucharist draws us together and, at least to a degree, makes manifest our everlasting communion with God and also with one another in Jesus. The Mass, one might say, is heaven breaking into our experience here and now.

B: The Purposes for Instituting the Eucharist

As we have said, the Council of Trent distinguishes five purposes for which Jesus instituted the Eucharist (see DS 1638/875), and this teaching is restated by Vatican II (cf. *SC* 47).

Trent says first that the Eucharist is a memorial. This does not simply mean that it reminds us of something Jesus did in the past.

The Eucharist is a memorial which makes his action here and now present for us to participate in, while at the same time keeping present and building up the covenant community he formed.

Jesus' action was not individualistic. He established the new covenant so that others could enter into it, and the Eucharist keeps it present and living. True, Jesus' community-forming act began in the past, but the act itself is *not* past. It did not—and will not—end. As a moral reality, any human act lasts until the one who has chosen to do it changes his or her mind, and in this matter Jesus will never change his mind. For our part, we join in his covenant-forming act in baptism, but we bring our participation to maturity and experience our sharing in it in the Eucharist.

In the Old Testament Passover readings, the people are exhorted yearly to remember the Passover events and the Exodus. This remembering is more than just recalling something that happened long ago. It is an affirmation that the people today are still the community of the Passover and the Exodus; it is a renewal of commitment. The Eucharist transforms and perfects that covenant community. It replaces the old with the new, as the Epistle to the Hebrews says (see Heb 8–10). It makes Jesus' sacrifice present for us to participate in by the offering of our lives—our selves—along with his self-offering to the Father.

This brings us to the second of the purposes for Jesus' instituting the Eucharist which Trent distinguishes: to be spiritual food. We consume Jesus' living, bodily self. But he is not transformed into us; instead, we are transformed into him (see *LG* 26). This must be understood in its depth, not simplistically or sentimentally.

Human life operates on more than the moral plane, involves more than choices and what pertains to them. People are more than intellects and wills. They are bodily beings whose willing and acting involve bodily action and bodily contact. For example, two people who choose to be friends not only will good to each other but express their friendship in outward ways like exchanging gifts and bodily contact: shaking hands, embracing, and so on.

Similarly, in the Eucharist, the head, Jesus, and the members of the new covenant community act together by bodily contact and cooperation in a central human act—a meal—but one which is sacred because it consists of Jesus and also perpetuates his sacrifice to God and enables us to share in it. In the Eucharist we are joined bodily to Jesus and, in Jesus, with one another. Our unity in the body of Christ is real bodily unity, though obviously unlike any other. We also share in Jesus' human acts and in divine life, and are united with one another. These several kinds of union and sharing depend on or are sustained by bodily unity with Jesus in the Eucharist.

How it all works is a mystery, but Jesus assures us that it is real and necessary: "Very truly, I tell you, unless you eat the flesh of the Son of Man and drink his blood, you have no life in you" (Jn 6:53). Bodily unity with Jesus and, in him, with one another is a real, irreducible aspect of the Eucharist. It is fundamental to our cooperation with Jesus' work of redemption and to sharing in his divine life.

Third, the Eucharist is a kind of medicine and immunization against sin. It motivates us to try to be more like Jesus. This is easy to understand, since the more we love someone else, the more we want to be like that person.

In this way the Eucharist helps us to avoid mortal sin and overcome venial sin. One thinks: "I do not want to commit mortal sin, for then I will not be worthy to receive Holy Communion. I want to struggle even against venial sin, so that I can receive communion more worthily." Or, in a more mature form: "I do not wish to be unfaithful to Jesus, for then I would be unfit for bodily union with him."

It is not unlike a good husband's or wife's determination to be faithful, so as not to be unworthy of marital intimacy. But the situation is different for someone who reasons: "It doesn't matter if I commit this sin—I'm only human, after all." That is the attitude which leads both to infidelity in marriage and to sacrilegious communions.

On a deeper level, the Eucharist is at the center of a kind of "virtuous circle" of love. Receiving gifts from God in the Eucharist and experiencing receiving them, we are motivated to respond with gratitude and with gifts of our own. But no sooner do we begin to give gifts to someone than we begin to feel more attached to that person—we have, as it were, a greater stake in him or her. In ordinary human experience, the people we love most are those for whom we have done most—children, other family members, close friends. So it is in our relationship with God.

God loves us so much because we are, and are good, by reason of his gifts in us. To speak in human terms, God the Father sees himself in Jesus, sees Jesus in us, and loves us on that account. And we, loved by God and experiencing his loving gifts, are moved to love him in return, which is itself a gift of God. So in the Eucharist we are drawn into a continuing exchange of gifts with God, and the more we give, the more we care for him. Thus, as Vatican II puts it, "the mind is filled with grace" (*SC* 47).

Living and acting within this virtuous circle increases unity. That brings us to the fourth purpose of the Eucharist enumerated by Trent: to be a pledge—a downpayment—or anticipation of heaven.

The ideal consummation of any process of growing closer is perfect unity. To take a simple case, if a young man and woman find themselves becoming steadily friendlier and friendlier, they are probably on the way to getting married. In the Eucharist there is no doubt about the matter: if growth in intimacy continues without interruption, it can only end in the perfect communion of heavenly fellowship.

The Eucharist joins us to Jesus not as he once was but as he now is: we are united with him in resurrection life. This unity with the resurrected Christ comes to completion in full sharing in his life and in our own rising from the dead. The Eucharist is central to the process; in the Mass we really experience the fellowship of everlasting life.

Fifth, and finally, Trent points to the unity of the Church—a unity which it perfects—as a purpose of the Eucharist. In being perfected in unity with Jesus, Christians are also perfected in unity with one another. The process begins in baptism and comes to fulfillment in the Eucharist.

Vatican II expresses this very clearly in its decree on ecumenism:

> Baptism, therefore, constitutes a sacramental bond of unity linking all who have been reborn by means of it. But baptism, of itself, is only a beginning, a point of departure, for it is wholly directed toward the acquiring of fullness of life in Christ. Baptism is thus oriented toward a complete profession of faith, a complete incorporation into the system of salvation such as Christ himself willed it to be, and finally, toward a complete participation in Eucharistic communion. (*UR* 22)

Our covenant with God not only joins us to him but makes us

more and more united to one another. The Eucharist brings us together as a covenant people, unites us in bodily communion in Jesus, and allows us to experience our unity. At the same time, nevertheless, the Eucharist is primarily a sacrament of unity with Jesus, not of our unity with one another. Although our union with him does unite us, heavenly communion will be primarily a matter of union with his resurrection life.

In practical terms, then, there is far more to the Eucharist than our coming together, sharing a meal, and having a religious experience with other believers. To be sure, in one aspect the Mass *is* a sacramental meal, the Church does come together for this celebration, a social act, and participating in the celebration should be a worthwhile religious experience. Moreover, pastors must work to develop genuine community and their flocks should cooperate in this effort so that everyone will experience fully the consolation and joy of sharing in the communion of the Church. Still, our union with Jesus clearly takes priority over our unity with one another, and the reality of communion is more important than the experience. As St. Paul says, "we, who are many, are one body in Christ, and individually members one of another" (Rom 12:5). Unity *in Christ* is the basis of unity with the other members of his body.

Even more concretely, this means that a good, vital parish or faith community of any sort is one where unity with Jesus in the Eucharist has priority. It is *this* which brings people together, not manipulative—though well-intended—attempts to "build community" on the basis of merely human solidarity, in the hope that sociability will lead to something authentically religious.

The danger in the latter approach is obvious: it risks reducing the Church to a club. Even where it succeeds, the success is shallow and distorts the Church's reality. But where unity with Jesus is the starting point and basis of community, people are led to consider how they can share with one another in practical ways, give mutual assistance and support, and build solidarity on a variety of other levels, especially by cooperating in apostolic living and works. This does not happen automatically, however; it requires catechesis regarding the practical implications of Eucharistic unity. But where these are explained, understood, accepted, and lived out, people have the firmest foundation and best motive for true religious "community" in all its aspects.

C: The Extension of the Eucharist through Daily Life

The Eucharist acts as an organizing principle of Christian life in many ways. Faith, prayer, the other sacraments, sacramentals, and devotions all find their center in the Eucharist. Everything else in Christian life prepares for, extends, carries out, or shares in this central reality: Eucharistic communion with God in Jesus and, in consequence, communion with one another.

However, two other ways in which the Eucharist extends through Christian life are especially noteworthy because of their liturgical character. They are the Liturgy of the Hours and the sacrament of matrimony.

The Eucharist organizes Christian life through the Liturgy of the Hours in a very simple manner. At best, one's participation in the Eucharist is limited to a brief time daily; yet, as we have stressed repeatedly, the whole of a Christian's life should be Eucharistic. The Liturgy of the Hours, which is liturgical prayer and therefore the prayer of the Church, brings this about by, as it were, extending the Mass throughout the day. As the General Instruction of the Liturgy of the Hours expresses it:

> The Liturgy of the Hours extends . . . to the different hours of the day the praise and thanksgiving, the commemoration of the mysteries of salvation, the petitions and the foretaste of heavenly glory, that are present in the Eucharistic mystery, 'the center and apex of the whole life of the Christian community'. . . . The Liturgy of the Hours is an excellent preparation for the celebration of the Eucharist itself, for it inspires and deepens in a fitting way the dispositions necessary for the fruitful celebration of the Eucharist: faith, hope, love, devotion and the spirit of self-denial.[26]

Of its nature, then, the Liturgy of the Hours is not only for clergy and religious but for lay people, too. In seeking its renewal, the principal objective of the Second Vatican Council was that it be the daily prayer of the whole Church, celebrated in parishes, neighborhoods, and homes. It is different from devotions like the rosary and the stations of the cross, good and important as these are, in that it is part of the Church's common and universal prayer life.

Yet the Church has not mandated it for everyone, for not all are ready to participate in it. For the Council's vision to become reality, the Liturgy of the Hours must be well understood and appreciated by bishops, priests, and religious—who have a strict duty to say it on behalf of the Church as a whole—then shared with others. Up to now, this sharing has not even been attempted in most places.

How the sacrament of matrimony extends the Eucharist through daily life is more mysterious, but that it does so is no less a fact. Obviously, marriage does shape the lives of married couples: most husbands and wives spend the greater part of their time on their duties as married people and parents. They set up and maintain a household, work to support themselves, raise their children.

But how does marriage extend the Eucharist through daily life? Start with the fact that the choice to be married and the commitment to carry out the duties of marriage constitute a Christian vocation. To live in fidelity to this vocation is to live an apostolic life, consecrated by the sacrament of confirmation.

But how is that different from any other vocation, and why is it specifically Eucharistic? St. Paul points to the answer in the epistle to the Ephesians: The marriage bond symbolizes the unity of Christ and the Church (see Eph 5:21–33).

Love means personal fulfillment in interpersonal relationship. The more perfectly persons are united in love, the more they are also distinct and perfected; they are, one might say, both more themselves and more in communion. The perfect model of this is the Trinity, whose persons are perfectly in communion with one another but also perfectly distinct, completely themselves. The situation is similar in the heavenly communion of divine and human persons which God is building up in Christ: the more united we are with Jesus, the more our own distinct identities are perfected. And as the divine persons are inseparable from one another, so Jesus and his Church are indissolubly united forever.

Marriage mirrors that. The union of husband and wife is a "great mystery," St. Paul says, adding: "and I am applying it to Christ and the Church" (Eph 5:32). A married couple are really one principle of generation, one organism, biologically speaking, for the purpose of begetting a child. Indeed, as a marital covenant, the whole relationship fosters unity and distinction of persons in procreative love. The more united the couple are, the more the individual personhood of each is fulfilled. And their union is lifelong.

Today many married people do not see it that way. Implicitly or explicitly, they approach marriage in an individualistic spirit and reject the idea of self-fulfillment in and through the communion of an indissoluble marriage. The result is self-alienation. The "liberated" man or woman seeks fulfillment in possessions (which tend to dominate the one who has them), in pleasurable experiences (which are not the lasting self), and in status and power over others (which make one's identity depend on one's inferiors).

Yet marital union remains a sign, a sort of natural sacrament, of the everlasting heavenly communion which God is bringing about. This is scarcely an accident. It is not as if God, having created sex, only then noticed that it somehow mirrors the Trinity. Rather, as three persons in communion who wish to bring us into their eternal fellowship, the Trinity creates sex as an experience and beginning of that relationship for us.

In short, marriage is a commencement and a symbol of the Eucharistic communion which will last forever in heaven. It is in this way above all that the sacrament of matrimony extends the Eucharist into life. When a married couple live within the Eucharistic communion of the new covenant, what they naturally are—an enduring human communion and sign of heavenly communion—becomes *part* of that of which they are a sign. In the fellowship of marriage, an interpersonal relationship pertaining to heavenly communion is made actual and experienced in a particular way.

Someone might object that in heaven there is no marrying or giving in marriage (see Mt 22:30). That is true. But why is there no marriage in heaven? Not because bodily communion and personal fulfillment by relationship will be absent. They will not.

In heaven, however, bodily communion will not be limited as it is in this life. Even as the sexual character of bodily communion drops away, the reality of "two in one flesh" will be universalized; all the saints will share in the bodily communion of Jesus' resurrection life, not only with him but with one another. The interpersonal communion of sharing in bodily life, in a single commitment of love, and in divine life will continue forever in heaven, but no longer marked by the exclusivity which is part of the reality of marriage. In heaven the union of the blessed will be fuller than the fullest union of married couples—that union which now is a sign and token of what is to be.

34. Christian Life Animated with Hope of Everlasting Life

We have seen how Christians follow Jesus by prayer, by living out their personal vocations, and by receiving the sacraments. Now it is time to summarize the vision of Christian life which we have been developing since chapter nineteen.

Life in this world is related to life in the next. How we live now has a bearing on our fulfillment in heavenly communion with Christ. But what is the connection? How is this present life both related to eternal life and distinct from it?

We consider three topics: first, three inadequate views of this relationship; then, how Christian humanism improves on these inadequate views; finally, how the Christian should view human goods in this life. The teaching of the Second Vatican Council is central to this treatment.

A: Three Inadequate Views of the Relationship between This World and the Next

The three inadequate views are the classical view, secular humanism, and liberalized Christianity. The first two are diametrically opposed, while the third is an unhappy compromise combining their worst features. As for the Christian humanism which we shall examine later, it is the diametric opposite of liberalized Christianity, and it avoids the failings of the classical view and secular humanism while incorporating their strengths.

The first position, called "classical" here, has its historical roots in neo-Platonism. This was a philosophical-theological school influential among intellectuals in the early Christian centuries. Its basic tenet was that everything comes from a transcendent One.

A Christian might wish to call this "God," but in fact the One of neo-Platonism bears scant resemblance to the God of Christian belief. Rather than creating, the One radiates like the sun. In diffusing its essential goodness, the One brings about things more or less distinct from itself, including those we call creatures; but they are not creatures, since the One does not create—it only gives rise to other things through a process of self-diffusion about which it has no choice.

Material things are on the furthest edge of this process. As for human beings, they stand at a certain distance from the One, and can either slip further away, toward nothingness, by becoming more immersed in matter, or else can turn from the outer world to the interior life, and move from the lower toward the higher, until finally they are reunited with the One. The multiplicity and individuality of finite human selves will disappear when merged into perfect unity with the One. This is not redemption; it is simply finding one's way back to where one came from and being reabsorbed into the One.

Obviously, no Christian can accept all this. Yet it does offer a seemingly coherent account. Needing a theological framework for their reflection on revelation, the intellectuals among the early Christians naturally turned to neo-Platonism. Some of the Greek Fathers were heavily influenced by this way of thinking, among them the so-called Pseudo-Dionysus, a Christian thinker who wrote under the name of a disciple of St. Paul and whose works were prized all during the Middle Ages.

St. Augustine, before his conversion, also was much taken with neo-Platonism. Eventually he came to realize that he, and the school to which he subscribed, had made the disastrous mistake of leaving Christ out of account. Even then, however, imbued with the thinking of the neo-Platonists, he continued to hold to their ideas insofar as they seemed consistent with Christian faith. In moving beyond neo-Platonism, he worked out a profound Christian theology; but because of neo-Platonism's role in his intellectual development, his theology also embodies a great deal of its way of thinking. His enormous prestige helped carry it into later Christian thought.

Hence the "classical" view. In general terms, it is as follows. Human beings must turn away not only from sin but from material things, then turn back to God and move toward the divine—from the outer to the inner, the lower to the higher. What we do in this life is not important in itself; it has merely instrumental value, as a means of reaching heaven. And heaven? It is intellectual union with God, understood in a largely individualistic way. (Note, though, that Augustine was a much better theologian than many of his followers, and so, nourished by Scripture, he sometimes speaks of heaven as a community, even a banquet. Also, his great appreciation for the Incarnation helps introduce healthy humanistic elements into his thought. Unfortunately, that cannot be said of all those who came after him.)

In this view, religion became confused with the divine life in which Christians share by adoption. As a result, the good of religion seemed not only supreme but the overriding good, taking precedence over every other human good—justice, human friendship, knowledge and scientific truth, even human life. This mentality naturally found crusades and inquisitions reasonable and good, for it seemed reasonable and good to set aside, even violate, other goods for the sake of the religious good. This was not far removed from the view that, where religion is concerned, the end justifies the means.

Without ever denying bodily resurrection, this classical spirituality tended to give it short shrift. Indeed, it is difficult to see how bodily resurrection fits into its scheme of things. Where the emphasis is on saving one's soul so as to enjoy intellectual union with God in heaven, what good purpose does bodily resurrection serve? This way of thinking also tends to foster legalism. Good human acts cannot bring about the Beatific Vision, but mortal sin can prevent one from reaching heaven. So, the relevant practical question becomes: "What must I do to stay out of hell?" That is a very important question, but many positive things drop out of sight and a legalistic outlook takes over when it dominates moral reflection.

Then Christianity becomes vulnerable to those who, fleeing the truth of the gospel because of the judgment it passes on them and their way of life, wish to rationalize their behavior by attacking the faith. The more intelligent such people are—and, historically, some have been very intelligent indeed—the more persuasive their critique is. For, to repeat, the classical spirituality leaves the Church open to such attacks. Thus, the critics accuse Christianity of denying authentic human values, paying little attention to justice and the goods of this life, and fostering a false otherworldliness which discourages people from struggling against human misery and thereby makes it easier for exploiters to go on exploiting. Even making allowance for hostile exaggeration, there is a good deal of truth in all this, if by "Christianity" one means the classical view.

In this way secular humanism emerged as a reaction to classical piety. During the late Middle Ages and especially in the Renaissance one finds a humanism which, though not antagonistic toward faith, does lend support to the search for an alternative to an exclusively religious appreciation of the human. This humanism evolved through the Enlightenment, with its rejection of miracles and revelation and its skepticism regarding transcendent religion generally, into the thoroughgoing atheism of nineteenth- and twentieth-century secular humanism.

The differences between Marxist secular humanism and the secular humanism of Western liberal democracies are not important for our present purposes. What matters are the likenesses.

In the name of human values, secular humanism holds that there is no source of meaning and value beyond the human. It considers looking and living for any life beyond this one to be a distraction and a delusion. This is the only life we have, and we must make the most of it. To be concerned with God, heaven, and immortality is an evasion of the real challenges and problems of living. "Yes, man is his own end," says Albert Camus. "And he is his only end. If he aims to be something, it is in this life."[27]

The values emphasized by this antireligious humanism are real ones: human dignity, justice, freedom. Marxists and Western secular liberals agree in wishing to make the human person godlike, the ultimate source of meaning and value. As Camus says, "To become god is merely to be free on this earth, not to serve an immortal being."[28]

But despite all its talk of freedom, secular humanism denies the reality of free choice. In its place it sets the dialectic of history, psychic or social evolution, or some other deterministic developmental process thought to explain the human condition. With free choice gone, personal moral responsibility naturally is denied. Thus, paradoxically, secular humanism radically undermines the dignity of the person which it set out to uphold and promote. Ultimately, individuals do not count; one may—perhaps even must—kill some people in order to make this a better world for others. Thus, in the twentieth century totalitarian regimes killed tens of millions of persons and the worldwide holocaust of legalized abortion wiped out hundreds of millions more.

Secular humanism is appealing not only because it affirms some real values but also for other, less attractive reasons. Its denial of free choice and the responsibility it entails is attractive to people who commit sin and do not wish to repent. If one has no personal moral responsibility for what one does, one might as well relax and enjoy oneself in doing it.

Moreover, the high status of creator and arbiter of meaning and value which secular humanism assigns to human beings readily leads to arbitrariness and despotism in society, and this is attractive to those who have power or hope to get it. Since differences about meaning and value cannot be settled by appealing to God (who does not exist) or to human nature (which is only raw material to be shaped), and since differences cannot always be settled by persuasion leading to consensus, they often must be settled by deception, manipulation, or force. Intellectual, moral, and cultural life are radically politicized in secular humanist societies; the ultimate struggle is the struggle for power. As the Freemason Ludovico Settembrini puts it in Thomas Mann's *The Magic Mountain:* "The friend of humanity cannot recognize a distinction between what is political and what is not. There is nothing that is not political. Everything is politics."[29]

Liberalized Christianity emerged gradually as secular humanism grew increasingly powerful. While there are undoubtedly many explanations for that, one concerns the academic environment in which this version of Christianity arose. Many academicians in other fields were moving away from faith, and theologians wished to be accepted as members of the academic community. They also felt it their duty to salvage what they could of their religious traditions, and to make faith as respectable as possible to cultured modern people. Therefore, the academic theologians began making concessions, partly in a quest for more defensible positions and partly for the sake of academic respectability.

Why not? Neither classical piety nor biblical fundamentalism seemed defensible. To the complaint of old-fashioned believers "You're denying the faith," the natural response of academic theologians was, "You unsophisticated believers don't get the point"—after which further concessions followed in the cause of appeasing secular humanism. Through such a process as this, liberalized Christianity arose in European universities, beginning in the seventeenth century, peaking in the nineteenth century, and continuing into this one.

At first liberalized Christianity resembled the classical view in taking seriously matters like heaven and hell. To be fair about it, even today liberal Christians continue to believe in something transcendent, namely, God. But hell was a great embarrassment, and over time liberalized Christians managed to dispense with it. By doing so, they detached life in this world from serious consequences in the next world, while moving closer to secular humanism in emphasizing this world.

At the same time, liberalized Christianity came to downplay, even deny, the idea that there is anything fundamentally wrong with this world, anything which cannot be repaired by human effort or the working out of some evolutionary process. In this account, the problem with the human condition is not original and personal sin; it is that we are at an early stage, a comparatively low level, of human development. Perhaps people who act badly have psychological problems or lack information, or perhaps defects in social structures prevent them from behaving better. Progress is bound to correct such problems.

With sin de-emphasized, it next becomes easy to ignore or deny free choice and moral responsibility. Original sin is a myth, while personal sin is not "sin" at all but only a flaw in a developmental process. Excluding moral responsibility also suits theories of grace according to which grace does everything and good works are unnecessary. With hell denied and forgotten, life becomes a golden escalator carrying everyone automatically to heaven. But one need not think about something far in the future that is a sure thing, so the significance of heaven also fades. Indeed, in this view everything having to do with an afterlife comes to have value (to the extent it has any value at all) as symbol rather than reality.

No freedom or personal responsibility, no heaven or hell, human life caught up in an evolutionary process or historical dialectic leading inevitably to betterment in this world: that does make Christianity a cozy and comfortable system. Just the sort of system against which figures like Kierkegaard and Newman were warning during the nineteenth century.

It is, of course, a system with no place for the cross. Suffering is meaningless for those who suffer, the moral significance—the sacredness—of bodily life is frequently ignored, and the reality of bodily resurrection is called into question. It is a system which empties life of moral seriousness because human acts have neither the everlasting significance they had in classical piety nor the ultimate this-worldly significance they have for serious nonbelievers. Still, this world view gained liberal theologians a measure of respectability among their secular humanist academic colleagues.

Liberalized Christianity became even more acceptable when its leading theologians began to agree with secular humanists that meaning, value, and moral requirements are human constructs, established by society, by public opinion, by cultural consensus. The theory that it is acceptable to sacrifice some human goods for the sake of a greater good made headway. An emerging moral theology adopted legalistic devices for dispensing people from accepting responsibility for their behavior. Where the "rules" are not clear and certain, people are entitled to follow their "consciences," and of course there are very few clear and certain rules in a system like this. At the same time, political and social schemes are accepted which, assuming the perfectibility of this world, are at once grandiose in their goals and questionable in their means. This fits in well with the current emphasis in some theological circles on "liberation" understood largely in socio-political terms.

Liberalized Christianity does emphasize this-worldly values while retaining a residue of traditional Christianity—those aspects of it which are most easily accepted. But it is not an adequate synthesis of what is true in secular humanism and in classical piety. Instead it combines the worst features of both.

The secular humanist, after all, attaches ultimate importance to this life, but liberalized Christianity still must acknowledge something after death. Lacking classical piety's belief in hell as a real possibility, however, it is comfortable and complacent. It caters to self-indulgence and spiritual laziness. Its characteristic vice is sloth. To avoid a fatal boredom with religion itself, its adherents find themselves needing stimulation, either from emotionally exciting religious experiences or from involving religion in the socio-political causes approved by secular humanism—or both.

B: How an Authentic Christian Humanism Improves on These Inadequate Views

Plainly there is need for a better alternative to classical piety and secular humanism. Such an alternative does exist. It is integral Christian humanism.

One finds it beginning to emerge in the writings of Pope Leo XIII and still more clearly in Pius XI and Pius XII. It is articulated authoritatively by the Second Vatican Council, especially in *Gaudium et Spes*. Pope John Paul II not only constantly repeats the Council's humanistic teaching but draws out its implications and adds many details, for example, in his encyclicals *Dives in Misericordia* (on divine mercy) and *Laborem Exercens* (on work).

Where classical piety emphasizes, to the point of exclusivity, fulfillment in divine life, Christian humanism emphasizes integral human fulfillment in Jesus. But fulfillment in Jesus, as we have seen repeatedly, is more than fulfillment in divine life. Since Jesus is not only God but man, and now man with a glorified, resurrected body, union with him also means fulfillment in human life and in human goods, including bodily resurrection life.

As this authentic Christian humanism emerges, Christian life comes to be seen more clearly as communal life. So, for instance, Pius XI, stressing the restoration of all things to God in Jesus, established the feast of Christ the King; the implication is that Christians are fellow citizens of his kingdom, which is already present (though imperfectly so) on earth. Similarly, the Church comes to be seen not simply as an institution providing spiritual services, but as the community of Christian faith and apostolic life. Pius XII presents it as the Mystical Body of Christ, Vatican II as the People of God. These are communal, corporate concepts: the Church is one bread, one body, one people.

As for secular humanism, while it emphasizes some human goods, it overlooks others and more or less distorts those it does recognize. But integral Christian humanism honors all true human goods. Bodily life is not viewed as instrumental to happiness (whether "happiness" be understood in this-worldly or other-worldly terms). Truth is not subordinated to justice, as Marxism has no qualms about doing. Human creative work—art, poetry, and the rest—is not instrumentalized for the sake of selling products or political propaganda; it is given its due. So also with other human goods.

Christian humanism views integral human fulfillment as an attainable ideal which will be realized in heavenly fulfillment in Christ. While liberalized Christianity finds it hard to say why human acts are significant, and so tends to trivialize life in this world, the fulfillment of everything in Jesus—an attainable possibility—makes human cooperation in God's redemptive work imperative and urgent. One has a fresh incentive for living a serious life when one knows that one is sharing in God's work and that what one does here and now will have an impact forever and ever.

Even as it stresses the continuity between this life and the next, however, Christian humanism also recognizes the discontinuity. It is important to make clear wherein lie both the continuity and the discontinuity in all three ways of being united with Jesus—that is, in divine life, in human acts, and in bodily union.

In general, the discontinuity is of two kinds. One is the discontinuity of maturation, the imperfect becoming perfect. There is also a more radical discontinuity of reversal. The evil now present in creation will be eliminated or overcome in the heavenly kingdom: there will be no injustice, no death, no evil at all.

The basic principle of continuity is that the goods we share in by being united with Christ persist. Let us consider each one in turn, along with the relevant discontinuity.

First, we are united with Jesus in respect to divine life. Continuity here concerns the fact that we are now children of God and will remain his children in heaven. The only discontinuity is that of maturation. That which is now imperfect in our divine filiation will be perfected in heavenly communion with God. "We are God's children now; what we will be has not yet been revealed. What we do know is this: when he is revealed, we will be like him, for we will see him as he is" (1 Jn 3:2). In other words, when faith gives place to sight, we shall grow up to the status of mature, adult members of God's family.

Second, we are united to Jesus in respect to human acts. We shall be included in heaven as his loyal members, self-constituted by acting in him, through the grace he won for us. Our self-determination by the commitments of faith, vocation, and appropriate relationships with other people will last. Hence continuity: We shall be the persons we have made ourselves, and our bonds with other people—spouses, friends, fellow members of the Church—will not be discarded but perfected. But there will also be a twofold discontinuity. First, of maturation: In heaven the possibility of choosing wrongly or betraying commitments will be outgrown. Second, a radical discontinuity: The sin and imperfection which cripple our personalities, twist our relationships, and cause misery to us and other people, will be completely overcome.

Third, we are united with Jesus in respect to bodily life. In the Eucharist we share even now in Jesus' resurrection life and enjoy true bodily union with him; we are "incorporated" into him. The continuity here concerns the fact that we shall rise in our own bodies and share perfectly in the resurrection life of Jesus. The discontinuity of maturity means that in heaven we shall enjoy positive immortality—we shall never die again. The radical discontinuity lies in the fact that God will do away not only with sickness, suffering, and death but with all the evils arising from sin which now infect the human condition, including defects in the products of our work, in our culture, and in our interpersonal communication.

In sum, the heaven for which we hope does indeed signify the maturation of divine life in us; but it also signifies the restoration and perfection of our human action, bodily life, and everything else which pertains to us. Our fulfillment will not be individualistic but communal, a true heavenly banquet, corresponding to the vision set forth by Vatican II in a passage which, with good reason, we have cited before.

> For after we have obeyed the Lord, and in his Spirit nurtured on earth the values of human dignity, brotherhood and freedom, and indeed all the good fruits of our nature and enterprise, we will find them again, but freed of stain, burnished and transfigured. This will be so when Christ hands over to the Father a kingdom eternal and universal: "a kingdom of truth and life, of holiness and grace, of justice, love, and peace" [Preface of the Feast of Christ the King]. On this earth that kingdom is already present in mystery. When the Lord returns, it will be brought into full flower. (*GS* 39)

C: How the Christian Should Regard Human Goods in This Life

Good human acts ennoble us. We fulfill ourselves in respect to human goods by our choices and our actions—by doing good and living well. Among the human goods which last is our friendship with God, into which we enter by the covenant of faith. But our good acts also contribute to the fulfillment of *all* things in Jesus, a fulfillment in which all good human relationships and whatever perfects human persons also will last.

As we have just seen, Vatican II clearly teaches that in the res-urrection everything worthwhile in our lives will be perfected and raised up. As real cooperators in carrying out God's plan, it is important that we do our best.

Plainly, then, human actions and human lives have a more than merely instrumental relationship to heaven. Life in this world is not just a kind of test which one must pass in order to be saved. It is one's contribution to the building up of heaven itself. As the Council says, everything good in human work and human culture has a place in heaven.

From this point of view, we can understand how a good life in this world merits heaven, without being merely instrumental. The Eucharist gathers in all the good fruits of human nature and ef-fort, which provide material for the kingdom. At the same time, human acts in their Eucharistic aspect are gifts to God. He will raise us up in response to that gift. For we do not simply give our works to God—we give them in Christ and in the unity of the Spirit. Small as our part is, the Eucharist would be emptied of much of its meaning if we did not live good human lives and offer them united with Jesus' offering.

The importance of human life becomes still clearer when we consider Jesus' life. Not even God could have brought about his human life without his living it. But suppose he had *not* lived it? Without having lived, suffered, and died, would he live now in glory? God could not have raised up Jesus in glory if he had not lived and died.

And now we, in our diverse ways, go on doing what Jesus did. The heavenly kingdom is still being built up by him in the life of his Church on earth, that is, in the lives of us who are the mem-bers of the Church. Here is the significance of Christian life on this earth, the essence of Christian humanism.

400 FULFILLMENT IN CHRIST

Obviously, then, a faithful Christian will have a distinctive attitude toward this world and toward human goods.

The Christian will love human goods indiscriminately. That does not mean pursuing them randomly, for such behavior would be contrary to vocation and commitment. No one can do everything; each of us must devote himself or herself to the service of particular goods and particular people. At the same time, all of us should have a deep appreciation and reverence for all the goods, just as we should love every neighbor as ourselves. One should not regard religion, say, as tremendously important while dismissing the physical well-being of people as unimportant; one should not prize truth while viewing the lives of the unborn as insignificant. All human goods are important. And because no good intrinsic to persons is a mere means to something else, the Christian must hold that there are some means which no end can ever justify.

Christians will detach themselves from everything not required by their personal vocations. This means more than giving up bad things, more even than giving up good things which interfere with fulfilling one's vocation. It means giving up everything which lies outside the range of personal vocation, because anything else will be more or less a hindrance. Yet even while the Christian cultivates this detachment, he or she seeks and uses everything legitimately available for fulfilling personal vocation.

Christians will be as energetic as the most energetic of nonbelievers. They will not be troubled or work any less hard if their personal vocations call for them to play modest roles. They will be eager that human goods be realized, in others as well as in themselves, but no more ambitious than their vocations require. Ordinarily, people either are energetic and ambitious with an eye on winning recognition and power, or else they lack ambition and settle for undemanding positions because they want to avoid hard work and struggle. The Christian, however, is able to combine these seeming opposites—ambition and energy on the one hand, selflessness and readiness to occupy a small role on the other—in light of the first and second modes of responsibility which rule out inertia and individualism.

For such a person, success is unimportant by comparison with faithfulness. Indeed, what passes for success is worthless if its price is unfaithfulness (the fourth mode). Failure does not matter, provided one keeps faith. Recognition and respect by others—superiors, professional peers, and so on—count for nothing if they require that one be unfaithful.

To think and live this way places faithful Christians in a position of alienation from much of the surrounding culture and many people with whom they come in contact. In one way or another, they will suffer. But they will not seek revenge. In the fallen human condition, people hate those who hurt them and make them fail. But the faithful Christian combines a healthy disdain for human opinion with a nonretributive attitude. Helping one's enemies is the Christian thing to do; one does not try to destroy evil but to heal it and to save those who do evil to oneself, just as Jesus did.

35. The Truth of Christ Lives in His Church

Having completed our treatment of Christian moral principles in chapter thirty-four, we turn now to a kind of appendix. In this chapter and the next we defend the theological sources we have used and how we have used them.

We have assumed throughout that it is possible to engage in theological reflection on the basis of what the Church teaches and on the basis of Scripture and tradition as the Church understands them. Catholic theologians took this for granted until the recent past, but today it is rejected by many who also reject various elements of Catholic teaching.

We shall not attempt to *prove* the truth of the Church's teaching here. These two chapters are a theological clarification rather than an apologetic. They should nevertheless help readers understand what the issues are and why many of the arguments used by dissenting theologians fail.

The present chapter proceeds constructively, by addressing five questions: the general idea of infallibility; the inerrancy of Scripture; the notion of magisterium; the infallibility of nondefined moral teachings; and religious assent to noninfallibly proposed teachings. Chapter thirty-six presents a critique of radical theological dissent.

A: The General Idea of Infallibility

To understand infallibility, one must begin with the apostles. They were Jesus' companions and friends, but also something more. Their unique role was to be the authorized recipients of God's revelation in Jesus.

Authorized recipients were needed. The communication of God's revelation in Jesus would not have been complete without someone to receive it, and this "someone" could not have been just anyone. Jesus communicated divine truth to many people, but only a few—the apostles—had the responsibility of being the *official* recipients, who would keep his revelation intact and hand it on, so that it would be available to all humankind.

Humanly speaking, however, even the apostles could have made mistakes in matters of faith. But if these authorized recipients had misunderstood it, revelation would have been thwarted. Thus, some special divine intervention was required to prevent this from happening. In the New Testament, Jesus frequently promises to send the Holy Spirit, and eventually does so, for just this purpose. "When the Spirit of truth comes, he will guide you into all the truth" (Jn 16:13). The Spirit ensures that the apostles do not and cannot err in believing.

That sure gift of recognizing revealed truth is essentially what is meant by infallibility. Although the term itself did not come into use until the Middle Ages, the reality was present from the beginning. The apostles received and believed only what God wished to communicate, and they received and believed all of it.

Not that they all believed and preached identically the same things. As individuals, they naturally tended to emphasize different aspects of Jesus' message, calling attention to particular words and deeds of his which they found especially significant. John emphasized things which Peter did not; Peter stressed things John did not stress, and so on.

The gospels and epistles reflect this diversity. The New Testament embodies a harmonious pluralism rooted in unified apostolic faith. Conflict and incompatibility among different apostolic beliefs were precluded, while at the same time the apostles' collegial unity and communication with one another were required to encompass the whole body of revealed truth.

Yet the apostles did not compile a list of revealed truths and transmit it to those who came after them. At first, much that Jesus had revealed was only implicit in the practice and worship of the apostolic Church. One searches the New Testament in vain, for example, to find the seven sacraments named, and indeed it took many centuries for the very idea of sacrament to be worked out clearly. It does not follow, however, that the seven sacraments were ever lacking in the Church. Even though it was not fully articulated, the reality was present in the community's worship and life from the start.

This point is important to the idea of doctrinal development. Because it was precisely the apostles' appropriation of their experience of Jesus which constituted Christian revelation, revelation was complete with the death of the last apostle. As Vatican II says, repeating a traditional point, "we now await no further new public revelation before the glorious manifestation of our Lord Jesus Christ" (*DV* 4). But development neither implies nor requires new revelation, for it is an unfolding, a making explicit, of what is already implicitly there.

Today's Church is founded on and continues the apostolic community, and its faith is the faith of the apostles. Just as in the past, of course, individual Christians can and do make mistakes. Popes and bishops, as individuals, can err. But the Church as such cannot err in its faith. For to the extent it did, revelation would be lost, and so God's communication would have failed. But God cannot fail in what he sets out to do, and in revealing divine truth in Jesus, he set out to communicate to all humankind, down to the end of time. In carrying out this task his appointed instrument is the Church, whose mission is "a continuing one" (*AG* 5), extending to all generations.

Thus, the gift which made the apostles incapable of mistaking the truth revealed in Jesus must still be given to the Church. This gift of the Spirit is the infallibility of the Church. As Vatican II expresses it:

> The body of the faithful as a whole, anointed as they are by the Holy One (cf. Jn 2:20, 27), cannot err in matters of belief. Thanks to a supernatural sense of the faith which characterizes the People as a whole, it manifests this unerring quality when, "from the bishops down to the last member of the laity," [note to St. Augustine] it shows universal agreement in faith and morals.
>
> For, by this sense of faith which is aroused and sustained by the Spirit of truth, God's People accepts not the word of men but the very Word of God (cf. 1 Thes 2:13). It clings without fail to the faith once delivered to the saints (cf. Jude 3), penetrates it more deeply by

accurate insights, and applies it more thoroughly to life. All this it does under the lead of a sacred teaching authority to which it loyally defers. (*LG* 12)

This should not be understood triumphalistically, as if the whole Church always lived up to what it believes or as if it had immediately at hand the correct answer to every new question. Nor, as noted earlier, does it mean that individual members of the Church, including popes and bishops, cannot err. It only means what it says: The Church as a whole does not and cannot make mistakes in matters of faith and morals.

But how does the Church as a whole believe and teach something? One suggestion must be rejected at the start, namely, the idea that the "sensus fidelium" (the views and opinions of lay Catholics) stands as an independent witness and norm of truth, so that if "the faithful" hold a position different from that of received teaching, the received teaching is mistaken and must be corrected.

This, Pope John Paul II points out, is not the teaching of the Second Vatican Council. "The 'supernatural sense of faith' . . . does not consist solely or necessarily in the consensus of the faithful. Following Christ, the Church seeks the truth, which is not always the same as the majority opinion."[30] Rather, as the Council understands it, the sense of faith is that of the whole People of God, the whole Church—including, and under the leadership of, the pope and bishops.

While members of the Church might be said to participate in the infallibility of the Church as a whole as long as, in a traditional phrase, they "think with the Church," the fact is that not every Catholic always thinks with the Church. Indeed, "the Spirit expressly says that in later times some will renounce the faith by paying attention to deceitful spirits and teachings of demons, through the hypocrisy of liars whose consciences are seared" (1 Tm 4:1–2).

Within the Church, however, the episcopal college, with the pope at its head, continues the apostles' work of discerning and communicating the divinely revealed truth. Vatican II, for example, prefaces its treatment of papal and episcopal infallibility with the statements that bishops are "successors of the apostles" who receive from Christ "the mission to teach all nations" (*LG* 24) and that, "teaching in communion with the Roman Pontiff,

[they] are to be respected by all as witnesses to divine and Catholic truth" (*LG* 25). The Council makes the crucial point that the Church's infallibility is founded on the infallibility of the apostolic college—an infallibility in which the college of bishops now shares under its head, the pope. This is what guarantees that, while individual members of the Church can err regarding faith, the Church as a whole cannot err.

At the same time, of course, both papal and episcopal infallibility must be understood in the context of the infallibility of the whole Church. Otherwise the infallibility of the pope and bishops takes on a magical character, as if certain persons were preserved from error by occasional, miraculous divine interventions into the normal course of things in the Church.

To repeat, however: Unless the Church as a whole is always infallible in discerning what is revealed from what is not, revelation—that is, God's communication to humankind—has failed; for communication which is misunderstood is failed communication. To deny the infallibility of the Church is to deny the continuity of revelation, and that is tantamount to denying revelation itself.

B: The Inerrancy of Scripture

Scripture is an expression of the faith of the Church, that is, of God's people. But God's people of the old covenant were already the Church (though obviously not in a fully developed form), and Jesus did not abolish the old law but brought it to perfection in the new covenant community. Thus, in speaking of the inerrancy of Scripture, one is speaking both of the New Testament and also of the Old.

Scripture both expresses and bears witness to divine revelation. As Vatican II says, it is "the word of God inasmuch as it is consigned to writing under the inspiration of the divine Spirit" (*DV* 9). Moreover, the Bible expresses not just belief *within* the Church but the belief *of* the Church. The New Testament is a unique, normative expression of apostolic faith, and thus a continuing norm of the faith of the Church; the Old Testament, too, is normative for Christian faith inasmuch as the New Testament presupposes it and builds on it.

Vatican II, reaffirming traditional belief, teaches that the books of the Bible have God as their author. But they also have human authors who truly are authors of what they have written. There is no contradiction here, provided one bears in mind that a human author and a divine author plainly will do their work in very different ways. The human authors of the Bible wrote what they wrote—their human causality was at work. But God's causality also was at work, through the mysterious process called "inspiration," so that one correctly speaks of God as the author of the Bible.

In practical terms, then, these humanly written books contain precisely what God wants. The Council says:

> Therefore, since everything asserted by the inspired authors or sacred writers must be held to be asserted by the Holy Spirit, it follows that the books of Scripture must be acknowledged as teaching firmly, faithfully, and without error that truth which God wanted put into the sacred writings for the sake of our salvation. (*DV* 11)

The assertions of the human writers are the assertions of God; whatever Scripture asserts is without error.

This is what the "inerrancy" of the Bible means. While Vatican II does not use the word (perhaps because it had taken on polemical overtones and had sometimes been given inadequate theological explanations), *Dei Verbum*, 11, restates traditional Catholic belief about Scripture's inerrancy.

This Catholic position on inerrancy must be distinguished from fundamentalism. A fundamentalist rightly holds that what the Bible asserts is true, identifies the propositions he or she personally considers to be asserted, and accepts them as true. A liberal Christian holds that some less important things asserted in the Bible are not true, establishes personally acceptable criteria for distinguishing important propositions from unimportant ones, and believes some things the Bible says while disbelieving others. A Catholic, believing that everything asserted in the Bible is true and that the whole Church cannot err in identifying divine truth, tries to share in the Church's understanding of Scripture and the Church's faith in the divinely revealed truths found there.

In all this, "asserted" is the key word. An assertion is a proposition proposed as certainly true. All assertions in the Bible are true, but not everything the Bible says is an assertion. For instance, some passages are poetic formulae of adoration, others merely report what somebody said or thought, and so on. Thus, in the book of Job, the human author constructs a theological dialogue, in which he recounts the views of Job's friends concerning his troubles and Job's attempts to defend himself. Since these several views are more or less in conflict, the author obviously cannot be asserting them all, and in fact he most likely is not asserting any of them. At the end of the book, however, Job acknowledges his inadequacy to understand, much less criticize, the ways of God (see Jb 42:2–6). This presumably constitutes the point of the dialogue, and, considering it in context, one must disengage from it what the author means to assert.

What is not asserted in the Bible need not be true, and *Dei Verbum* and the Church's teaching in other places do not suggest otherwise. In reading Scripture, one must try to determine whether and when the human author is saying, in effect, "This certainly is true; you ought to believe it." It is to these assertions, and only to them, that biblical inerrancy applies. Vatican II does not say there are no mistakes in the Bible; it says no false propositions are *asserted* there.

This distinction also applies to the moral teaching in Scripture. The Bible does propose moral norms, and those which are asserted are true. But one needs to examine the text and take into account the Church's traditional reading of it to see whether a particular norm is being asserted or merely reported (as if to say, "This is how people thought about the matter" or "That is how they acted").

Even the fact that certain norms are taken for granted in the Old Testament does not necessarily mean they are asserted by the sacred writers. In some cases, the authors may simply be describing accepted beliefs and practices, without asserting them. One must also bear in mind that, when a scriptural author does assert a moral norm, he should not be supposed to be asserting it beyond its limits. For example, as we saw in chapter ten, affirmative norms are never absolute—there are situations where one should *not* do what is positively enjoined; thus, a true affirmative norm asserted in Scripture will always admit of exceptions.

Thus, the presence in the Bible of norms which seem unsound or which admit of exceptions does not lead to the conclusion that the absolute norms asserted there are unsound or untrue. Like everything else really asserted in Scripture, such moral teaching is inerrantly true.

And clearly some absolute moral norms are asserted in sacred Scripture. The Decalogue is not only presented as the very words of God (see Ex 34:27–28; Dt 5:22, 10:1–4) but often reaffirmed in the Old Testament. It is also repeated in the New Testament: Jesus interiorizes and deepens it in the Sermon on the Mount (see Mt 5:21–37) and reaffirms it as indispensable for entering eternal life (see Mt 19:16–20; Mk 10:17–19; Lk 18:18–21); Paul also assumes the Decalogue's truth and permanent relevance, for in urging the superiority of love he makes the point that "love is the fulfilling of the law" (Rom 13:10). In short, no reasonable reading of the Decalogue and its treatment throughout the Old and New Testaments can escape the conclusion that the Decalogue and its norms are fundamental revealed moral truth. Common Christian practice in moral instruction always has accorded the Decalogue that status and has interpreted its negative norms as exceptionless. So, to take one example, it is inescapably a revealed moral truth that adultery is always wrong.

C: The Notion of Magisterium

It is a matter of faith that the pope and the other bishops are successors of the apostles in regard to the elements of the apostolic office which could be handed on. Of course, not everything it meant to be an apostle could be communicated. Only the apostles themselves could be the official recipients of God's revelation in Jesus, and so they are the foundation of the Church as the pope and the other bishops cannot be. But other elements of the apostolic office are communicable: being leaders whose faith and preaching are normative for the rest of the Church, acting sacramentally in the person of Christ, and so on. These things could be, and were, shared and communicated. We see this happening in the New Testament, for example, in the "pastoral" epistles (Timothy and Titus). The earliest Fathers of the Church similarly make much of the fact that they not only belong to the Church founded by the apostles but are in continuity with them.

The First Vatican Council teaches solemnly and definitively that, by the will of Christ, the pope is Peter's successor as head of the Church (see DS 3058/1825). The Second Vatican Council confirms this teaching and adds to it that the bishops are the apostles' successors:

> Just as the role that the Lord gave individually to Peter, the first among the apostles, is permanent and was meant to be transmitted to his successors, so also the apostles' office of nurturing the Church is permanent, and was meant to be exercised without interruption by

the sacred order of bishops. Therefore, this sacred Synod teaches that by divine institution bishops have succeeded to the place of the apostles as shepherds of the Church, and that he who hears them, hears Christ, while he who rejects them, rejects Christ and him who sent Christ (cf. Lk 10:16). (*LG* 20)

Thus, the pope and bishops succeed Peter and the apostles as authorized guardians and teachers of the truth revealed by God in Jesus. This role of theirs is called "the magisterium" (teaching authority or teaching office). Although the term was given its technical meaning only in modern times, the reality is present in the Church from the beginning.

But what does "authority" mean here, and why is it vested in the bishops?

Infallibility, as we have seen, belongs to the Church as a whole; individuals, as such, are not infallible. But even though the Church as a whole is infallible in what it believes and teaches, the question remains how one can know what this is.

We have no complete, definitive list of doctrines dating back to apostolic times. Nor is it enough to say, as some Protestants do, that one can find the Church's belief in Scripture. Certainly one *can* find the belief of the Church there, but simply leaving it at that offers no scope for authentic doctrinal development, which is essential for the faith to be explained and applied in relation to new questions and new contexts. Scripture says once and for all what it says; alone, it cannot be the norm for determining whether something said to be a "development" is authentic—that is, whether it is part of God's revelation. Moreover, Scripture does not interpret itself. Something else is needed.

This "something else" is the magisterium of the bishops in union with the pope. Vatican II expresses it this way:

The task of authentically interpreting the word of God, whether written or handed on, has been entrusted exclusively to the living teaching office [magisterium] of the Church, whose authority is exercised in the name of Jesus Christ. This teaching office is not above the word of God, but serves it, teaching only what has been handed on, listening to it devoutly, guarding it scrupulously, and explaining it faithfully by divine commission and with the help of the Holy Spirit; it draws from this one deposit of faith everything which it presents for belief as divinely revealed. (*DV* 10)

As that makes clear, the magisterium does much more than

find a consensus and give voice to it. It decides—that is, judges—what does and does not belong to revelation. The members of the magisterium obviously must make their judgment by using their own faith as a sample of the Church's faith, yet they make the judgment not in a personal capacity but precisely as the Church's leaders, speaking in Jesus' name and assisted by his Holy Spirit, and so their judgment is authoritative. Consequently, when all the bishops together and in union with the pope propose something as the Church's belief and teaching, these successors of the apostles are pointing to what *is* the Church's belief and teaching. Those who reject what they say place themselves outside their communion, that is, outside the Church itself. (There are, nevertheless, degrees of union and disunion—the "separated brethren" are not totally separated.)

To put it another way: The community of the twelve apostles, who were the authorized witnesses to Jesus, was the core of the Church as an identifiable human community; in apostolic times, communion with this apostolic community constituted others as members of the Church. Now, too, the communion of the pope and the bishops in union with him distinguishes the Church from every other group of people; to be in communion with them is to be a member of the Church, while not to believe and teach what they believe and teach is to separate oneself from the Church.

But how do the pope and bishops express belief and teaching? In several ways.

One way is in an ecumenical council. Here the pope and bishops deliberate together, reach a conclusion, and formulate a common position. Even if the pope is not physically present, the council cannot exist except as a gathering of the bishops in collegial union with him, and his agreement is required to validate its conclusions.

Also, the pope, as center and principle of unity within the communion of the apostles' successors, can define a proposition of faith or morals which is to be held by all. Then, according to Vatican I, what he says is irreformable and must be accepted, because he teaches with the infallibility of the Church (DS 3074/ 1839). He is, one might say, the official spokesman for its faith.

A papal act of this kind presupposes the Church's faith and the collegial unity of the apostles' successors. The pope cannot simply make things up and define them as revealed truth. Rather, as head of the college, he acts for the whole leadership of the Church and solemnly declares what the Church believes. Because of God's gift of infallibility to the Church, his act of teaching participates in that infallibility. His teaching is infallible not because it is his personally but because it officially articulates the Church's faith.

D: Infallibility of Nondefined Moral Teachings

There is, however, another way, much more interesting for moral doctrine, in which the pope and bishops teach together. It is teaching proposed infallibly by the ordinary magisterium—the bishops' united witness in matters of faith and morals, given in their day-by-day teaching.

Vatican II states clearly the criteria for an infallible exercise of this kind of teaching authority by the bishops:

> Although the bishops individually do not enjoy the prerogative of infallibility, they nevertheless proclaim the teaching of Christ infallibly, even when they are dispersed throughout the world, provided that they remain in communion with each other and with the successor of Peter and that in authoritatively teaching on a matter of faith and morals they agree in one judgment as that to be held definitively. (*LG* 25; translation supplied)

For obvious reasons, this is not a thought which theological dissenters receive with great enthusiasm. Efforts to discount it have therefore been underway for a long time. What exactly does it mean?

It means that, quite apart from solemn definitions, ecumenical councils, and papal declarations *ex cathedra*, the bishops around the world teach infallibly when they all, being in communion with the pope, teach the same position on a point of faith or morals, and propose it definitively as the view which Catholics must hold. Each element of this conciliar statement deserves examination.

The first condition, that the bishops be in communion with one another and with the pope, does not mean they must act in a strictly collegial manner—formally, that is, as a single body. In their day-to-day teaching, they plainly do not act that way, and from the evolution of the text it is clear that what is envisaged as necessary and sufficient is simply that they be bishops in the Catholic Church.

Authoritative teaching on a matter of faith or morals means the bishops are not expressing personal opinions but acting officially in their capacity as teachers. As for "faith or morals," nothing in the expression's long history suggests that "morals" does not include specific moral norms, such as the norm forbidding adultery.

That the bishops "agree in one judgment" signifies universality in episcopal teaching. This is not absolute numerical unanimity but *moral* unity. Furthermore, if the condition has been met in regard to some teaching in the past, it is not necessary that it always be met in the future; otherwise one would have to conclude that it can *never* be met until the end of time, since there is no way of knowing in the present what bishops in the future might conceivably say. In other words, what has once been taught infallibly remains infallibly taught, even if disagreements break out later.

"Definitively" in Vatican II's formula clearly does not refer to a solemn definition, since the Council is speaking here about ordinary teaching. It means that the point in question is not being proposed as merely probable but as certain, not as something optional but as something which bishops are obliged to teach and Catholics are obliged to accept.

What Vatican II says is not substantially new (one finds attempts to formulate the same idea as early as the fifth century). But in the Council's very clear and specific formulation it comes as a surprise to people unaccustomed to adverting to the infallibility of the ordinary magisterium and perhaps not eager to do so. It should be borne in mind, however, that infallibility is not something extraordinary and occasional, nor is it a property of particular persons and documents; it is a gift from God by which the Church consistently receives, believes, and hands on all of God's revelation. It follows that, when the pope and the bishops in communion with him around the world, acting as the official teachers in and of the Church, believe and teach the same thing as Jesus' teaching, what they believe is the Church's faith, what they teach is the Church's teaching, and their belief and teaching participate in the infallibility of the Church.

One should also bear in mind that bishops "teach" in various ways. Obviously they do this by preaching, publishing pastoral letters, and the like. But they also teach by authorizing textbooks for use in their seminaries (assuming they actually involve themselves in this matter, as they used to do), by making it clear to their priests that something is to be treated as a norm in confessional practice, and so on. On moral questions, they teach as definitively as they can when they take a position, tolerate no other, and make it clear that what is in question is the matter of grave sin. The last phrase is important, because bishops almost always are very careful not to say that something is a grave matter unless they are sure it is and convinced they must insist on the point.

There is an extensive body of Catholic moral teaching, including many specific moral norms. One finds this body of teaching in many places, among others in the New Testament, the Fathers of the Church, lists of sins used by confessors, canon law, the works of doctors of the Church like St. Thomas Aquinas, catechisms, individual and collective statements by bishops, the documents of ecumenical councils including Vatican II, and many documents from popes and Roman congregations.

That this body of teaching includes exhortation and nonabsolute norms taught without explicit qualifications, and reflects variations of emphasis and even substance on some matters, is true but beside the point. The point is that for many centuries Christian teachers, including the bishops of the world in communion with the pope, did condemn certain acts absolutely and without exception—for example, adultery, direct abortion, contraception, remarriage after divorce of persons who were sacramentally married.

To see that this is so, one need only examine the textbooks used in Catholic seminaries between, say, the years 1700 and 1950. Evidently this body of teaching was an obligatory standard, known and approved by the bishops, for the education of priests and for confessional practice. It was also the consensus—broken only beginning around 1960—of modern theologians, whose agreement, at a time when theologians were understood to be, and acted as, authorized agents of the bishops, progressively eliminated whatever vagueness or inconsistency had existed in the tradition on various details pertaining to acts condemned as immoral.

Thus, at least for several centuries, the conditions for an infallible exercise of the ordinary magisterium were met in the case of this common body of Catholic moral teaching—or, rather, *Christian* moral teaching, since up to the nineteenth century Orthodox

Christians and Protestants taught most of the same norms. That does not mean this body of teaching was not infallibly proposed *before* then, but only that, during these centuries, the evidence is exceptionally clear.

Repeatedly, the norms which make up this body of moral teaching were proposed as being divinely revealed. The Ten Commandments and other passages in Scripture were cited in this regard. For example, the story of Onan (see Gn 38:9–10) was used in support of the teaching on contraception. Here, it makes no difference whether the evidence used to show that these norms were divinely revealed did or did not prove the point or whether, for instance, the story of Onan does or does not mean what it was taken to mean. Our point is a limited one: In teaching moral norms in this way, bishops and theologians were by implication calling on people to make an assent of divine faith; they proposed these norms as truths which Catholics were obliged to hold, since to deny them would be to deny the faith. In doing so, the bishops of the world together with the popes most surely proposed these norms as truths to be held definitively. Thus, this body of moral doctrine was proposed in a manner which satisfies the conditions identified by the Second Vatican Council for an infallible exercise of the ordinary magisterium.

As Vatican I and Vatican II make clear, even when a doctrine is defined, nothing is added to divine revelation. The Church's infallibility in believing and teaching extends only as far as revelation extends; it pertains to those things "which belong to the revealed deposit, or are required to guard it as inviolable and expound it with fidelity" (*LG* 25; translation supplied). Still, the latter phrase—"required to guard it as inviolable and expound it with fidelity"—rules out limiting the object of infallibility to truths explicitly contained in revelation as it has already been articulated. Such a limitation would block development of doctrine and prevent the Church from rejecting new errors which are incompatible with divinely revealed truth.

Finally, against the claim one sometimes hears that the Church has never defined any moral doctrine, it is important to note that it has. The Council of Trent specifically condemns polygamy and teaches the indissolubility of Christian marriage (DS 1802/972, 1805/975, 1807/977). Since some moral teachings have been defined, others can be. That up to now the Church has not often done so (presumably because it was not necessary) does not limit its ability to do so in the future.

E: Religious Assent to Noninfallibly Proposed Teachings

Vatican II teaches:

In matters of faith and morals, the bishops speak in the name of Christ and the faithful are to accept their teaching and adhere to it with a religious assent of soul. This religious submission of will and of mind must be shown in a special way to the authentic teaching authority of the Roman Pontiff, even when he is not speaking ex cathedra. (*LG* 25)

Popes and bishops do not always teach by doctrinal definitions and infallible exercises of the ordinary magisterium. Here the question of religious assent arises. As the passage just quoted makes clear, in some circumstances it is an obligation for Catholics. But the obligation has limits.

A bishop may have opinions on matters outside the area of faith and morals, and may badly want people to agree with him, but no one has to give religious assent to what he says on those matters. Again, a bishop may express views on faith and morals without presenting them as truths which must be accepted. Here, too, no one is obliged to give religious assent. For example, the U.S. bishops' collective pastoral letter on war and peace (1983) says many of its concrete recommendations are proposed only as "prudential judgments." From the context it is clear that, as the bishops see it, on those matters there also are other, alternative positions which Catholics can legitimately hold. Thus, these "prudential" elements of the pastoral letter do not demand religious assent, although they do require respectful consideration inasmuch as the bishops state them. (We shall see below when the views expressed in such collective documents do require religious assent.)

But suppose that, in the absence of both a solemn definition and unity of teaching by the whole episcopal college in union with the pope, he and/or some bishops do propose some teaching on faith or morals as certainly true. Not all the conditions for an infallibly proposed teaching are met; the teaching *could* be erroneous. Yet the pope and/or bishops, speaking as pastors and teachers, are saying that something which concerns faith or morals is certainly true and that the faithful must accept it. In such a case, the teaching could be recognized as infallibly proposed, except that the whole college has not agreed in one judgment. Here religious assent short of faith is required.

By no means is the possibility of this happening merely hypothetical. New issues arise and, in fulfilling their duty, popes and bishops must teach what has not been taught before. New questions also arise out of disputes concerning things already taught infallibly. In reaffirming the teaching, popes and bishops are likely to assert things not previously taught by the magisterium, since this is part of the dynamic of any dispute. Although a unanimous judgment by the whole college is lacking, Catholics have a duty to give religious assent.

Sometimes, too, collective statements by bishops require religious assent. This is so when, as often happens, they teach something which on other grounds requires religious assent, or when what is said is endorsed by the pope and/or one's own bishop and meets the other conditions under which religious assent is required.

Lumen Gentium, 25, describes religious assent as a "submission of will and of mind." The teaching could be mistaken, but, because it is proposed authoritatively by one's bishop, or especially by the pope, one accepts it. The acceptance is real, but, because what is involved is not clearly a matter of faith, it is not accepted as matters of faith are. At the present time, for instance, this is the case with the question of in vitro fertilization. Pope Pius XII, some bishops and groups of bishops, and the Congregation for the Doctrine of the Faith, with the approval of Pope John Paul II, have taught clearly and authoritatively on this matter, but up to now the whole college has not become involved. Similarly, much of the Church's constantly developing social doctrine falls into this category when it is first proposed.

In such cases, the teaching concerns something which could eventually be recognized to pertain to revelation and turn out to be a matter of faith. Bearing in mind that the pope and the other bishops have a responsibility to safeguard the Church's faith and to direct Christian life, Catholics will be ready to give religious assent to what they teach. Catholics will also be mindful that, as we saw in chapter twenty-three, one important reason for forming conscience in accord with the Church's teaching is that dissension and a pluralism of incompatible life-styles make it harder to communicate Christ's truth to the world.

Under the appropriate conditions, then, faithful Catholics will agree with what is being taught and try to act accordingly. Perhaps, left to themselves, they would consider a different view more likely; perhaps they do not understand or agree with the arguments advanced in support of the teaching. Even so, they will not dismiss it on the grounds that it is "noninfallible" and therefore possibly mistaken.

Preconciliar theological manuals argue the need for religious assent, using either that term or another. Often, though, they make the case legalistically, as if the issue were simply obedience. What is most fundamental to religious assent, however, is not obedience but the possibility that what is being proposed pertains to revealed truth. There is good reason to suppose this is so when, even in the absence of a common judgment by the whole episcopal college, the pope or a bishop firmly teaches something on faith or morals. That reason is the divinely given office of the pope and bishops, and the grace which accompanies it. And because these latter realities are matters of divine faith, religious assent, though an act of human faith, is grounded in divine faith.

Still, there are limits to the obligation of religious assent. The duty comes into play only when the pope or one's own bishop, acting in his official capacity, proposes a teaching which pertains to faith or morals and calls for its acceptance as certain. Vatican II suggests this latter condition—the teaching must be proposed as certain—when it says, in the case of the pope, that Catholics must assent to papal teaching of this kind according to his "manifest mind and will, which he expresses chiefly either by the type of document, or by the frequent proposal of the same teaching, or by the argument for the position" (*LG* 25; translation supplied).

Briefly, then, religious assent is *not* required: to opinions which the pope or bishops express on anything other than faith or morals; to their merely private views on faith or morals, which they express when not acting in their official capacity; to teachings they propose in their official capacity but only tentatively rather than as certain; to the supporting arguments and observations they offer for a teaching without insisting that these be accepted as the teaching itself must be; and to disciplinary directives, including those about what should be taught or how to teach it, which stop short of demanding assent to the teaching itself. But even though in these five kinds of cases religious assent is not required, one should give respectful attention, try to understand what is being said, and, in the case of disciplinary directives, obey them.

There are times, nevertheless, when a teaching falls in none of these five categories and yet an individual is unable to assent to it. Sometimes that is because the teaching presupposes a factual claim which one who knows the facts knows to be mistaken. Imagine, for example, that a bishop, having been told that a certain medical treatment involves the use of tissues from aborted babies, firmly condemns the treatment on that basis. But in fact the treatment only involves the use of tissues from nonhuman embryos. In that case, anyone who knew the facts would be unable to assent to the bishop's mistaken teaching (and, obviously, should tell him the facts so that he can correct his mistake).

Also, and more interestingly, if a higher source drawn from faith itself makes it clear beyond reasonable doubt that some teaching, although proposed authoritatively, is mistaken, one can only judge according to the higher source. But one should be slow to trust one's own interpretations and, when interpretations conflict, should prefer those of the magisterium to others. Moreover, one must be careful about qualifying sources as "higher" than the authoritative teaching of the pope and bishops. Scripture, defined doctrine, and teaching proposed infallibly by the ordinary magisterium are higher sources; a consensus of dissenting theologians and a "sensus fidelium" contrary to received teaching are not.

So, to take a fanciful example, if some bishop or bishops were to teach, or even to insist, that adultery is sometimes morally obligatory behavior, the teaching should not be accepted, since there is a higher source to the contrary: namely, Scripture and the continuous teaching of the Christian tradition that adultery is always wrong—a teaching clearly proposed infallibly by the ordinary magisterium. Similarly, if a few bishops teach something contrary to a clear but (up to now) nondefinitive papal teaching, the papal teaching should be followed, because in these circumstances it, too, is a "higher" source.

As a practical matter, does all this provide a loophole to justify the kind of radical dissent we shall examine in the next chapter? Not at all. For, in the first place, that *dissent* is much more than *nonassent,* as we shall explain. And, in the second place, the limits on the obligation of religious assent are simply not relevant to most moral issues currently disputed in Catholic circles: abortion, contraception, adultery, remarriage after divorce of persons who were sacramentally married, masturbation, premarital sex, homosexual behavior, and so on. Bishops for centuries have universally taught the norms on matters like these. The question of withholding religious assent only arises with regard to matters where that kind of consensus is lacking.

36. A Critical Examination of Radical Theological Dissent

As we saw in chapter thirty-five, one sometimes need not, and indeed cannot, assent to a teaching, although the pope or one's bishop proposes it as certain and it concerns a matter of faith or morals. We do not maintain that one must always assent to whatever popes and bishops say. Our critique instead concerns radical theological dissent.

Three assumptions underlie radical dissent: first, that, defined doctrines aside, the Church's teaching is only one factor among others which Catholics should consider in forming their consciences; second, that theologians should judge moral questions by their own scholarly standards rather than by what the magisterium teaches; and, third, that dissenting moral theologians may and should propose their views as norms which people may follow in practice, despite constant and most firm Church teaching to the contrary.

A statement published immediately after *Humanae Vitae* by a group of theologians and others led by Charles E. Curran provides a clear example of radical dissent: "Spouses may responsibly decide according to their conscience that artificial contraception in some circumstances is permissible and indeed necessary to preserve and foster the values and sacredness of marriage."[31]

But radical dissent extends to much else besides contraception. Within a dozen years of *Humanae Vitae*, some theologians were arguing that virtually every kind of act which the Church condemns as intrinsically evil can sometimes be permissible or even obligatory for the sake of realizing greater goods or avoiding

421

greater evils. Their views were generally associated with the method of proportionalism, criticized in chapter six.

Other views linked to radical theological dissent have also been criticized earlier. Chapter twenty-three dealt with the obligation to form conscience according to the Church's teaching; chapter thirty-five with the infallibility of the Church and the obligation of religious assent. In this chapter, therefore, we consider only certain arguments for dissent. We shall treat four topics: some specific grounds used to justify radical dissent; the theory of the magisterium used to defend dissent; dissent as alleged reformulation and development of doctrine; and why some seek to change the Church's moral teaching.

Only a few theologians are mentioned here by name. This is not meant to single them out for special opprobrium, but because they are representative figures whose views are shared by a substantial number of others. We take for granted their sincerity and good character. The question, however, is not whether they are sincere and have good characters, but whether they are right.

A: Some Specific Grounds Used to Justify Radical Dissent

The statement by the Curran group quoted above contains this assertion: "It is common teaching in the Church that Catholics may dissent from authoritative, noninfallible teachings of the magisterium when sufficient reasons for doing so exist."[32] By 1978 Curran had laid down the general principle that dissent from any specific moral teaching can be legitimate.[33] He and others maintained that common teaching in the Church justifies this position.

Practically speaking, this assertion was based on what standard theological manuals in use before Vatican II had to say about this matter. But an examination of these manuals shows that they do not justify dissent. They discuss something different—nonassent; that is, cases in which someone might be unable to assent to a teaching which has been proposed. They do *not* envision theologians challenging received, constant, and very firm teaching, and telling Catholics to follow their dissenting views rather than the magisterium.

Since this fact soon became apparent, dissenting theologians shifted to another argument: Vatican II justified dissent. But since the documents of the Council, and especially *Lumen Gentium*, 25, offer no support for this assertion, it was necessary to appeal to the spirit of the Council or something of that sort. Evidently, however, this "spirit" of Vatican II could not be harmonized with what Vatican II actually taught. So, Curran and his associates said "that the documents of Vatican II were 'dated' on the first day after solemn promulgation,"[34] while Richard McCormick, S.J., wrote in 1977 that *Lumen Gentium,* 25, embodies a "very dated and very discussable notion of the Church's teaching office."[35] Such claims are a tacit admission that Vatican II does not support dissent.

Appeal was then made to certain declarations by bishops' conferences. Many issued statements after *Humanae Vitae* appeared, and these have been collected and translated into English.[36] Most not only support *Humanae Vitae* unambiguously but, on the whole, fail to support radical dissent. Some, to be sure, do take a view of dissent which cannot be squared with the previous teaching of the Church, but they also tend to contradict and cancel out one another.

Actually, the most important collective episcopal statement on dissent was not published after *Humanae Vitae* but before it—by the bishops of West Germany in 1967. They note that the ordinary magisterium can propose teachings infallibly, and they insist that when it does, there is no room for dissent. However, they also discuss "the possibility or the fact of error in nondefined statements of doctrine on the part of the Church," along with the possibility that a theologically well-informed individual could adopt a dissenting position "in his private theory and practice."[37] This is not necessarily inconsistent with what was said in chapter thirty-five, but it is incomplete insofar as it fails to clarify the very limited reasons why one might be unable to assent; it also confuses matters by using "nondefined statements of doctrine" as if it were equivalent to "noninfallible teachings"—thus not consistently recognizing the infallibility of the ordinary magisterium.

Undoubtedly, however, the events of the late 1960s did leave a certain residual confusion and disharmony within the magisterium. That may be one reason why marriage and family life was chosen as the theme of the 1980 assembly of the Synod of Bishops.

Various views were aired on that occasion, and eventually a consensus took shape. It was expressed in propositions which the synodal Fathers submitted to Pope John Paul II. He in turn stated this consensus in a synthetic document, the post-synodal apostolic exhortation *Familiaris Consortio*, which reaffirms traditional Church teaching on contraception, remarriage after divorce, and other such matters; insists that preaching, teaching, and pastoral practice be in accord with the teaching of the magisterium; and says that, while theologians have an important role, it is mainly to help people understand and accept the truth which the Church teaches. "It is useful to recall," John Paul remarks, "that the proximate and obligatory norm in the teaching of the faith—also concerning family matters—belongs to the hierarchical Magisterium."[38]

In sum, the Synod assembly of 1980 and *Familiaris Consortio* supersede whatever disarray existed in the magisterium immediately after *Humanae Vitae*. Therefore, episcopal statements from that era can no longer reasonably be used to support radical dissent.

The statement by Curran and his associates immediately after *Humanae Vitae* said: "The Encyclical is not an infallible teaching."[39] But they did not consider whether the teaching it contains had already been infallibly proposed by the ordinary magisterium. Since then, of course, the argument "not infallible" has been used against received moral teaching on many matters besides contraception. Not surprisingly, the defenders of radical dissent have generally ignored the infallibility of the ordinary magisterium.

Yet, as we saw in chapter thirty-five, many specific norms in the body of received moral teaching do meet the criteria for teaching proposed infallibly by the ordinary magisterium. For example, in collaboration with John C. Ford, S.J., one of the authors of the present work presented the evidence in the case of contraception in a long article which has not been refuted up to this time.[40]

On this point, it is interesting to recall that, ten years before *Humanae Vitae*, Karl Rahner, S.J., made the general argument for the infallibility of the ordinary magisterium in very clear terms. The Church teaches God's commandments with divine authority, he wrote, not only through *ex cathedra* definitions of a pope or a general council, "but also through her *ordinary* magisterium, that is in the normal teaching of the Faith to the faithful in schools, sermons and all the other kinds of instruction." He added: "In the nature of the case this will be the normal way in which moral norms are taught, and definitions by Pope or general council the exception; but it is binding on the faithful in conscience just as the teaching through the extraordinary magisterium is."[41]

B: The Theory of the Magisterium Used to Defend Dissent

Predictably, the effort to justify radical theological dissent gave birth over time to broader arguments implicating increasingly fundamental issues. Eventually a new theory of the magisterium began to take shape.

Richard McCormick, S.J., noting that Vatican II had contributed to a more participatory, less legalistic approach to teaching in the Church (as indeed it had), contended that in order to teach, the magisterium must persuade, that the correct immediate response to magisterial teaching is "docile personal assimilation and appropriation . . . rather than an unquestioning assent," and that theological reflection is essential for the magisterium to function.[42] (He further contended that if one had to accept what the magisterium taught on the basis of its authority rather than its arguments, one would have to agree with everything the magisterium said.[43] We have already seen that this is not so.)

Along with this view of the limited authority of the magisterium, the idea arose that theologians have a magisterium of their own which in practice is superior to the magisterium of the pope and bishops; certainly, it was said, the episcopal magisterium could not firmly reject an opposed theological consensus. Avery Dulles, S.J., contended that the episcopal magisterium should teach nothing without first consulting theologians and, at most, in the absence of theological consensus, should express its own opinion while conceding that good Catholics were free to disagree.[44] McCormick, following Dulles's lead, set rules for the use of theology by the magisterium: Bishops may not choose theological advisers on the basis of their assent to received teaching, may not teach contrary to a significant theological consensus, and may not object to theological dissent.[45]

In applying this view of the magisterium in the moral field, McCormick and others apparently made one or both of two assumptions.

One is that the moral norms which the Church teaches are not revealed truths; rather, Christian moral teaching reflects the mentality of New Testament times or is a cultural accretion acquired in the course of centuries. But if no moral norm is part of God's revelation, then any norm, or all of them, can be repudiated. If that were so, of course, there would be no reason for thinking that the magisterium has any special competence to settle disputes about moral teaching (though whether in any particular time and place it had the power to enforce such determinations as it might make would be another question).

The other possible assumption is that the magisterium resembles public authority in civil society, which can deal effectively with problems to the extent that it seeks and takes the advice of people with appropriate technical expertise. Administrators who act in this way tend to make sound decisions and please the public.

This, however, is not an appropriate model for understanding the magisterium of the pope and bishops, since it leaves out of account the sacramental role of the bishop, ordained to teach in the name of Christ and given divine assistance in doing so. In fact, it denies the magisterium the status enjoyed even by established academic theologians. The latter are free to consult and collaborate with whomever they please and to say what they wish, but in this view the pope and bishops could not do the same.

What of the claim that only experience and arguments can settle moral issues, so that the pope and bishops must be guided by the consensus of the academic theological community? Implicit in this is the idea that theologians have access to moral truth which other Christians do not have. But, to say the least, it is hardly clear what this access is.

Moreover, the so-called theological consensus to which dissenting theologians appeal is actually quite limited. Many able theologians and philosophers do not share the views of dissenting theologians. The latter naturally ignore these others as much as possible while commending one another's views; but the politics of academic theology (and the interventions of media glad to publicize views at variance with received Catholic teaching) can hardly be said to constitute a "consensus" in theology.

In any case, one is obliged to ask why theologians who have detached themselves from the authority of the collegial magisterium should be believed. No one is required to believe a theologian in preference to the pope or a bishop; on the contrary, as we saw in the preceding chapter, the testimony of faith and the teaching of the Church are that on matters of faith and morals the judgment of the collegial magisterium should be accepted.

To be sure, both in times past and at the present time, theologians have had an important role in the Church. Historically, too, there were times when they participated in the work of the magisterium in ways they no longer do. In all cases, however, their status derived from their service to divine revelation and their cooperation with the pope and bishops.

But when theologians set aside the Church's teaching and throw off the authority of the hierarchy in favor of their own opinions and authority, why should any Catholic rely on what they say? Intelligence and training, experience and arguments? For every position taken by a radically dissenting Catholic theologian, someone else as well trained and intelligent—often a nonbeliever—appeals to other experience and arguments and takes a more radical view. Adultery sometimes acceptable? One can find academic intellectuals who hold that marriage is a bad thing. Presumably Catholic dissenting theologians do not wish to go that far, but once one accepts the idea that technical expertise must be followed in the field of morals, there is nothing in the dynamic of dissent to stand in the way. For all their intelligence, training, and good intentions, dissenting Catholic theologians, in rejecting received teaching and the authority of the magisterium, rejected the basis of their own credibility. Hence, no one should *believe* them; their opinions are no better than the arguments they offer for them. And the arguments dissenting theologians offer are not impressive, as even they implicitly admit when they try to buttress their opinions by appealing to the authority of other theologians who agree with them.

Besides laying out their claims, of course, it was necessary for radically dissenting theologians to put forward arguments showing that they enjoy an authority superior to that of the magisterium. The arguments were of several kinds.

It was said, for example, that the view of the magisterium's authority which they contested was an aberration of relatively recent vintage. So, for example, Avery Dulles states: "In the post-Tridentine Church, and in the Neo-Scholastic theology of the nineteenth and twentieth centuries, the dialectical tension between the charisms in the Church is virtually eliminated. All authentic teaching power is simply transferred to the episcopal order."[46] In other words, it happened after the sixteenth century. Daniel Maguire, however, finds the trouble beginning in the eleventh and twelfth centuries, after which "there is a tendency to see the teaching acts of popes and bishops as divinely guaranteed."[47] Hans von Campenhausen, a Protestant scholar, holds: "In the course of the third century the exclusive authority of office attains its full stature."[48]

When *did* the aberration begin? In the New Testament, one not only finds Jesus teaching "as one having authority" (Mk 1:22) but handing on teaching authority to the apostles (Mt 16:17–19, 18:18, 28:18–20). There is no point after apostolic times when the apostles' successors *began* to exercise teaching authority, for it was conferred on the apostles and their successors by Jesus himself.

Dissenting theologians also argued that the magisterium made errors in the past and so can be in error now. This requires examining the alleged instances of error. While some did not involve teaching but administrative and technical matters, others indeed were errors in teaching. We do not contend, however, that the magisterium can never err, but only that it cannot err when it teaches in a way that meets the conditions for infallibility.

Did the magisterium err in some instance where these conditions were met? The Galileo case is frequently cited. In 1616 Galileo was told, by the authority of Pope Paul V, not to continue to hold and defend the Copernican view that the earth revolves around the sun, because it appeared to conflict with some passages in Scripture. In 1632 Galileo published a book defending the Copernican theory. The following year he was tried by the Inquisition for violating the order given him in 1616, was convicted, and was sentenced to life imprisonment (though in fact he spent the rest of his life under house arrest rather than in prison).[49]

This episode is certainly not to the credit of the Church authorities, and it provides a good argument for not judging new questions too quickly. But the events of 1633 were disciplinary in nature, and are therefore irrelevant to the assertion that the magisterium erred in teaching. As for the 1616 decision, with Pope Paul V's authority—that the Copernican view is at odds with Scripture—clearly it was an error. But it was neither an *ex cathe-*

dra pronouncement nor a teaching meeting the conditions for the infallibility of the ordinary magisterium. The Pope was wrong, but not in a way that touches on infallibility.

A similar analysis can be applied to other cases of real or alleged error—certain decrees on interpreting the Bible issued early in this century by the Pontifical Biblical Commission, nineteenth-century papal teaching on religious liberty, and so on—with the same results: where there was error, the circumstances were not such as to call into question the authority of the magisterium when it teaches in a way that meets the conditions for infallible teaching.

Radically dissenting theologians also contended either that moral questions are outside the competence of the magisterium or, at least, that its authority is limited in such a way that it cannot propose any specific moral truth definitively. Charles Curran, for example, argued that a specific moral issue like contraception, "so removed from the core of faith can never be the place where the unity of the faith is to be found."[50] Josef Fuchs, S.J., held that because faith and love are central, specific moral questions are "only a secundarium," so that diverse and conflicting moral norms could be acceptable in different cultural situations.[51]

The first view—moral questions are outside the magisterium's competence—is at odds with the very character of faith. Faith accepts the covenant with God as a way of life, and any way of life has moral implications. If the magisterium, and therefore the Church, has nothing to say about morality, it has nothing to say about this essential aspect of the covenant and therefore this essential aspect of faith.

As for the second view—the magisterium cannot teach specific moral norms as definitively true—we have already dealt with this question in chapter thirty-five. It will be recalled that at least one concrete norm has been solemnly defined, by the Council of Trent ("If anyone says that Christians are permitted to have several wives simultaneously; and that such a practice is not forbidden by any divine law [cf. Mt 19:4–9]: let him be anathema" [DS 1802/972]), while a substantial body of other specific norms has been proposed in a way that meets the conditions for an infallible exercise of the ordinary magisterium.

There are, moreover, at least two good reasons why the magisterium must teach specific moral norms definitively.

One is that the Church has the task of guiding people on the way to salvation. Following Jesus requires leading an upright life; commitment to human goods is the authentic humanism by which people achieve fulfillment. But without the help of the magisterium teaching specific norms, ignorance, confusion, and self-deception would make this a practical impossibility.

The other reason concerns the Church's identity. Moral norms express the identity of any community, but if the Church's magisterium did not teach specific norms definitively, people would be entitled to ask, "What does this community really *stand* for?" The answer, of course, is the truth of the gospel, but what this means in practice is the Christian way of life in just those aspects which set it apart from the moral standards of the surrounding secularized culture. Moreover, while in any other community a pluralism of conflicting norms is acceptable about matters outside the community's limited purposes and ends (though about some matters, uniformity always is required), the community of friendship with God concerns persons in their entirety, so that Christian morality necessarily takes in the whole of life. The Church therefore must teach on many specific moral questions about which other communities could rightly tolerate divergent views.

C: Dissent as Alleged Reformulation and Development of Doctrine

Often enough, radically dissenting theologians have acknowledged that their views on moral questions are not consistent with the received teaching of the Church. In 1978, however, Richard McCormick adopted a new line, arguing that he and others who disputed the magisterium's teaching were changing not the substance of received teaching but only its formulation.

According to McCormick, both Pope John XXIII and Vatican II in the Pastoral Constitution on the Church in the Modern World, *Gaudium et Spes,* "explicitly acknowledged" the difference between substance and formulation. At the same time, he added, there is "an extremely close, indeed inseparable connection" between the two—"They are related as body and soul"—so that it is "difficult to know just what the substance is amid variation of formulation."[52]

McCormick took as an example the received teaching against premarital intercourse. Its substance, he contended, is: "It is morally wrong, scil., there is always something missing. Hence, it should be avoided." (Other things which the magisterium has said about the matter—such as "It is intrinsically evil" and "There is a presumption of serious guilt in each act"—were philosophical-theological addenda, not part of the substance.)

McCormick drew three conclusions: Substance and formulation are distinct, and the magisterium must take part in a process of teaching and learning to arrive at appropriate formulations; it is "not a stunning theological putdown or an insuperably serious objection against an attempted formulation" to point out that it is contrary to a recent, authoritative statement of the Holy See; and the pope and bishops "should not formulate their teaching *against* a broad or even very significant theological consensus," since the existence of such a consensus is a sign that "the problem has not matured sufficiently to allow an authoritative formulation."[53]

There are several things to be said about this.

To begin with, McCormick gives the game away by saying substance and formulation are "related as body and soul." For when body and soul are separated, as McCormick's procedure separates substance and formulation, the result is death. McCormick might reply that he was only using a metaphor, but this is a case where the author of the metaphor spoke more truly than he knew.

The claim about John XXIII and Vatican II rests on a serious misunderstanding. In an address at the beginning of the Council, the Pope did indeed call for suitable restatements of Catholic doctrine; he added that these are only possible because "the deposit or the truths of faith, contained in our sacred teaching, are one thing, while the mode in which they are enunciated, keeping the same meaning and the same judgment, is another."[54] The Council made these words its own (in *GS* 62).

Often omitted in translations, the phrase "keeping the same meaning and the same judgment" (*eodem sensu et eadem sententia*) is crucial. It takes for granted that identifiable truths of faith are found in different formulations, since otherwise it makes no sense to speak of keeping "the same" meaning and judgment when replacing one formulation with another. Where does this phrase come from? It is taken from Vatican Council I, which quotes it from St. Vincent of Lerins. He used it in the fifth century to call attention to the continuity which must characterize authentic development of doctrine. Vatican I adopted it in reference to its definitive teaching on faith: that the "meaning of the sacred dogmas that has once been declared by holy Mother Church, must always be retained; and there must never be any deviation from that meaning on the specious grounds of a more profound understanding" (DS 3020/1800).

McCormick's handling of the example of fornication suggests what is really happening when radically dissenting theologians say they are simply reformulating the "substance" of Church teaching: they want the substance to consist in what is common both to the received teaching and to dissenting views. This approach was made familiar—though on dogmatic more than on moral questions—by liberalized Christian theology throughout the nineteenth century. It need hardly be said that it is arbitrary—one determines the substance of doctrine by what one finds acceptable in received teaching, then discards the rest. But it also involves certain other difficulties.

For instance, in teaching that those who commit mortal sin lose the grace of justification, the Council of Trent also teaches: "This assertion defends the teaching of divine law that excludes from the kingdom of God not only those without faith, but also those with faith who are fornicators. . ." (DS 1544/808). This is in fact the position of the whole Catholic tradition. In order to defend his view, McCormick would have to argue that Trent (and the tradition) only mean that there is something lacking from premarital sex, and so it should be avoided. Naturally, McCormick gives no explanation of why his formulation is a better expression of the substance of the received teaching than others far better grounded in Scripture and tradition than his.

As for McCormick's three conclusions, they do not follow from what he says about formulation and substance. If one denies that the magisterium can judge whether formulations are faithful to the substance of the Church's teaching, one must deny that the magisterium has the right to do so. But the magisterium has always claimed precisely that right—and duty. It comes down again to the question: Whom are Catholics to *believe*—dissenting theologians or the pope and bishops? Chapter thirty-five made clear what the answer is.

What then of development? Are the views expressed by dissenting theologians not reformulations but developments of the tradition? Catholic moral doctrine, like Catholic teaching in general, does develop. Might not a large-scale development be occurring now in the field of morals?

Some development is merely refinement, while in other cases (for example, the question of slavery) it is a movement from what was tolerated, without a firm judgment, to a clear condemnation. For the present question, though, cases like these are not really very interesting. Much more interesting are those in which the development seems to be a reversal of what was previously taught.

But because merely contradicting what was previously taught would not be developing it, dissenting theologians who wished to argue that their views represented development faced the problem of showing how their apparent denial of the tradition did not contradict it. In general, they argued along the following lines:

> Basic human values underlie specific moral norms. What the values require in practical, behavioral terms can vary with circumstances. If protecting a value requires proscribing certain behavior in certain circumstances, the Church rightly proscribes it. In different circumstances, concern for the same value may make it permissible, or even obligatory, to engage in the very same behavior which was previously proscribed. In this case the behavior is not really the same act which the Church formerly forbade; although it looks the same, from a moral point of view it is different.

Actually, there is a good deal of truth in this. As we saw in chapter ten, most moral norms are not absolute. Affirmative norms are never absolute, since they can always be specified further, and negative norms are usually not absolute either. So, it is quite possible to encounter a true norm whose further specification seems to lead to its reversal.

The case of usury is often cited in discussions of these matters. John T. Noonan, Jr., who published a study of scholastic theories of usury before the contraception debate began, later argued that as the Church once condemned the taking of interest and later changed its teaching, so, even though the Church now condemns contraception, change in that teaching is also possible.

But what really changed in the case of the teaching on usury? In his study, Noonan himself concluded that there was no change in the Church's central teaching on the taking of interest. He put it this way:

> Moreover, as far as dogma in the technical Catholic sense is concerned, there is only one dogma at stake . . . that usury, the act of

taking profit on a loan without a just title, is sinful. . . . This dogmatic teaching remains unchanged. What is a just title, what is technically to be treated as a loan, are matters of debate, positive law, and
changing evaluation. The development on these points is great. But
the pure and narrow dogma is the same today as in 1200.[55]

In other words, the moral teaching on the taking of interest,
which would appear to meet the criteria for an infallible exercise
of the ordinary magisterium, has not changed.

The teaching about usury is precisely that it is always wrong to
charge people interest simply for making them a loan, because
that amounts to charging them for their need: for example, by
lending a poor man facing a family crisis fifty dollars until pay
day, on the condition that he then pay back a hundred dollars. In
a modern economy, however, money serves many purposes—for
example, as venture capital. Thus, lenders can rightly charge interest in proportion to what they give up by not putting their
money to some other use. So interest taking, within limits, can be
morally acceptable. For a more specified act there is a different
norm. This is a legitimate development.

Why is the case of contraception any different? Simply because
it is impossible to choose conception-preventing behavior for its
conception-preventing effect without choosing to prevent the
coming-to-be of a new life; and, as far as the good of human life is
concerned, that is contrary to the eighth mode of responsibility
(one may never choose to destroy, damage, or *impede* any basic
human good). Circumstances cannot alter this fundamental fact
about choosing to do something for its contraceptive results. So
the specific negative norm against contraception is absolute (in
the sense that it admits of no exceptions).

In his book *Contraception*, nevertheless, Noonan argues that the
norm is nonabsolute (though he does not put it that way). He
contends that its purpose was to defend certain human values—
procreation, love, and so on—under conditions which existed in
the past but do not now exist.[56] But Noonan does not prove his
point, while analysis of contraception along the lines sketched
above, as well as (and especially!) the constant and very firm
teaching of the Church, show that the norm is absolute.

Some dissenting theologians have attempted to argue that their
views on an issue like contraception are a development. Charles
Curran supported this position before 1968. In an article pub-

lished in 1978, however, he admitted that the argument was never really plausible. "One must honestly recognize," he wrote, "that 'the conservatives' saw much more clearly than 'the liberals' of the day that a change in the teaching on artificial contraception had to recognize that the previous teaching was wrong."[57]

Development can indeed occur with respect to many nonabsolute moral norms. But, considering what they dissent *from*, that is of no help to those who engage in radical theological dissent, since the norms which forbid the choice to kill the unborn, the choice to engage in sexual behavior outside marriage, and so on are not nonabsolute but absolute.

D: Why Some Seek to Change the Church's Moral Teaching

Avery Dulles provides a rationale shared, it seems, by many radically dissenting theologians. Development of doctrine as described above is not adequate for his purposes; rather, he wished to allow room for outright revisions.[58] The central Christian mystery, he holds, is God's saving work in Christ. Those doctrines which express this mystery are primary. As for other doctrines, not everyone should have to accept them all. It is reasonable to require acceptance of the minimum needed to prevent "harmful deviations from the gospel" from occurring, but otherwise people should be free to accept or reject what the Church teaches; and no one should have to accept anything in which he or she can "as yet find no meaning, relevance, or credibility."[59]

Dulles gave a clear reason for proposing this program, namely, "to lighten the burden of assenting to doctrines handed down from the past."[60] It will not do simply to dismiss this concern out of hand. After all, many people have drifted away from Christianity in modern times, especially in the West. Pastoral concern naturally leads one to wonder whether lightening the burden of faith and Christian life might not be a reasonable step. It certainly appeared so to the liberal Protestantism of the nineteenth and twentieth centuries.

The program of Pope John XXIII, Vatican Council II, Pope Paul VI, and Pope John Paul II is, however, profoundly different.

They recognize that over the centuries the Church has acquired many merely human, and in some cases unattractive, accretions in its structures, practices, and even in the manner in which it teaches. They agree that whatever is merely human and counter-productive should be eliminated or at least modified so that the Church will be more acceptable and effective. Hence the strategy underlying such things as the reform of the liturgy since Vatican II.

But all of them—Council and popes—distinguish sharply between merely human accretions and essentials, and insist that the latter be retained, not modified or discarded. This reflects the conviction that the Church *may* not change or set aside any of the essentials of Christian faith and moral teaching, because these come not from the Church but from God.

In chapter twenty, considering revelation and faith, we saw that faith has a definite propositional content. It is arbitrary to separate most of this content (all of which is essential) from a few core doctrines, as Dulles suggests, and to insist only on the latter, while leaving it to individuals to reject the rest of the Church's teaching if they wish. On the contrary, Vatican I says:

> Moreover, by divine and Catholic faith everything must be believed that is contained in the written word of God or in tradition, and that is proposed by the Church as a divinely revealed object of belief either in a solemn decree or in her ordinary, universal teaching. (DS 3011/ 1792)

Some truths of faith *are* more important than others, but that does not mean we can knowingly ignore or reject any of them, for all of them are essential.

The program put forward by Dulles, or something like it, was needed to sustain the radical dissent of McCormick, Curran, and others, since it allows one to change or discard the Church's teachings more or less at will. But it is based on an unacceptable theory of revelation and faith—unacceptable, that is, to one who believes that the Catholic Church is what it claims to be. In the end, the project of lightening the burden of faith comes down to picking and choosing among the teachings of the Church, using as the standard for selection something entirely independent of faith, so that even the "core" which one retains is retained because it meets one's own standard, not because it is God's truth.

In our review of the field of morals we have seen a multitude of diverse theories—proportionalism, subjectivist notions of conscience, untenable understandings of fundamental option, and so on—advanced by various groups of contemporary moral theologians. Some of these theories contradict one another (for example, subjectivism and proportionalism) but have nevertheless been supported by the very same people. Why is that?

The radically dissenting theologians are intelligent individuals. Undoubtedly they recognize that some of their theories are mutually incompatible and none is very plausible. Yet in their various ways all these theories do lighten the burden of faith. They accomplish this by allowing people to act contrary to the constant and very firm teaching of the Church without giving up hope of heaven.

Lightening, indeed. But at a great price.

Notes

1. See *De veritate*, q. 17, a. 3 and a. 5.
2. St. John of the Cross, *The Collected Works of St. John of the Cross*, trans. Kieran Kavanaugh, O.C.D., and Otilio Rodriguez, O.C.D. (Garden City, N.Y.: Doubleday, 1964), 174.
3. Marriage and family life is not included in the list of basic human goods in *The Way of the Lord Jesus*, vol. 1, *Christian Moral Principles*, because it was mistakenly thought to be reducible to the other goods—friendship, the new life of the children, and so on. However, the substantive aspect of the good of marriage is not reducible to the reflexive good of marital friendship, and many people do marry and have children for no reason beyond the intelligible goodness inherent in this way of life.
4. For a book-length treatment of the ethics of deterrence: John Finnis, Joseph M. Boyle, Jr., and Germain Grisez, *Nuclear Deterrence, Morality and Realism* (Oxford and New York: Oxford University Press, 1987).
5. Karl Rahner, S.J., "The Problem of Genetic Manipulation," *Theological Investigations*, vol. 9, *Writings of 1965–67, I*, trans. Graham Harrison (New York: Herder and Herder, 1972), 243.
6. Pius XI, *Mit brennender Sorge*, AAS 29 (1937) 157.
7. On monogenism: Pius XII, DS 3897/2328; Paul VI, "Original Sin and Modern Science: Address of Pope Paul VI to Participants in a Symposium on Original Sin," *The Pope Speaks*, 11 (1966), 234; *AAS* 58 (1966) 649–55. Paul VI, however, also approved a treatment of this problem, prepared to amend the teaching of the "Dutch" catechism, which renders the Church's essential teaching on original sin and polygenism compatible: Edouard Dhanis, S.J., and Jan Visser, C.Ss.R., "The Supplement to 'A New Catechism': On Behalf of the Commission of Cardinals appointed to examine 'A New Catechism,' " *A New Catechism: Catholic Faith for Adults* (New York: Seabury Press, 1973), 534–37.

8. St. Augustine, *The Lord's Sermon on the Mount*, trans. John J. Jepson, S.S. (New York: Newman Press, 1948), 43.

9. The false assumption that Trent teaches "that man cannot have any real and absolute certitude about the state of his own conscience and his state of grace" served as a premise in an argument that the "ultimate quality of a free decision" is an "unreflectable" reality: Karl Rahner, S.J., *Theological Investigations*, vol. 3, *The Theology of the Spiritual Life*, trans. Karl H. and Boniface Kruger (Baltimore: Helicon, 1967), 108.

10. *AAS* 68 (1976) 87.

11. Pius XII, "De Conscientia Christiana in Iuvenibus Recte Efformanda," *AAS* 44 (1952) 275–76; *The Pope Speaks: The Teaching of Pope Pius XII*, ed. Michael Chinigo (New York: Pantheon Books, 1957), 97.

12. *De peccatorum meritis et remissione et de baptismo parvulorum*, 2, 6, 7, in William A. Jurgens, *The Faith of the Early Fathers*, vol. 3 (Collegeville, Minn.: The Liturgical Press, 1979), 91.

13. In section 34, *AAS* 74 (1982) 123–24.

14. See *The Mystery of Death* (New York: Herder and Herder, 1965).

15. "General Instruction of the Roman Missal," Introduction, 2.

16. *AAS* 71 (1979) 317.

17. See William A. Jurgens, *The Faith of the Early Fathers* (Collegeville, Minnesota: The Litugical Press, 1979), vol. 1, 99 (St. Irenaeus, *Against Heresies*, 5, *Preface*) and 322 (St. Athanasius, *Treatise on the Incarnation of the Word*, 54, 3); vol. 2, 16 (St. Basil the Great, *The Holy Spirit*, 9, 22); vol. 3, 17 (St. Augustine, *Enarrationes in psalmos*, 49, 2).

18. St. John of the Cross, *The Living Flame of Love*, 3, 78, in *The Collected Works of St. John of the Cross*, trans. Kieran Kavanaugh, O.C.D., and Otilio Rodriguez, O.C.D. (Washington, D.C.: ICS Publications, 1979), 641.

19. *AAS* 72 (1980) 1225.

20. St. Francis de Sales, *Treatise on the Love of God*, trans. John K. Ryan, vol. 1 (Rockford, Ill.: Tan Books, 1974), 268.

21. See *S.t.*, 3, q. 63, a. 2.

22. See *S.t.*, 3, q. 72, aa. 5–6.

23. *Mystici Corporis Christi*, *AAS* 35 (1943) 235.

24. *The Rites of the Catholic Church* (New York: Pueblo, 1976), 347.

25. *The Rites of the Catholic Church*, 583–84.

26. "General Instruction of the Liturgy of the Hours," *Liturgy of the Hours*, vol. 1, 29.

27. Albert Camus, "The Absurd Man," in *The Myth of Sisyphus and Other Essays* (New York: Vintage Books, 1959), 65.

28. Albert Camus, "Absurd Creation," in op. cit., 79.

29. Thomas Mann, *The Magic Mountain* (New York: Alfred A. Knopf, 1952), 515.

30. *Familiaris Consortio*, 5, *AAS* 74 (1982) 85–86.

31. Charles E. Curran et al., *Dissent in and for the Church: Theologians and "Humanae Vitae"* (New York: Sheed and Ward, 1969), 26.

32. Curran, et al., *Dissent*, 26.

33. Charles E. Curran, "Ten Years Later," *Commonweal*, 105 (7 July 1978), 429.

34. Curran, et al., *Dissent*, 100.

35. *Notes on Moral Theology: 1965–1980* (Washington, D.C.: University Press of America, 1981), 667.

36. For example, *Humanae Vitae and the Bishops: The Encyclical and the Statements of the National Hierarchies*, ed. John Horgan (Shannon: Irish University Press, 1972).

37. The text of the relevant segment of the document is in Karl Rahner, S.J., *Theological Investigations*, vol. 14, *Ecclesiology, Questions in the Church, The Church in the World*, trans. David Bourke (New York: Seabury Press, 1976), 85–88.

38. John Paul II, *Familiaris Consortio*, 73, *AAS* 74 (1982) 171.

39. Curran et al., *Dissent*, 25.

40. See John C. Ford, S.J., and Germain Grisez, "Contraception and the Infallibility of the Ordinary Magisterium," *Theological Studies*, 39 (1978), 264–69. On criticisms of this article and replies to them see Germain Grisez, "General Introduction," in John C. Ford., S.J., Germain Grisez, Joseph Boyle, John Finnis, and William E. May, *The Teaching of "Humanae vitae": A Defense* (San Francisco: Ignatius Press, 1988), 12–21.

41. Karl Rahner, *Nature and Grace: Dilemmas in the Modern Church* (London: Sheed and Ward, 1963), 52.

42. Richard A. McCormick, S.J., "The Teaching Role of the Magisterium and of the Theologians," *Proceedings of the Catholic Theological Society of America*, 24 (1969), 245.

43. McCormick, *Notes*, 221.

44. Avery Dulles, S.J., *The Resilient Church: The Necessity and Limits of Adaptation* (Garden City, N.Y.: Doubleday, 1977), 110–11.

45. McCormick, *Notes*, 784–85.

46. Dulles, *Resilient Church*, 102.

47. Daniel C. Maguire, "Moral Inquiry and Religious Assent," in *Contraception: Authority and Dissent*, ed. Charles E. Curran (New York: Herder and Herder, 1969), 136.

48. Hans von Campenhausen, *Ecclesiastical Authority and Spiritual Power in the Church of the First Three Centuries* (Stanford, Calif.: Stanford University Press, 1969), 299; see 192–93 concerning teachers and theologians.

49. See Stillman Drake, *Galileo at Work: His Scientific Biography* (Chicago: University of Chicago Press, 1978), 252–56, 330–57.

50. Curran, "Ten Years Later," 428.

51. Joseph Fuchs, S.J., "The Absoluteness of Moral Terms," in *Readings in Moral Theology No. 1: Moral Norms and Catholic Tradition*, ed. Charles E. Curran and Richard A. McCormick, S.J. (New York: Paulist Press, 1979), 102. A critique of this important article: Germain Grisez, "Moral Absolutes: A Critique of the View of Josef Fuchs, S.J.," *Rivista di Studi sulla Persona e la Famiglia: Anthropos* (now *Anthropotes*), 1 (1985), 155–201.

52. McCormick, *Notes*, 744.

53. McCormick, *Notes*, 744–45.

54. John XXIII, "Allocutio habita d. 11 oct. 1962, in initio Concilii," *AAS* 54 (1962) 792. Not only has this passage often been mistranslated, but some have claimed that the critical words were added to the text published in *AAS* against Pope John's better judgment. But those words are in the text published immediately after the allocution was delivered: *L'Osservatore Romano*, 12 October 1962, 2, col. 3, beginning 10 lines from the bottom.

55. John T. Noonan, Jr., *The Scholastic Analysis of Usury* (Cambridge, Mass.: Harvard University Press, 1957), 399–400.

56. John T. Noonan, Jr., *Contraception: A History of Its Treatment by the Catholic Theologians and Canonists* (Cambridge, Mass.: Belknap Press of Harvard University Press, 1965), 532–33.

57. Curran, "Ten Years Later," 426.

58. Dulles, *Resilient Church*, 51–54.

59. Dulles, *Resilient Church*, 57.

60. Dulles, *Resilient Church*, 51.

Index

Citations of documents in the Denzinger-Schönmetzer collection are indexed under Chalcedon, Council of; Florence, Council of; Trent, Council of; and Vatican Council I. Citations of the documents of Vatican II are indexed under Vatican Council II documents, citations of. Citations of Sacred Scripture are indexed separately, at the end.

Names and subjects

Abortion, 4, 33, 71, 139, 144, 146, 147, 148, 180, 200, 216, 243, 277, 393, 414, 420

Abraham, 162, 246, 249, 260, 342

Absolutes, moral, 46, 92–96, 128, 180, 248, 319, 321, 335, 431–35; doubts related to, 136, 142, 144, 145–47; nonabsolute norms and, 111, 115–19, 121–22, 321, 408, 414; proportionalism and, 60–74

Absolution, 369

Adultery, 36, 73–74, 79, 81, 82, 175, 176, 177, 183, 186, 187, 189, 192, 204, 247, 248, 321, 371, 409, 413, 414, 419, 420, 427

Almsgiving, 320, 375–76

Anger, 26, 92–93, 201, 202, 204

Anointing, sacrament of, 376–78

Anxiety, 27, 33, 89, 90, 96, 112, 167, 175, 203, 308–9, 376, 377

Apostles, 238, 249, 250, 260, 268, 269, 276, 346, 357, 358, 365, 380, 381, 402–6, 409, 410, 411, 428

Apostolate, 300, 325, 329, 380, 385, 387, 396; confirmation, personal vocation and, 356–66; conscience formation and, 276–78

Apostolic succession, 405–6, 409–10

Aristotle, 56–57, 123, 182

Athanasius, St., 283

Augustine, St., 9, 32, 57, 283, 289, 404; neo-Platonism of, 390–91; on sin, 155–56, 181, 209, 215

Authenticity, 54–55

Authority, 18, 24–25, 112, 124; Church's, 3, 134–35, 137, 276, 278, 354, 405, 410–20, 422, 424, 425–30, 431; in civil society, 131–34; defined and distinguished, 125–30; Jesus', 259–60

Bad, 49–53

Baptism, 24, 163, 171, 188, 196, 232–33, 266, 267–68, 277, 284, 292, 304, 344, 348, 351, 360, 373; basic sacrament, 352–55; confirmation and, 356–57, 359; Eucharist and, 380, 382, 384–85; penance and, 367–68

Basic commitment, Christian's and Jesus', 256–57, 262–64, 270, 272–76

Sacred Scripture